For God and Country

The authoritative story of Haym Salomon

An Epic Biographical Novel

by

JAMES ARCURI

"He was a son of liberty that gave his all for God and country, from being a courageous spy to coordinating the financial obligations which allowed the promise of America to be violently born, against the wishes of the most powerful monarch and army in the world."

This book is dedicated to all Patriots then and now.

For Lauren, my lovely wife, my life.

This book is an account of actual facts based on the life and times of Haym Salomon, as researched by the author. Some characters, incidents and dialogue are drawn from notes, interviews, decedents, and also from recorded historical fact.

Identity Features Publishing, 1812 Hemming Way, Orefield, PA 18069
Tel: 646-725-4000 Email: IdentityFeatures@gmail.com

TABLE OF CONTENTS

"But with respect to future debt; would it not be wise and just for that nation to declare in the constitution they are forming that neither the legislature, nor the nation itself can validly contract more debt, than they may pay within their own age, or within the term of 19 years." - Thomas Jefferson

"Our country is in danger, but not to be despaired of. Our enemies are numerous and powerful; but we have many friends, determining to be free, and heaven and earth will aid the resolution. On you depend the fortunes of America. You are to decide the important question, on which rest the happiness and liberty of millions yet unborn. Act worthy of yourselves." - Joseph Warren

PROLOGUE

"The cause of America is in a great measure the cause of all mankind. Where, some say, is the king of America? I'll tell you, friend, He reigns above."   Thomas Paine

Through wrinkled, weary eyes, the old man gazed up at the 365 polished marble steps leading to the unfinished dome of the United States Capitol Building. He leaned on his cane, took a deep breath, and sighed. It had been a long journey— a life's journey. With trembling fingers, the elderly gentleman took a large, gold pocket watch from out of his vest. He pressed the tiny release mechanism and the cover effortlessly popped open. It was 1:27pm. "Good," he thought. That left him plenty of time to make it to the Senate floor for his appointment at two o'clock.

It was 1864 and the country was noticeably tired from the long, three and a half years of the ravages of civil war. Although the afternoon sun was shining bright that glorious spring day, there was an almost gloomy pall cast over the white city. Sorrow and sadness weighed heavily on both heart and mind. While the nation was still locked in its desperate struggle for the union and mourning its brave fallen, the distinguished, white-haired gentleman was also noticeably exhausted from having been locked in his own desperate struggle: fighting for but a modicum of justice— in his eyes, against an unappreciative government.

Haym* M. Salomon, 79, had been here many times before. He climbed those steps on dozens of occasions over the previous half century without any favorable outcome or success, and he was praying that this was going to be the last time he, or anyone in his family, would have to do so. The thin, frail old man desperately wanted to end the quest while his heart still remained passionately beating in his chest. This was his bequeathing— an inheritance of unpaid debt, a life's justness pursued on the declivitous balance of justice and penury. He certainly did not want to see the burden pass to his own children and grandchildren, as it had been passed to him. Haym closed the pocket watch and placed it back into his vest pocket, then tucked the leather case he had so cherished and guarded with his very life under his arm. With confidence and great determination, Haym M. Salomon, fourth child and second son of Haym Salomon, native of Leszno, Poland, began his last ascent up the glistening marble.

Winded and wheezing, with his left leg throbbing, Haym finally reached the set of large, wooden double doors leading to the Senate chamber and hobbled down the side aisle to the front of the room. His cane thumped with each step against the solid, hardwood floor. Men of authority resided here: powerful men.

However, he was neither intimidated nor deterred. He looked around the stately room admiring the framed artwork as he hobbled to a seat in the third row and sat down. He was early. The only other individual in the chamber was a neatly dressed clerk seated at a small desk to the right.

Haym placed the leather case on his lap and opened it. Inside were various documents; several signed by past U.S. Presidents, as well as a small, frayed siddur, a daily prayer book. He gazed upon the unraveling and wears of a thin Star of David on its cover, fully grasping the profound meaning of his heritage. Gently, the old man picked the handwritten book up with both hands and placed it against his heart. He clasped it tighter and closed his eyes. A teardrop followed.

"I have lived a full life not knowing you or understanding who you were." He whispered.

***

*(pronounced Hi-yeem)

1
BLOOD

"They who can give up essential liberty to obtain a little temporary safety, deserve neither liberty nor safety." Benjamin Franklin

Central, Poland, 1758. A sparse amount of snow was gently falling to earth in the taciturn stillness, drifting between the indiscernible electricity in the heavens. Even the atmosphere seemed to be waiting in nervous anticipation— the calm before the storm. The air was nearly motionless; uncharacteristic for the time of year in the modest, little textile village of Leszno. It was still winter and the wind usually came howling from the northwest off the great Baltic Sea, but the temporary reprieve from the bitter cold was assuredly welcome.

The world should have seemed fresh and alive with anticipation of the coming spring, but to eighteen year old Hayim Shelomo, relegated, like all Jews in Leszno, to the most squalid industrialized section of the city— spring, summer, winter, or fall, the air of the world seemed to hang heavy with the suffocating tension of exhaustive sweat, the smoke of smoldering arson, and the constant pressure of national subjugation. Their racially segregated quarter or ghetto, though cramped, was an economic powerhouse among the collapsing cities and industries of the Commonwealth. The section of the city was a merciless mix of contradictions— felicity and misery, kingdom come and purgatory.

The history of Jews in Leszno dated from the second half of 16th century when the city was the private estate of the Leszczyńsk family. They did something extraordinary among European nobles; they offered all religions sanctuary and permeant residence. Jews flocked to the estate and gradually dominated the economic force of what became a standing city. In 1626, as religious tensions heightened among the Calvinist, the Catholics and the Jews; the latter were granted a special privilege governing relations between their own outlined suburb, the municipalities, and to owners of the castle. Under this privilege, the Jews were a distinct population of a district and permitted to construct a cemetery and a synagogue. Separated from the larger Christian whole of the town, they were relatively free from persecution. The community became one of the largest Jewish centers in the Republic and distinguished in economic and cultural activities. Their trade reached Turkey, Persia, China and Russia and the most importantly— the fairs in Leipzig and Frankfurt. For the next 200 years, wealth particularly abound among Leszno's Jews. In contrast over the same period of time, the failures of the Commonwealth steadily tightened a racist, economic, and military grip around them.

By 1758, there were still in excess of one hundred very wealthy households with the majority of the population a contended third estate of craftsman, shopkeepers, and clergy, and yet the streets were execrably overrun, by interloping beggars. On one hand the streets sparkled of cleanliness and pride. On the other, many of those among this virtue and dignity were reprobate unhygienic wastrels. Charity was an ideological custom among the Jews, a glorious act, a mitzvah, and the responsibility of every community, but on the other hand, it could be an enormous burden on a community's budget. Therein, after twenty years of mendicant influx, so accumulated were the alien vagrants in Leszno that the parnas asked the voievode to issue a ban that would prohibit begging by the poor who were not native residents; for the majority of these hordes were Jews and non-Jews alike who came as far as the region's capital Poznan, simply to solicit alms. Yet still, this was a cloistered paradise by comparison to ghettos around the world, but at it's heart, the compulsory and coerced component of taxes was the contradictory element that sustained it.

Taxes were fixed and assessed to every aspect of life. Varying from year-to-year was a significantly heavy lump-sum poll tax levied from on high to the community as a whole. And to not pay was to risk the legal pyro manic destruction of every building and the confiscation of every piece of property that had even the slightest value. The government's excessive taxes were a burden to the community's financial well being but paradoxically were also the ransom paid for protection from the occasionally rampaging gentiles. To understand Leszno in the mid-eighteen century is to be acutely aware that life is Janus-faced— double masked, a trade-off of sorts, compromises in paragons; standing for both purity and sin, pleasure and pain, old and new, right and wrong. The welkin and the pit, and so was the district— there was more beauty and the wafting scent of perfume among the residents of Leszno than of all the Jews of Wielkopolska, though the concentrated smell of mingling crafts from tannery to silversmith infused the air into an unhealthy acrid chemical compound all its own. The main vocation of the Leszno Jews was trade in wool, linen, silk, furs, and spices, both local and with other lands. Behind the vocation was the occupation, and main calling of the Leszno Jews was religiosity — be it of the faith, their vocation, or the social advancement of the peoples. The heart, the mind, and the body were one in spirit to a greater degree in the population of the district than was common among the diaspora. Seeking for what was relatively common, it could go without saying, but many resentful regulations were issued by town authorities tirelessly attempting to limit the activity of Jewish traders, e.g., they were prohibited from door-to-door selling and retail trade was limited only to the days when a market was to be held. Other restrictions were also imposed. In crafts, the most common among them were tailoring, animal slaughter, shoemaking, and goldsmithery. Nevertheless, Leszno and its Jewish industries played an exceptional even if not appreciative role in the trade of the entire Commonwealth. The restrictions themselves, serving no truly economic advantage or purpose were more petty punitive bulls in the exercise of power than they were anything else. Yet, the one indignity that couldn't be overlooked or reconciled by finance was the threatening presence of occupying Russians in the quarter; herein laid the greatest aggravation for the Jewish community as a whole.

The community was characteristically divided on their occupied status. The elderly among the population complacently whittled away at time rather than risk blood — to them, when had it ever been historically different for the Jew? The ghetto's leading patriarchs knew all-to-well the cheapness of their lives to the armed and the nobility, plus they valued the well-established industrial systems that kept them wealthy, thus they sought to stir no trouble that would upset their profitable economic network. The fellow rising associates of scions of industry may have been of a younger and more energetic generation, but they saw their own artisan future on the horizon and merely carried on praying for better. For most, as long as money could be made until it was their opportunity to be in power, than the politics of change be damned. But, it was the young disaffected idealistic Jews that simmered and marked incursions with truculent defiance. So it was, in Leszno and for many Polish Jews, and certainly no different for young Hayim — as the eager boy was crouched behind a wall with six other rebellious minded teenagers and young men from his ghetto district. Protected as they were by a wooden wall — on the other side, it was obscenely carved with a familiar antisemitic image, compliments of the artistic and assiduous Polish Catholics of the city and militaristically guarded by the Russians. The image had been a popular woodcut since the Middle Ages and this local version showed three Jews, two rabbis, and a third marked by his garlic bulb and moneybag, debasing them-selves around a sow. As one of the Jews suckled at the animal's teats, another lifts the Judensau's tail, whereby allowing the third to drink the animal's excrement. The carving eluded to the tale of Simon of Trent, a murdered boy in the year 1475. It was also an insinuation of Jews being a bloodthirsty people and a local warning to them that everybody knew who and what they really were. Not to mention that it served as a fitting reminder of the times: they could be so disparaged in their own quarter; that it had been 200 years since the Leszczysk family gave them welcome and now they were no longer welcome or protected by an overlord, but scarcely tolerated and extremely vulnerable. On this day however, the smoldering of the teenagers lying in wait was not aimed at their denominational countrymen, but rather ignited by yet another assault by the occupying Russians. In addition to their imposition of high contributions required against the Jews, payment didn't always rescue the local population from a little arson— a noncompliant house fire here and there, or as the Russian saw it, smoking out rats from a burrow. The neotentic conspirators— or patriotic heroes as they saw themselves, waited for the signal from the most senior visage down the line, and the only one presently capable of growing a full beard, Noah. While the order to advance balanced in the measurement of Noah's mind, Hayim quietly rolled his shoulders, letting his coat slip down as he incommodiously peeled off his fur-lined cover and placed it on a wooden barrel. It was cumbersome and he was concerned that it would restrict his movement— he certainly wouldn't do that! No inapposite lee of fabric against the cold was going to hinder his resolve— no! Hayim Shelomo would be ready when the signal was given! As for the man, who would give the signal? When it came to the simple about Noah— at around thirty-four or thirty-five, he was a seasoned guerrilla but in reality possessing only mediocre leadership qualities. With his limited skills, however, he banded together the naïve; the undisciplined, and the willing young. His overall aim was to make a stand against what he and the entire community believed was tyranny— and show the imperial crown exactly what he personally thought of them and their ever-increasing slavish taxes, including a recently enacted consumption tax on Jews. However, his greatest ire was a white-hot seething hatred of the Russians and their conquering presence since the Great Northern War. The objective of his open attacks was Russian exasperation and arising local support. He hoped in displaying the courage of his convictions by the righteousness of his cause that he would eventually be supported en mass. Through the years, his hopes went unfulfilled, as no widespread support was ever forthcoming. As a matter of fact, by many in the community he was derided as a dangerous menace but tolerated because through him they could vicariously carry out their anger and wage a pittance of vengeance.

The other boys, barely young men, one after the other, placed their woolen scarfs over their faces and nodded to him. Next to Hayim was his childhood friend Yankel, who tied his scarf tightly and nudged his friend to follow his example. Ultimately, it wasn't so much an act of solidarity, as it could be construed merely a heed for survival— the cardinal rule being: "Don't let them see you!" Hayim wrapped his scarf across his face, tying it in a loose knot behind his head— a face of wool showing only his determined deep-set amber eyes. Every conceivable precaution was always to be taken, getting recognized meant a sure, painful, and fruitless death.

Although having no formal education, Hayim was an incredibly intelligent individual. He read voraciously and studied in detail many topics on his own. He understood the underpinnings of his society and astutely grasped the political nature of the times. The bit-by-bit, turn-by-turn, Russian machinations— owed to the decaying Commonwealth's political anarchy squeezing the life out of the society at large, but especially for the Jews. The western half of Poland was overrun with Russian forces in a brutal, conquering annexation. No friend of the children of Israel, the Russians were openly hostile to the mass Jewish population with utter indifference to their life and death.

***

As a child, Hayim was both loyal and energetic to his God and his Father— his father, god, and God, his Father. By parental instruction he was to read aloud at least one book of the Torah each night before a Shabbat candle burned to the bottom of its wick. He did so with implicit inspirits. And in the name of El Shaddai, God Almighty, he faithfully absorbed every word read— even if on most nights the candle continued to glow and the book remained open in his little hands under the overwhelming victory of winsome slumber. Withal, the child's upbringing was characterized by a willingness to overcome obstacles others would quickly retreat from. If called upon, no shelf or roof was too high, no distant needed too great— and, if success brought with it his mother's affection or his father's approval, happiness was at hand. As he matured in mind and perspective, he wanted to utilize the strength of his being, the character of his conviction to not only better his own future, but to stout-heartedly serve the historically abused and battered community in which his blood ran through. Even though he came from humble beginnings, Hayim was an exceptional talent; the type of talent that isn't focused but apparent in everything he did. He believed in his abilities and confidence from on-high; and below, in his own hand, he was unwavering. Yes, he was of the Hebrew nation— the diaspora, having the olive complexion of someone from Middle Eastern descent with neatly combed uncut, jet-black hair. However, his thin, straight, Sephardic nose betrayed his Jewish ancestry to anyone north of Italy and east of France.

***

As Hayim crouched behind the wall, a small group of heavily armed mounted dragoons and Russian regulars were canvasing the area posting curfews and other orders from the Czarina onto building fronts, rock walls, and doorways. Their form-fitting, dark green, ruffled uniforms stood in stark contrast to the bare trees around them as the soldiers unsuspectingly marched ever closer toward them. From their secure vantage points, the revolutionaries were poised and ready to spring into action.

"Easy. Wait for the others. Just a little closer," Noah whispered in a self-venerable susurration.

The neatly dressed professional soldiers conversed with strained stiffness amongst themselves, but not letting their guard down for a moment, always, there was an underlying readiness; an ever watchful eye. Even with strength in numbers and having the advantage of being armed, they understood that discontent and strife was great within the rickety, fragile bounds of the impoverished community — and since tensions ran high, they remained attentively on their guard.

Suddenly, a second group of disguised rebels charged from behind a hedgerow and ripped the newly placed posters off the establishments while yet others distracted the guards by pummeling them with the only weapons they had in their possessions: large chunks of wood and rocks! The soldiers quickly turned in formation, moving to action! They each opened their shot and powder pouches, discharged a match, and readied to light the pan. Just then a well-thrown rock whizzed past an unflinching conscript, missing him by a fraction of an inch — the lucky soldier immediately responded with an expert raising of his weapon! The soldier's eyes followed the rock thrower — patiently he watched the agitator with the strong arm, waiting for the callow combatant to hoist a second armament. When he did, the confident soldier steadied his weapon — the rope burned, and finally the flint struck the frizzen! A loud bang ruptured the anxious silence! Small nesting birds instantly took flight! Each soldier, in turn, raised his rifle, took careful aim, and pulled the trigger! The reports echoed loudly as they unhesitatingly continued to discharge their weapons!

A charging dissident was thrown backwards as a round shot ripped through his right shoulder, creating a gaping hole! He looked down at the cavernous well in his upper chest — gradually his eyes rolled backward and he calmly relinquished his puny ordnance, followed by his inalienable right to the living presence of his physiology, and mortally fell to the ground, dead. While, still another skipped between spilling over and scurrying for cover clutching a wound in his left leg — much of it below the knee shredded flesh and splintered bone. Steam rose from the cold, boot-trodden ground as warm blood mingled with packed snow draped about the fallen young men, turning the holy-colored ice crystals into a deathly pink. The occupying soldiers — never breaking ranks — quickly lowered their weapons and went down on one knee to reload their single-shot muskets. Seizing the moment, the rebel leader signaled his men. With fire in his eyes, Noah shouted —

"Now!"

Simultaneously, all six boys jumped over the wall; primitive weapons in hand!

Hayim's heart was pounding— blood and thrust, as he raced toward the uniformed Imperial Infantry of Regular Irregulars; white-knuckled with plank of wood tightly gripped in his right hand! He felt like David, only he wasn't going up against a singular Goliath, but many. All the while, with the collective guttural howls of aggression, the rebels converged on the surprised soldiers and recklessly threw themselves forward before the men-at-arms could finish reloading their spent rifle guns. Hayim watched as Noah, his confederate leader, who unknown to him, was also an unwitting stooge burnished in the miserly lacquer of the Golden Liberty; champed at the bit and focused on a stripling soldier marching forward. Noah, was already dropping a second and third round into his three-barrel turnover and crouching low behind the wall. Squat as he was, when it came to the complex about Noah: he stood on low order and finance from a loose secretive consortium of the oligarchy's legally privileged noble class. They rewarded his hyperbolic offers of cheap heroic resistance backed by a riled schoolboy militia, to which they knew would be easily, if not comically overcome. However, in the event it might unnerve the Russians, they'd have off with a florin or two. For his part, the rebel-for-hire drew his inspiration from his people's own theology of Chosenness and recruited his youthful subordinates by demagoguery of their very real everyday oppression. His message was simple, his rationale factual, but his methods basically suicidal— and at point blank range, he rose, raised his own weapon and fired into the approaching and suddenly terrified face of his adversary. Bang!

When the grey veil of spent gunpowder cleared, the stripling soldier had been blown away backward, twitching on the ground with half his face missing. In that moribund state of life, the remaining eye stayed open; staring upward in forgotten memory. Blood, blood, and more blood pooled around him as his still beating heart tried valiantly to feed his oxygen-starved brain. On the frozen, snow-covered turf, that escaping blood quickly coagulated— becoming a thickened gel rendered horrific and useless when outside of the body.

Hayim was mortified. He had seen death before— but he had only viewed it in its pristine state, sanitized by the natural covering of the body; lifeless but whole. Now though, before him, its inner workings were laid out in intimate detail. The outward gore— bits of scrambled brain tissue soaked in flowing arterial blood matted into the deceased soldier's hair, making it stick together in sickening moist clumps. The gravity, the graveness, and the gruesome reality dawned upon him in a soft, rising awareness, that he too might soon kill a soldier or possibly be killed himself. Suddenly, he saw Noah turn toward a blinding glint of light— another Russian lunging at him with blade drawn! Noah's weapon was spent; he was no longer in a position to strike first. Helpless as he was— there was no time to think, and Hayim simply reacted! He quickly raised the plank and, as the blade in the soldiers' grasp started its downward thrust, he swung! Hayim's aim was true, striking the guard squarely on the head as the soldier's blade came down for the kill! The trajectory of the knife was altered just enough by the heavy blow, before causing his leader serious injury. Noah lost his balance and fell to the ground clutching his injured arm. Venous blood oozed between his chilled fingers. Seeing the rich, dark maroon color, Hayim went to him— jumping over the unconscious but still living Russian.

"Is it bad?" he asked, helping Noah rise from the cold unforgiving surface.

"Blood! It's only blood!" he triumphantly yelled over the roar of the skirmish.

But suddenly, a look of concern came to his face, but not for his own injury—

"Gdzie jest twój szalik?"

His scarf? His scarf!— Hayim put his hand up to his face. His eyes grew wide. Silent panic! In fact, a Russian soldier stopped loading his weapon and glared at him. Their eyes met and immediately both the solider and Hayim knew, from that moment on, they would forever recognize one another, anywhere.

"He saw you." Noah declared!

In a bedlam of echoing gunfire and smoke, the fighting was getting the better of the rebel gang. A few soldiers were almost finished reloading their weapons, and—

"C'mon, we have to get you outta here," Noah, shouted!

He waved his arm in "retreat" and the men ran for the wall. Hayim ducked behind it just as more sounds of rifle fire rang out— simultaneously a round struck the wall, missing him by inches! He could hear the ball ricochet off the warped wood as he dove behind it! Hayim desperately retrieved his coat, and incautiously did so by the skin of his teeth, and caught up to his leader!

***

For Hayim and Noah it was a long and potentially dangerous retreat to the leader's cottage. Hayim was mired in a stark disillusionment all the while Noah, adrenalized, reveled in a future to come. From the torchbearer's own fantastical perspective, he succeeded at putting the Russians on further notice that blood, and bloodshed was the price paid for their bearing suzerainty. Hayim struggled to wrap his own understanding around Noah's frantic fanaticism, for it seemed to him that the only thing they had accomplished was raising the Russian's level of alertness and in the exercise, two of his friends were lost.

Noah's shirtsleeve had become a dark crimson from the wound down to the cuff and a trail of blood left tell-tail signs of their progress in the hard-packed snow, marking each step, except those few they purposefully brushed away to conceal their course. A number of dark spatters of blood— Russian blood, had soaked into the new shirt Hayim's mother had just sewn for him. For a moment, he considered how she was going to be upset that the shirt was ruined, to be more exact— heartbroken, but that trivial thought was quickly eclipsed. In the representation of the Slavic blood was the threshold Hayim had crossed, from just another adolescent rock thrower among the ghetto youth to an actual revolutionary crossed with a swath of evidence about his clothes and the newly cast impression in elephantine memory of the Russians.

***

Noah opened the door of his cabin home and the two compatriots stepped inside. What was supposed to be a cozy cottage was more an arsenal depot— highlighted by a wall of obsolete snaphances. Noah's wife, carrying an infant child, upon seeing the blood on her husband's arm, coolly went into service as though more of an expecting duty nurse than a surprised spouse. The rebel leader took off his frayed hat and set it on a wooden peg in the wall— his long, thinning hair was left wildly standing up. Noah rubbed his head, smoothing his hair back deep in thought and plunging still deeper. Finally, he crossed to a battered, old, oak desk. He rattled open the unhinged drawer; a handful of .67 caliber musket balls clumsily rolled forward. At first, the head of the household reached for a tarnished copper tobacco box, but noticed a small crimson pouch with an embroidered coat of arms. He quickly turned it upside down— empty. Together, with the box, he raised both out of their confinement. Upon opening what may have well been the most expensive commodity in their quarters, he lifted a rough, hand-carved pipe, followed by a wad of cut tobacco, which he packed into the bulbous end. Noah then crossed to the fireplace, kissed his kneeling wife— who was knelt in wait for the water to warm, on the top of her well-brushed head. Then, to her surprise the pouch was suddenly dangled before her attention and she was silently scrutinized with a gazing chastisement that brought with it a distinctly powerful blow across her face for leaving such an incriminating article about. The display of dominance was brought to an end with Noah spitefully tossing the object into the flames. She ashamedly pressed her hand to the point of contact and watched the lovely little bag burn. With intended insensitivity to her quaint and starved sensibilities, he lit a thin stick upon the burning contention, which he contentedly brought up in a lit flame to the pipe. The older of two men, looked long and hard at his brethren, as he drew deep breaths and considered what more cruelly needed to be done next.

The contemplation took the form of billowing puffs of gray smoke floating upward to the thatched ceiling. Through most of this, Hayim remained obediently silent, a bit afraid, and angled away.

In contrast to Noah's relaxed manner, he suffered a certain unexpected tension tinged with an inexplicable fear. To a degree, the anticipation seemed worse to him than it did just before the skirmish with the Russians. Now, he was nervous and extremely anxious to get home, but he didn't dare leave the man's side until his brutally violent de facto leader excused him. His wait was nearly over when the young wife was ready to apply a tepid towel to her husband's gash of a wound. Noah followed her to the handmade dinner table and sat.

His wife, like many married women of the day, was young; several years younger than even Hayim. But, she dutifully and expertly went about cleaning and dressing her husband's wound in explicit deference, rarely looking up, while a meal simmered in a huge, black, cast-iron pot. She took great pains, and a healthy amount of pride in pleasing the man she was married to; always patching him up to make him whole again. The baby began to cry, but foremost she would concern herself with the obliged marital task at hand.

For his part, Noah was thinking how best to handle Hayim's serious matter and paid little attention to her devotion or the infant's wails; finally —

"That was a brave thing you did back there— stupid, but nonetheless, brave. You saved my life, but you were also recognized. Now, they'll be looking for you."
The end of his injured leader's words trailed into a grave expression before growing into a growl. Hayim sat silently, head down in submission.

"You have to leave, tonight," Noah announced.

"What? Tonight! Where? Where will I go?"

"Anywhere," Noah winced, as his wife bandaged his arm. "I don't care, but anywhere, anywhere but here."
Then, he puffed his pipe, staring long and hard at his bewildered, valiant lifesaver.

"If you're captured", he continued, "do you have any idea, any idea what you're in for? You will be tortured... mercilessly—"

"They can torture me all they want, I couldn't leave—"

"Not the way they inflict their justice!" Noah interrupted. They will twist you; break you... until eventually, you beg them, and give us all away."

"I will do no such—" Hayim started.

"They will finish you like a dog!" Noah shouted!

Hayim saw the look on Noah's face: no remorse, no compassion, no time for tomorrow. He meant each of his words, not as colorful illustrations but as plain facts.

"Hayim, I tell you true, if you don't leave tonight, I'll have no choice… but to kill you myself."

Noah, as was his habit, brought a leg up and tapped the pipe on his leather boot. He kept his eyes to the ground and plaintively murmured —

"Go now."

But still stunned, Hayim didn't move. Noah's wife completed her detail — lovingly rushed to the baby and quickly brought it to her breast.

"Go now, I say! Go now!" Noah said.

Finally, Hayim knew he meant it, with speed. He rose and walked to the door, neither backwards, no forward, but more sideways, never taking his eye off of his leader. Noah met his gaze with unnerved puff and grit. And once he reached the door and began to open it, Noah raised his voice again in measured fact —

"And tonight, Yankel will meet you at your home with instructions. Be ready!"

***

DISGRACE

"I have never yet made, and I hope I never shall make, it the least point
of consideration, whether a thing is popular or unpopular, but whether it is
right or wrong. That which is right will become popular, and that which is wrong
will soon lose its temporary popularity, and sink into disgrace." Thomas Paine

It was nearly sundown. Hayim began his trek home where his father was presumably not so patiently waiting for him in preparation of the Sabbath. When it came to the Sabbath, or any one of the Jewish feasts, Hayim's father was intolerant of excuses or tardiness, all things were done according to pattern. It was his duty, his great commission to preside over solemn rituals. He was the type of man that kept a keen eye on his congregation with a calculated sternness.

One did not cross Rabbi Moses Shelomo. Missing a service would bring a sure knock at the door wondering why a Sabbath was not observed. The Rabbinic master was the same way with his own unliberated family. From his prideful perspective, he not only had a reputation to uphold but doctrine to fulfill.

Hayim slowly walked the snow-covered cart path toward his home. The young man was not at all anxious to inform his father that he had to flee. When provoked to anger, Rabbi Shelomo was harsh, sparing not the 'rod' or his maxims, "He who puts up with insult invites injury." He was a man of much social respect, but not one who was known to be extolled. The core of his love was layered under a parchment of piousness and mucilage of austerity. His coldness appeared to be calculated to an idiosyncratic measurement of his own oneness with God. However, his humanity lacked the Godhead's touch of Heaven; whereby, many followed him in a collective flock but only few would allow themselves to be lead individually. Hayim, had no such recourse and in the last two years of his relationship with his father had sadly devolved from veneration, to at times: antagonistic. Hayim crested the small high ground, near his parents' home. From this vantage point he had a clear view of the entire kehilla — not to mention, that behind him, he could even spot the street that the day's fighting took place and at even closer inspection still: the spent blood across the ground. Though, in truth, he knew it was too great a distance for the eye to see such fine detail… but his memory knew it was there. Just the same, the juncture bound within the occasion ceased the expansion of his forward momentum, and in the beauty of sheer wonderment, he stood perfectly still, faintly underwhelmed by the overwhelming magnitude of the predicament he faced. Lost in the moment, he stood there, arraying the comportment of nothing more than yet another young man en route. Though, in fact, he was numb, desensitized, immersed in a transcendental sensation; feeling for a brief period that he was floating above it all, locked in that inimitable, boundless in-between space of temporal human regard and ephemeral omniscience — an undulating peace that unifies the heart, the brain, and the mind, before the raw moment that a new certitude is revealed and whatever was understood as truth in days gone by will now, never be as true again. It was from there that he fixed on the rows of homes and shops and surveyed the district of about five thousand packed in ever-so-tightly. In Leszno there was nowhere else a Jew could go, live, and work — the quarter was the gilded cage. Officially, it was asserted to be a partition to protect the Jews' life, limb, and property. Yet, in point of fact, at it's best, it served as a designed segregation to separate them from the majority Catholic population in which anti-Semitism actively ran high. Thereby, they were banded together into a neatly self-possessed industrial center for the Crown's benefit and the society's liking. Again, this was at it's best. At it's worst, the district functioned as a single center of hostility to be conveniently served pitchfork hot or blade-thrusting cold, in the calculations, machinations, and rationalizations of the political class as the excuse du jour to the evermore worldly serfdom that increasingly failed to accept witchcraft as an explanation, and yet sought answers to their economic and social contentions. For Hayim, still standing still, a consideration glanced his conscientiousness, which it could possibly be the last time he would see that vista spread before his eyes. In the thought alone, the familiarity of his childhood already seemed to appear slightly different, considerably harsher, vaguely unreal, as though it never was what he remembered it as. Nevertheless, he carried on, before he slowed again— then paused, as though momentarily preventing the hands of time from continuing before he faced the projection of his father's unforgiving expectations. The anticipation of the task that lay ahead of him detonated in his mind's eye. "My God," he thought with butterflies, goosebumps, and palpitation. Vacillating, he bent to pick up a stone; bounced it in his hand, feeling the smoothness of its ovular dimensions. He studied the crystal-like flecks and imperfections. Seeing his own imperfection in them, his thoughts circled around his father, the man he respected more than all other men, loved the least among his family, and feared more than the Almighty YHWH!

"Disgrace!" the word silently screamed in his conscious thoughts! "Disgrace!" He presumed he would hear it again and again. However, it was questionable to him if he had actually disgraced himself— his spirit, his subconscious, his repressed true self… waveringly told him otherwise!

Although he knew it would be the first word his parents would use to associate his behavior. "Disgrace!" God forbid! "Disgrace!" What was he thinking? "Disgrace!" Here shalt thou lodge! "Disgrace!" How could he? "Disgrace!" Where else do they have it better? "Disgrace!" Warned, he was warned, again and again— so shall they remind him!

***

But to Hayim, he was fighting for much more than the old grievances— the lack of security, the discrimination in the law; he was taking up arms for justice, justice none would disagree had all but disappeared from the quarter! What life was there without justice? What hour did it await? What exertion did their God still seek sacrifice of them? Academic questions or clarion calls? To his mind, he was throwing rocks and swinging boards in aggression for spiritual freedom— even if it was by the dint of religion and flesh. And so, in the young man's own muddled, unsophisticated, naive judgement, he stood by his noble convictions and acted accordingly. Yes, it was a revolutionist cause, but only because he and many like-minded were convinced that rebellion was the only method to obliterate the injustice that wasn't going to destroy itself! Elizabeth wasn't going to abdicate the Russian throne! The Catholic Poles traditional tolerance of Jews was not guaranteed to last indefinitely— not while they were being swallowed whole! And yes, the day brought blood and death— maybe even unfair and futile slaughter! But, wait... what had they really accomplished? "God forgive me," he slowed his mind enough to shamefully implore. However, the tragic loss of life altered little in how he felt about the cause and his belief behind it. Still, "Disgrace," weighed heaviest on his mind. Yes-yes-yes, he knew his actions were going to prove to be a huge disappointment to the man who had instilled integrity in the virtues of temperance, prudence, honesty, and the value of hard labor. Ugh. Just the same, in the end, he reasoned, action was preferable to inaction!

***

Hayim continued on his hesitant way, stepping at times more to the side than straight ahead and contemplating the delivery of his extraordinary asseveration. Finally, he accepted that a degree of disgrace was called for. He was not fleeing in triumph. He could not stand tall in his participation of the afternoon, unless he sought to stand suspended from a rope. Yet, for as long as he could remember, he had been instructed that nearly 3,000 years of religious persecution had been inflicted on his people. It was etched in his mind— stigmatized in his heart.

Pharaoh, Nebuchadnezzar, Caesar, inquisitions, blood libels: three millennia of strife— no matter where his people roamed around the globe, sooner or later they were persecuted for their beliefs. Why did his people not retaliate, not fight? Often, he pondered; questioned in disarranged emotions: even the Christians, who claimed the same true God; why did they capriciously victimize them? Hayim didn't understand how his ancestors could just lay down and let this go on century after century and do nothing when he had read about great warriors, such as Joshua and Gideon. To him, it was unacceptable. Certainly more than his own Rabbi father, Hayim believed in the teachings of Israel ben Eliezer, the Baal Shem Tov. His aim was not so much to change the belief itself, but the heart of the believer. The Rabbi's teachings had a profound, psychological effect on him. It called him and like-minded individuals personally, not only to keep the rites and rituals of their faith, but more so, it was a call to action! Young Hayim Shelomo wanted to believe that self-determination was preferable to the eternal timetable of God. Though, he knew as such was a trap of the devil— a slip into his own identity of spirit and soul and away from the memory of God. The world seemed lost and what the kehilla, and the elders, and the functionaries, and the rabbi's all resolved to was a compromise of their projected selves for scraps of breath, bread, and time. Did not men die for true country? Did not the Maccabees revolt?

In his emancipated heart, though yet unarticulated, Hayim yearned, longed for a place; a land; a country, that removed the shackles of identification and the restrictions of worship— a cultural tillage where all would have religious freedom to openly adore the god of their own choosing— not having to resort to dank cellars or cold, musty, back rooms. In his mind, he, and his people worshiped the one true God with meekness, while the rest of Poland did so unafraid of their heritage. Beyond the unanswered prayers, camouflage of theory, and the compromises of light for fear of the dark, there was a present reality that was implacable and unforgiving. Every few months, or so it seemed, a new law or restriction was contrived.

Enlightened Prussia and Imperial Russia were working together to divide and weaken Poland, flooding the country with counterfeit money in an effort to devalue it, while imposing imperious illegal tolls and tariffs to recoup the cost of the Seven Years' War. The more rules the Jewish community obeyed, the more were added. For Jews and Poles alike, one thing was certain, allowed to continue, its aggressive neighbors would consume Poland and cease to exist. Until that very day, Hayim never did anything to disgrace his family name, stand out in the community, or cause physical injury to another human being. But now, the splotches of brown oxidation on his hand proved otherwise, indicating that the years of pent up frustration and anger as an immigrant Jew in the mutually exurb and paradoxical ghetto was too great a force, as is nature in full fury.

Straightaway, Hayim could see the front door of the home where he was raised. The time had come and he would give anything not to know his father's disappointment, but he could never take back the deeds of that afternoon— it was soaked into the fabric of his shirt. The next time he stepped through the door he expected it to be his last for a good long while. The young man didn't know where he could go, where he should go, or even how he was going to survive. He only knew he couldn't stay where he was: the same way, years before, his parents couldn't stay in Portugal— clearly illumined as being sons of Abraham by the flickering light of the auto-de-fes, the fires of the Portuguese inquisition.

Every step he took brought on a flood of new and varying dispositions, considerations, and lamentations. Considering it further, to his own astonishment, he concluded he didn't want to stay in Leszno, nor anywhere in Poland— anywhere he, as a Jew, wasn't welcome anymore. He reflected— why would anyone stay tied to the yoke of financial bondage? Why continue to make roots when so many are determined to uproot you? The wind began to pick up and Hayim raised the fur collar on his coat and turned away from it. Puffs of sweat and steam evaporated into the atmosphere with every labored breath he took. He, too, was glad winter was almost over.

The young man didn't embrace his predicament, but he didn't see any point in being fearful, either. The more he thought about it, the more he was resolved to go wherever the Lord led him. This was to be looked at as a positive experience, a beginning and not an end. Hayim turned a corner and walked up the worn cart path to the home of his youth for what he already knew could be the final time.

III

RENT

"Children should be educated and instructed in the principles of freedom."
John Adams

Hayim Shelomo opened the door to his parents' sparsely furnished home— already believing it was no longer his. He, like Noah before him, somewhat smugly placed his hat on a wooden peg; but kept tightly and rather boyishly, the fur-lined coat he was wearing, buttoned. It was the first season donning it and he cherished the rich, dark-brown covering. He had watched his mother, Rebekah, the previous summer hand stitch it from the animal skins a member of the congregation had trapped. The man had given the treasured pelts to Rabbi Shelomo as a payment for services performed. Piece-by piece, he witnessed her painstakingly push the needle through the tough leather hide. But, the value Hayim placed on it was more than simply for keeping him warm when chopping wood on cold winter days. His mother had made it and he felt dignified because of her doing so. However, that still wasn't the reason for his leaving it on. He had blood on his clothing— a great deal of blood; and it wasn't his. The coat was concealing those conspicuous, reddish-brown stains he received from the scuffle with the soldiers earlier in the day.

He walked toward the rapidly darkening dining area; the aroma of Challah bread was distinctly permeating the entire home. He saw the warm glow of the Shabbat candles he knew his mother had lit, flickering in close proximity to the two loaves of steaming bread. Hayim could hear his father in the dining area blessing the wine, chanting in his high-pitched melodic singsong voice. He had always thought the way his father prayed and sang psalms was beautiful; an earnest, rich, far-reaching call. Yet, that was the only earnest, rich, and far-reaching aspect of the man. Rabbi Shelomo was a miser. Their home was sparsely furnished in the vainglorious demonstration of piety, thrift, and purity. Where and what money he might have actually accumulated and saved, Hayim knew not. The hypocrisy— being arguably whited sepulcher, as it could have been suggested he was, would have been lost on the man. For not only was he a miser, but he was an uniquely rare individual who sought to serve, not with his heart, but through his judgment.

Hayim consciously tried to be completely quiet as he walked toward the room where his family was located, but the floor; those old, wooden floorboards creaked with every step he took and prevented him from doing so. It was never as though he was going to just stroll in unnoticed, but he did want to be as inconspicuous as possible.

His shadow drew across the room before his physical body entered. Hayim anticipated his father ceasing his prayerful melody to rebuke him; demand him to sit and take his proper seat. But the melodic song, his father was singing continued without so much as a wavering note, even as his disapproving glare met Hayim's creeping gate and chagrined expression. His mother, grandfather, and seven year-old sister, took notice as he slinked into the dimly lit occasion. The slight smile on his mother's kindly warm round face let him know she was relieved he was home. His sister was amused that her older brother was, as she figured, "in for it," while his slightly slumped grandfather silently gestured for him to move it along and quickly take his unoccupied seat. Rabbi Shelomo's song continued, but was oddly interspersed with the scrapes and squeals of the wooden chair against the also ligneous floor. This rackety disturbance repeatedly brought Hayim and his father eye-to-eye. Nevertheless, the ritual went on with his father punishingly staring at his son with a steady glare that pushed beyond mere disapproval. It was a postulating look, a menacing regard, suggesting at the behest of being late that Hayim wasn't even there, a ghostly stripping of importance or even membership in the family. For his part, Hayim merely sought to overcome his failing by joining in accordance. He sang under his breath along with his father until his voice rose in resound unison. Finally, Rabbi Shelomo's mien changed to a more approving manner, and as the song ended, the tension around the table settled— order temporarily restored.

This was the Sabbath: it was a time-honored tradition, a faithful observance honoring God as creator of all things. Hayim had been taught that it had literally been that way for thousands of years. And, just as faithfully, every week, as he would have performed it in the temple; the beit k'nesset, his father performed the exact same steps in seraphic order over his own family's holy meal. It was done the same way without any deviation every Friday night at sundown for as long as Hayim could remember-- that is, until that evening. In Rabbi Shelomo's home, Hayim knew there was one thing as a member of the family, which was strictly forbidden: absence or tardiness from a Sabbath observance. Punctuality was a must. Tardiness reflected a lack of reverence, a self-grandiose pretension of disrespect. Worshiping the God of Abraham, Isaac, and Jacob was taken seriously. Rubric order was understood as implicit to loving God. Aaron's son's had been killed instantly at the powerful hand of God because the Almighty's instructions were not done specifically in accordance to His demonstrative commands. This rigid devotion was instilled in Hayim at a very young age. Anything less was not tolerated and came with severe consequences— and Hayim never had the displeasure of discovering what those consequences amounted to. Even though he was considered a man in his own right, still, Hayim was afraid, realizing he was about to discover what those consequences were.

***

Rabbi Shelomo was dressed in his tallit; the traditional prayer shawl and yarmulke. Hayim sat directly opposite from the other side of the table and looked back at the way his father looked askew at him— in the stillness of his slender frame and the slightly raised eyebrow.

"Do you want to explain yourself?" his father asked in rather measured quality above rhetorical, in the range of edictal decree.

"Well," Hayim stared witlessly in momentary silence.
His father in droll mockery assumed it would take a moment or two for his son to formulate his unforgivable excuse and he went about sacredly storing away their Torah in the holy. It was a Sefer Torah, older than the man himself, and he gently handled the parchment scroll; an ancient copy of the first five books of the Bible— cradling it as if it were a fragile infant. It had been in the Shelomo family for generations and was always treated with utmost care— the singular most venerated item in their home. Eventually, Hayim responded to his father's understated directive by merely bowing his head— an act of acknowledgement that he had committed a serious transgression. Rabbi Shelomo, dismissed the inarticulate response and continued his derisive admonishment with his back purposefully turned to Hayim—

"You wear your coat at the table, now, too?" Shaking his head, "Late for Sabbath and—"

"Take your coat off, Hayim," his mother kindly encouraged him. Hayim turned and profoundly looked deep into her eyes—

"Hayim, take your coat off," she said a second time with surprise and insistence; unaware of the depth in which he stared into her.

Still, her son didn't quickly comply. Yet, he knew, eventually there was nothing else he could do but consent. Finally, Hayim arched forward and painstakingly — one arm at a time slowly pulled back the sleeves of his coat, until his mother suddenly gasped at the sight of dried blood! Rabbi Shelomo turned and he too became witness to something he never expected —

"What happened to you Hayim, have you been hurt?" his sister innocently spoke.

"No, I'm all right," he coolly stated.

Notwithstanding, his coolness and calm was antithetical to the underline sight, and his parents and grandfather waited for what seemed an eternal second for further explanation.

"It's not my blood," Hayim assured them.

Hayim's mother gasped yet again!

"Were you in a fight?" his father asked.

"Yes, father."

"Someone attacked you?"

Hayim didn't have a ready answer before his father continued —

"You attacked someone?"

The son didn't speak but his timid peering up at his father answered in the affirmative for him.

"Who? Who Hayim?"

"The soldiers," he finally admitted.

"'The soldiers?'" his father questioned as though it were impossible that he meant 'The soldiers.'"

"The Russian Soldiers, at the edge of the district," Hayim explained.

The rabbi could not believe it. This was an inconceivable proposition.

"Their wont?"

"No, father."

"What business?"

"They had no business! I had no business! But I made business! With others! We wont," Hayim confessed with a tinge of shame but a full bore of truth.

It was all incredible, unimaginable, and simply maddening! The rabbi, beyond belief, was beside himself. A ghostly shade of incredulity suffused up his neck and washed over his face, leaving him looking more apparition than a bearded red-blooded man. Hayim's body never felt so cold and so formless as it did in that moment in which his father was almost speechless, until—

"Are there dead?" the rabbi brought himself to ask.
Hayim brought himself to answer in stark truth—

"Yes, father, there are dead,"
His mother howlingly gasped! His sister shuddered! His grandfather, already in a permanently degenerative slope, bowed his head but a little lower— and all the while, the rabbi tempestuously transitioned from disbelief into fury! However, it was the kind of fury that has to simmer to a boil in nervous gestures before it detonates into a froth—

"What have you done?" his father hissed through his teeth, "My son, God forbid— what have you done?"

***

Hayim had no choice, he had to quickly tell all; everything that took place only a few short hours previous. The longer he spoke, the angrier his father became. The man's once ghastly white graduated into an inflammation of color on the scale of a chameleon resting against a rose hip. His hands involuntarily shook— regardless of the amount of times he desperately clasped them together, they wouldn't stop trembling! Fully grasping the magnitude of the situation, Rabbi Shelomo collapsed on the bench and turned away from his son. He wasn't disgusted. He was terror-stricken. There was absolutely no fixing the problem.

"Hayim, I don't understand," his mother said.

"Leave the boy to his own," his grandfather quavered in an indistinct defense.

"But Papá, I don't understand. Hayim—"
She grabbed his face and desperately held it in her hands. Mystified, she looked at him— unabashed, she still saw the young man as her little boy—

"Mother—" he said.

"Why? What were they—"

"You see what they do to us!" Hayim said with pleading aggression.

"Do you know what you've done? What have I told you and taught you about the hand raised in anger? Do you think you're safe now just because you are home?" his father said sharply rebuking the plea!

"No matter, I'm leaving tonight," Hayim spoke up!

His mother almost fainted. His father rose —

"'No matter?' That is of what is no matter! You have put us all in danger. Do you not think they will come, come here looking for you, tearing this place apart, taking what they will, destroying as they wont, and God forbid if they decide to punish you by punishing one of us!" Then and there it all sunk in. In the course of his fading adolescent, Hayim never thought so deeply or so far ahead when he sought to stand against the vague, ill-defined notion of "Injustice." Maybe reprobate, if that was all he was. The pragmatic structural actualities of reality substantiated that his father was direly correct. Ergo, Hayim's previous concern about disgracing the family was baldly transmuted into abject indignity. "Oh my God," he thought. Yes, what had he done?

"Do you know where you are?" his father thundered! "Do you know where you are, Hayim Shelomo?" Fury and froth! In it's wake the echo of stillness was embodied in the rest of the family's taciturn stiffness. The room was as hush as the deepest vacuum of space. The rabbi held unbroken a mean wordless stare to thoroughly dress down his son. In the glaring ignominy the young man just might as well have been bare naked in front of a firing squad. He indefensibly came to regret his recklessness in the solemn emotions of utter shame and guilt. The people he loved so dear — and now, he was their greatest detriment to life. His father continued to roar in the register of rolling thunder!

"Fool! My son — the fool!"

"No!" Rebekah pleaded to her husband! Immediately, the rabbi reflexively wiped his face, cleaned his lips of spittle, and disengaged the belligerent onslaught whereby bestowing upon his wife due respect. However, he wasn't finished with his son and he approached him in a seething self-controlled rage.

"Injustice? You want to be a hero? What do I see? Tell me? Moses? David? Samson?," the Rabbi said as though profanely cursing at his child. "Is your self-devised plan of salvation also going to save us from the Czarina and the King, the Grand Inquisitor, the Russian Orthodox Church — the Holy Roman Empire! Or God forbid, French Pox and the plague?" His father sneered —

"It is injustice you despise, is it? Such a small little principle of fruit from the tree of knowledge, or would you not agree, my foolhardy son?"

Hayim could have merely retreated further into humiliation, but he stood his ground and spoke respectfully that he may give understanding to his less than fortuitous act—

"It is no excuse, father, but they bleed us dry."

Rabbi Shelomo was not pleased by Hayim's words.

"I see I have taught much, but conveyed little."

"I have learned much from you, father! Please forgive me!"

"What have you learned?" the rabbi asked rhetorically.

Hayim was heartbroken by the inference that he learned nothing, that he sat at the foot of his own biological creator and did not retain the glory poured upon him— an assertion it was, that he was, after all his love and devotion: worthless. Anguished, the "words" surged forth—

"How long is it going to last? When you sent the dove out of the ark in the time of the flood, You gave it an olive branch so that it might have support for its feet on the water, and yet it was unable to bear the water of the flood and returned to the ark— whereas my children you have sent out of the ark into a flood— and have provided nothing for support where they may rest their feet in their exile," Hayim recited from memory.

In that soliloquy, the rabbi's own teachings abruptly met him before his face. However impressed he could have been with his son and student, he was not—

"What more good did you think you could have done?" the rabbi asked.

Hayim was silent.

"You do not know where you are… but this my Sephardic son… child of the flames of the Inquisition… developed in the womb of his fleeing mother—"

The rabbi pointed to his wife's abdomen. She clutched it, tears welling in her eyes!

"At one month in the cavity of her body, like the child under the dominion of Herod, they sought you, too, scorched— burned in her act of faith."

Rebekah was overcome with tears; a weeping she couldn't hold back any longer. Hayim had seen her cry, but never like this. She whimpered inaudibly; the uncontrollable twitching of her wetted face sounded in the profundity of affliction. Piled with the most disturbing anguish, her tears welled and ran in streams— in the vein of salt poured into the wound of a soul.

"I know of no heroes in your kind. None as vigilant in their love and as patient in their faith as to carry it with such care treated no better than pigs in a cargo hold onto Italian shores. We traveled the indignities and the abuses that you might be born in the relative safety and security of a country you find so unjust. My dear son, to have gleamed half an education is to have knowledge but understand nothing at all. They had nowhere to rest in their exile, you say, but thereupon, God took a piece of the Land of Israel, which he had hidden away in the heavens at the time the Temple was destroyed, and he sent it down upon the earth, and said: 'Be My resting place for my children in exile.' Yahweh be thanked, so then existed Poland. You stood safely and securely on that ground— by her labor— you were born here! This is the land where we wait— though you do not yet taste the milk and honey."

Hayim remained silent, and might have done so forever, but—

"Speak up! Look around— look around you, see— see before it is all ablaze by the Russians whom will surely return your favor!"

His sister burst into tears!

"I'll give myself up," Hayim desperately declared!

"No, Hayim!" his mother screamed!

Suddenly a quiet rap came to the door and everyone jumped in fear! After a moment, Hayim realized it might be Yankel, yet still, he approached cautiously. To everyone's surprise the knocking was not only quiet but after a few quick taps— all together stopped. Surely it wasn't Russians, because it if were, the knocking would not have stopped but would have crescendoed into a pounding, and then into a violent forced entry. Be that as it may, Hayim slowly opened the door, and thankfully it was only his boyhood friend, Yankel. His thick dark bushy hair poured out of the sides of his second-rate sheepskin ushanka. Yankel knowingly entered, respectfully doffing off his hat; ready as commanded.

"I'm to help you get out tonight," he said to Hayim.

"Where?" Hayim's mother screamed!

Before speaking, the boy looked to Hayim, who indicated that there was nothing to hide—

"Just far enough I was told, as far as I could go without freezing," he said to her but all the time looking back to Hayim. "You are to leave the country altogether, and never return, 'never' I was told to tell you."

A long silence hung over the entire house until it was broken by Hayim's sister openly weeping—

"I don't want you to go! I don't want you to go!" she cried! Now suddenly, it seemed time itself was no more. Hayim stepped toward his father and bravely spoke—

"It is not a sacrifice to me, father, to sacrifice myself for all of us. Please forgive me for what I have done— please forgive my head but not my heart."

Rabbi Shelomo held his gaze into his son's watering eyes. Hayim was bravely willing to take his punishment but that didn't mean that his soul was not rent. He knew he would be rent from his family or from the earth, and he held back his tears but couldn't hold back his body's natural quivering of fear. Rabbi Shelomo pulled his boy tightly into his chest and squeezed him with all of his might. Then, he turned to the familiar face of Yankel—

"Please, take him as far— as far as you can."

The entire family, including Yankel, huddled in the moment in shifting embraces, until finally time beckoned and they reacted to it as expediently as required!

***

Hayim effusively kissed his mother and sister, combining his tenderness with devoted whispers of "It'll be all right." The females cried in anguish; yet he purposefully squeezed back his own developing sorrow and straightened every muscle into rock-hard self-assurance— even though he himself was utterly terrified. But suddenly, there was no time to waste and his mother leaped from his embrace and jumped into action! First, she gathered a satchel for her son. While doing so, her eyes met both her father and her husband— clearly this was it, the bitter good-bye. Yet, but nobody was suddenly stronger and wiser than her!

Yankel was anxiously waiting, still shivering from making his way in the frigid temperatures. Rebekah rushed about, and Hayim looked up to his father in the most adult state of self he had ever possessed.

"Father, one day— one day father, change will come, and I will play a part in it, I know it, I just know it," he painfully claimed.

"God makes changes, not men!" the Rabbi quickly corrected him. Hayim knew those words were a censure to his actions, to his discernment that had suffered an abrupt enlightenment— and he respected the artful reprimand because he knew he had done wrong trying to do right.

However, he lent Hayim a word of faith he never conferred upon him before—

"My son, the change you seek, the righteous atonement you want, the treasure of the heart and of man that abounds it, even it on this earth— is not worthy of you."

With that concession, whatever strength Hayim Shelomo was going to need now to survive and possibly even thrive, was dearly bestowed upon him. He heard the words and he understood their magnificent meaning, but that meaning paled in comparison and amazement to his father's actual and unexpected outward expression of a deeply profound love and approval toward him. It was all he ever needed and Hayim was intensely awe-stricken in tender silence. Nonetheless, the moment was short-lived—

"Come on! We have to go now!" Yankel shouted!

Hayim's mother had thrown open nearly every trunk, cupboard, and drawer they had and hastily stuffed what she could into the simple satchel. Bread! Socks! Candles! A wooden-handled knife! A mezuzah! A pot! Potatoes! And various other constituent items. She dropped the bag into Hayim's arms; then threw herself at him and hung on for dear life! The weeping on his shoulder soaked into the blood stained fabric.

"Kocham cię," she cried! "Kocham cię!" letting him know that she loved him in an immensity beyond what words could express.

Then, remembering something highly important— she pried herself away from him and went to the one old chest in the bedroom she hadn't flung open, the one that she had to unlock. The old hinges creaked as she opened it. But there, under two handmade quilts just where she placed it, the woman found what she was looking for.

"Let's go now," Yankel insisted and opened the thick wooden door into the frosty night.

Hayim began to follow his comrade's insistence when he felt a gentle tug on his arm. He turned to see yet again the loving eyes of his mother.

"Take this!" she said, after glancing to her husband for approval— and getting the nod.

Hayim's mother placed a small pouch in his open hand.

"It isn't much, but..."

But she couldn't finish her words without sobbing again—

"What if I never see you again?" she wept.

One of his own tears flowed freely as he opened the small, leather bag. It had a few lower denomination coins inside and a few pieces of silver.

"I cannot take…" he began, when his father, standing behind them, offered his approbation—

"You must," he said tenderly.

Hayim gazed back into his father's face and saw a tear welling. His father quickly turned away but that developing tear told Hayim of the true depth of his father's affection for him, and it bridged the spatial gap in Hayim's heart that had grown between them since he had come of age.

Hayim hugged his mother and raised his sister off the floor, repeatedly sweeping back her exceptionally beautiful and long brown hair. He held her in his arms as she looked up at him with blurred vision. He kissed her softly on the cheek and wiped away her tears. Sobbing, she squeezed him tightly around the neck as though to never let go.

"I will be back. I promise. We'll be together, again," he said to her. But, it was a promise Hayim Shelomo in fact would never be able to truly keep.

IV

DARKNESS

"These are the times that try men's souls." Thomas Paine

Before Hayim hurried out the door with Yankel leading the way it was already a black, starless night. Everything about it was dim, dark, and enigmatic. By the winter's tilt of the sun, the clock was still at late evening but boarding on night— all the while the temperature had increasingly fallen in the hours since Hayim had returned home. The air was bracingly crisp, as a three quarter moon hid behind thick, incoming cloud cover. Even before Hayim felt the full effect of the gelid air, he knew it was bone-chillingly cold by the portentous sound of the packed snow crunching under the thin threadbare soles of his shoes. He stepped in advance to an open-ended horse drawn cart that was waiting for him. Nonetheless, the gravity of the situation and the dire foretoken affair wasn't lost on him by the imperative call to action. Everything, inwardly and outwardly seemed black-on-black. The sky was black, his heart felt black, it was a black day for his family, Yankel was dressed in a black smock-frock, and coming upon the cart, he sighed— noticing with dread that even the horse pulling it, was black.

"Get in. Cover yourself." Yankel instructed as he climbed onto the horse's back. "Stay low, stay quiet, and don't let yourself be seen!"

The soon-to-be fugitive Shelomo was about to scale his transport when he heard the door of his home shut behind him. Hayim turned. It was his grandfather. He was dressed in a dark cloak-like garment. The old man hobbled up to his departing kindred, surreptitiously pulling something forward from the inside of his cloak.

"Here... take this. Careful!" he said, his hands trembling with the premature age of shaking palsy. The patriarch was holding out an old little book to his grandson. Hayim dutifully took the soft, leather-bound book. On the cover was stitched a six-pointed star— the Star of David. He had never seen the book before. Hayim mournfully looked at his grandfather cocked in his flexed posture, before he looked again at him inquisitively, and gently touched the star on the cover. Even in the low light, he could see that it had been repaired and re-stitched several times. It must have been a very old book. Hayim peered at the thoughtful, old man and opened the pages. He saw writing but could not decipher its meaning. It was only a minute in which they had stood but already the temperature felt as if it had dropped a few more degrees. The old man started to shake and his teeth to chatter. He opened his mouth to speak but first he had to overcome his body's involuntary mechanisms to stay warm.

"Take it with you," he managed. "Study it. Keep it. Pass it on to your..."
But feeling pressed— feeling cold, and ultimately fearing for his life, Yankel interrupted—
"We must leave, now!"

Hayim was awed and amazed; here was his grandfather bravely baring the cold just to give him this... "Book?" However, his grandfather was less sentimental and quickly pushed his numb quivering fingers across the pages to a folded piece of parchment tucked inside. Hayim unfolded it. It was an address, but just as Hayim lifted his lips to ask whose it was, a hell baying wind whipped through the physical space of separation between he and his grandfather, as though nature itself was separating them prematurely! The elder wobbled and the deafening howls unnerved the old nag to rear and stir in agitation! Eddying snow followed and there was simply no time left for extended sentimentality. Hayim quickly embraced his grandfather and kissed him on both cheeks— as was customary, and then prodded him the few steps needed to catapult the man back into the house where Hayim's mother and sister were despairingly watching out of the window. Finally, Hayim hurdled into the wooden cart and found a dark blanket. He laid flat and covered himself. Yankel yelped something unintelligible that Hayim assumed was directed to the horse and immediately the cart lurched forward.

In minutes, Hayim found a tiny hole in the scratchy, woolen blanket, and through it he could only see where they had been and not where they were going. Nonetheless, he quickly realized they were headed toward the main part of the city, and at a good pace. The cart was bouncing and bounding along the uneven terrain. Over the wind, Hayim could faintly hear Yankel fitfully yelling instructions to him; among what he could hear, telling him that he was never to come back to Leszno and that if he were to get caught, he was to give the Russians a fictitious name. Eventually, the cart slowed almost to a complete halt, then lurched forward with even more urgency. Hayim stayed low.

***

The cart, loaded with a bewildered and motionless passenger tucked safely in back, raced into the city proper as an unenthused Russian soldier stepped onto the snowy wind-blown street—

"Ostanovit!" he shouted in Russian!

The guard apathetically had raised his hand to stop the galloping horse, but the foul weather immediately brought on the decision to wave through what appeared to be a harmless lone rider pulling a hapless lone cart. Fate is the invisible feature of the human synthesis, and he that is born to hang shall never drown— so it was that the Russian waved them forward and Yankel gladly sped past. Surely, if it had been warmer, if the weather patterns had been different, he would have given a more valiant effort. But, since it was only a singular rider with an empty cart, the guard considered it could be of no consequence and went back to the guardhouse as if nothing happened. As Hayim peeked through the hole, which stared into the past, he saw the same Russian solider that he had made eye contact with, and without doubt, would have known him in an instant. Maybe fate was on his side, but luck was another issue altogether.

Hayim heard the extraordinary sound of shoed hooves clopping against evenly laid stone streets; the howling wind whistling past. Through the same tiny hole in the wool blanket, he saw the cleaner, urban, Baroque architecture of closed shops along the darkened district streets of Leszno's better class. There was absolutely no one on them, nor was there any sane reason for anyone to be out on them— it might have well been the coldest night of the year.

He watched the snow swirling in enormous, horizontal circles and began wondering if Yankel stopped the cart anywhere less than a place of lodging, how was he supposed to travel through this evolving blizzard? God help him, it was not going to be a good night to peregrinate the unknown and Hayim knew it. Still, the horse galloped on....

For his part, Yankel was as nervous as the mare he was riding. He knew the bitterness of the air, the way it seared his lungs as he inhaled; it was not conducive to traveling on foot for great distances. Yet, that is what he was instructed to do: leave the young rebel in his charge at the far end of town— no further. He told Mrs. Shelomo as far as he could go without freezing, but that's because it sounded more compassionate and was his personal intent. But that's not what Noah commanded him. "Just to the edge of the city," he ordered. "Any further— both of you will be dead ice by morning," he warned.

But Yankel was ashamed to just leave his friend in the elements to die, and by the inclement feel of the lording darkness, he surely would— although, point of fact, Yankel was given no choice. To him and many of the boys, the cause took precedence over his own conscience, the circumstances dictated that he couldn't go too far without risking his own well-being, and retribution if Noah discovered that he disobeyed his orders could be brutal. Two years older than Hayim, he had his own wife and child to think about, otherwise, he might have risked it all in valor— to take his lifelong friend, the days of journeying to the border himself; far away from the bitterness of both squall and country. Yankel drove the horse onward past the last business; a seamstress, into the pitch-blackness and fearsome darkness of the forest's wintery night.

Finally, the aged well-ridden mare was stubbornly reigned in to a quick halt. Hayim could hear the horses' nostrils flaring to take in air. He heard his friend jump down from the animal and approach the rear of the cart. Yankel whipped the blanket off of his lone passenger. It seemed almost immediately that Hayim was covered in a thin but complete veil of snow.

"I think... this is far as I can go," Yankel sheepishly said.
Hayim didn't oppose him, but Yankel continued—

"I went farther than they told me to go, I did," he ashamedly and proudly confessed.

Hayim understood and held nothing against him. Yankel stood above him frozen to the bone. His face was blue; tiny icicles formed from the snot that ran from his nose, and he was trying to conceal a trembling numbness. He gave all he could and both of them knew, the elements or a more earnest soldier too, might overcome him on his return. Hayim wasted no more time and half-heartedly jumped out of the cart, remembering to pick up his satchel. He watched as Yankel quietly steered the transport around. The biting wind had the horse quivering — a colubrine ripple moving back and fourth, up and down, all along the steed's body. Pacing, she stood in direct contrast to the falling snow around her — displaying her instinctive sense of humanity with what appeared to be remarkable understanding, whereby she nervously circled her pace around Hayim. In any case, coaxed and cajoled, Yankel focused the sable mount the other direction. Instead of taking a last good-bye, still weighed in guilt, he hurried away in a dusted cloud of white powder, heading out of the forest of naked arbor on the treaded route in which they had come. Ultimately, Yankel was typical among the young rebels, foolhardy but not daring; pained but not troubled. Hayim stoically watched the rider and the horse disappear. In their vanishing, so too his youth legitimately receded. For what felt like the first time in his young life, the present was free of all past associations and the moment that had just evanesced was bunched into a new sentiment for him, one that would last forevermore, "I remember before…."

***

It was a late winter bombardment, the true darkness of March before the dawn, and as Hayim stood there, the storm continued to swallow the atmosphere — reeling in the sight of the air and the land, and the whole of the past, present, and future tightly around him into a zero visibility. Which way was he facing? Which way should he go? Hayim needed to leave his native country far behind and the quickest course was to the west, through the ever expanding Empire of Prussia and beyond!

Maybe that border was his River Jordan where he could enter the promised land of freedom— freedom to worship as he chose; freedom to make an honest living without government persecution and torture at the hands of detestable, angry mobs. Then again, maybe it was no different under Fredrick the Great than it was under Catherine II. Hayim suddenly wondered, what was the address his grandfather had given him? Which direction did it lead? Though he couldn't simply reach into his satchel against the conditions, no matter where it was, it couldn't have been close enough at that moment. However, he had to move. If he stood still vacillating any longer, surely he would be overcome by the unseen weather of the darkness and die.

In no time, Hayim was on a lonely stretch of snow-covered road; miles beyond Leszno but still somewhere, in the dangerous military reaches of Southwest Poland. A fading beam of moonlight silhouetted the landscape as he trudged westward with the wind having shifted, suddenly coming almost due north and with it— more snow— a great deal of it. Though he couldn't see beyond his hand in front of his face, to the left and to the right, he continually glanced, hoping to catch the sight of a residence or any form of shelter; seeking someplace to ride out the ever nearer full blizzard conditions. But nothing less, than bare trees caught his impaired sight.

The hours elapsed; it became harder for Hayim to make his legs move through the thickening white drifts. It was midnight, though Hayim didn't know it, and he could feel a tingling sensation in his legs and was barely able to feel his feet. He had turned the fur collar up on his coat to protect his ears, but they were painfully numb.

Until an hour previous, only a steady wind interspersed with howling gusts, but suddenly, as it can sometimes do at those latitudes, the wind picked up and the snow started whipping horizontally. In the blink of an eye, the weather had intensified beyond the capacity of common human endurance. The dim moonlight was no more. Darkness. True darkness had fallen. Walking in blindness. Collapsing in drifts of snow. Whipsawed by branches. Slamming into trees. The winter could be heard. The weather could be felt. But nothing could be seen.

In shorter and shorter careful steps, Hayim tried to take his mind off of the freezing temperatures by reflecting. He reflected about how loving his mother was, yet, in contrast, how strict and unbending his father could be. Hayim saw his mother as being a gentle, kind individual who took the time to understand her children, whereas, his father only wanted his children to understand him. Despite the recent rejoining they had just shared and the betterment of his heart, a deep well of misgivings between his father and he still perplexed him. The rabbi was a strong traditionalist, but Hayim never understood why the man insisted on being so, when before his eyes, his people were being tormented, persecuted, and killed. Hayim remembered growing up and seeing violent mobs rounding up many of neighbors and his parents' friends; accusing them, berating them, and occasionally beating them. His mother tried to shelter him from the wickedness, but he saw — he saw much. He witnessed homes aflame set by the enraged mobs and murderous rampages in which residents of the quarter were burned at hastily erected stakes.

As he grew older in adolescence, he asked his parents why it was happening. His father would only explain in non-sequiturs the complicity of hate — that there were differences in the outlooks and perspectives between themselves and the Catholics. He still didn't quite understand, but he knew well-enough not to ever press his father any further. He was left to simply assume they were fundamentally different; but were the differences so much so, that they warranted the negative consequences? Jewish cries of injustice rang out to the sympathetic Kingdom and Grand Duchy, only to fall on ears influenced to be deaf by sponsoring Russia. A repressive monarchy that ground, both its small people and its small protectorates under its heels. At the time, he didn't know it was policy, governmental pogroms; state financed massacres, which allowed for the maltreatment of Jews — but not without the tacit cooperation of idle indifference from the Polish Catholic community. Hayim didn't understand why absolutely nothing was being done to stop the carnage. Was it really the land of milk and honey?

***

The Haidamacks were paramilitary bands, best known for hanging a Pole, a Jew, and a dog, on one tree and placing the inscription, "A Pole, a Jew, a hound — all the same faith bound." However, most of the attacks made by the Haidamacks and other various mobs the government would occasionally incite in an effort to deflect responsibility for the state of the state, were directly targeted against Jews — usually taking the form of robbery and the murder of merchants traveling on the highway and assaults on Jewish tenant farmers living in isolated places or on the inhabitants of small defenseless towns. On any given day, you'd hear about seven dead here or ten dead there. To these boys, almost to a one, except for Hayim, they were rebellious against the stricter order of the Ashkenazic tolerance they were brought up in — and since the government was going to condone and supply hordes of ruffians with the means to destroy and look the other way, they were going to fight fire with enduring pride. That was how he met Noah, thanks to Yankel.

***

In darkness there is no light. Darker of darkness there is no sound. The night that was already cold grew colder. The storm had stopped. In it's halt, silence eclipsed everything. The wind that howled now did not even whistle. There was no rustle of animals, nor chirps of a bird, or even that of an insect. The timbre of Hayim's movements, his legs, his shoes, and his breath — any of it should have made a sound of some sort, but insulated within snow, nothing made a single tone. The silence was even more frightening than that of the storm, then — he fell!

***

Hayim lay there sweating and freezing at the same time. The darkness that knew no bounds invited him to stand, but promised to show him nothing but itself. He had to rise, though even if he did — in blindness, where was he forward to go? The wind howled as Hayim tried to remain upright — the yowl of nature that at most times hummed in a wail of terror now sounded beautiful, that it was sound at all. He came to his feet, heavier with snow and staggering in the frozen darkness. He was numb from the biting wind and bitter temperature and yet sweat made him as wet under his clothes as if he was in the sea. He had been in the elements for hours, but still the night lingered, itself young. Hayim thought he would never see daylight again. His hands were without sensation and beginning to turn purple, though he wouldn't have known that. Likewise, his thoughts were becoming more scrambled with each step. His body shivered uncontrollably and Hayim Shelomo knew he needed to find shelter — and fast. He was moments from arrant collapse.

The beam of moonlight returned and the young man laboriously ascended a snow-covered hill. In the distance, through squinted eyes, he thought he could see the outline of a large structure. As he toiled along, he wasn't sure what he was seeing or not seeing. He decided it didn't matter. He would will himself to the distance, whatever that distance was, but he wouldn't and couldn't will himself any further. If it was a structure, then maybe he could survive the night. If it wasn't, he was prepared to lie down and allow the elements to consume him. With his body temperature dropping fast, Hayim forced his legs to pick up the pace. He teetered on, tottering between reality and insanity. Was he looking at a structure or merely a figment of an overactive imagination that could only be conjured up by a delirious mind exposed to the wrath of nature for too long? Was his mind, in fact, seeing an oasis in a blizzard of snow?

Hayim was pelted by tiny frozen beads that stung his face, further obscuring his blurred vision. Again, he fell! He didn't know how it happened — one second he was upright, the next, he was on the ground. Thousands of needle-like sensations pricked into his body. He raised his snow-masked face above the white fluff — and encouragingly, the structure hadn't disappeared. It was real! It had to be real! He tried to stand — but collapsed yet again in a heap.

To not move meant to die. It was not a matter of minutes any more, but any given seconds. Hypothermia had set in. His core body had permanently fallen below the heat required for his organs and muscles to function adequately. Hayim willed himself to claw and crawl through the snow itself, as though crawling against quicksand. His fingers, hand, and his arms all felt as though they were supernaturally disconnected from his body. The extremities only moved to a limited degree in delayed response to his brain's staggered firings. The character of a man is built in his bravery against nature and trust in himself. So, it was, that Hayim forced his debilitated synapses to fire in sequence and willed his muscles to respond accordingly. He brought his legs up and pushed his throbbing hands into the thick snow. With a guttural howl, which the wind immediately dispersed, Hayim forced himself to a standing position. He staggered unsteadily the first couple of steps, nearly falling once again, but, finally was able to find a workable gait. As he plodded on, the dark looming edifice only increased in size and became clearer until he was able to feel the seasoned wood under his stinging hands. Through the blinding snow he was looking at a barn. Above the howling wind, Hayim Shelomo actually laughed!

***

The barn was open at one end, but at least it was the end opposite the direction of the buffeting wind. It wasn't ideal, but he knew it was going to provide essential shelter away from the roaring squall. Hayim walked up to a large pile of hay near a few cows. They uttered a sound of nervous acknowledgement, but overall didn't seem to mind him there. The hay seemed to call to him; beckoned him. Hayim dove into the loose straw; disregarding the possibility of rodents, and completely covered himself in the hay. He could hear the crunching and snapping of the dried grain against his cold flesh and with his body temperature close to altering him lifeless, the straw felt as if tiny knives were stabbing into the exposed portions of his skin.

Slowly, a proportion of calefaction at a time, he warmed— just enough that the blood vessels dilated and the pale white of his expiring face blotched in red patches of life. His breathing, which fell through the night into slow and shallow draws rose steadily to lifesaving respiration. Hayim, unable to simply sleep with a heart that seemed determined to continue beating, began to reflect on the events of the previous day. While he was deep in thought, wallowed between hypothermia and a mild state of unconsciousness, the world finally began to feel both lighter and heavier at the same time. His attention wandered and flickered in and out of awareness. He had witnessed the horrors of death first-hand; watched a man, who couldn't have been much older than himself, collapse to the ground— his face eviscerated! He saw fellow rebels, ones he had spoken to earlier in the day, whom he would later see drained of life. He was actually wretched that he hadn't thought about them before that moment. The events of the day and the horror of the night did not permit him to ponder the boys' deaths at great length. And he chastised himself, believing each sacrifice and each person who died, rebel or Russian, deserved no less than his undivided reflection. Hayim wondered if they had families; even wives— maybe a child on the way! Of his friends, he naturally felt more sympathy and gradually became saddened by their ultimate sacrifice… a most noble, worthy cause— that is, it was only appropriate to think of it that way for the moment; in the face that they died for it and all. Though, in point of fact, they were a bit younger then him and he never even knew their names.

Hayim internalized everything and pondered the idea of his own demise— how his mother would have been devastated to learn of his fate, if it was him lying on the frozen ground and steaming from a gaping rifle wound. All the while his teeth chattered and the sound of the blizzard beating on the walls scared him. He looked around his dark, almost black, unfamiliar surroundings— hay, sickles, anvils, rope, and animals. He didn't have to contemplate very much to see what his actions lead to. He was staring up from the very bottom of his own valley of the shadow of death. He could go no lower. No family; no home; little food or money. He fretted what tomorrow or the immediate days after would bring in terms of fate to his family. He thought maybe he shouldn't have left them, that it was the cowardly thing to do. He could have stayed and let himself hang— that they would knowingly live. They had made such a sacrifice for him. His mother, now he knew, twice had given him life. He could safely condemn himself— he was as low as a man could get.

From his satchel, he extracted a piece of his mother's bread and his grandfather's siddur. He took a bite of the moist center, letting it melt on his tongue and then he placed the prayer book on his chest. The folded piece of parchment fell out onto the straw bedding next to him. He lifted and unfolded it. It was a hastily written address in his grandfather's crabbed hand. To his surprise it was an address in Holland. Holland! Holland?

Hayim looked through the rest of the book. Most of its contents he couldn't understand. It was written in a language he couldn't read, Hebrew — ironically, that of his own people. Toward the back, though, he noticed something different. Names! Names of Shelomo's dating as far back as 1218! The thought of why his grandfather would give such a treasure to him and not his father bandied about in his evermore tired and clouded mind. Finally, he couldn't think any longer. The night's survivor leaned his head back, closed his eyes, and let sleep envelop him.

Mercifully, the wind stopped kicking the walls and door. It gradually started to become light in the East. Hayim hadn't noticed it because he was locked in a deeper rest, but morning had finally arrived to that part of the world. Around him creeping shadows emerged, objects turning from black to a rich dark brown in the pre-dawn light. Outside the barn, in absolute confirmation of a brand new day, the snow and wind diminished and the clouds parted. As quickly as it came, that was how speedily the storm dissipated. The sky suddenly brightened to enhance the crisp, unspoiled, virgin white Polish landscape. The sunlight was glistening like millions of tiny stars on the freshly fallen snow. He was about twenty-five miles from his escape, far enough that for now he was safe. Darkness was no more.

***

V

HOLLAND

"The only ground of hope must be on the morals of the people."
                                                    Gouverneur Morris

The Low Countries— endless tractable miles of beautiful spectral colors— row after meticulous row of delicate petals among the iconic, flour-producing windmills— spring doused in blooming perennials. From a birds-eye view, solid patches of primary hues weft with vivid variegated colors swaying in unison at the force of balmy ocean breezes. Winter had collapsed long ago, crushed under the hand of spring; presently turned over into the open palm of summer across the tiny northern European nation of the Netherlands.

Hayim stood at the door of the undisclosed address his grandfather had courageously given him. He raised a hand to knock— he didn't exactly know where he was or whose door he was about to knock on, but it did seem to him as though he had "arrived," arrived somewhere, a new person, inhabiting a new life, in a whole new world. For a protracted moment, he held his hand suspended in hesitation as he reminisced, bearing in mind, the long four month sojourn that brought him there— the snow rapidly melting as he made his westward journey through the Prussian countrysides of dying winter, rising spring, and raging war. In his travel and travails, Hayim had spent nearly all of the money his parents had bequeathed him, but had managed to stretch it out by eating only once a day. Luckily, the barn, he had stumbled into on that harrowing first night, was owned by a sympathetic, Polish farmer.

He was a dissenter among the more common regressive Catholic peasants and toll farmers— raised in the urban setting of Kraków, he considered himself a cultured mind of the enlightenment by hungrily consuming books and pamphlets of various leading luminaries such as Kołłątaj, Kant, Wolff, Voltaire, the poetry of Krasicki, and of course, the Stolnik officer: Stanisław August Poniatowski. He detested those fellow farmers that benefited from policies that forced the various Jewish agriculturist to pay an additional eight gulden in taxes, which frequently lead to foreclosure and the spectacle of a bloodsucking menagerie on the meat and bone of cheap acquisition. Moreover, he oft unsolicitedly spoke in favor of the Jew against the practiced systematic prejudice that routinely favored the non-Jew in local land squabbles.

The middle-aged bachelor took exemplary care of his guest for just over two weeks, taking full advantage of the unusual gift of company— fattening him up, turning his home into an extemporaneous coffee house for two— reciting, if not actually preaching from his small library of written words and rhapsodizing of the new found fad: Polish nationalism. By the time they parted, Hayim was warmed, rested, confident, and packed with kołbasa.

People along his route were generally generous. At times, as well, meagerly feeding him in exchange for menial work— especially those farms owned by wealthy aristocrats. Spring was a busy time of year; a crucial time, and owners were always looking for additional able-bodies to prepare for the oncoming planting season. However, toward the end of his journey, as he crossed the border into the Netherlands, Hayim had become gaunt— the toll of the work often required the burning of more calories than those provided as payment for services rendered. Yet, other than the drastic weight loss, he was no worse for the wear. In fact, he felt he had become tougher; a bit wirier.

***

With his hand suspended to rap the door, he stepped a bit closer and finally— meekly tapped on the entrance at 24 Warmoesstraat— the address written in his grandfather's hand and folded inside the fragile prayer book. He had put the address to memory in case he lost it, but it turned out to be an unnecessary exercise. The door opened wide, something that also would not have happened in the Polish quarter. People of Leszno were leery of strangers. No one dared open the door of their home without first hesitating to make certain the one standing on the opposite side meant them no harm. It was remarkable to witness the foreign behavior. It conveyed to him that the people of Amsterdam did not live in fear… of anyone or anything! On the other side of the threshold, to Hayim's amazement, were distant relatives he had never met nor heard much of. Those from his mother's side who had also escaped the Iberian Peninsula during the Portuguese inquisition, but had relocated in the sprawling city below sea level to work building the Grachtengordel; the famous dike system constructed primarily to reclaim land the relentless sea had swallowed up. Because of its strong policy for religious tolerance, many Jews escaped Spain and Portugal and settled in Holland. In some ways, Hayim was home again.

***

In the summer of 1758 when Hayim Shelomo arrived in Amsterdam it was still one of the financial centers of the world. Although waning in its power and influence over the European trading centers, Dutch banking institutions as well as the revitalized speculation based Futures markets, again on the uptick since the boom and bust of Tulip Mania— which augmented the oldest continuously functioning stock exchange, were all still prospering and making the tiny nation a global powerhouse. Companies in Amsterdam had reinvented and reinvigorated how investment trading was conducted. The country was a wealth of capital. High profits were being earned. Interest rates were lower than anywhere else in Europe. The bourgeois enjoyed the highest savings ratios in the world. The private sector was awash in surplus. The Dutch East India Company in Asia and the Dutch West India Company in the Americas and Africa were titans of global industry and trade. This was where Europe's money was being doubled, tripled, and beyond— the financial capital of the world!

For Hayim, at first Amsterdam merely appeared as a confusing homogenized enormity. Yet, in reality, on the heels of the prosperity of war that the Netherlands and all of Europe was enjoying, it was a model of modernity encompassing 200,000 inhabitants in a bright colorful culturally and visually diverse metropolis. By stark contrast, it was a community of heaven in comparison to Leszno, a suburb at the gates of Hell. It was in this global marketplace Hayim Shelomo thrust himself.

Hayim was up early one morning, relaxed; strolling the city— so lively, even at the hour after dawn— thriving, pulsating in an organic rhythm similar to a giant human body. Everywhere he saw people and transactions. The air smelled of fortune. The milieu, the redolence of birth— promise and possibility, the impossible and the unlimited continually taking new shape. Into the bargain, here he was, threadbare, ill educated, foreign, and Jewish. However, he would learn soon that he was the right kind of Jew, but for now he needed to exchange his unsanctioned Russian rouble, Polish zloty, and szelags for some of those shiny copper Dutch duits he saw as numerous as the tulip.

Hayim's aimless path leads him to the waterfront. It was even busier than the inner city, a far greater density of people in a much smaller scale of area. He watched as thick-muscled men hastily loaded and unloaded ships off wooden gangways onto thronged docks. In the gathering there was nothing of the earthly natural sounds such as a river gently rolling, rustling reeds, or the "kree-ar" call of the black-headed gull, the docks were a cacophony of harsh swearing men, heated in threats and ambitious detail. To the eye, two and three-mast ships spread across the water just as buildings fan side-to-side across the land. And, as the wind blew, they swayed and rocked in gigantic waves of hand-made nature. "Teaming with life" couldn't even begin to describe the chaotic flow of the waterfront. Hayim stood planted in one spot for minutes at a time with child-like excitement and fascination. He would be rudely bumped into, sneered at, questioned, but ultimately undisturbed and crystalized in profound awe. It was nearly an hour before he was able to pull himself away and in good spirits went in search of a bank.

Hayim gazed upon a somewhat lavish, three— story building of golden-brown natural stone, across from where he happened to be standing. Between the pillars, engraved above the entrance was the moniker: "De Neufville Brothers Banking House." It was unquestionably the nicest edifice he had ever seen and surely the most imposing he ever considered entering. He crossed the street and walked through the doors unmolested. It suddenly seemed remarkable, the individual freedom of movement he was enjoying, coupled with a relaxed atmosphere thereabouts in a brave new world. No prying eyes. No standing soldiers. No restricted districts and underlying fear.

"How can I help, sir?" was the next thing he heard that brought him out of his quant trance.

***

For the de Neufville Brothers, it was boom times, just two years into the world war waging between what seemed to be every known nation in the world, and the Dutch commodity markets that were thriving from it. The marbled and ornate first floor was a bustle of young men to and fro. Hayim turned to the voice that spoke behind him. He wasn't one of the young men, but instead a rich-featured fellow— stalwart, patrician in appearance, but gentlemanly without airs. His smile continued to extend after his lips had already closed, while his eyes were furiously saccading between the poor-looking young Hayim and the fantastic order of business whirling around him.

"How can I help you, sir? He repeated.
Speaking in Dutch, Hayim wasn't sure exactly what the aristocrat-looking man was saying so he cautiously approached. He continued pleasantries and other elements of conversation, all of which were similar to words Hayim had recently been hearing from his relatives, but nevertheless remained elusive to his own comprehension as to their exact meaning. Finally, the young immigrant unveiled his coins on the man's desk and spoke in Yiddish, but it was to no avail. He followed the effort with broken Russian, but the language barrier still wasn't broken. In a desperate attempt Hayim assumed would be for not, he requested an exchange of his money in his native Polish.

"Excuse me, but are you Jewish?" the man put forward.

Imagine a lion tamer and the lion frozen, staring into one another's eyes. And so it was with Hayim and the de Neufville Brothers' representative. They stared into one another's eyes. Hayim couldn't translate the question in exactness to his full linguistic understanding, but every Jew innately knows all the derivatives of the appellation of their race. He was sure the man wanted to know if he was a "Jew." He didn't know why, but he didn't expect that it was a welcoming question.

"Ye," Hayim said proudly in Yiddish.

Well, the man easily smiled and called over another chap, who came clicking across the marble floor wearing a kippah. The fellow Jew held out his hand, introduced himself, and kindly inquired as to Hayim's intentions with his motley collection of money. Following a deep sigh of wonderment, Hayim reached into his pocket and pulled out the small leather pouch his mother had given him. He opened it and dumped the few remaining coins onto the desk.

"Gelt enderen," he said in Yiddish.

The Jewish man sifted through the small pile, then picked up the singular piece of silver, a Russian rouble. He looked long and hard at the coin before he pulled out a small piece of paper, and ran his finger down it. Quickly, he swept the zloty coins into a drawer and replaced them with a few duits. However, he continued to look at the silver rouble. The man who first greeted Hayim said something to the Jew, and they both agreed. The Jewish associate stepped away and quickly returned with a long piece of paper. The stalwart gentlemen spread it over the desk and, he too, ran his finger downwards, until he came to the what he was looking for. Suddenly, he exchanged Hayim's rouble for a significant amount of duits, stuivers, and guilders. Interestingly, even though the shiny new specie lay there in a small pile, all Hayim could focus his attention on was the strange chart that appeared to have calculated his net worth.

Slowly, he reached for the vellum instrument, expecting the men to stop him. By the time his fingers came upon it, they hadn't. So, he daringly picked it up and raised it straight before his eyes. It was an Exchange Rate Chart.

To Hayim it might as well have been a map of the whole wide world. Neither sailor nor captain was ever so transfixed by longitude and latitude exacted over a charted position than Hayim was to the multitude of currencies listed in relationship to one another on the piece of paper he held. So fascinated was he by it, that the two men standing opposite chuckled in merry amusement. Hayim scanned the lengthy sheet of parchment; studying the numerous denominations before his inquisitive, but vacuous stare — Spanish doubloons, British pounds, Swedish S.M.'s, Russian roubles, Persian abbasids, Ottoman akches: every coin and currency imaginable, representing nearly every nation on the planet, from every corner and continent on the globe having a monetary system. Each had a brief description along with the valuation of the Dutch equivalent. His eyes glistened and grew ever wider as he tried to make sense of it all. He was stupefied; fascinated! It was painfully obvious that monies of the world were systematically listed, but he could not comprehend their values or how those values were so exactly calculated. He had to know! He had to learn!

Chance? Luck? Fate — Divine intervention? Whatever it was that had brought him to this point in time, Hayim Shelomo had indeed found his passion; his life endeavor — finance!

***

Hayim spent the better part of the next half-hour suggesting he should be put in employe; proposing he spoke some of the languages that were reflected on the chart by denomination, foreign tongues that others didn't readily know — though it was evinced to him that he didn't speak the most important one of all, the native Dutch. Hayim's pleading insistence, and the fact he was clearly just a boy turning into a young man, finally brought the employees to bring him in front of Mr. Leendert Pieter de Neufville, the bank owner. There, they figured, Hayim could continue to babble on — either talk his way into a position, or finally be thrown out on his ear.

***

At twenty-eight, Leendert and his brothers had already built a successful banking business from the ground up in less than a decade. Actually, they were speculators, taking global risks other forms of investment bankers shied away from. De Neufville's balance sheet revealed an extensive range of projects — in manufacturing, goods trading, shipping, insurance and other financial activities. There was nothing they weren't willing to turn a profit on. Thus, as well as being bankers who acted as the guarantors of a loan, being the drawee of bills, de Neufville was a debt-financed entrepreneur in his own right. The size of their balance sheet relative to capital was incredibly large, and at the time Hayim Shelomo walked into Leendert de Neufville's office, it was speculatively growing larger by the day.

Hayim was introduced in a cheerful, almost jeering manner. His own claims of his potential worth repeated before him in mocking tones that brought laughter throughout the room. Hayim laughed along, unaware they were laughing at him. However, Leendert de Neufville seemed interested immediately. Languages he thought could expand partnerships and create new far-reaching ones. Leendert was willing to give the young man the opportunity to prove himself but he had one reservation. What kind of Jew was he?

Leendert was not overtly prejudice by nature. However, all of Holland, including Jews who had immigrated from Spain and other parts of the Iberian Peninsula centuries before were harboring a bias against the influx of Ashkenazim, or "German Jews." Ashkenazic and Sephardic Jews represent two distinct subcultures of Judaism. They are all Jews and share the same basic beliefs, but there are some variations in culture and practice. Ashkenazic Jews are the Jews of France, Germany, and Eastern Europe and their descendants.

The adjective "Ashkenazic" is derived from the Hebrew word "Ashkenaz," which is used to refer to Germany. Sephardic Jews are the Jews of Spain, Portugal, North Africa and the Middle East and their descendants. The adjective "Sephardic" is derived from the Hebrew word "Sepharad," which refers to Spain. Historically, Sephardic Jews have been more integrated into the local non-Jewish culture than Ashkenazic Jews. Sephardic Jews have been seen less as "Jews" than the Ashkenazic.

It was a question; many believed, of work ethic, cleanliness, skilled versus unskilled laborers, and overall worth to the country. The larger truth was, it also had to do with appearance. The Ashkenazic Jew represented the stereotype of the bent nose like the number 6, the puffy lips, the receding foreheads, the "deceitful" eyes. In racist form and academia, it was attested too that you could smell their unpleasant sweetish odor. Likewise, everyone knew they brought with them deathly plague and intrinsic greed. Or so, these were the rueful descriptions that differentiated the European from the subhuman that was the Ashkenazic Jew. By contrast, in Northern Europe, the Sephardic Jew was considered pleasant and somewhat handsome, with chiseled features, well-kept manners, and their courteous use of the native tongue.

All of this was nothing new to Hayim, where as a Sephardic Jew, he was surrounded by Ashkenazim Jews in Poland. Often there were tensions over the importance of certain values; there were differences in observing holidays, but more recently a clear rift rend between them at the rise of the Hasidic movement. However, in the Netherlands, the Sephardi Jews were the majority subculture and they, like the Dutch, did not care for refugees they, too, considered dirty, lazy, and without expertise. Ashkenazic Jews had been pouring west ever since the Thirty Years' War and Hayim had already been witness to the divide while being there. In the synagogue, the congregants were separated on each side of the aisle by subculture at the behest of the Sephardic Rabbis and well established laity. To Hayim, the type of Jew he or anyone was, mattered not, but be that as it may, he answered the question honestly and proudly, that he was a Sephardic Jew, from one of the few families as such in Poland. This seemed to assure Mr. de Neufville that he could be trusted, relied upon, and was of a better class of people. He was getting a job because he was a Jew, the right kind of Jew, that is. For the first time in his life, prejudice was working in his favor.

He would have to start at the bottom, a mere bookkeeper. And, he was expected to learn Dutch and learn it quickly to retain his position. Hayim couldn't have been more agreeable to the conditions, nor happier. He was truly embarking on his life now. His childhood behind him, his passion ignited — the unfed flame of Hayim Shelomo was now burning.

***

VI
THE DEAL

"The modern theory of the perpetuation of debt has drenched the earth with blood and crushed its inhabitants under burdens ever accumulating."
Thomas Jefferson

Five years later, by February of 1763, the conflict throughout Europe and the world had come to an end. In Amsterdam, on the third floor of the de Neufville brothers banking house, Hayim Shelomo had risen in his position to that of broker. He was the head broker of accounts and collections. There was no transaction or aspect of the company's merchant banking business that did not require his judgement or consent. In the five years since the serendipity of Hayim exchanging his species, he had immersed himself into the vast economic workings of commerce. As a simple bookkeeper, by day, he took in coin, granted credit and receipts — accumulating vast deposits of precious metals from all over the world. By night he studied Dutch, talking on-and-on with his usually affable but frequently worn-out cousins. Periodically, the relatives would carry on conversations that boarded on the absurd or downright silly, just so he could learn every occasion for any word or to keep them interested enough to continue on when they'd naturally lost interest. Incontrovertible, moderation was not Hayim's strongest suit, and a little of something was never enough for him. He was relentless in everything he did, be it to better himself, better the bank, better the world, or as the determined best use of time — and of course this applied to the learning of Dutch. For this task, besides his books and cousins of contemporary age, there was one cousin in particular whom he adored and she thrived on his attention. Elka. When everyone else in the very full household had had enough of the language lessons and were too bored or fatigued, Hayim — always wired for more — would turn to little Elka.

At only eight years old, she was the baby of the house and his favorite pastime was to go out into the garden where she played and get down on her level. As other's in the family didn't include her in their conversations, often going to the extreme of spelling out words so as to talk over her head, Hayim got down in the dirt and played tea-time with her. There were days in which they would play for hours at a stretch. Here he was, a grown man, pretending to be drinking from tiny little cups and sharing conversation with wood and wax dolls. As it was, Dutch was the only language that Elka knew, and she spoke it mumblingly fast, like many eight year-olds will do. She didn't carry the slightest regard for his actual lack of comprehension, and for her older cousin, it was a real-world simulation of everyday conversation with a stranger, or someone who didn't know he wasn't a native speaker. This was how customers and colleagues spoke at the bank. Elka did not know it, but she was his greatest language teacher. Conversely, in Hayim's presence, the plucky child benevolently received the adolescent attention and acknowledgment she innately needed and desperately craved. Regrettably, her parents' love was dulled by the over-ripe maturity of parenthood. She was the seventh child, and it had been ten years between her birth and her youngest older sibling. Put into perspective, her parents' tenderness was unalloyed but their affection could not match her youthful enthusiasm. Her older brothers and sisters only went out of their way to make time for her in the distribution of chores or the self-serving commands of sibling hierarchy. The child was loved but lonely, accepted but misunderstood, and needed but not required. In this family dynamic, she and her cousin, Hayim, developed a remarkable bond. For one, they would play a myriad of adolescent games, from graces to tops. Moreover, he was keen on assisting in her education, sure to exercise her developing memory in mathematics and the study of the Torah. Through all of it, his mastery of the Dutch language expanded. As it would turn out, he was a natural in languages— a master of the foreign tongue. Dutch would only be the beginning of his linguistic competency. As for Elka, time went by and he traveled extensively. Whenever he returned, he would share countless tales of the lives, customs, styles, and ever-so-interesting people existing beyond Amsterdam. He was her window to the world and more importantly, the engrossing presence, which preoccupied the lacuna in her emotional self-development. Likewise, she furnished him something others didn't, an unquestioning ear and an unconditional interest. His world was anything but childish, it was money.

For all others the "money," and the accumulation thereof, or the possibility of being in relation to it, seemed to take a greater precedence than the applied mechanics of fiscal affairs, which was Hayim's personal and professional proclivity. He was a man of finance while finance was not looked at as a discipline. It was the theory and practice he was interested in most, not the making of money for the sake of self-enrichment. However, at times, Elka, too, would tire and fall asleep, sometimes very cutely so, in mid-sentence, just as Hayim used to do reading himself to sleep. When even she couldn't keep up with him, Hayim read Joseph de la Vega, a Dutch Jew that had preceded him among the financial industry in Amsterdam. In 1688, he wrote the seminal book on the stock market almost a hundred years before Hayim held it in his hands. Confusion of Confusions was not widely read nor regarded— no bestseller, but it would be the second most important bound bit of paper of Hayim Shelomo's life, next to the one his grandfather had given him for safe keeping and travel. Joseph de la Vega showed Hayim the way. A pious charitable man, he set fourth the rules of finance that young Mr. Shelomo would quickly adopt and implicitly live by.

> The first rule in speculation is: Never advise
> anyone to buy or sell shares. Where guessing
> correctly is a form of witchcraft, counsel cannot be
> put on airs.

> The second rule: Accept both your profits and
> regrets. It is best to seize what comes to hand
> when it comes, and not expect that your good
> fortune and the favorable circumstances will last.

> The third rule: Profit in the share market is goblin
> treasure: at one moment, it is carbuncles, the next
> it is coal; one moment diamonds, and the next
> pebbles. Sometimes, they are the tears that Aurora
> leaves on the sweet morning's grass, at other
> times, they are just tears.

> The fourth rule: He who wishes to become rich
> from this game must have both money and
> patience.

However, his biggest success as a bookkeeper was to fix forward rate quotes of paper money at a certain specified amount based on the value of the foreign government money — not simply by the old chart which calculated the length of a voyage and the precious metal content of the coins. This was a revolutionary idea that up until that point neither existed nor was immediately adopted by the other Amsterdam banks. There was no fixed exchange rate quoted between Hamburg, Paris, London, or St. Petersburg, not until Hayim Shelomo devised such a chart. Once the other finance houses saw the beautiful simplicity and additional money made by the de Neufville's — one-by-one, they borrowed upon Hayim's tabulation and it became standard practice around the banking world. However, by that time, Hayim was already an agent. He had learned Dutch eloquently and was traveling Western Europe on behalf of the de Neufville brothers. His range of fluency exploded by four more languages, French, Spanish, Italian, and German. Now, he was older, in his early twenties, established, professional — an international man on the rise.

***

Until recently, the De Neufville Brothers were making exceptional money. Company assets had tripled in the five years Hayim had been in their employe, ballooning to 4.2 million guilders. Then, the war ended — The Seven Years' War — a conflict that ignited a long fuse of worldwide explosions — detonated on the charge of petty trading interests, ceaseless territorial disputes and despotic hegemonial conflicts. This was, for the first time in history, truly, bloodshed on a global scale. From the whole of Europe, to the colonies, Portuguese and Spanish South America, all the way east to the Spanish protectorate of the Philippines under insurrectionary British occupation. The international campaigns were characterized by punctuations of conquered towns aflame, sieges that lasted months, and battles that left legions of blood to slowly drain into the soil of the earth. All n' all, in excess of a million people died until it came to a halt with treaties in the order of St. Petersburg, Hamburg, Paris, and Hubertusberg.

As it were, in the ensuing peace, the whole of northern Europe was gripped by a financial crisis, countries bound together by highly leveraged institutions, liquidity drains, and the intertwining of credit risk and market risk. Hayim Shelomo was in fact an integral part of financial innovations that allowed de Neufville and other nimble market players to increase leverage in buoyant financial markets and amass rapid gains at the expense of the increased fragility of the economic system. The war years were good to de Neufville and other merchant bankers. They were not restricted in their practices by impeding government policies on the commitment power to borrow, such as in Germany. Nor were they bound by trifling traditions as other banks in Amsterdam which accepted deposits but did not extend loans with institutionally held money. The Netherlands, and Amsterdam in particular, was the largest single creditor nation, where capital was a dog always looking for a bone. While Hayim was a bookkeeper, the de Neufville's and other speculators were busily trying to devise methods of expanding the markets. In turn, Hayim ingeniously fashioned a new form of credit, the Acceptance Credit. In the normal course of business, bills of exchange were instruments in the payment system, facilitating trade in goods. However, with the acceptance credit, a banking house would make their own creditworthiness available to another person by allowing the other person to draw a bill on them, which could then be used for payments to third parties. As cleaver and pioneering as it was, Hayim pleaded for caution against the interlocking sets of claims and liabilities binding the numerous markets together. He oft warned, if one domino fell, they all would fall. But from Amsterdam to Scandinavia to Hamburg, the aggressive speculators thrived on the easy credit and unwittingly linked their balance sheets, even though there were no underlying transactions in terms of trade in goods between them. Not surprisingly, de Neufville's business practices were initially viewed with suspicion, and even condemned by the two most powerful banking houses in Holland: The Bank of Amsterdam and Hope & Co.. Nevertheless, their apparent triumphs ensured their further meteoric ascent in banking circles and gave rise to many imitators. Hayim openly forewarned his bosses of credit exceeding liquidity, but with the de Neufville's— known for their lavish lifestyle, his warnings fell on opulently deaf ears. But now that the war was over, the economic boom that spread throughout Europe during those seven years was essentially built on the expansion of credit. With the return of many soldiers to the farm and the tide of normality rising, the regular rhythms and seasons of harvesting and marketing restored itself, and prices immediately declined in exotic goods, such as cocoa, tea, and sugar, which hit the speculators particularly hard.

At first, even though invested in many of the falling commodities, this didn't effect de Neufville to any extent that caused great alarm— so much of their portfolio was diversely invested. Nonetheless, Hayim brought to the brother's attention the warning signs, that even the goods that did not show strong declines were reported to be unmarketable. The de Neufville's, as always, remained overly optimistic. However elsewhere, there was bleeding in the speculator circles and some of the merchant houses were forced to sell their goods in public auctions at very low prices in order to stay liquid, just as Hayim had predicted.

Hayim spent the spring frantically juggling the overextended bank house's books. He was forced to borrow at a high spread to keep enough capital on hand in case of a minor crash and a small rush. These were difficult days for Hayim and his immensely conscientious conscientiousness. Now, at twenty-three, he was confident but cautious, amenable but discerning, unassuming but shrewd, and since he had a hand in the past, he believed he could see the future fairly clearly— and it was rather bleak. He realized he had constructed a monster, an unstoppable force of human rapacity— wisselruiterij, as the easy uncollateralized lucre had become known as. It was credit madness all throughout the Low Countries. And now, with the commodity prices plummeting and monetary debasements smoldering from the wreckage of the former antagonists, the bullion trade was disrupted— credit upon credit was being extended, banking houses were expanding their acceptance of the Bills of Exchange that were not covered by corresponding shipments of goods or bullion. These Acceptance Credit bills depended on the drawing of further Acceptance Credit bills to prolong the extension of credit, until it was hoped that real assets could be liquidated to cover the final chain of bills. It was a bough bending, ready to break. Nevertheless, Hayim continued to faithfully tend to his responsibilities but was also astutely constructing his exit. Many nights he further busied himself sending inquires to the various financial institutions outside of the volatile markets of Amsterdam and Hamburg, to the more wilderness reaches of global finances— banking houses in Berlin and even further, Frankfurt. Then, the deal arrived!

**

April of 1763. Hayim was managing to keep the de Neufville Brothers Banking House afloat amid a turbulent sea of uncertainty and price fluctuations. Truth be told, he was the great life-saving surgeon and they were the patients hemorrhaging money.

On one particularly fateful night, located in the Keizersgracht canal house of the de Neufville's— where he and the other most esteemed officers of the company were newly situated, Hayim was in his office, writing by the light of his lamp when three shadows pitched across him and made the entire room as dark as night.

Leendert de Neufville and two Berlin merchants, Leveaux and Stein entered the office. Hayim looked up. From what he could make out, the three men were in very good inebriated spirits. There was a party going on the main floor, which Hayim was aware of, but felt more comfortable in the study of saving the company than reveling in what appeared to be flush times. They entered and business was suddenly the toast of the hour! Leendert wanted Hayim to buy a large quantity of grain from the granaries of the departing Russian army in Poland. The purchase price was a cool one million guilders. Hayim who had just replenished the coffers on borrowed money said that it couldn't be done. This was a capital sum of money equal to entire countries. De Neufville was undeterred. He, with the excited assistance of Leveaux and Stein explained the deal. They were sure; this was a killing waiting to be made. De Neufville assured Hayim that actual capital wasn't a concern; their equity stake was only going to be six percent. Leveaux and Stein were responsible for the substantial part of the deal. Though Hayim respectfully retorted that they were extending acceptance loans to Leveaux and Stein, making their actual capital participation obviously much larger than six percent. But de Neufville had it all figured out, and done so earlier when he canvassed his own party for the right participants. How? Well, the plan further called for drawing bills on other Amsterdam bankers, spreading the risk without spreading the reward! Again, Hayim respectfully dissented; suggesting that it was a cynical scheme based on the cyclical rise in the price of grain, and furthermore, he pointed out that the grain market in Prussia was already artificially inflated because the farmers had been holding back their product during the war.

For Hayim knew exactly what was going on in the world, more than likely, better than most, if not all. He was well traveled and keenly still followed Polish politics, which included Russian and Prussian statecraft. At the time, he was afraid the wobbly reign of Augustus would lead to a coup d'état by the Russians. He didn't trust all the machinations involved in cornering a market and successfully exploiting it for gain, not to mention the tendency of the Prussian Crown to place its imperial fingers in everybody's pies. De Neufville didn't need Hayim's approval but he wanted his validation. So, he brought in a figure that he was sure would change Hayim's mind.

Moments later, Johann Ernst Gotzkowsky stepped into the large opulent office of Hayim Shelomo accompanied by an almost bacchanalian staggering de Neufville. Hayim looked over all the players, Leveaux and Stein, Gotzkowsky and the individual he held in the greatest admiration, the man who gave him the opportunity to be all that he had become. He wanted to see intelligent businessmen in front of him, great minds at work, titans of commerce. Instead, in their gleaming drunk faces, he perceived unfettered avarice stuffed in the innards of these men like a duck too gorged to fly.

Gotzkowsky was introduced, but wearing his nobility on his persona, offered neither his hand nor his pleasure. De Neufville boasted that Gotzkowsky was the man who conceived one of the greatest money making schemes of all time, the "Seven Years' War," then he went on crowing that Gotzkowsky was a nobleman and in the commission of King Frederick II of Prussia — that he could assure not only the farmers' surplus but that the King's stores would not be released to market. Hayim controlled his incredulous laughter as he asked — "How?"

Gotzkowsky moved into the low light and sat down as though an actor proudly taking the stage.

"Because any intelligent man can be convinced of the intelligent thing to do," Gotzkowsky confidently stated.

"Such as war?" Hayim asked.

"Especially war." Gotzkowsky triumphed!

Hayim mused for a moment. He knew he didn't have to agree but he had to be respectful.

"Well then, what about the farmers?" Hayim queried. "How intelligent are they? What will you do about them?"

"Farmers aren't intelligent, or they wouldn't be farmers, correct?" he chuckled saying. "Of course, they want to keep the prices respectable, themselves." Gotzkowsky assuredly retorted.

"But I hear they're hungry in Hohenzollern."

"Not everyone, just those who don't have food," Gotzkowsky glibly quipped.

If it were up to Hayim, he would have tossed the man out the window right there and then, and probably dumped his chamber pot on him for good measure. But he was in the service to de Neufville and was obliged to hear how the dubious conspiracy was to work.

"Has he—"

"The King?" Gotzkowsky interrupted!

"Yes, the King. Has he already mentioned the harvest or the prices?" Hayim inquired.

"Frederick is not concerned with the lesser orders. He knows they will take care of themselves."

"Then, what does he concern himself with," Hayim lisped with disgust.

Gotzkowsky thought a moment, and with pleasure came upon his sure answer.

"Art!" he said with aplomb.

"Well then, war must surely get in the way of that study." Hayim quipped as though quickly moving a knight on a chessboard into a winning position.

"You don't know a good Prussian then, my boy!" Gotzkowsky just about shouted, blocking the knight.

Laughter accompanied him all around but he followed with—

"War, too, is a form of art, quite possibly even the highest."

"Yes..." Hayim mannerly sighed.

Hayim was tired of the self-assured Gotzkowsky, but he did want to know something that Gotzkowsky could enlighten him on.

Furthermore, he knew what de Neufville wanted to hear and he dutifully complied.

"I'll say, this might be a great investment—" Hayim started, lying through his teeth.

De Neufville was thrilled, but Hayim quickly continued, turning his full attention to Gotzkowsky—

"'Might,' I repeat. But there are many undulating parts to this snake," Hayim said and then took a deep breath. "But, you sir, let me ask you," he directed to Gotzkowsky. "Now that war is abated, what concern does your King have in regard to the country of Poland?"

Gotzkowsky laughed, a chortle, which could have come from the bowels of Mephistopheles—

"Poland? Why he loathes Poland— so great is his loathing, I can only envy him! But more to your point, it is well known among court, that when he is done, that is before— by the grace of God his ascension to the angels— Poland and as a word, as a land, as an empire, will be forgotten for the ages, a forgetfulness replaced by just a greater expanse of the almighty Kingdom of Prussia!"

Hayim was stoically silent, not surprised but neither was he pleased. The deal was done. De Neufville led the standing of all parties except Hayim who sat behind his desk, his head slightly bowed. They made their way out. The broker knew what his next task was— to expedite the deal. He could only think to himself, that if nothing else, he loyally did his job as expected. However, on the way out, Gotzkowsky happened to turn back to Hayim and spoke rather earnestly—

"I must say though, I don't know why, but my King does look quite favorably on the Jews."

***

On July 29, 1763, the first to fail was the Amsterdam banking house of Aron Joseph & Co. but, most spectacularly, was the Brother de Neufville. So it was, in the best-laid schemes of rats and intemperate speculators with little elitist designs— all but two banks, The Bank of Amsterdam and Hope & Co. suspended payments. In all thirty-one banks and the seven largest merchants banks were bankrupt, including the de Neufville Brothers. In total, 27 million guilders of debt were dishonored.

***

As it turned out, Gotzkowsky was right on one count, the wholesale grain merchants held firm and kept the grain supply artificially low. However, the King warned them and advised the merchants to not hold their stocks. Frederick set forth stated goals to lower the price and quell a simmering public fear— watermarks that could have adverted the crisis though they would have depressed the profit. In hindsight some profit is better than insolvency. Yet, the merchants in connection with the speculators called the king's bluff and Frederick the Great, acted every bit his epithet— he interfered in the market greatly, beyond anything that could have been imagined. He flooded the Empire of Prussia with grain, grain, and more grain, until the prices collapsed and the bottom fell out.

***

VII

ROTH SCHILD

"The greatest ability in business is to get along with others and to influence their actions."   John Hancock

The majestic facade of Saint Bartholomeus' Cathedral, once to the top of it's stout spire, a distance of 312 feet separated firm footing from the Germanic sky. As of the middle of the eighteenth century, it reached for the clouds as the highest structure for over hundreds upon hundreds of miles across the Holy Roman Empire. Its monochromatic construction enthusiastically began over the Merovingian foundation of a simpler construct of worship in the thirteenth century and did not cease for more than one hundred years into the future. Distinguished as consecrated ground by the availing ostentation of anointments and crownings, it just happened to be the exact geographical center of the free Imperial city of Frankfurt am Main.

One-third the size of Berlin, it was a small distinctly non-cosmopolitan town on the river bearing its name. By definition, the cathedral was in an extremely fortunate position, being the gateway between two rivers and sitting dead center to the east-west, north-south of the Central European trade routes.

Frankfurt was a medieval city-state still maturing, balanced in between the antediluvian past and the moment ago present. It was distinctly paralyzed within a social structure that was profoundly rooted in the estates and ruled directly by the Holy Roman Empire of the German Nation. These cerulean blue bloods had withdrawn from the rigors of work, trade, and commerce centuries before and now were subtly living decadently off their resplendent tax-free properties while ruling the city's municipality in grand entitlement. To perspicaciously understand them, is to understand that they were almost exclusively confessional Lutherans contemporaneously tossing in the potent tide of Rationalistic Illumination.

To God alone be glory, but as their pietism degenerated very rapidly into their own apologetic and socinianistic moral decay, it was those who swore they truly embodied the Christian faith who were often the ones who ended up compromising it the most. Underneath the generational divide of dogmatic subtleties, capital bourgeois interest, and patriarchal elitism that delineated this religious nobility— like the bed of coal a diamond lays upon, there was a wholly independent and exploited stratum of thriving society subordinate to them: the mercantile class. They, like all non-lutherans, were forbad from owning land or holding office, and further inhibited with limited civil rights. Nonetheless, guild after guild they consisted of shop owners, tradesman, and craftsmen— Calvinists, Huguenots, and Catholics! In the whole organism of the community, they functioned as a respiratory system to the aristocracy's cerebral and academic discernment. Furthermore, some of the inspired inhabitants of Frankfurt made for a serendipitous collection of mighty aspirations— Goethe, Mozart, Nicolai, Fröbel, and Bethmann, to name a few.

In this incognizant zeitgeist of February 1764, Hayim Shelomo under a light snowfall waited at the gate of Eschenheimer Turm, the high gothic tower erected during the Dark-Ages to deter invasion— waited with his well-traveled satchel and stared at the high point of the imposing hallowed edifice that Saint Bartholomeus' presented.

***

He had been waiting over the better-part of the afternoon, when suddenly the clomping sound of hoofs and the after note of wooden wheels turning-over cobble-stone streets brought his attention outward. Not many carriages had passed him during his wait, but the ones that did, did so without pause. This one however stopped. It wasn't particularly fancy but it was outfitted with glass and painted on the side with a prominent roth schild, or red shield, highlighted with a simple gold-colored, emaciated-looking eagle— not to mention, that it appeared to be in anticipation. The driver shouted toward him—

"Herr Shelomo?"

Hayim nodded, flung his satchel over his shoulder and obeyed the driver's cue to enter. He straddled into the coach. His eyes had yet to adjust to the sudden shade which made the stranger already inside— seated opposite, seem partially invisible. Hayim settled in and the stranger said in a rather almost pubescent voice and unfamiliar dialect—

"Shl dvar haben sie?"

Hayim strained to understand the mash of words. They were a unique mixture of Hebrew and German. Finally, he arranged them in his head and assumed to understand the question of his arrival.

"Shl dvar haben sie, shl dvar?" the all but invisible stranger impatiently asked again, pressing like a boarder guard would to see a passport.

Hayim quickly retrieved his post in the form of a reply that was sewn into his coat— thereby the man knew for certain that he was Hayim Shelomo. A terse command to the driver followed and the carriage swiftly moved on.

In the fullness of time, Hayim's vision adjusted and to his surprise the person riding next to him looked vaguely more than an overgrown kid. The "kid" freely held out his hand and enthusiastically introduced himself—

"Nice to meet you, I'm Moses!"

Hayim was startled by his appearance. He had traveled almost three hundred miles, by a combination of foot and carriage, in just under two weeks of sometimes less than cold comfort, all with a vague expectation of being received by a strapping, confident, and established organization, similar to de Neufville. Yet, here was a boy with rosy cheeks and a cherubic appearance— so youthful, nary a facial hair! Before Hayim courteously and finally extended his reach, he asserted a peek at the dispatch he coveted— coveted so highly that he had it sewn into his coat.

"I am my brother's brother!" Moses said to be as reassuring as he could, seeing that Hayim was confusedly glancing at the letterhead, which clearly displayed the same shield, as did the coach.

Hayim offered his hand in the exchange of a greeting, but was little less relieved.

"All affairs are in order?" Hayim inquired.

"Ye-ja, I have arrived and here you are," Moses cheerfully replied.

"And you… and your brother, you need a bookkeeper, right, yes?" Hayim said with a kind of disbelief.

"I would say much more than a 'bookkeeper,' but that is more the business of my brother than I."

"I see— well good," and Hayim tried to settle in, but he was still unsettled. "But, excuse me if you may, Moses, right?

"Ye, I'm Moses."

"Right, thank you. - But just how old might you be?"

"Why, I'm eighteen!"

"Eighteen?"

"Ye!"

"Hmmm," Hayim thought.

"I see. Then it stands to be— you're by far the youngest of the siblings?" Hayim now said rather reassured and with the eminent conceit of a still young man, but of one who had already eclipsed the tender ages.

"Oh why yes, my brother is much older than me," Moses said. "He just turned twenty this month!"

Hayim's mouth almost fell to the floor.

***

In transit— just inside the city's obsolete and crumbling walls, the first impression was the viridescent presence of flora. A multitude of planted saplings were remarkably numerous and small promenades seemed to be freshly laid over disintegrated ramparts. This appeared to be a city in the process of verdured redevelopment from an anachronistic military fortification. Then the carriage came to a fork in the road, between a wide roadway laid with stone and a drovers' way. It turned onto the roadway, and before long, it rode through the main artery of the city. The way that Amsterdam splashed of color and newness, Frankfurt stood distinguished in a stately assortment of stone grays, brick reds, and Dark Ages black. It was immediately obvious that Frankfurtian movement was frenetic, on pace with unconcealed lightening in a bottle. The urban stew was a metropolitan racket of sound and senses, a mash of commerce— a carnival of vendors barking their wares; the pestilent stench and disturbing noises of steer, goats, sheep, swine, driven to market— spillways of blood from being slaughtered on site. In a catechismal din of flourishing Western European cultural there were farmers, merchants, customers, officials, voice after voice consistently and furiously rising over one another. Products and wares were cheap. Services were efficient. And life was good.

76

The carriage continued down the street, revolving over the square inlay of parquet cobblestones until it reached the wooden barrier of Fischerfeld gate. The brick archway tunnel was guarded by an armed warden; quite sour of disposition. Once into and passing through the darkened tunnel, before hoof and trot was again exposed to the sun— the previous municipal splendor dissolved into an unremitting aggregate of squalor. They had entered Juddengasse, or Jew Alley, the enclosed ghetto where the Children of Israel, quasi-citizens of Frankfurt, were reluctantly permitted to live and dubiously encouraged to die by the illiberal society and city council. Hayim had seen elements of dilapidation and the black bile of abject poverty his whole life, but this was a more systematic modernity of defiled Israelite captivity that he was not prepared for.

First, there was the undeniable putrid stench— Hayim gagged; struggled to withhold the reflex to vomit. The pungent smell caustically emanated from the mud-caked river of raw sewage that overflowed both the channels that ran behind the homes and the open shallow ditches from which it freely flowed along the street— human and animal excrement, solid waste, the toxic and alkaloid runoffs of blacksmiths, stonemasons, and tanneries; the entrails and decomposing by-products of animal processing... and the thin bacterial film that gave it all it's mustard coated tinge. Thirteen feet wide, 1,200 feet long, and a quarter of a mile square, the alley ran at a curved angle that ultimately manifested into a half-paved semi-circle with numerous twisting tendrils. All along each side, formless heaps of hovels and dirty dilapidated cottages, built one top another, atop another, between two others, and always a mansard roof extending over the street for just a little more space above. Some of the buildings still showed signs of fire damage from many decades before which gave the overall impression of rows of matchboxes with a few extinguished match heads protruding out. These stacked residents were so compacted; close together to one another, that neither sunlight nor fresh air penetrated the living quarters. What started out as 100 Jews pushed out of the main walls of the city in 1462, was now thriving with thousands upon thousands, upon thousands, of residents crowded into exactly 195 actual houses. It seemed as though the whole of European Jewry was overcrowded into this filthy deafening marshaled humanity.

Nevertheless, no matter the conditions, business was the main business at hand. Human enterprise thrived on both sides of the narrow lane in a weary and ravaged patchwork of peddlers hawking everything from Nürnberg wares— cheap chotchkies, to rag collectors, junk dealers, grocers, and wine merchants trading in homemade spirits as redolent as cough syrup, not to mention the busy but furtive traffic in human sexual gratification. Even ghettos have class structures, and the aforementioned peddlers in the Judengasse were the lowest. Ranking above them were the partially skilled enterprises. Often operating family business directly out the decrepitude they called "home," setting up shop on what was the oldest and always most crumbling layer of disrepair: the first floor— the crockery, drapery, fur, flour, iron, and leather, merchants— and butchers, carpenters, caterers, clockmakers, shoemakers, bookbinders, and tailors. But these were just some of the professions. Even though only a quarter-mile square and encased in 30 foot high walls, besides the invariable doctors, schoolmasters, and rabbis, the Judengasse was truly it's own municipality with even mail carriers and lottery collectors— and of course, not to be forgotten, gravediggers. By comparison, the higher class was comprised mainly of goldsmiths and merchant bankers, the latter called as such because banking and mercantile capitals were inexorably intertwined. Even though, in point of fact, very few made any money— the ones that did were the men with access and privilege, either bought, or gained through time immemorial. Nevertheless, they were still Jews, and still forced to live in the indigence of Judengasse. It was the timeworn discrimination— the universally inequitable policies of Christians against Jews that forced them into the precarious occupations in which they were so reviled for, despised upon, and cursed, as is a tick satiated with blood. Yet for the moneylender, in particular— the well financed one, that is, he simultaneously served a social and financial interest that trumped both race and religious beliefs for the Lutherans and mercantile class alike. As a legal and moral ready source of coin, even a digression into this infernal realm wasn't too much for a gentile to venture. However that venture— neigh, click— clank, and clomp, for Hayim was still only just past the gates, and already he had resisted the involuntary urge to purge his stomach of its contents, all the while his eyes painfully burned from the rotten mixture of acrid smolder that hung in a thin veil of artificial fog— the diaphanous vapors of cooking smoke, the light white emission of heat producing wood and the burning exhaust of flaming garbage and disposed carcasses ablaze which only added to the unnatural humidity.

Nevertheless, if first was the smell, second was the noise. It was beyond deafening. The rattling vegetable carts, street musicians, the screaming of playing children and the crying of neglected ones— starved bundles of rags; the moaning of beggars, the barking of dogs, the shrieking of hucksters, the wailing of vendors, the whimperings of death, unfought anymore! This, in the heyday of the Age of Enlightenment, at 50 degrees north latitude and 41 degrees east longitude by the irresistible grace of God was but a concert of all the imposed sounds of the human race in a casual incongruent symphony of crucifixion. So much Hayim could gaze upon straightaway, but so much more he couldn't immediately know. Located outside the Frankfurt walls, the Judengasse spread to the edge of the city mote, it was gated and locked on two other sides than the Fischerfeld Gate he had entered— a fortress of contained pestilence and managed malnutrition, it had seen the bubonic plague and other waves of epidemic right along the whole of the pandemically cursed continent. For the residents, Christian beadles at the employee of the city council, but ironically paid for compulsorily by the Jewish community, made sure no entrance nor exit was permitted after sundown, or Sundays and of course blessed Christian Holidays. Within, the Judengasse walls, a jealous Hell hath never known equivalent. Everywhere, death lived inside the body of the breathing, and walked among time— yet always wearing, by law: the badge of a yellow star.

The Judengasse was not a settled transpiration. The municipal officialdom reigning over the alley carved out this perdition on earth. Furthermore, they regulated every aspect of these lives that many never saw with their own eyes, but would only hear of in literary compendiums. From the collection of deliverable goods to the number of weddings per year— twelve to be exact, and only for those over the age of twenty-five, was under their complete control. Frequent visitations— the random extraordinary knock of city officials upon a family's unsuspecting door was the means of control to make sure all these regulations were kept.

Upon these visitations or inspections, the residents were often molested in the streets, harangued with the cry "Jew pay your dues!" These dues of course, were essentially the right to live in existence by state allowance. And those who did want to so exist knew best in the passing of these sanctioned agents of despotism to take off their hats, step aside, and bow. In the passing of these men, the herded souls were forbidden to leave for any reason other than business, and at a great cost. In a hard-boiled town, the Jew was to be feared, his commerce, his competition, and his willingness to sell below cost. And, these were the predominate reasons, the protectionism, used to rationalize the savage nature of their treatment. However, this was not the only Judengasse on the planet. Vienna. Venice. Prague. Worms. Leipzig. Rhodes. Rome. Istanbul— to name a few. But, no other European city treated its restrictions on its Jews in its Judengasse so harshly.

***

Hayim could barely breathe, but he looked to Moses, and just as Moses seemed so young and vibrant in the bright sunlight, inside these walls and stacked apartments that blocked out the sun, Moses' face, covered in shade, was still youthful but his eyes suddenly looked with an aged tenderness of a perspective accustom to the sight of a world without, cheated of common humanity. Eventually they arrived at the aesthetic exteriors of rows of buildings housing first floor storefronts, which supported upper floor living spaces. These were also dilapidated, but less so, window-lined fronts consisted of the same various family endeavors— suppliers, money-lenders, large-scale merchants, and the few rich Jews who dealt in luxury goods such as jewelry and silk. They reached the address of: 188 Judengasse and emptied out of the carriage. It was a two story, two family dwelling in which the bottom floor was a tasteful storefront, marked explicitly with the sign of a red shield, the same emblem matching the carriage and the letterhead in which Hayim's letter offered him welcome. Above the cerise washed coat of arms and traced golden bird of jove, in gold letters it read simply: "A.M. Rothschild."

Moses led the way through one dreary narrow room into another, which eventually lead into an office. The curtains were all drawn keeping out the natural sunlight. However, the room was outfitted with several burning oil lamps— strategically placed as they were, they illuminated the room only so much, enough that one could read, but left the feeling of being in the lair of a wily animal. Moses and Hayim stood there; the smell of fresh paint odiously lingering in the thick miasmatic air. Behind the desk, outlined in stacks of ledgers was a short wiry fellow, concentrating between two sets of open registers. Moses let out a short cough, which brought the man to look up!

"Mr. Shelomo, meet my brother, Meyer." Moses proudly spoke. Meyer quickly acted as though apologetic for his lack of inattentiveness and came around the desk and eagerly shook Hayim's hand.

"You got my letter!" he said.

"Yes," Hayim affirmed, displaying it.

"I was impressed with your inquiry," Meyer continued. "It was fluid. It read of a man that's honest, but it smelled of a man that knows money."

Hayim wasn't exactly sure what Meyer meant by his assured judgement. Meyer moved some books around and stacks of papers, as to tidy up a bit, but it was more a matter of calm dramatic business than efficacious action.

"Do you still need a man like me?" Hayim asked.

"Need?" Meyer said, ending with a slight chuckle. "Did you know, that you couldn't love and also need? Have you ever thought about that, Mr. Shelomo? Need is the one instinct that interferes with emotion." Hayim certainly wasn't sure as to what he should say. Though four years younger, Meyer already seemed older and more powerful, if simply not more aggressive and lyrical.

"Need? No," Meyer said. "I specifically want you. I know from bankers in Berlin the extent to which the good fortunes of your former employer rest upon his former employee before me."

Meyer Rothschild, standing slender, with receding thick black hair and burgeoning sideburns, was the first son and fourth born of Amschel Moses and Schönche Rothschild.

Sadly, his father passed on nine years earlier during a smallpox epidemic that swept through the Judengasse; inhaling and exhaling his final breath in the same room in which he and Hayim stood. Tragically, his mother would follow his father less than in an extension of a year's time. The elder was a traveling merchant, silk trader and moneychanger. His most lucrative source of income was his excursions in which he dealt in beads and trinkets that he would sell to the servants of Wilhelmsburg Castle, in excess of over a hundred miles distance from the Judengasse. Once of age, Meyer would accompany him on such long sojourns. Before passing, Amschel Rothschild secured for his son an apprenticeship under Wolf Jacob Oppenheimer, at the Jewish banking house started by Simon Wolf Oppenheimer in Hannover, a city without a delineated Judengasse. Wolf Jacob and Simon Wolf were descendants of Samuel Oppenheimer, the Court Jew to the Austrian Court.

Meyer inherited a rather simple and mildly profitable storefront from his father. Combined with his entry into privileged society, known and trusted sources of wealth, experience in foreign trade, learnedness of currency exchange, and knowledge of rare coins through the bank's rare coin collection, he was poised to make his mark on the world. For the time being though, he was cleverly expanding the Rothschild empire that was physically no larger, but substantially more profitable.

General von Estorff was a patron of the Oppenheimer Banking House. He dabbled in collectable coins. His collecting began as a small interested aside. Though as time went on and he came to know a young enthusiastic employee name Meyer Rothschild, who would go to great lengths to ever impress him with rarer and still yet rarer coins, lucrative medals, quaint jewels, and other curios, the general energetically immersed himself into the trade and Meyer as his personal broker.

By the time the orphaned Rothschild commanded full control of his father's business, employing his two younger brothers, he did what all Jews in Frankfurt were known to do, he sold his wares at a discount. In his case, his central customer was General von Estorff.

As Moses and Kalmann were relegated to continuing the local trade in silk cloth and moneychanging, Meyer exclusively concerned himself with rare coins and medals. The reason why he wanted Hayim would soon be clear. For Meyer recently made the deal of a lifetime. Through General von Estorff, newly named to the court of Prince Wilhelm of the Principality of Hanau, heir to one of the wealthiest fortunes in Europe, he was able to shrewdly sell precious medals and almost invaluable coins to the Prince at a price so tempting he could not refuse. The Prince, too, was quickly an ardent collector and admirer of Meyer Rothschild, whom he granted addition to the Wechselstube, the currency exchange of the kingdom — officially making him an instrumental cog in the imperial financial system. Mayer's status further grew as court after court bought and traded in rarities through him. He was aggressively buying and trading at coin fairs all across Prussia, but always close enough to be back home before sundown, when the Judengasse gates were locked.

He took every opportunity possible to buy out the entire inventory of his competitors, thus owning not only their stock, but by fact-of-the-matter, their customers, too. And when there were no others left to challenge him, he created the most stunning, the most beautiful, the most enchanting catalogues — scripted, word by word, line by line, with the strictest detail and delicate care worthy of the biblical Moses chiseling the Word of God, which when laid open exquisitely described his precious coins and gold medals. By design, these books would find their way into the hands of prospective clients all over Europe and bestow upon the still only twenty year old, the foundation of an ever-expanding fortune.

***

As Hayim stood there awaiting to hear Rothschild's plans, expectations, and final offer of his employment, already a new sign, a new roth schild, freshly painted, that same deep-red color with the gold gangly eagle — was drying on the desk they stood over. It read anew in golden lettering: "M.A. Rothschild, By Appointment Court Factor to His Serene Highness, Prince Wilhelm of Hanau."

***

VIII
HOME

"The reformation was preceded by the discovery of America, as if the Almighty graciously meant to open a sanctuary to the persecuted in future years, when home should afford neither friendship nor safety."   Thomas Paine

"Hayim, in the six or so years we've been acquainted," Meyer started under his own hilarity.

Meyer was not a man prone to amusement, a jack-in-the-box personality — wound tight, all business, no clowning around whatsoever. However, sprung open, his amusement was like that of a coughing fit — a surprise, very personal, out of the blue, and always ceasing abruptly.

"I could not testify to your thoughts," Meyer said.

"I have given you my opinion many times," Hayim responded, somewhat casually taken aback.

Bouncing and swaying in a light rain, as they rode in a dry comfortable carriage, slightly larger, but no more ornate than the one that had serviceably delivered Hayim years before. The Rothschild was still in prominent display as the quartet of horses struggled to climb the juniper-covered Zoller Mountain, nearly 3,000 feet steep en route to the Medieval castle of Hohenzollern of the House of Hesse in one of their common visits with Prince William.

"Yes, that I know," Meyer said indicating that they must have had some real differences of opinion over the years but with the utmost respect.

Meyer was now twenty-six and his hairline quickly reaching toward the back of his head while his sideburns had become as telltale as the family crest. Hayim, too, was looking older but unlike the additional paunch circling around Mayer's abdomen, he was still as slender and angular as ever, maybe even more. His face had always been shaped in a taunt alignment of high cheekbones and a thin pointed nose. But now he grew into a distinguished mien, clearly appearing as a learned, well traveled, well-to-do man. Both, dressed as such, cut striking figures, representative of their age and good fortunes.

"You're not always right, you know —" Hayim jabbed him with a spunky needling that only two men who have grown into confidents can assert.

"And neither are you," Meyer responded in kind and cheer.
But both men had short jocundity spans. You could think of them as plow horses with blinders and endless stamina. However, Meyer came back to the theme of his exchange.

"I speak truly, though. I know you're opinion of long and short, hot and cold, coin and medal, but I know not your opinion of yourself."
Hayim looked across from him, curiously.

"Of yourself, of your experiences — maybe of your expectations," Meyer said in all sincerity.
Hayim had to think, trying to understand the line of questioning, but eventually he added —

"I think highly of myself," he said with a rather dry undefensive tone but defensive body language.

"But tell me, what do you think of this moment, this hour, but not within the hour but the hours that lead to this hour, the course you trod that receives you in grace now, in the passage of your life, what you hold in your hand and what has slipped through your fingers?"
It was a mouthful and Hayim was more concerned with the nature of the inquiry than the question itself. So, with impassivity, he turned it back on Meyer —

"No, but what of you and yours?"
Meyer understood and respected his friend and employee's wariness; he respected it as he did any competitor willing to do anything to win. Therein, he honored the question —

"I was born in the Judengasse, in the house we, both you and I, presently reside. I despise my surroundings. And as I soon take Gutlé as my wife, I shall make unprecedented arrangements to live on the other side of those walls."
Hayim was shocked by such brazen plans but he was also mesmerized with the boldness and certainty in which Meyer spoke.

"I am the blood of Bauer, yes, I tell you as such, we, like you, are Ashkenazi — somewhere within, we are as one, and I despise those other brotherhoods — of cardinals, of popes — of the whole of the whorish Dominican Order. I despise those who make the laws — in this land and every land afar! Do you think it is the natural order that some should be slaves, that others should be cursed; that even others should be arraigned and slaughtered… in vain exercises of power? How many Gods can be at war with other Gods and still without victory be God? I doubt every mechanism of man! I doubt and despise every order, every writ, every precept and warrant of the law! I believe and trust in natural law, as Newton and Galileo did! I respect gravity and space! I honor the sunshine and the rain. But I despise and am bound to a vow only spoken within the set of my ears, to destroy the forces of man's power. Give me the control of a nation's money and I care not who makes the laws. I have been born a Jew and of that I am proud! I am a Jew and of that others despise! I shall not parish as a king or as a ruler of principalities, but as infinitely more, as a creator— oh less than Yahweh, but more— much-much more, than mere men."

Hayim had never known such puissance in one man, such a definition of purpose. Here was truly a life of spirit pregnant with cause, donned in flesh and grounded in self-interest.

"Be not trepidatious, you need not entertain my suspicions. Maybe you have no answer, no matter," Meyer flippantly said.
Hayim accepted the partial assumption and relaxed in expectation that they would travel on, carry on, and be simply as they had always been. However—

"But I have a second, a new question for you," Meyer asserted. Then Meyer stopped; looked over the view spread before them. It was an endless vista from high atop the entire world.

"You are from Poland, no?" Meyer asked.

"You know as such," Hayim quickly replied with less a smile.

"And did you flee in cowardice or heroics?"

"I protest that question," Hayim said, but only after getting over his shock.

"Because it is one, or it is the other, or it is both?" Meyer pressed forward.
Hayim simmered with a subdued anger, an emotion he rarely felt. His natural or adopted habit was to neatly fold his emotions as would a tailor sew a stitch, and then wrap the garment for the customer and present himself as though there was never a tear. He kept everything at an emotional distance, including emotions, but he could also do this with ease because his life was bereft of any emotional attachments. Suddenly, he was more or less trapped, bearing little control and being called to consider the nature of his starved feelings.

"I fled —"

"In the night," Meyer interrupted.

"Yes, in the night," Hayim bitingly admitted as he wondered why his "friend" was saying these things. "But I was neither filled with cowardice or heroics."

"Then what were you filled with?"

"Why do you ask me these question, Herr Rothschild? What else do you question about me?"

"Nothing. I hold you in the highest regard I can hold anyone other than a member of my family," Meyer said in complete honesty.

Hayim was defused and out of earned and owed respect, he mused and then spoke his mind —

"I say the word 'impressionable' if I say about myself then. I say the word 'young.' I admit to the word 'irresponsible.' I had to flee! What would have happened if I had not?" he said rather uncomfortably.

"And what did happen?"

"I don't know!" burst from Hayim's lips.

Meyer would not normally accept such an outburst directed at him, but he mercifully granted leeway —

"Excuse me, Herr Rothschild, please excuse me" Hayim said apologetically; truly embarrassed.

He, too, took the moment to look out over the vista and at the castle slowly emerging larger in his vision. But in actuality he did not see what he looked at, instead he was stewing in his own disapproval over his unbecoming lack of self-control. He was shocked by his own outburst. He was discombobulated, as though momentarily divorced from his faculties.

"When was the last of your engagements with your family?" Meyer asked.

"I've had no word."

"Not even in Amsterdam?"

"There was no word."

"You wrote?"

"Of course."

Meyer almost felt pity for Hayim, but he felt even more victorious for himself, and competently continued to his endgame.

"Do you like living in the Judengasse?"

"I hate it," Hayim said ever so sharply, in a voice Meyer had never heard before — a helpless loathing.

"But you never say so."

"What difference would it have made if I had?"

"But it is your home, no?" Meyer asked.

Hayim just silently stared back at him.

"I tell you of my intrigues— my proposal for a new home. If you listened well— those expectations do not involve my old home. But, I put to you, Herr Shelomo, 'do you... want to go home?'"

"I am a man without a home," Hayim evenly spoke.

Meyer held his breath, allowing the ambiance, the air, and the sounds— the grunting horses, the chirping birds, and the pounding hoofs, all to penetrate the gravity of the moment and weigh the emotions into an even balance.

"A man must have one of two things to be alive, to be beyond the act of his breath, being merely an instrument moving in and out. That is to have a home or to have a purpose."

"I have neither," Hayim said straightaway, tired of the discourse. "I have no family, no home. I am hired to make money and I make money for others and for it I get only money in return. I have enough money that I could sleep on a bed of gold coins or cover myself in a blanket of the highest notes, but little else I have, less the beat of my heart and the functions of my body— my breath you say, in and out."

"Good," Meyer reflected in that common German expression— relaxed, respectful of Hayim's impressions.

"What is it that will satisfy you, Hayim?" Meyer offered the question as one offering a sweet.

"I don't know. I don't know," Hayim, said refusing to even muse it over.

"You thirst?

"Thirst for what?"

"What all unsatisfied and discontented men thirst for... redemption."

Without intention, Hayim absorbed the word "redemption" and quietly feasted on it as though it was a rag soaked in fresh water given to a man wading at sea.

"I want you to go home," Meyer said.

"For a time?"

"For me, for profit."

"There is no profit to be made in Leszno."

"Warsaw."

"Or any of Poland."

"I believe there is, simply because there is not," Meyer confidently retorted.

"It is not a safe country for Jews, Poles, or money."

"That may be. But I want you to set up a bank. I want you to run a bank for me."

Again, Hayim just silently stared back at him.

"This I promise will be the beginning of a dynasty."

***

IX
DAMNED

"That God, from the beginning, elected certain individuals to be saved, and certain others to be damned; and that no crimes of the former can damn them; no virtues of the latter save."   Thomas Jefferson

In the atypical flush of evening sunlight, the typically shimmering blue waters at the mouth of the Danube were flecked with nymphaeaceae, or water lilies— herbs that are commonly called lily pads. That is, human nymphaeaceae, that is to say, that the typically shimmering blue waters at the mouth of the Danube were flecked and glut with human lily pads. At the confluence of the river Prut, on it's left bank, in what was the village of Frumoasa, the defeated damned stayed afloat, dead. Salonika blue bloated in bubbles of fabric; waterlogged cotton uniforms of tens of thousands of retreating and routed Islamic arms. The Turkish damned was composed of all ranks: the light infantry, the janissaries, and likewise the kapikulu corps to boot— even the whole of the military band, which consisted of a single kidnapped twelve year-old boy and his drum. Faced down, drum stick still in hand, his lifelessness freely floated and bumped against one drowned static soldier after another— swept in the ancient current that would eventually take him in body and burial to the cold depths of the Black Sea. However, where his soul went was a matter of holy interpretation. In the name of Russian westward expansion and Turkish belligerence in support of Polish nationalism, that divine interpretation was held in the balance.

On September 25, 1768, Sultan Mustafa III declared war on the Empire of Russia. The declaration was in response to a rampaging detachment of Cossacks in Russian service that crossed into Ottoman territory in pursuit of a Polish Bar Confederation force. The Cossacks, as they were known to do, didn't simply chase their prey in a straight line, but distracted themselves en route with the razing of a little town called Józefgród— and in cold-blood, mass murdered it's Jewish population. The act was obstinately denied by the Russian Crown, but to the Turks, the dead spoke in sufficient volume from the sight of their motionless lips scattered in slaughter. Two years later, invested with twice as many men and ammunition, plus an alliance with the vicious Crimean Tatars, the Battle of Kagul, as the victors named it, was another surprising defeat for Mustafa III and the struggling antiquated Ottoman Empire. Notwithstanding, this was war with the Russians— nothing new. For the tenth time in exactly 200 years, the two belligerents would be so belligerent.

"The Perpetual Treaty of Friendship and Guarantee Between Russian and Poland of 24 February, 1768," was the checkmate of a quarter of a century's old chess match between Frederick II and Elizabeth and Catherine of Russia, respectively. The treaty gave rise to the unofficial death of the Kingdom of Poland and the Grand Duchy of Lithuania, or as it was better known: the Union. The Union, a Polish–Lithuanian Commonwealth was in practice a dual state of the dominions of Poland and Lithuania, unified in rule by a common monarch but separated by state boarders. In sum total, the two countries combined to be one of the largest and most populous territories in Europe. If the Union stood on two legs before, hamstrung by the Treaty, it thereby precariously stood on one. By accord, the purpose of Poland was little more than for the exclusive betterment of Russia. Immediately, revolts, riots, and uprisings on a massive scale erupted throughout Poland. No strata of society were unaffected. The inflated, or unusually vast Polish nobility were essentially stripped of political power. The church was under attack from Russification— the intended conversion of Polish Catholicism to Russian Orthodoxy. And for the peasant, who already had no rights, no land, no goods, and no service which they conducted that was not ultimately at their lord's disposal— had no love for their country, but even less for the historically hated Russian empire. Five days later, in the city of Bar in the Podolia region, the independent wealth and influence of Poland met with the distinct intention to defend the Union at all cost against internal and external capitulation to the Russians. Proclaimed under the slogan, "For God, Country, Faith and Freedom," this would include against the vein intellectual puppet king and former lover of Catherine the Great, Stanisław Augustus Poniatowski. The names: Casimir Pulaski, Father Marek Jandołowicz, Walenty Łukawski, John Strawinski, Jan Kuźma and Adam and Michał Krasiński, were names that were to mean forevermore: "civil war."

Kagul Lake, or Jelly Lake, connects to the Danube by the Vekita Channel. However, the soft mushy rain-soaked battlefield was 15 miles north on the Dobruja steppe, in Gagauzia, agricultural land that was not a virgin to armed bloodshed. Politically, the site was situated in Bessarabia, a principality of Moldavia. The region or parts of it continually changed hands, almost with the seasons, frequently switching between, either the Principality, Austria, the Russian Empire, or the Ottoman Empire. Ironically, the Battle of Kagul didn't take place at the lake; it was merely the closest Russian named land feature that the Empresses's forces could identify. And, just as pre-dawn light cast a glow, enough that silhouettes could be seen, the Russian commander Pyotr Rumyantsev tactically arranged his army of grenadiers and life-guards. 40,000 soldiers fit with 118 guns were arrayed into solid squares.

Rumyantsev was a military child. His glory began as he reached the tender age of eighteen when he ceremoniously carried the Peace Treaty of Abo to the Empress, a treaty concluded by his father Count Alexander Rumyantsev. That is if the rumors weren't true that he was in actuality the illegitimate son of Peter the Great. By this date however, he was truly a dazzling and rightly gloried officer, few had ever done more militarily for the Russian cause than he. Tactically, his decisions varied from battle to battle. He based his stratagems more on the implied momentum of a campaign than most military men whose decisions were rooted in numbers and topographical conditions. Moreover, it had been a fortnight since his triumph over the same foe at Larga. Thirty-three of his one hundred and eighteen cannon came by way of that decisive battle. Finally, with his troops squared, Rumyantsev surveyed the plateau and though outnumbered, he surprisingly grasped the initiative and took the offensive. Daring to say the least, because opposing him was an allied force of the Khanate of Crimea and the Ottoman Empire, which directly consisted of 30,000 infantry and 45,000 cavalry, plus the little drummer boy; not to mention the additional 80,000 Tatar cavalry within striking distance.

It was 5:00 am, August 1st, 1770, but July 21st to Russians and March 9th, to the Turks. Finding the approach of Russian troops, the Turks opened artillery fire, and the cavalry was thrown into the attack! Stubborn fighting continued for hours. The Turkish cavalry being repulsed by Russian infantry and artillery fire, retreated in disorder to their base camp.

It appeared the general's gamble had paid off. Then, Rumyantsev went for the deathblow.

He personally led the attack on the bulk of the Turkish units stationed in the camp. Heavy blows of the Russian troops on the flanks and in the center were supplemented by a blow from the rear of the column bypass. Victory appeared in sight but in the midst of storming the camp, the Russian life-guards were counterattacked by a force of 10,000 raging janissaries, the musketeer unit that formed the personal royal guards of the sultan. Rumyantsev neither bent nor broke, he organized a counterattack on the counterattack! Two batteries of Russian artillery opened fire with buckshot; a detachment of cavalry led the counter charge on the janissary flanks, and two battalions of grenadiers threw a bayonet attack! Nevertheless, the balance of offensive to defensive turned as the superior number of Turks outweighed the might of the Russians. That was until Brigadier Ozeov and the First Grenadier Guard was called upon. Known for their exceptional tenacity and renowned for their heroism, they heedlessly attacked the attacking janissary without any tactical forethought, just sheer outrage! They did so with such unbelievable recklessness and savagery, that the janissary transmogrified from offensive positions to simply turning tale! Ivazzade Halil Pasha, the Turkish commander abandoned camp and all guns, ordering a desperate withdrawal to the other side of the river. On the raging battlefield, the Turkish soldiers also knew, treading upon the great losses absorbed under their footing— tripping over, falling on and dying among each other, one-after-another; and behind them their camp suddenly captured! En mass, the Islamic and Tatar antagonists disregarded all baggage and stampeded in herds seeking to cross the Danube to temporary geographical safety. As they ran like wildebeest, the Russians chased like lions. Alas, those who did not die from wound back to front reached the riverbank and the "beests" had no choice but to attempt to wade in safety. However, by the weight of their clothes, the panicked disorganization of jostling bodies, and the depth of the river, their escape was not temporary but permanent, from not only the Battle of Kagul, but from life on earth. The final tally was Russians wounded and killed: 1,500. Ottoman wounded, killed, drowned, and damned: 20,000. This was the dramatic backdrop in which Hayim Shelomo arrived in Warsaw August 1770.

***

Alone, as a singular representative and officer of M.A. Rothschild, Hayim entered Warsaw riding in a roths child emblazon carriage— a black Grand Tour with post chaise. Inside he was alone in the elegant carriage. Outside of it, he was escorted in numerous company. Two armed men rode on the chaise, with arms purposefully on display, while the driver was sandwiched in between two additionally equipped men, who most probably were the largest and strongest goons the Judengasse could provide. Charged with the task of protection, it seemed they were instinctively more concerned with the survival of the small fortune they were guarding than with the man dually appointed to invest it. Though only two hundred miles from Leszno, Warsaw was a cultural universe away. Hayim had seen all of Europe's great capitals and been impressed by the greatest marble and stone. Here though, he marveled at the edifices of polished granite being as Polish as he was. They made the trip in great speed and for Hayim, deep reflection. His months old conversation with Meyer riding up the slope of Hohenzollern Castle remained with him. He was confronted by the recognition of his own emotional vacancy. In the twelve years since Yankel drove him out of the city and abandoned him in the dead of winter, he never gave anything more than a cursory thought to his family, his past, or anything personal. It was his habit to "garden," to tend only to what was presently in time. Outside of the world of finance with it's estimations, predictions, analysis, and forecast, if an event in Hayim's day-to-day life was more than a week old, it either fell from his memory, or maybe in truth, it was consigned, but either/or, it was salted away in forgottenness.

In many ways, for this aspect of character Hayim was well liked. He never became temperamental over a point of fact or argument. He was agreeable even in disagreement, though not wavering in conviction. Nothing seemed to affect him personally; all encounters or exchanges appeared only to be a matter of enterprise. Conversely, even those who did slight him, and there were many over his years of travel and obligation through Europe, were amazed upon a second assignation. As it would turn out, he never held even a consideration of any of the grievance or slights, even in particular to the ones racially based. Yes, he recognized them, but they meant as much to him as the shifting of a single grain of sand on an unseen beach. His singular and unbroken focus was his position as a bank representative, be it de Neufville or Rothschild. Nothing else held a matter to him. His mind was like that of machinery cogwheels constantly turning and grinding integers into fractions. War? It wasn't his business to opine and discuss. Extended family? They would get along, with or without him as they always had? The integral welfare of the financial system of the whole of Western Europe? That held his attention and greased those cogwheels. Concisely, he could readily seem like a human without a heart.

For some, this was a quality of the man that left them confused and privately unsatisfied; in particular, his extended family in Amsterdam who utterly adored him. Hayim was not only quick-witted, exceptionally intelligent, and exceedingly kind, but he also furthered their financial affairs. He was a blessing more than he was ever a burden. However, many evenings, after the conclusion of a meal, ones in which Hayim would occasionally speak eloquently and sometimes riotously of his day at the banking house— when pressed to his concerns or thoughts about his father, mother, sister, grandfather, or any extension of the past, he was politely silent— ceasing to partake; eerily disengaged. It wasn't Hayim who wrote letters back home, it was his cousins who did so on his behalf. He never knew what the letters pertained, he only knew they were neither returned nor replied.

Hymn lived with his relatives five of the six years he resided in the Netherlands and as much as they admired him, they could not emotionally connect with him no matter the effort. Nay openly, nay privately, did he share his feelings, nor did he seek to inquire upon another's. It wasn't that he was unfeeling toward his cousins— on the contrary, in many ways he couldn't live without them, but it was out of a mutual respect in which he hoped if he did not query them, that they would not query him. Astonishingly, the young man never lied, he was honest to the core, and at times brutally so with a self-deprecating emphasis. Despite that compunction, he refrained from asking in kind or any affectionate curiosity. Often his cousins sought to relieve his unvoiced pangs of conscience with suggestions of hope, but it only nurtured him to become more insular. In short, he could have been described as a social hermit, though not an outcast.

Socially, Hayim Shelomo was a man of convincing power and influence, neither of which he abused or personally used. He was good in company and favored to be around, but he sought no one out of anything other than the pressing matter of business. His affairs came only as others sought him. This is without mention of how rather handsome he was, possessing a certain natural distinguished countenance in appearance and manner. Many young women found him desirable, but he failed to approach or seem to have any deciding interest in them. At times, "friends" or acquaintances took it upon themselves to introduce him with the express expectation of a flowering romance. None would ever be forthcoming. Yet, it wasn't because Hayim was shy or awkward. No woman could penetrate his ungiving emotional welcome or his habitual work habits. In fact, he was lonely. Yet, his type of loneliness was steeped in self-condemnation and disesteem. It was those self-debasing opinions that he sought to avoid sharing, even at the cost of sharing nothing of himself at all.

He was a free man, and yes: a Jew, but in many ways, infinitely freer than most. He had no responsibility to spouse or children. He seemed to have a kind of "freedom" in the sense of having no one to answer to, merely the work in which he was obligated. But he did not find liberation or deliverance in his "freedom." In fact, he merely incurred isolation. The rebelliousness he displayed in his youth, though still in his youth, was quelled. There was a fire inside, but he regulated that flame. He regulated it out of fear, the fear that it might drive him to another reckless act for which he could not defend. The journey from Frankfurt was seven hundred miles long and much of it was spent in the solitary consideration of his deeper, darker, self. Of the many things Hayim acknowledged within, one was that he was not dead inside. However, emotionally he had been brought to a standstill— paralyzed, years ago. He was still frozen in the day after he left Leszno. Frozen in the morning of the following day— not in the barn, but in wonder of what fate befell. Were they safe? Did his escape conclude the danger? It was there his memory lived, his heart vested— fallen into his belly, lodged in his gut, wound in twine, knotted to strangulation! He knew not of what the next day brought, and nervously, to know could be cause for celebration or reason for self-annihilation. Hayim Shelomo's emotions, guarded and stolen away as they were, had been arrested as are the hands of a broken clock. Of the heart, the time remained, as always, the same, and when the hour would strike— he would suppress the memory, cancel the question; deny the possibilities! Furthermore, he realized that he never looked back through the passage of time. He hated time. He hated it for what it was in the aggregate of events; what it meant in the accumulation of it's materialization, and what it represented in the totality of space in which it dominated.

But now, he was going home! Thus, along the journey, aside from these clusters of consideration, he drew the strength to symbolize his willingness to change. Whereby, he chose to view the road staring back through the window, at the trek already trod. Yes, he was going home—not Leszno, but close enough that he could call it "home." Yet, his real home would not be far. He could return. He would return! He could redeem himself— and face the past while honoring it at the same time. He came wedded with riches, though that didn't matter. As for the riches, he had a task to accomplish of which he knew much would be required.

Finally, he would look out of the window facing east, to the present he was arriving upon, not the past he just proceeded by— Warsaw was in his view. Further, it was a city without a Judengasse! That alone, made it a kind of heaven.

It must have been the most beautiful day of the year; at least it was to him. Hayim Shelomo, thirty years old was excited, again. However, he had no idea what lied ahead.

***

The plan was simple. Hayim was supposed to set up a bank. Operationally he would issue promissory notes that could be paid against estates. He was instructed to be lenient with credit in particular to the new and heady Jewish mercantile elite, many of whom had crossed into banking and had begun to dabble in the funding of military arms. Meyer wanted to control this market, to not only in-debt these men but thereby restrain their activity. Furthermore, Hayim was charged to under cut the competition in the age-old usury of currency exchange, even at the expense of losing money. It was about volume. To have everyone involved in dealings with the Rothschild bank, to quickly rise to prominence, and to wet the peckish appetite of paucity, before offering the main course garnished in avarice. The real business at hand was in subtly enticing the Poles, the Lithuanians, or even the Russians to borrow— to bring them into the sphere of Mayer's financial influence. The pitch and the assurance would always be the same: that the money is ostensibly "free," a privileged advance on if need-be, a fitting increase in taxes. Receive what you need now; remunerate on-time. Enrich yourself and your endeavors, pay for them by the labor of subjects, the defined cost of the kingdom. Taxes represented the security of both the government's means to pay and the Rothschild ability to collect, not to mention, the respective rulers' capacity to rule at will without the dam of the inopportune cyclical financial limit.

Hayim was alone, his back to the door; he happened to be shuffling through a fresh batch of trade cards he recently had printed at a rather exceptional cost. It was an English tradition he had discovered in his travels. They were small square pieces of thick paper with the illustration of the mansion and Rothschild's gold-colored eagle— both a calling card and an advertisement of sorts. In the six weeks since he landed by carriage, he had unfailingly taken the Warsaw markets by the proverbial storm. The location for the exchange was a large building on Miodowa street that Hayim bought outright. It was set directly across from the recently constructed and enormous palace of Crown Marshal Jan Klemens Branicki. It wasn't a storefront. It was a modestly lavish mansion. Notwithstanding, it was keeping in the restrained style of Mayer's understated manner as it wasn't as ornate or equal to the architectural wonders surrounding it. Yet still, it stood squarely as a sign of newly minted power. Already, there wasn't anyone in the know that wasn't aware of the name M.A. Rothschild and the face of Hayim Shelomo.

The large, tall, and thick, Polish Lancut-styled doors crept open. Undisturbed, Hayim casually turned to see who sought ingress. Two distinctively different types of men, numbering four, entered self-assuredly. The first, the second, and third were older men, boarding on elderly. They were Father Jandołowicz— most notable as the only one with a beard, followed by brothers, Adam Krasiński and his older sibling, Michał. The latter were undoubtedly nobles. The last to enter was a somewhat short but dashing figure more than half their ages and even younger than Hayim, Casimir Pulaski.

"Are there others about?" the younger Krasiński inquired from far across the room, an expanse large enough that there was a tiny echo to his words.

Hayim was not easily unnerved and comfortably moved from concentrating on the trade cards to coolly strolling toward them with his shoes clicking across the marble.

"The room or the house?" Hayim calmly replied.

"Casimir— Drzwi!" Adam Krasiński quickly ordered!

The young man, in his mid-twenties, did as he was told and guarded the door. Both parties were briskly closing the palatial gap until they at last came face-to-face.

"I am Adam Krasiński— this is Father Jandołowicz, and my brother, Michał."

"You are Polish, no?" Michał quickly interjected before Hayim could even say anything.

Cautious or coy, Hayim inquisitively shifted his sight from one man to another—

"We already know everything about you Mr. Shelomo," Michał's brother sought to preeminently inform him rather than waiting for a pat answer.

"You are a Jew," said the Father in his own uniquely subtly disparaging tone.

"Yes," Hayim breezily but sarcastically remarked, "Then, I guess you do know everything about me—"

"But you are a Pole, first?" Adam interrupted.

He indefatigably said so less genuinely as a question and more in a self-comforting assertion for all parties involved. Hayim knew these men sought to intimidate him but he was not intimidated nor was he going to be. Yet, out of respect and astute caution, he partook and entertained their unexpected arrival.

"I was born a Jew and a Pole," Hayim started, unamused. "If I would have been born in Bohemia, I would have been born a Jew and a Bohemian. If I would have been born in Finland, I would have been born a Jew and Finnish. I cannot escape my heritage— if you know anything of anatomy, it slouches and spills in arterial channels throughout the body. But of heart and nationality, I am certainly and proudly: Polish— if that is what you wonder."

Just as well, a certain air of agreement descended among the visitants and they relaxed just enough—

"That is good, quite good" said Adam. "Porozmawiajmy— Porozmawiajmy!"

Two of the old men took to sitting in ornate high-back silver chairs, something their bodies had been aching for, leaving Adam standing in de facto leadership. Father Jandołowicz turned and motioned for Casimir. He came forward and handed the old man a box the clergy had entered with. The aging cleric opened the wooden crate and extracted a bottle of homemade vodka— that is, "homemade" in the vestibule by Father Jandołowicz.

"We want you to befriend us," said the ever-so good man of the cloth in a conniving tone, much like the devil when he said to Jesus on the mountain top, "All this I will give you, if you will bow down and worship me!"

He handed the bottle to his companions and they opened it without further ado. Hayim, though not fearing them, was not so cavalier as to dismiss them outright and possibly suffer an unbecoming wrath, so with glasses raised high, Michał and Adam lead the forced cheer—

"Na zdrowie!"

As the men slowly wet their gullets with the high proof water for life, Casimir desperately threw his back and dutifully returned to manning the door.

"As the Father, said, 'we want you to befriend us!'" Adam spoke cheerfully.

"I see... but, how more could I befriend you other than how I already have?" coolly asked Hayim.

"You deal in the interest of money," the priest hissed as if he was spitting out a bad seed.

"What do you say of the cause of Russia?" Adam queried.

"What do you say of the King?" Michał followed.

Hayim thought for a moment as he finished his dry liquid endowment.

"I do not say anything of them, as I do not say anything of anyone," Hayim declared.

"Do you then agree? A Pole you say— agree that the Union should be whittled and defiled by the malevolent hand of Russia?"

"So... you are the rebels," Hayim somewhat delightfully realized.

"If you have made an agreement with that illegitimate and dethroned potentate, we will cut your throat here and now," the Father asserted.

"I have made no agreements," Hayim said with amused fearlessness, "but have you consulted the butt sunk on the pillow of the throne, that it is not, as it is?"

No one found it funny that he poked fun at one of their meaningless declarations in Podolia. Nevertheless—

"Have you been in congress—?" Michał inquired.

"Neither have I been in congress or conference of your cause, for or against. I deal exclusively in the service of finance," Hayim forcefully maintained!

"Well then, we are here in just that service, the service of finance," Adam proclaimed!

But the Father was already threateningly pointing his finger at Hayim—

"Have you not morals? Have you not a regard for law? Absent are you of right and wrong? You are, no— no, what do I say— you are a Jew. You are like all other Jews. You discern only care of your enrichment. Like the tentacles of the octopus, you squeeze your victims of life and like the cannibal, you eat indiscriminately of your own kind!"

The tension had certainly raised when suddenly the door began to open. Casimir held it closed and frantic knocking followed!

"Herr Shelomo!" a voice on the other side cried! "Herr" denoting Hayim's marked status, even in his home country. The banker knew he was being strong-armed, at least to a degree, and relented enough that he threw his voice toward the door—

"Gwidon, I am in private consul! Let it wait!"

Then, there was silence. Everyone stood perfectly still until they all heard the clacking sound of footsteps going away.

"What do you want to hear from me, that I am a sworn enemy to the crown, to the King of Poland— that I am hateful of the power which he derives? Do you want to hear that I support your movement? Well, I no more support any rebel than I support any illegitimate king. I treat all no different then I treat the present bout of plague erupting in the streets— with as much avoidance as possible."

"Did you think you could simply come upon this country in rent and profit without taking sides, Herr Shelomo?" Michał said snidely, lisping the foreign salutation. "You meet with us, but do not be so foolish as to think the crown will not be walking through your hall into this room just as we are walking out."

"He is a Jew," the Father sneered!

Hayim instinctually knew what they were saying was more-than-likely true. Glancing at the portraits that came fastened upon the wall with purchase of the mansion— oils of past Polish rulers, distinguished nobility, and scenic panoramas, Hayim quickly realized that Poland was a den of vipers and that he would be bitten by one viper or the other, unless he was able to walk very carefully in between the nests—

"Just tell me now, tell me what you want."

"Your support," Adam humbly suggested.

Suddenly, Casimir rushed forward as though his hair was on fire and his tongue rolled out like carpet—

"Believe as we do— that Poland should not be a protectorate or a slave to Russian designs! The Confederation needs champions—"

"You mean money?" Hayim quickly retorted!

"Champions! The will by which to campaign, to make war against, to fight on equal terms, and to win! Without us, Russia will crush Poland until it is less than the ground of a peppercorn!"

The Rothschild representative clasped his hands behind his back and dramatically walked in a few unconnected semi-circles, before delivering a deferential charge—

"Your cause is worthy, but fear do I that I am not an investor," Hayim shrewdly suggested as a tactic.

"We do not come in labor of alms and entreat for investment. Righteously, let us all benefit, let us all prosper, let us all be on the side of God," argued Adam.

More-or-less cornered, Hayim mused, and finally asked—

"And tell me, what does God not have, but need?"

"What does God always need, Pan Shelomo? He needs the will and might of men," the Father spoke convincingly.

"Bear us a loan," Adam put-forth in request.

"A loan? And how should I suspect to be guaranteed of this loan?"

"We will come bearing all the motherly holdings of Poland. Anywhere that is green, in deeds," his brother triumphantly professed.

Hayim almost laughed and gave away enough of a smile to bring wrinkles of displeasure about their faces—

"Those deeds of lands could be worth less than not only the paper they were printed on, but the bark in which they were pressed— that is if you fail in your endeavor. Be it by confiscation, destruction, dispossession, or of course, your untimely executions."

"We shall win!" Casimir shouted!

"How do you know you shall win?"

"You are truly a Jew!" the Father roared in anger!

Forcefully Hayim submitted—

"I ask again to those who ask me for the means to fight, 'How do you know you shall win?'"

"We shall take the King! And make them beg us for self-restraint and mercy!" Casimir wildly pronounced!

Michał and Father Jandołowicz jumped to their feet!

"Take the King?" Hayim said in shock!

Quickly, the Father dismissed Casimir back to the door, but this time he wouldn't so easily acquiesce. Though, he did step behind the man, but not to the door. Blushed and constrained, four of the five men found themselves standing in a long silence. The host, the fifth, forced his silence, that it be known, he heard well.

"Disregard what was shouted," the Father calmly spoke and even kindly poured Hayim another glass of spirits. "Please, I made this of my own hands, like a farmer, in my palms so you may say is my heart. I say, do you not believe it is possible that we shall win?"

Hayim held on to his full glass, but staring into the man's eyes he purposefully would not drink. The insult grew with every second that passed. It was a friction of enmity, a standoff, a match of mettle. For his part, Father Jandołowicz would not sit. They continued burning stares into one another, until finally Hayim sipped ever-so-slightly and the man of God victoriously reclined into a pleased lounging position. However, Hayim was no feeble opponent.

"Do I believe you will win? My dear Father, I am not in the business of faith and the artful slight of spirit, as you so bountifully are." The Father was flabbergasted but was surely not going to make an ass out of himself by standing again in the face of the aspersion.

"You seek from me terms of wherewithal in which I cannot lay claim to title of possession. I am a little more than a manager of other's wealth," Hayim finished.

"We are supported in earnest by the Kingdom of France!" Adam pleaded.

"But not enough earnest that you seek measures of my earnestness," Hayim responded.

"War is expensive!" Michał exploded!

"And who are your leaders? Your great generals that have held the reigns of pitched battles and won?" Hayim vigorously vocalized!

"I am one of them!" Casimir proclaimed. "I am a marshal of the confederation forces in the Łomża region! As is my father and brothers! We, all of the vanguard, have fought already bravely for two plus years— I have been victorious, I have been defeated, I have been captured, and I have been freed! The pulsing waves of war, of riptide and low surf, there is nothing I have not glimpsed, though everyday I see something new! We are not inexperienced— we are the might of the Will of God!"

For his part, Hayim was unimpressed—

"And what do you have to say of confidence?"

"I was victorious at Slonim. I was victorious at Kukielki."

"And of the recent past?"

The marshal took a long breath; the kind in the uneasy unraveling of an uncomfortable truth. Then, he held his right hand before Hayim's face as might a solider his medal in proof of valiant service. The appendage was swollen and deformed to the degree in which it was unnaturally curved and debilitated. Clearly, he was living in continual agonizing pain.

"Grab!" he said, referring to the village in west-central Poland. Then Casimir pointed to a small growth, a discolored tumor developing below his left eye—

"Fortifying Berdyczów— I felt nothing but humor as the Russian's knife penetrated all the way to the bone. And I howled, I did, in great laughter, as I slit his belly from right to left, and back again— from left to right."

The morbid nature of his boasts or his conviction, you might say, momentarily silenced the conversation, until—

"Your valor goes unquestioned," Hayim calmly remarked. "And so does my question go unanswered."

"I have made my way here from retreat to Austria," Casimir finally admitted.

"There are always gains and losses," Hayim respectfully said, yet also knowingly— "but what have you and the others held?"

"We have sought Krakow and Lvov."

"But you hold them not—"

"Throughout Lithuania there is uprising after uprising!"

"Uprisings! Uprisings!" Hayim shouted back! "Where are the victories? The strongholds?"

"We have captured and maintain a monastery at Jasna Góra!" Casimir shouted back in frustration.

Hayim bellowed in laughter from even the mere mention of the meager success of storming and occupying a monastery, "monastery?"

"And how many men do you have?" in all seriousness, Hayim followed.

"Many! But not enough!"

"You ask me for money, give me numbers!"

"More than a thousand," Casimir said through gritted and grinding teeth.

"And what do the Russians have, a million?

"Of course you exaggerate—"

"But they have more, many times more! I would see more than a mere thousand as a child! And how many cannon—"

"Yes! We need more cannon—"

Hayim glared at the man almost with pity in his eyes—

"And what do you expect to do? To fight them, like children in the street? Chase them with sticks and stones? Are you that benign a horde?" Casimir immediately drew his sword and in one fell swoop, deftly brought the tip of it to the skin of Hayim's throat.

"We are soldiers," he said in all seriousness.

Just wanting to make his point, Casimir dropped his weapon and adeptly slid it back into its sheath. Hayim swallowed hard but was not dissuaded from his argument, just prudently more composed.

"How many Polish-Russian wars have concluded in our victory over the Russians? You ask me if I am Pole. I am Pole and I know our history and it is bereft of even a single moment of triumph over the archenemy. But it is fraught with a succession of losses. And what battlefield victories have you won so far, safe from the skirmish of an unfortified monastery— what trust can you inspire in me?"

Casimir was silent as Hayim waited for his response. Hayim had continued the exchange with a steady composure but after the sword was erect to the soft indentation above his collarbone, on the pique of the tip of Casimir's pride and corresponding instrument of authority, inside, he privately shook like a leaf. In the completion of his discourse, he certainly wanted the full contents of the glass of vodka he left but slightly sipped— anything to anesthetize the nerves. He drank as Casimir admitted—

"None."

"And, why should I support you with anything more than encouragement? And do not threaten me with life or Russians. If my life fails, there will be no means and he who sent me will support your enemies in destroying you for destroying me. Now, I thank you gentlemen for your vodka and your company—"

Hayim stood expecting them to simply turn and exit. Such was not forthcoming.

"You forget something, bankier" Michał said. "You could refuse to support our righteousness, and just as so, we could send word to our foe that we have been favored by you. Jew, have you ever seen a fish flapping in a dry pond?"

Hayim had seen more than his adversary knew and didn't bristle at his feeble metaphor or menacing tone.

"What do you think he who sent you will do if it is the Russians who take it upon themselves to destroy you, as you say? Might in turn, he finance their enemy?" Michał concluded.

Again, Hayim wasn't impressed with the logic, even though it was sound. In fact, he knew from his long journey that Meyer would not likely lose sleep over his demise, nor would he finance a lost cause.

"In closing, are you denying our appeal?" Adam asked.

Hayim knew better than to refuse them outright. Anything was possible, and possibly, they just might impulsively slit his throat.

"No. I am not. I am to travel over the next week. And, when I return, I vow, I shall honor you with a thoughtful decision."

***

The dawn of the next day saw Hayim begin three days of westward travel en route to Leszno. He rode in his emblazoned Rothschild carriage, bringing along armed protection and spending the night in Łódź and Kalisz. All-in-all, it took seventy-six hours, but at long last he came upon some of the lazily spinning blades of a few of the windmills in Rydzyna. Once and for all, he knew exactly where he was. The windmills cast down his vertical line of sight, stretching until they reached the axis of the horizon; circling, going round, spinning on the pleasure of the wind, as natural as the birth of a child... and they did so for him, en mass— as far as any human eye could see on a bright clear day. Thereafter, in one eagerly lived hour more, he geographically arrived in the city of his physical genesis.

Entering, there were no more occupying Russians. Entry was unmolested. He rode into the town square and in many ways, the city appeared brand new to his sight, as once did Amsterdam, Paris, Vienna, and Frankfurt. All the wooden buildings that still stood next to brick and stone emanated a charming quaintness that Hayim hadn't been surrounded by since the farmer's barn. Oddly though, the old-world urban rusticity to the once small town boy who was now a worldly man of means mined an untapped vein of vanity. Maybe it was the truth, an actuality, one, which Hayim could no longer turn his attention from— he was successful, and he was primarily proud of that success. For in point of fact, there he rode, not on a donkey but in splendor.

The morning seemed radiant, summery, and the market and the Wieniawa so magnificent— to Hayim, ever more so than Warsaw, which it certainly wasn't even by any lucid stretch of the imagination? He knew that, too, but it felt irresistibly magnificent, otherworldly, or just simply: eternally beautiful— in a winsome resemblance to true love lost and that same true love divinely regained. Who knows, maybe it was because the last time he rode down those cobbled streets it was in fear for his life, in the dark of night, in the imprudent obedience of adolescence. Whatever the unreasoned reason, the morning felt beyond belief.

His affinity stirred, he gazed and beheld with desire the spectacle of tableau vivants, wishing to see something truly familiar. However, nothing was actually familiar and he merely settled for remembering that he remembered this or that. Ultimately, it was in the expectation of entering the Jewish section in which his greatest hope of visceral rapport was placed. Be that as it may, there was a more material ambition he held— to see his family again. And, if nothing else, to locate exactly where they were.

***

Hayim crested the small high ground, near his parents' home. From this vantage point, he had a clear view of the entire kehilla, the community made up wholly of Jewish nationals. With the carriage swaying as they were wont to do— he reached into his satchel and reverentially lifted the tattered siddur stitched with the Star of David given to him by his grandfather; his stomach pulled taut and ached in a gnarled knot. The boundless joy of only a matter of moments ago— by way of a few left and right turns into the future, abruptly devolved into breathtaking internal terror. Suddenly, he never felt so low, so afraid, so uncertain of his course in his whole life. He tried to buoy himself with the vision of being reunited with his family but the dark side of his mind played upon his fears of their death or worse— their outright rejection of him. First, what if he stepped into his home and they did not recognize him? "Impossible!" "Impossible," he thought, and tried to shake it out of his mind. But, second— what if they recognized him immediately and were genuinely disgusted by the sight of him? What if his success, riding in a grandiose carriage as he was, was seen at the cost of their welfare— and brought them to rightfully applied hatred from a bubbling cauldron of acrimony? Thirdly, what if he found them in abject poverty, wandering the streets— but then he would save them, he thought! But what if they did not care anymore to be saved, like many of the shuffling lost souls he encountered in the Judengasse? What if his salvation was past the point of deliverance and his redemption past both its mortal and divine expiration? It can be said that the return of Hayim Shelomo to the Jewish District of Leszno, twelve years after his departure, was the most nerve-racking moment of his life, and never could anything compare.

Finally, the coach traveled gingerly down the street in which Hayim had been born and with no further roads to traverse, he knew if nothing else— he was home, again. It was a rather great distance before he would reach the actual domicile. The wheeled rotation of steam-bent hickory— round n' round, the horse clomp and hoof, nostril and inhalation, inch by inch, foot after foot, the swaying reigns and the metal tire to stone, measured in the measurement of yard upon yard— whereas all together were bound with time and space, it was in that peculiar context and transient dimension that Hayim surveyed each side of the street as the horses cantered forward. He noted a vivacity, a spirit, a freedom that was self-evident. Surely, this was his youth in residency but not in reflection. In the time since he had been away things had clearly improved for the Jews, just the same as he had taken notice of in Warsaw— they lived in a veritable bounty of prosperity. As he continued in passing, many gawked and wondered who this was in the majestic calash. He intentionally tried not to stare into anyone's eyes, while at the same time, he looked to see if there stood anyone in existence he knew. Much of the district was striated with the lingering effect of fire damage from three years before. A conflagration broke out in the town and burnt down the whole Jewish district. Due to the tragedy, the town officials decided to write off all the fees paid by the Jewish community for the period of six years. It was a cost in afford to their being secretly subsidized by the Prussians and the Italians— a precursor of the machinations of foreign interests to come. Nevertheless, free from taxes, the community thrived. At that moment, unknown to Hayim, he had entered the Lion Cave, as Jewish Leszno was newly so called, because it was the dynamic center of Judaistic learning. When he resided there, it was simply known for Jewish craft and trade, but now it was appreciated as the heart of Jewish academia. The closer he came to his home, the less the fire damage lingered. Row after row of houses had been rebuilt and were quite radiant. He grew steadily more excited. His fears were alleviated enough that he began to imagine a type of joy that was unspeakable! However, again though— just as quickly, the darkness set in. Why hadn't they written? Were they protecting him? Did the letters of his cousins ever reach them?

The horses trotted past one house after another, ones in which he recognized alone by their structural shape, if not their newly painted color. Then, without further ado, he came to the front of his own home…, and, almost literally, his heart sank into his stomach.

***

Between two elegantly rebuilt facades was his family's place of residence: burned out, gutted of fire— not from the recent blaze, but an old inferno, so old that weeds and wild vegetation had over taken some of it from the inside and under the foundation. This damage was clearly not new, but years or decades bygone. Hayim instructed the driver to stop. In further consideration, he decidedly placed his most holy possession, the prayer book, back into his satchel and left it on the seat of the carriage. Then, he slowly disembarked— his eyes never breaking sight of the blacken hollowed habitation. About the sidewalks, residents froze in uncommon scrutiny at the vision of this wealthy stranger slowly approaching the remains of a tragic day. What was left were three crumbling walls, buttressed by concrete firewalls. The front had no door, no wall— no partition whatsoever. The whole edifice had been disavowed, abandoned— forsworn like that of a ghost town. But why?

It was the height of the afternoon as he entered over crunching brittle wood that instantly blew into ashes on the heel of his step. The nature of the fire damage made it appear as if the house had been smelted. Everything that was of material form, at its center had been burned to dust, while its structural integrity lingered like ghostly remnants, palled frames— thin trace hints of spectral apparitions caught in the ephemeral kairotic transmutation of human handiwork. Those non-existing existential material objects, those molted elements of matter, those delicate vestiges of withering shells, those otherwise charred corners and ends as they were— all seemed to be balancing in supernatural phenomenon. Everyone in the district knew they were unambiguously, signs and wonders.

As he carefully stepped forward one after another drew their purpose to a close and dissolved into nothing more than common dust— the tables, the chairs, the chests, and the holy. He walked among the ruins, the world outside watching in amazement. There was no doubt in his mind, this was the fire of his home, not another who lived in it after him. The desire to recognize something familiar was suddenly a nightmare in progress. Much he became familiar with again: their mezuzah— heat warped and lying on the floor; the unburnt fringes of one of his father's tallits, their pure silver family menorah— which he raised and wiped a thick layer of soot from its base. Mournfully, he wished the inscription had not read: "Shelomo." Yet, how did he know they didn't escape— maybe fleeing before the fire? Then, in the far corner of the room, he made his most gruesome discovery.

Not all that glitters is gold— not all that is burnt is black. With his eyes as transfixed as they say the sight is on the light upon death, carefully he took each step toward the object of his gaze; his auditory range narrowly locked on his heartbeat. What he could not hear was the wood cracking in thunderous blasts under his feet as the floor gradually disintegrated. He reached the far corner. He glanced back at the rest of the room and the entire home. It was there, in that far corner, that of all the area, the strange sense of being the last refuge of safety emanated. The other corners were more exposed, situated as such that they invited a flow of direction. This corner however, off of the kitchen, was singularly unique— where the wall declined from the perpendicular a little inward. This was where you would hide if your back were to the wall. With his heart in his mouth, Hayim reached down and lifted a half-burnt clump of exceptionally beautiful long brown hair.

Instantly, he fell to the ground, which still contained him enough that only his knees were buried in rubble, and then he wailed in the most desperate cries of pain that any man has ever howled! He held his sister's hair in his hands and he died inside, over and over again, one guilt-ridden memory at a time. This solemn self-immolation continued witnessed and unabated until evening fell. Hundreds stood outside the house weeping along with him.

If Hayim could have forced his body and soul to elapse, he would have. However, his heart failed him and continued to beat. His excretory system failed him also, and he could cry no more. Unwilling to actually bring himself to expire by his own hand, there was nothing left for him to do but rise to his feet and exit what was dead of him for good.

He rose, clinging tightly to his sisters hair— to what remained of her persona. Outside in the deepening dark light of late summer, strangers' eyes endued him the most beautiful pity. Weighing a million times more with the heavy heart of sorrow, he placed his sister's remains securely in his coat pocket and made his way through the house, which for a second time in his life no longer appeared to him as his. Now it was precisely just aged debris. With each step he came closer to the crowd they superstitiously reeled backward. As he reached the street, his driver awaiting— an old man approached with a small bowl of water and a towel. He spoke no words and would not look at Hayim in the eyes but for a second. Nevertheless, he kindly insisted that the sorrowful man wash his hands of the dead. So most likely, everyone knew that the Shelomo's did not escape the fire, and in honor, horror, and respect, no one ever laid foot, claim, or touch upon the property again, that is once the bodies were excavated. It was the house of the dead. It was the house of the damned.

Hayim laid his tear-soaked hands into the bowl and looked at the man, but the man would not look up. He would not look into the eyes of he who had just stared at death. Hayim removed his hands from the bowl and in haste merely let the water slowly drip off of them. He had washed his hands of death, and now it was time to resolve the washing of his hands of Russians.

***

X
"WE ARE THE DAMNED"

"Men will ultimately be governed by God or by tyrants."
                                        Benjamin Franklin

Scads of shiny silver portraits of Peter I easily slid in the potent disposition of a loose pyramid of accumulated roubles.

"I suspect soon, you will need more," Hayim impassively stated. He sat in full command— the king of trusts, the lord finance, at a small mahogany bankers desk in his own piddling private office. Unpretentious— intimate, it was one of the otherwise unoccupied residential servants' quarters of the mansion. The intention was uttermost privacy. Obviously, the room was a much smaller chamber than the first meeting between he and the floundering confederation. This time, with the airs and graces, similar to the fealty tone of liege homage, Hayim was the doyen of the duration. The overly anxious dissidents stood around him, pressed nearly shoulder-to-shoulder. Of the four, Hayim already knew Casimir and Michał. But the pleasure of this second encounter was to bring him into acquaintance with Walenty Łukawski. He was yet another noble, dressed to the nines with a fantastic mien— a permanent countenance of the cat who ate the canary, and evidently found it quite delectable. In addition, there was a man unable to control his giddiness at the sight of such riches, Jan Kuźma. Kuźma was little more than a man who actually looked dumb. Therein, his face spoke honestly of his authentic intelligence.

"And if we shall?" asked Michał.

"Then we shall have an arrangement," Hayim replied. "A man is to come, come here— a plain man— and be he a different man, on every occasion of his arrival. He is to bring these—"
Hayim placed on the desk an open sack of silver Javan rupees. Only something from interstellar space could have been more exotic looking to the rebels.

"Three of them, and he is to seek but a simple exchange of currency. Any more or less than three, and I shall turn him away. But with three, I shall exchange them for one Spanish dollar. That specie is to be brought by a man entrusted, but not a solider or noble— a Jewish merchant, a common merchant— anyone outside who is of wares— be he unknown to you, but surreptitiously approached. When such a fellow arrives upon my desk with the coin in hand, I shall enrich him thusly. Then, it is incumbent upon you to quietly and peaceably retrieve your welfare from his service."

***

By the evening of November 3, 1771, the laws of nature by which the body of an object increases in volume or in actual size by heat, and diminishes or contracts by cold had not changed since the degassing of the planet's interior. Pendulum rods, usually crafted of metal or wood, suffer from this inevitable consequence of fluctuating temperatures and subsequently alter in length. Such variation on the length of the pendulum will at once be seen to increase or decrease the number of oscillations in a given measurement of time. The average clock as of the aforementioned date was incapable of going nearer to accurate time than about 40 minutes within a 24 hour time period. Therein, sometime between nine and ten o'clock at night, Stanisław Augustus Poniatowski, in all, the seventy-eighth ruler of Poland and the Grand Duke of the Polish-Lithuanian Commonwealth, excused himself from an intimate and informal soirée at the house of his uncle, Prince Fryderyk Michał Czartoryski.

The King was a rather handsome monarch with a sharp, candid, interesting face highlighted by a strong masculine bone structure. His height was neither too short for common liking, or so tall as to be commonly noted. Coupled with fit proportions, he was striking upon entrance and impressive upon exit. He was a charismatic leader that could be defined by a biography of diverging contrasts. Born of the noblest station— yet his reign rose on the behest of the most degrading patronage. He was an ardent nationalist but a puppet king tied to a long slacked string. Pedigree from a Princely House, he was naturally a benevolent leader, just as he was personally vainglorious and easily led. Stanisław sought absolutism in rule at the cost of civil liberties and opposed the newly fashioned Polish Constitution, though he himself not only drafted a large portion of the document but also gave the country's most stirring speech on behalf of his vow to uphold it. He undermined the Polish Army but he also established the Corp of Cadets. But, above all, he was a man of the arts in the name of the Enlightenment. He founded the national theater; took great interest in architecture and the remodeling of historic palaces.

He launched the Monitor, the leading periodical of the Polish Enlightenment. He hosted weekly fantastic social functions, known as the "Thursday Dinners" and the "Wednesday Dinners." The middle of the week brought together educators, scientists and political activists while Thursday, his favorite of the two— painters; sculptors; poets; and artists of every walk! They were combined and intermingled with intellectuals and statesmen— all convoked for scrumptious culinary and pedantic delights. Maybe in a different time, during a different era, Stanisław would have been the model of the great patron of modernity— the demarcation of human intellectual advance from external conquests to civilized insight. But instead, he was trapped in the most graven hour of his country's existence— Poland's hour of extinction.

It was an evening of intense political discourse. The conversations mainly consisted of a deeply genuine discussion on the possibility of reconciliation with the Bar, which Stanisław privately sought to invoke. From there it drifted into a dialogue on the abolition of the liberum veto before lightheartedly being capped in private drunken chagrin revisiting the night sixteen years ago that the young man who would be king, Stanisław, was kidnapped by the ugly angry little figure of the Grand Duke, and forced to confess his carnal transgressions with the man's wife and second cousin, the Grand Duchess Sophie Friederike Auguste von Anhalt-Zerbst-Dornburg, renamed, Ekaterina Alexeievna, or later to become better known as: Catherine the Great. However, in good spirits, the last laugh of the night was on the old Grand Duke, who became the short-lived czar, Peter III. For his promiscuous Catherine eventually had him arrested, forced to abdicate, and assassinated with the cannibalistic deftness of a black widow spider.

The opulent baroque palace was just across the street from the King's own palatial residence, and less than a brisk ten minute walk from the mansion in which Hayim had established the Rothschild bank, and was theretofore presumably sleeping on that night. Stanisław relaxed and in good cheer, was accompanied by his usual retinue of guards and a small escort of mounted guerrilla fighters or "hajduks" as they were called. In all, seven bodies protecting one. Beyond the courtyard, they passed the great ornate guardhouses of the residence that bookended the great iron gate. The King was helped into his carriage and the party had only to turn the horses and trot across the street when suddenly from a safe distance,

Walenty Łukawski— donning his great-exaggerated smile, gave the signal and dozens of men sprang out upon them in ambush!

The barrage and volley; the shrieks and squeals— undiscriminating gunfire ripped through the night; one hajduk fatally fell dead in the snow! Mayhem and confusion! A skirmish— the air aerated in adrenaline— jumpy and edgy halfwits, buffoons, and dolts! Scared, witless, and incompetent regal defenders and preserves of a potentate! A fray of chaos! The King— desperately gripping to the upholstery of the carriage when he was wrenched and heaved into the center of the madness! He shouted with authority! But everyone shouted! Though, en mass, they weren't hollering in words, but— grunts— groans— bewilderment— surprise, and indubitably: fear! They were all yowling in terror! Instead of nobly protecting their sovereign with the integrity of their lives, the mounted guerrilla and all the king's men, except for one, turned tail and ran! However, the organized attackers of the Bar Confederation were no more magnanimous nor courageous. They, too, more than a handful, caught in the turbulent storm of assault and its raging ire of gunfire became frightened and fled! Almost everybody was running away from one another in the cold night. The exception was the one man who couldn't run, a fearless hajduk that intercepted a bullet with a trajectory toward his king. It was fired by John Strawinski, one of the two nobles, leading the attack. As the ball exploded into the hajduk's left temple, the corresponding blood splattered Stanisław in advance of the wobbling projectile continuing it's course of blowing the mercenary's brains out of the back of his head and grazing the top of the king's skull! Strawinski, too, maybe overwhelmed by the mortal power held in his own hand— tossed the gun and scurried into the night! At the same time, the face of a heavy blade crashed down over Stanisław's head. He crumpled at the blunt blow and lay nearly unconscious over the dead man who at least momentarily saved his life. The ambush that combusted in sound and fury, suddenly was eerily silent— and there stood, the feeble-minded pea-brained, Jan Kuźma holding the sword. The whole ordeal was anything but an extraordinary feat of planning, ingenuity, and courage— it was a daft exercise of fundamental amateurishness. Nevertheless, the Bar figuratively held what they wanted in the palm of their thick, dull, imbecilic hands.

Łukawski, still at a distance, hushed Kuźma to follow through with the execution of the overall plan, and accompany him into the deeper reaches of the night. Kuźma lifted the groggy king, dragged, and tossed him over one of the hacks. Unlatching it from the carriage, the addled conspirator, with the King laid horizontally in front of him, hurried off at full speed into the forest of Bielany!

***

The Polish–Lithuanian Commonwealth is a uniquely singular example of a nation deliberately committing suicide for the sake of absolute individual liberty. However, the virtue of said liberty was narrowly defined to the self-preserving, self-enriching, self-interest of the landowners. Before the liberum veto, there were primarily only two classes of peasants, the free and the bound. In time, by an oligarchical consolidation of power by the Szlachta through an aristocratic political system in which the nobles ultimately controlled both the parliament and the king, the bound were gradually reduced to the condition of serfs with the aristocrats— for all intensive purposes having divided the population into two principle classes: the nobles and the ignobles. In reality they were divided into five classes: the political class of titled gentry, the all-powerful and land accumulating clergy, the wealthy bourgeoisie, the lowly peasants, and the even lowlier Jews. It was the hour of Poland's extinction— the death of so-called noble democracy, the demise of the intelligentsia culture, and the arrant destruction of national liberty. This calamitous hour began November 25, 1764 at St. John's Church, with the virtually dripping, well-greased greedy hands of Władysław Aleksander Łubieński, the Archbishop of Gniezno, placing the great glory of the Brave's Crown on Stanisław Poniatowski's undeserving head. However, the long day coming of that hour started on a Krakow morning ninety-five years prior when for the first time, the entire Sejm was prematurely disrupted on the strength of the liberum veto before it had completed its deliberations.

Poland's internal troubles rested on the liberum veto. It is a latin phrase, loosely translated, "I freely forbid." It was a parliamentary device that allowed any member of the Sejm, the Polish legislature, to force an immediate end to the current session and nullify any legislation that had already been passed at the assembly by shouting the simple negation: "I do not allow!" The parliamentary device made every session a house of cards, just waiting to fall by one disunited voice out of one hundred and eighty. Conversely, the country's external troubles began when Stanisław

I, King of Poland, double-crossed Peter the Great and his Tsardom of Russia in the heat of the Great Northern War. He was the first Stanisław to be a puppet king, but evidently not the last.

Stanisław I ascended to the perch of power on the heels of the military defeats of Augustus II the Strong, the Saxon Hercules. Maybe best characterized by animal carnage, Augustus was equally a voracious collector of Asian ceramics and a wildly enthusiastic patron of the arts. Standing strappingly at six feet tall, he insouciantly renounced his Protestant faith and converted to Catholicism for the unprincipled acquisition of a foreign crown; and whenever the opportunity presented itself, went to great lengths to demonstrate his physical prowess, as if it made up for his moral and intellectual vacuity. Unquestioningly, he was a lover of the arts but unfailingly a fanatic of the bloodsports. Reputably, he was able to break horseshoes with his bare hands and ghastly raised the decadent sport of fox tossing— slinging live foxes into the air, to a level of harrowing atrocity and danger supremely reserved for madmen. However, Augustus the Strong flung more than foxes for amusement— with the power of one finger alone, he hurled: boars, wolves, badgers, and wildcats! At times, it was a sight to see, the struggling and whimpering broken bodies of these creatures trembling in shock— while all around the triumphant king in an atmosphere of carnival delight, were little boys gifted with miniature clubs with which to gleefully play. They did so in the merciful delight of thrashing and bashing the skulls of the injured animals until the pulp of brain matter made for giddy laughter. At his prolific height, one afternoon in Dresden, Augustus, "the Grim Reaper of Wildlife" sent 647 foxes, 533 hares, 34 badgers and 21 wildcats into expiry. While he was mentally one of the most vacillating of rulers there is no doubt he was physically one of the strongest men of any age. Moreover, despite being trained for a military career, where it counted the most— intellectually and militarily, he was grossly outclassed by all of his contemporaries of such lowly weaker mesomorphic physiques.

'Tis the last feather that broke the horse's back, was the Battle of Klissow over a marshy field in Kielce. Led by the once child-king, Charles XII of Sweden, who around the time of the battle turned the ripe-old age of twenty, the Swedes out maneuvered the Polish-Saxon army of Augustus the Strong. The Poles had almost three times the man power of the Swedes and the advantage of the defensive position. Still, adeptly commanded by Charles, the Swedish army routed the Saxe-Polish forces and upon the subsequent capture of Warsaw, Augustus the Strong— now more-fitting to bequeath upon him the moniker of "The Defeated" or "The Weak," also double-crossed Peter the Great and hopelessly sued the Kingdom of Sweden for a pitying peace. However, Charles XII was uninterested in Augustus's contrition and pledges of fidelity. To his own liking and insurance, the young King dusted off the Polish royal throne for the unqualified and assumedly unassuming ambitious presence of the twenty-six-year-old governor of Poznan, Stanisław Leszczyński. In time, the two Polish kings, he and Augustus II— both initially brought to the throne by political dispensation, would alternately lose and regain their crowns. However, in 1709, after Charles suffered the worst of his agonizing military defeats in Russia, Poland was abandoned by Sweden, wholesale. Augustus II led troops to recapture the ancient northern Polish city of Toruń, where he met the great Russian czar Peter and hopelessly pledged his fidelity to a foreign sovereign a second time. The Czar shrewdly accepted his obsequiousness and Stanisław, much preferring to guarantee his life than chance death, promptly resigned his throne— thereafter, the perspicaciously generous Czar rewarded Augustus with the restoration of his.

The down payment, or terms for this ordained honor was low— the mere brutal prosecution of nobles who supported Sweden and the Stanisław reign. Eventually, this left the country politically ruled only by nobles who supported the tsardom, or at least supported themselves by suggesting they didn't support anyone other than the tsardom. Restored, revived, and enkindled, after the gentle purge, Augustus renewed his new reign by seeking to establish an absolute monarchy— subtly encouraged to do so by his benefactor. However, the King faced opposition from those who presumably supported no one but Russia in the face of self-preservation, but under no circumstances would support a reinforced ruler at even the slightest cost of their power— best exemplified in the liberum veto. Lo and behold, Peter the Great shrewdly seized on this opportunity to pose as mediator, even threatened the Commonwealth militarily under the auspices of the Sejm appearing to be anti-Russian. However, it was he himself who carefully crafted this wedge by his encouragement of the indebted king, all the time intending on inconspicuously squeezing the life out of his pray. Finally, in the height of the Great Northern War, raging into its seventeenth year, he forced Augustus and the nobility to sign an accommodation favorable to Russian interests, at the infamous Silent Sejm. Yet, that was only the second act of this three act machination. It was four years later that Augustus and Poland would realize how high the ultimate price for their artificial self-determination was. With the end of the war, Poland was left in the defenseless position of either being a well-behaved protectorate of the newly founded and proclaimed Empire of Russia or alternatively, to no longer exist, even in it's limited political form — absorbed as the new and fifth most western province of the infant imperium. Without second thought, Augustus, the now "Compromised," and the nobility immediately acquiesced to the purposed new world order that bound the Polish crown to the Russian will and the whole of the nation a foot on the precarious precipice of subsided dependency.

It was the liberum veto that was the Russians' strongest parliamentary tool to quietly control the outcome of Polish laws and political triangulations. One person alone, one dissenting voice, one bribe, and the passage of anything was impossible — even the best constructed plans and laws would go undone. There was no bill that could help or strengthen Poland that didn't find some foreign opposition in which a member of the Sejm could not be found by the Prussians, Austrians, Russians, or Swedes that would cause its inevitable defeat. Enter, the Bar Confederation.

***

Kuźma had done good, and raced the horse into the charted path through the Bielany Forest — mile after mile, shallow ponds of swamp water splashed all around as he blindly drove deeper into the timberland! Łukawski, also on mount, was continually shouting behind himself into the nighttime for Kuźma, "Ta droga — szybszy! Szybszy — ta droga!" By now, some of the Confederation cowards who had fled in ambush, had turned again and were rushing through the woodlands themselves — as previously plotted! Of the entire band of dozens, a handful found themselves in disarray between the dense pine and spruce going in disoriented circles. Kuźma could hear Łukawski but his first responsibility was to manage the horse while keeping his exsanguinating captive balanced atop. For his part, the King was slowly coming to; his head gashed, excoriated, and bleeding profusely. Kuźma began to concern himself with the possibility of the crowned head expiring and his own ill-fated hands left soaked and stained in murdered royal blood. A panic of "No's!" repeated in dire echoes from the inner voice of his mind. Even by his own judgement, he was just a simple little man.

At twenty-nine, Kuźma already felt that maybe half his life might have already been lived. He was a fatalist by nature. In all his best-laid plans, if something hadn't yet gone wrong, he worried that things weren't right. A native of the town Kuzmin in Volhynia, he joined the Bar under the influence of one of its most charismatic leaders, Joseph Sawa-Caliński. Kuźma wasn't a noble, he was just a peasant armed-body, an untrained solider, a denizen with no land, who believed to fight for whomever was a better proposition than to rot in the hope of some unforeseen seasonal change. Though he didn't expressly believe in miracles, he loved his country, he loved its land, but to hear him explain it, God did not bless him with "riches, holdings, or station" — "but birthed me out of a delicious stir of water and mortar dust of His greater human sculptings." His humor and his self-image were both pejoratively self-effacing. Born and raised a Catholic — except for his occasional sin of engaging a prostitute, sleeping all day, gorging himself on other's hospitality, petty displays of anger against landowners, frothing jealousy of Jews whom he couldn't understand made a living without working the land, indebtedness, drunken self-grandiosity, and kidnapping the King of Poland, he was otherwise an excellent Catholic. Now, though he superstitiously worried that he had done wrong; because from his perspective of responsibility in the ambush, so far everything was working out just right — that is unless the King were to die by his enterprise and under the duty of his care.

Łukawski tried to gather the disjointed voices calling out for guidance and direction! However, steering a ship at night caught on the top of a mountain is nearly impossible, except to teeter and fall over the side of the cliff — and so Łukawski quickly abandoned all efforts but that of connecting with the man who carried the prized possession. Furthermore, as was apt to happen, the palace guards had been alerted and all of Warsaw was abuzz in the great drama!

Łukawski, no more sure of where he was in the medieval forest, than anyone else, discovered himself to be on the bank of the glacially flowing Vistula unable to safely go any further. He too was lost, unsure if the old bridge at Zakroczym was still further north or further back in the direction of south. Then, he heard a horse in the distance and held back. Following the zigzagging pattern of hoofs was the whispered shouts of, "Łukawski! Łukawski!" It was Kuźma. Weaved into his call was the ad lib moaning of a man that might be dying.

Łukawski came out to meet him. Kuźma immediately squinted in the night—

"Where's the bridge?" Kuźma whispered.

"We have further to go," said Łukawski, without whispering.

"How much?" Kuźma whispered, still.

"Never you mind— what if it is one more foot than you have gone, will you stop going?"

"No," Kuźma said, though he didn't really understand the logic. Suddenly, by the disproportionate distribution of weight, Stanisław's body rolled off the horse and crashed to the ground! Kuźma was affright, either that the King was already dead, or that the care he was giving him was so negligent that he didn't secure the body and it succumbed to angle and gravity. Łukawski rushed to the fallen figure! The King's face was horrifically imbrued by a stream of blood that had descended from the top of his forehead and rolled down the center of his face on the plane of his nose before having trickled off his chin.

"He's still alive!" Łukawski said.

"Is that unusual?"

Łukawski looked up at Kuźma, and by the moonlight, glared into the half glow of the idiot's face and dryly suggested—

"Not for the breathing."

Stanisław's eyes popped opened! Startled, the two men jumped back! He looked up at his captors as they looked down on him. In time, they all individually moved to staring at one another in curiosity.

"Are you going to kill me?" Stanisław murmured.

"That's not for me to decide," Łukawski granted him through the grit of his teeth.

"Then who does?" intrigued, Kuźma asked Łukawski.

"Never you mind," Łukawski said.

Then, Łukawski grabbed Kuźma and took him aside.

"We have to get across the bridge," Łukawski said.

"Where is the bridge?"

"Never you mind."

"What do you want me to mind?"

"As I tell you, then mind."

"As you tell me, yes."

"They wait for us on the other side of the bridge. We will move faster as one than three. You will mind him and I shall come to the bridge and cross it and return with others."

"The ones who decide?" Kuźma innocently asked.

"Never you mind," Łukawski again repeated.

What Łukawski wasn't telling Kuźma was that he didn't know where the bridge was and the fastest way to find it was to go alone, especially if he went the wrong direction at the start. He grabbed Kuźma again and nearly dragged him back to the King. Then, Łukawski seized Kuźma's sword and stood over Stanisław with it pointed at his throat!

"Stand where I stand," he commanded Kuźma.

"But you stand there."

"Take this sword and stand where I stand, how I stand, now!," Łukawski shouted.

Kuźma did as he was told and stood over the King with the tip of his blade a minor thrust from a course of unalterable fate.

"If he moves— thrust!" Łukawski said.

"'Thrust?'"

"Kill him if he moves— where he lay, without mercy! He is an enemy of you, of me, of the Bar, of the goodness of Poland."

"Yes," Kuźma said, not necessarily in agreement but in obedience.

"I have given you an order."

"Yes."

"If he moves, comply with that order."

"Yes," Kuźma said, shaking.

Łukawski mounted the horse and whipped the reigns hard! Quickly he faded into the night. Kuźma was left to stare down at the King staring up at him.

"I will not move, I swear to it," Stanisław said.

"I am to thrust if you do."

"But I shall not," Stanisław assured him.

Kuźma held his ground but it was clear that Stanisław was well injured.

"I am thirsty— bitter the thirst." Stanisław strained to say. "Grant me water I beg you, grant your king water."

At the rustling of foliage, Kuźma turned and was astonished to see a familiar face, John Strawinski. He was haggard, out of breath, and flushed with fear.

"Kuźma!" Strawinski said before gasping, "The King!"

With hand, quivering, Kuźma made it a point to keep his sword held as directed. Strawinski approached somewhat cautiously until he could see the sweat beads accumulated across Kuźma's forehead and the trembling nature in which he was holding his position.

"Are you mad?" Strawinski asked him, then pushed him away from the King!

Kuźma stumbled sideways, holding the blade high enough to spare the monarch further injury and grave outcome. Now, Strawinski stood over the potentate and looked down with glee —

"I've never seen a king, that is — nose to nose," he sneered, slowly lowering his head and coming nose-to-nose with the Stanisław.

"Will you give me water," puttered from Stanisław's mouth.

"Get him some water!" Strawinski commanded Kuźma.

"But I am to mind and thrust!"

"Do as I wish you to do!"

Obediently, Kuźma handed Strawinski the sword —

"Thrust if he moves," Kuźma said meekly, respectfully and proudly passing on the order — or just as a safeguard against future accusation.

Again, Strawinski dismissively shoved him away. Kuźma scurried to the water. Strawinski stared into the King's eyes and sneered all the more, as though the act was an earned defiance garnered him as above the law both figuratively and literally! However, the King naturally or instinctively, radiated a charitable virtue of compassion. Strawinski mercilessly yanked Stanisław's head forward and examined his wounds. In the murky light he had to look closely but he felt how deep the gash was in the back of the man's head and how lucky Stanisław was to be no taller than his God-given height. Kuźma returned with water overflowing and dripping from within and through his hat. He rushed to bend down and cup his hands with the frigid request. Stanisław lapped it up and seemed to immediately raise in liveliness.

"It is not safe to remain here," Strawinski said to Kuźma. "The guards and the hounds are making their way."

"But I am — we are — to wait!"

"Wait?"

"Wait for Łukawski! And those who will decide!"

"Wait," he said somewhat amused. "And you wait to be beheaded, quartered, and burned! Do you invite that fate Jan Kuźma?"

"No."

"Then you will follow me."

"Where?"

"Across the bridge— and every mile with our comrades-in-arms, until the Confederation has reached Jasna Góra with the traitor of Poland— triumphantly as planned!"

Strawinski pulled Stanisław up, but quickly learned that the ruler was more damaged than he first thought.

Stanisław's clothes were tattered, filthy, and soaked with splattered blood and swamp water. The back of his coat was marked by a long trail of fresh blood from the gash to its tails. The blow to his head had also left him woozy and unable to independently stand on his feet. Nevertheless, Strawinski was undeterred—

"Help me carry him!" he called out to Kuźma.

"We should not leave. Who knows the way?"

Strawinski drew his finger across his neck, the sign of cutting the throat, reminding Kuźma that not doing so would likely end in such debilitation.

"Jasna Góra?" Kuźma asked softly and excitedly.

Strawinski nodded. He would know— only a month before, he was part of the brain-trust huddled in the basement of the monastery that concocted the audacious plan to abduct the King. Under the Hodegetria eyes of the Black Madonna, the primary authority and power of the Bar were in attendance, all the usual suspects and the tails that wagged the dogs— Father Jandołowicz; Adam and Michał Krasiński; Michał Jan Pac, Marshal General of the Lithuanian Bar Confederation; Szymon Kossakowski, the Bar's greatest commander; Antoni Barnaba Jabłonowski, the Bar's envoy to the Royal Court in Austria, Cardinal Angelo Maria Durini, the Papal's Apostolic Nuncio, and the Confederation's federal marshal— the most influential presence in the Bar's creation: Józef Pułaski, Casimir Pułaski's father.

***

The Bar Confederation— may be etymologically better understood as a conglomerate of disgruntled Polish nobles that were well-heeled, soused with time-honored power, made of money, and armed to the teeth. They hurriedly formed as such in Bar's castle fortress. The coalition was inaugurated with a memorandum in defense of the Catholic faith and independence of the Republic, directed against the guardianship of the Russian Empire, King Poniatowski and supporting it against Russian troops. The purpose of the confederation was to abolish the laws imposed by Russia, in particular, those giving equal rights for dissenters. At the time of their inception, the Russian army had in excess of 500,000 well-equipped troops, while at their height, the Bar was no more than a lightly-armed 100,000 strong. Essentially, the Polish civil war was an inescapable contretemps between the Age of Enlightenment and an epoch of established enlightened elitist entitlement, embroiled in an imbroglio of monumental self-interests.

The Monitor magazine, a royal subsidy of the intelligentsia came to prominence on a series of articles by its benefactor, King Poniatowski. On Ways of Effective Counsel, was Stanisław's treatise on the need to abolish the Liberum Veto and enact a simple majority rule in the Sejm. From afar and within the circle of nobles, many assumed that Stanisław was merely Catherine's marionette that was willingly manipulated and sweetly pleased by her freely availed seductive charms. But at the heart of the matter and the personage— he was also a man of big ideas in little ways.

Before Madison and Jefferson and ahead of Franklin's arrival in Paris— there was King Stanisław August Poniatowski. He reigned, but unlike the other kings, queens, and czarinas of his day, he ruled a Republic. The king sat on the throne but did not govern. His was a traditional monarchy, but an elective one— elected within a long-established system by which there was no guarantee the monarch of any royal house or noble family would be preferred to that of any other. Yet still, it wasn't a government for the people but a democracy of the nobles. The juxtaposition of the earth and moon, the contrast of the land and sea, the symbiotic solidarity of the honeyguide and the honey badger— and so it was, the Polish royalty and the Polish nobility; the lion and the hyena. From the view of the hyena, they were the cooperative clan that could be counted on to protect national interests and the true basis of faith and reason in Christendom. The Szlachta's view of Poland's independence from the static dynastic state systems of Europe and as a Republic was synonymous with their "Golden Liberty." In the bloody wake of a damnable order by Charles IX in what resulted in Paris' St. Bartholomew's Day massacre, the Szlachta sought to legally guarantee that no Polish king would ever be able to carry out such genocide upon them. They're instrument of warranty— a political bill of rights. At the Warsaw Confederation, January 28, 1573, the Golden Liberty was born— an incredible issuance of legal assurances. First and foremost was religious tolerance but second and just as unprecedentedly was the parliamentary apparatus of the "Liberum Veto." These and ten other unheard of rights were established for the first time in the human history of government!

1. Kings of the Commonwealth were all to be chosen by election by the szlachta, and his children had no right of inheritance with regards to the throne;

2. King marriages had to gain the approval of the Senate;

3. The king must convene a general Sejm at least once every two years for six weeks;

4. The king had no right to create new taxes, tariffs or such without approval of the Sejm;

5. Between sejms, 16 resident senators were to be at the king's side as his advisers and overseers. This Royal Council of 16 senators was elected every two years during the Sejm session. Four of their number (rotating every six months) were obliged to accompany the king and serve as advisers and supervisors to ensure that the king made no decision contrary to the laws of the Commonwealth. All royal decrees had to be counter-stamped by the chancellors or the deputy chancellors;

6. The king had no right to call a levee en masse without approval of the Sejm. Further, the Articles upheld the informal tradition that the king could not send those troops to serve outside the Commonwealth's borders without compensation;

7. Provide for the standing, royal army;

8. The king had no right to declare war or peace without approval of the Sejm;

9. The king must abide by the Warsaw Confederation's guarantees of religious freedom;

10. Finally, if the monarch were to transgress against the law or the privileges of the szlachta, the Articles authorized the szlachta to refuse the king's orders and act against him. Each king had to swear that "if anything has been done by Us against laws, liberties, privileges or customs, we declare all the inhabitants of the Kingdom are freed from obedience to Us."

***

With this, Poland was a framework of government that caused a rippled shudder and a sharp pang of fear throughout the European dynasties, not to mention it was the most democratic nation since ancient Greece. However, from the conviction of the lion it was an outdated, outmoded, backward, stifling, and ineffective approach to administrative government. Paradoxically, the lion was right.

Poland may have been moored to its rapacious neighbor, but Stanisław's intention was to raise the country's Slavic feudal consciousness and thereby spiritually deliver it beyond Russia's illiberal influence. However virtuous his vision, its plausibility was contradictory in nature. He sought to ennoble the country with enlightened republican ideals, all the while sapiently towing the line of political necessity by improving the privileges of the nobility. The devil was in the details but the angels were in the arching notions of Plato, Aristotle, Aquinas, Hobbes, Locke, and de Vattel and the concept of sub lege naturae— natural law! He would return Poland and the individual man back to his primitive nature— deliver him to his original freedom. Be he finally as divinity intended him— living independently, master of his own fate. So was Stanisław's claim, his promise, his stated ambition, article after article in The Monitor! He sought to expand property rights for peasants; simplify tax burdens; pave streets; reduce the scope of the judicial system, and strip guilds and municipalities of their bullying pretensions. But how was he to do this? At what cost of man, blood, flesh, or government? According to Stanisław there was only one-way: restrict the power of the nobility and instruments of the ruling class. Basically he sought to harmonize through balancing the scales of authority. That is to legally restrict the power of the szlachta and raise the might of the crown and the rights of the subjects of the kingdom. Notwithstanding of course, the lion was in effect an underling in reserve for sport of the mighty big game hunter that was the Russian Empire, the very top of the food chain. On this hapless point, the king's attitude was: nothing to see here— providence would eventually deliver them, as It had so many times before when they were threatened with complete collapse.

Stanisław took his position as king seriously and he knew the truth, that the wolves were at the door, and this he thought was the best chance to keep them at bay before their open and salivating mouths finally bit down on Poland. The lion was urgently trying to protect the kingdom from being overrun and destroyed by its own voracious scavenging hyenas.

At the opening of the Diet of 1766, Stanisław proposed to abolish the liberum veto entirely; and to increase the revenues and consequently the throne. Even the Czartoryski's, his own family which conspiratorially brought him to power, could not agree in full to such radical measures. Yet more significantly, inflamed, Nicholas Repnin, Russia's ambassador, openly scoffed in the session. A bevy of "I do not allow's" was shouted by numerous members! Ironically, it was the insidious liberum veto that nullified and ended any proposal and debate of its own termination. The unintended consequences were almost inestimable. First, Stanisław had to beg his former lover for forgiveness of his momentary lapse into open patriotism; secondly, the often-strange bedfellows of politics saw the nobles and the Russians in sudden accord. Further still, the stage was set for the following winter of discontent. Repnin, by direction and virtue of Catherine, was the effective ruler of the country. His standard modus operandi was coercion and bribes. However, before the next Sejm, he ordered, captured, and exiled some of the more vocal supporters of the King and opponents of his standard operational procedures. To assure a cognizant understanding of absolute political hierarchy and what was expected, he immediately stationed an additional 50,000 Russian troops in Warsaw, some even placed in the very chambers of the Sejm. Anger among the nobles was undivided. Fear among the nobles was categorical. Although, courage among the nobles was nonexistent, except for the lawyer, Józef Pułaski. He alone publicly confronted Repnin, face-to-face, with an angry diatribe. He vowed even if it even took the blood of 100,000, that the nation must be free. Soon, the country descended into upper-class civil war and the predicted blood of 100,000 was tragically shed. However, the nation was not free— on the contrary, it was decisively partitioned like a ham, and ruthlessly served to its neighbors on a victorious silver platter.

***

Stanisław could barely walk. Strawinski, Kuźma, and the King were trekking within the forestry of trees along the river's edge. Strawinski worried that with their plodding pace they would be caught. Kuźma suggested putting the King back on the mount but Strawinski feared that if he fell it could be fatal. However, there was no other option to their plight but to carry on. Even at the river's edge it was a coil of vines, a tangle of vegetation, and a clutter of trunks. Each step they took was circumventing one impasse after another, making every yard traversed five yards of effort. Kuźma served principally as a crutch for the King, all the while Strawinski, carrying the sword led the horse about a quarter mile ahead. Kuźma, in actuality, could not see him, except to hear his crackling steps and occasionally spot a shifting silhouette anywhere moonlight slipped through the canopy.

Suddenly, Strawinski and Kuźma heard an approaching rush— the ruckus of sniffing and barking hounds and the caterwauling encouragement of their masters! Panicked, Kuźma turned; fell with Stanisław into the short conifers and pressed his hand over the King's mouth! Strawinski was promptly fallen upon, by both dog and sword! He screamed as he was initially teared at and devoured! The dogs were pulled away and the force of broad swords and fists pummeled him until he was already half-dead— before they even asked him who he was and where the King might be. Maybe he would have spoken or pointed in the direction of their answer, but he was so drubbed that he simply collapsed and was violently dragged away.

Kuźma waited and listened. It was trembling hour of utmost fear before he finally rose, lifting Stanisław in hand. Most of Kuźma's nerves were obviously frayed and the dizzy but attentive king grasped the opportunity to subtly take his fortune into his own hands—

"I mean you no harm, do I," Stanisław said. "If you too were to have been apprehended, I, as King, would have seen that no harm came to you."

Kuźma wasn't sure what to make of such a declaration, he just wanted the ruler to walk with him, to be more able, that his efforts to come to a well-performed achievement on the other side of the bridge.

"Yet, if I am to die of my wounds, there will be no one to protect your interest," the King proceeded. "I believe I understand your motives — I harbor no ill-will. The truth be told, I find you innocent."

"Speak no more! Please!" Kuźma pleaded.

"Is it because my head is more valuable disengaged than being instilled with life? Like a high-stakes game of Tysiąc, no?" the King pressed on. "I understand. You are the innocent party of this charade. And, it is a charade, isn't it? You are, in candor, working with the Russians, no? This is a plot to discredit and undercut the Confederacy, no?"

Kuźma grew angry and defensive of his comrades —

"No more you speak!" he spat!

The King was clever, triangulating his argument in an effort to unravel the plot, to know the truth, to avenge the state. In a fit of rage, Kuźma might have thrust him then and there, but he was without his apogee of power. It mattered little, though, he was fitful but not enraged, and he knew the King could not physically bring harm to him. His wish was simple, to deliver or be delivered, King in hand.

"Yes, as you command," the King said, an ironic twist of expression for a sovereign. "I shall not speak, unless spoken to — be you, let you speak of your mind, of your heart, of the cause we are here."

"Please!" Kuźma appealed. "And say not those words of the Confederacy! I know not the plans of better men, but no plans involve cooperation with the sworn enemy! I have pledged to the Confederacy — therefore my nation! Hold your tongue even if you are to summon again the thought that I act on behalf of any tactic of Russia!"

Kuźma was at the end of his rope, no more waiting or being told what to do. The only possibility of success was reaching the bridge, but the possibility seemed ever-so remote. Nevertheless, he had to try and make his way —

"Come!" Kuźma said as he yanked the King forward, daring to overcome the odds.

The King gave no resistance and yet gave no assistance, allowing himself to be burdensome dead weight.

"I do not think I can go any further—"

"We must!" Kuźma angrily implored.

"What I see, if you could see as I see—all are circles in a round—"

"Come— you must come!" Kuźma directed, and with all his might he pulled the King to his unsteady feet!

But now, Kuźma was also tired— spent, and the King, unconscious and insensate— simply fell on legs that could no longer stand! Panic set in as the captor couldn't instantly bring him back to alert consciousness. Kuźma rushed to the river and with his hat brimming, returned and doused his sovereign with water! Stanisław's eyes fluttered open. Sighing, Kuźma couldn't have been more relieved that he wasn't dead.

"You have pledged? What have you pledged?" Stanisław asked him with a thespian inspired deathbed voice.

"My toil and my life."

"I will give your pledge in reward that your toil and your life are not in vein. I am your king. I, too have pledged, I have sworn fidelity to you and all within these borders," Stanisław wheezed. "I know not what reason I am a captive. Is it that I may be assassinated? For so it may be, but if assassination was of order, would I not be dead now? Oh, but you have spared me. Shot, yes, I have been— by errant chance or merely protected by our Christopher—"

Just as he rambled for benefit, he allowed his eyes to close and his voice to trail in mid-sentence. All that was left for him to do was to reel his dullard in.

"Wake! Wake!" Kuźma shook him!

Stanisław's eyes slowly reopened. However, only so much, leaving them to look ruefully sad and spurned. Kuźma feared he would for surely die. Thereupon, his guilt and compassion overcame him and he decidedly would tell Stanisław all he knew, though he knew next to nothing at all!

"I know no edict of death! Only your life has been spoke of. Many say to hold you in ransom for terms of better understanding. I know only that which I know."

"Who is your king?" Stanisław asked him.

"Why you are," Kuźma said after much thought.

"Yet, you have pledged another."

"I have!" Kuźma said in shame but true loyalty to the cause.

"Is it legal I ask you, to possess the unlawfully attained?"

"No, my lord!"

"See you not, that such a pledge of treason is not without validation in judgment of the Lord?"

"Maybe it is," said Kuźma.

"It is in the judgment of this lord, your earthly lord," Stanisław assured him. "You are innocent of placing your fidelity where it could never rightfully be."

"Oh, forgive me, my lord!" Kuźma cried.

"Oh, never did I condemn, thee, my most loyal subject."

"Jan Kuźma, I am! That is my name and who I am! Your most loyal subject from the region of Volhynia!" Kuźma pronounced before he suddenly sighed and dropped his eyes in disgrace, "But I am not loyal your lord!" he whimpered.

"You are the most loyal, for you are loyal to men! To be led astray is a testament to your capacity to trust, obey, honor, and seek the highest good! I know no other in the Kingdom as loyal as you!"

Kuźma was reeled in, hook, line, and sinker. He weeped upon the body of his king. He couldn't forgo the constant need to pray for forgiveness. As it became the earliest hour before the dawn, the King saw a light coming from a mill. Kuźma agreed to take him there that he might be spared the death or the bad spirits that awaited him in elements. Upon their entry, Kuźma allowed the King to send the mill owner for the palace doctor. The Cossack patrol shortly arrived and arrested Kuźma. Stanisław was taken back to Warsaw, a little dizzy, but no worse for wear. As the light of dawn arose, the entire city congregated outside the palace. The King refused to change his clothes or even close the gates or doors of his residency. Everyone was invited to see him dressed in the unvarnished scars of the ambush! It had failed and he was victorious; an undisputed child of providence. Or so anyone unfamiliar with the life and times of Jan Kuźma understood.

***

"In here," Hayim said softly.
He carried a small cake-pan candlestick and gently closed the door behind him. It was the same room, the tiny servants' quarters that served as his private office. It appeared surrounded in a gush twilight. Only the halos of their half-lit faces broke the interior shroud of darkness. The hour was the hush of night following the disastrous day the King was taken hostage and returned in triumphant safety.

"I warn you I'm already soaked, and I insist you be as drunk, if not drunker than I am to become," Casimir Pułaski said in rhapsody.
He unveiled a few bottles of wine, which he returned with, as he slipped back into town.

"I did not come possessed with shekels or farthings," Casimir joked and laughed at his own dark humor.

It had been a long year since they first met. Hayim had spent 32 million roubles of Rothschild gold— blood money of sorts, for the spilling of Russian blood. Casimir poured the spirits with a broken right arm suffered at Skaryszew, where his units were again scattered in defeat. Hayim didn't usually partake in inebriating intoxicants but Casimir insisted, and Hayim's worries were at such that for the moment it was soothing to relieve his mind of the storm gathering over his head.

"The Bar is doomed," Casimir said, laughing.

"Is it so funny?" Hayim responded.

"It's hilarious!"

"Excuse me if you will, but I fail to see the hilarity," Hayim was able to say with mild amusement.

"It has not come yet! You'll know it when it comes! When they have spilled all the guilty blood and what is left are those willing to unwrench the contents of their souls to save their corporeal lives! Laugh you will, like I, when those Szlachta feign ignorance, claim confusion, renounce the Confederation, and re-pledge their miserable beings to that miserable crown."
With that his laughter and mirth finally died. He looked sour, angry; and washed his brain in wine.

"Drink! Here, drink," Casimir, said as he poured Hayim another glass. "I must flee… I must flee."
Hayim acquiesced and partook in the wine with a stoutheartedness and reverence of fellowship for Casimir. He sat for a moment, swilling his glass and staring into his own projects, until—

"I regret nothing I'll have you know," Casimir chuckled with; again laughing and drinking more heavily.

"Why did you return?" Hayim asked, truly wondering if Casimir had a suicidal urge within him.

"We should regret— that we should, that this endeavor was an exercise in uncultured affairs.

"The Russians visited me again today. I've counted now fourteen times they come upon my person and property and accused me of malfeasance. Repnin, himself, the scrawny kozojeb—
Casimir exploded in laughter—

"Goatlover! - Goatlover!" the general repeated over and over.

"I think often it is more because I am a Jew that he suspects my involvement. But he came today, and orchestrated a most beautiful destruction of all my financial collections."

"Did the goatlover find what he's looking for," Casimir cackled rhetorically.

With the liberating effects of alcohol impressing themselves upon Hayim, he coolly unlocked a false drawer. Inside was a thin leather ledger and the siddur stitched with the six-pointed star. He brought out the ledger and slammed it down between them—

"Would we be in company, now?" Hayim said as though shouting from the rooftops in a hushed voice.

They hooted and howled and drank more together! It was like laughter at a funeral.

"You ask, why I returned?"

"Strawinski and Łukawski—" Hayim started!

"Kuźma, Father Cybulski—" Casimir added!

"Then why?" Hayim said after a shocked beat.

"To bestow what was earned. To grace upon you warning. It is the least that any of the Confederacy could do for you."

"Valor?" Hayim quipped.

"We owe our defeats to our own inadequacies, but the indebted of our victories is in part owed to you!"

Hayim Shelomo was truly moved.

"I must flee! You must flee! If they came today, they came only looking for the evidence in which to hang, drawn and quarter you! Tomorrow they will bring their own evidence and scaffold," Casimir gravely said. "Hayim, we are the damned. It is us they want, you and I. And as I began, I regret nothing but we should collectively regret that our's was an intensely political entity. In this war there are no heroes on either side, we're all villains fighting to keep what is dearest to us— power."

Hayim stoically drank the last of the second bottle. The thought of his own villainy was something to consider.

"We are all damned before we even began," said Casimir.

"Then why fight at all," Hayim said with irritation.

"Does a cornered boar just lay down and invite its demise or does it fight for its life?" said Casimir. "Poland could never have succeeded, either as we fought or that pompous ass sought. It is damned. All things are damned that cannot escape their past!"

"No accumulation can escape its measure, calculated in the quondam integer of formerly," said Hayim.

"Ignore my ignorance," Casimir said, completely unsure of the qualifier Hayim proposed. "I say, a country must have no past to enact these lofty ideals we discuss and execute in such minute portions that they couldn't feed a bird! - I drink to you, sir!"

"I know of no such compliment to your suggestion," Hayim said with sadness.

"Raise your glass, and I the bottle! You were the true guiding spirit of the Confederation! I drink to you!"

They drank the last of what remained. Finally, as the candle, too, came to the last of its remains, Casimir leaned very closely to Hayim and solemnly spoke—

"Hayim, even if it is not to your liking, consent to what I say. You must leave as soon as the sun rises. For myself, I shall take leave even before such an hour."

Casimir swallowed the last of their vintage and leaned back as defeated as he had ever looked in his life. Hayim reflected and finally returned Casimir's exhortation—

"Yes. We are the damned," Hayim said.

***

XI

LONDON

"He that rebels against reason is a real rebel, but he that in defense of reason rebels against tyranny has a better title to Defender of the Faith, than George III."

Thomas Paine

In the year of the Lord: 1492, the cresting advancement of human culture progressed over the delineating longitude that invariably marked the modern age of civilization— all that came before, was merely only half a world. The legendary year began on a Sunday. By the break of dawn Monday, in the more dramatic of fashions, Sultan Boabdil, the last Moorish King of Granada, surrendered his beleaguered city to the army of Ferdinand II of Aragon and Queen Isabella I of Castile. The future had just begun.

Since the spring of the previous year, Granada had been all that was left of the former Moorish Kingdom of Al-Andalus. The Moors were a virulent concoction of different nomadic tribes from a mixture of Arabs, Berbers, and Black Africans who came from north Africa, thread together primarily through Islam. The lengthy siege was effectively the last dramatic act of the 10-year Granada War and the Reconquista, the campaign by the medieval Christian states of Spain to drive out the Moorish invaders, which lasted nearly the previous 800 more. The conclusion and capitulation of this drawing of the curtain came rather suddenly and spectacularly. Dressed in full royal regalia, Boabdil marched out through the gates of the city, his vision clouded by the mist of his anguished tears, and he deferentially bended to one knee; upon which the Sultan submissively kissed Ferdinand and Isabella's victorious hands. It is said the sultan's mother chided, "Thou dost weep like a woman for what thou couldst not defend as a man." And so it was— from war it labored; and with a kiss, contemporary Spain was born.

With victory secured, the Spanish Catholics were now enthusiastic to redefine the country from the perspective of their enduring xenophobic vision. Ironically, with the same set of epochal juncture, for the first time in human history, the Torah was being creased, scored, and pressed into imprinted form for mass consumption. Again, it was the Spaniards at the axis of the action, but not the Catholics, but the pressing was being done so by the Sephardic Jewish citizenry of Spain. However, other presses were also driving a historical incunable to print that of an edict of expulsion, entitled the Alhambra decree. It read thusly:

> King Ferdinand and Queen Isabella, by the grace of God, King and Queen of Castile, Leon, Aragon and other dominions of the crown — to the prince Juan, to dukes, marquees, counts, the holy orders, priors, knight commanders, lords of the castles, cavaliers, and to all Jews, men and women of whatever age, and to anyone else this letter may concern — health and grace unto you.
> You well know that in our dominion, there are certain bad Christians that judaised and committed apostasy against our Holy Catholic faith, much of it the cause of communications between Jews and Christians. Therefore, in the year 1480, we ordered that the Jews be separated from the cities and towns of our domains and that they be given separate quarters, hoping that by such separation the situation would be remedied. And we ordered that and an Inquisition be established in such domains; and in twelve years it has functioned, the Inquisition has found many guilty persons.
>
> Furthermore, we are informed by the Inquisition and others that the great harm done to the Christians persists, and it continues because of the conversations and communications that they have with the Jews, such Jews trying by whatever manner to subvert our holy Catholic faith and trying to draw faithful Christians away from their beliefs.
>
> These Jews instruct these Christians in the ceremonies and observances of their Law,

circumcising their children, and giving them books with which to pray, and declaring unto them the days of fasting, and meeting with them to teach them the histories of their Law, notifying them when to expect Passover and how to observe it, giving them the unleavened bread and ceremonially prepared meats, and instructing them in things from which they should abstain, both with regard to food items and other things requiring observances of their Law of Moses, making them understand that there is no other law or truth besides it. All of which then is clear that, on the basis of confessions from such Jews as well as those perverted by them, that it has resulted in great damage and detriment of our holy Catholic faith.

And because we knew that the true remedy of such damages and difficulties lay in the severing of all communications between the said Jews with the Christians and in sending them forth from all our reigns, we sought to content ourselves with ordering the said Jews from all the cities and villages and places of Andalusia where it appeared that they had done major damage, believing that this would suffice so that those from other cities and villages and places in our reigns and holdings would cease to commit the aforesaid. And because we have been informed that neither this, nor the justices done for some of the said Jews found very culpable in the said crimes and transgressions against our holy Catholic faith, has been a complete remedy to obviate and to correct such opprobrium and offense to the Christian faith and religion; because every day it appears that the said Jews increase in continuing their evil and harmful purposes wherever they reside and converse; and because there is no place left whereby to more offend our holy faith, as much as those which God has protected to this day as in those already affected, it is left for this Holy Mother Church to mend and reduce the matter to its previous state inasmuch as, because of our frailty of humanity, it could occur that we could succumb to the diabolical temptation that continually wars against us so easily if its principal cause were not removed, which would be to expel the said Jews from the kingdom. Because whenever a grave and detestable crime is committed by some members of a given group, it is reasonable that the group be dissolved or annihilated, the minors for the majors being punished one for the other; and that those who pervert the good and honest living on the cities and villages and who by their contagion could harm others, be expelled from the midst the people, still yet for other minor causes, that would be of harm to the Republic, and all the more so for the major of these crimes, dangerous and contagious as it is.

Therefore, with the council and advice of the eminent men and cavaliers of our reign, and of other persons of knowledge and conscience of our Supreme Council, after much deliberation, it is agreed and resolved that all Jews and Jewesses be ordered to leave our kingdoms, and that they never be allowed to return.

And we further order in this edict that all Jews and Jewesses of whatever age that reside in our domain and territories, which they leave with their sons and daughters. Their servants and relatives, large and small, of whatever age, by the end of July of this year, and that they dare not return to our lands, not so much as to take a step on them not trespass upon them in any other manner whatsoever. Any Jew who does not comply with this edict and is to be found in our kingdom and domains, or who returns to the kingdom in any manner, will incur punishment by death and confiscation of all their belongings. We further order that no person in our kingdom of whatever station or noble status hide or keep or defend any Jew or Jewess, either publicly or secretly, from the end of July onwards, in their homes or elsewhere in our reign, upon punishment of loss of their belongings, vassals, fortresses, and hereditary privileges. So that the said Jews may dispose of their household and belongings in the given time period, for the present we provide our assurance of royal protection and security so that, until the end of the month of July, they may sell and exchange their belongings and furniture and other items, and to dispose of them freely as they wish; and that during said time, no one is to do them harm or injury or injustice to their persons or to their goods, which is contrary to justice, and which shall incur the punishment that befalls those who violate our royal security.

Thus we grant permission to the said Jews and Jewesses to take out their goods and belongings out of our reigns, either by sea or by land, with the condition that they not take out either gold or silver or minted money or any other items prohibited by the laws of the kingdom. Therefore, we order all councilors, justices, magistrates, cavaliers, shield-bearers, officials, good men of the city of Burgos and of other cities and villages of our reigns and dominions, and all our vassals and subjects, that they observe and comply with this letter and all that is contained in it, and that they give all the help and favor that is necessary for its execution, subject to punishment by our sovereign

grace and by confiscation of all their goods and
offices for our royal state house.

And so that this may come to the notice of all, and
so that no one may pretend ignorance, we order
that this edict be proclaimed in all the plazas and
usual meeting places of any given city; and that in
the major cities and villages of the diocese, that it
be done by the town crier in the presence of the
public scribe, and that neither one nor the other
should do the contrary of what was desired,
subject to the punishment by our sovereign grace
and deprivation of their offices and by
confiscation of their goods to whosoever does the
contrary. And we further order that evidence be
provided to the court, in the manner of signed
testimony, regarding the manner in which the
edict is being carried out.

Given in this city of Granada on the thirty first day
of March in the year of our Lord Jesus Christ -
1492.

Further than the eyes could see, above and beyond the organized,
characterized, and structural sequence of time and space— the event
horizon shone as blindly as the angular totality of the diamond ring effect
of a total eclipse of the sun... the Spanish Empire stood as the most
culturally significant political land mass in all the world— the initiation of
humanism— the first book of grammar— the Latin-Spanish dictionary— a
gilded age glittering like fine course gold flittering about the air; and
within this particle acceleration of the age of empire and the expansion of
the human mind was the inhuman barbarity of the forced conversion,
expulsion, and/or death to Jews! From the garrison at Gibraltar, to the
Pyrenees, welcome to the year 1492. With hard-earned conquest over the
Moors, the Kingdoms of Aragon and Castile damned the subtleties and
personally sought an accouchement of a divine divinity in an untainted
holy Catholic dominion. This grand deranged vision of purity— of a
cultivated tract of Heaven on earth, was motivated principally by
arguments of a political and religious nature, for the sake of which the
crown was willing to sacrifice every other practical consideration. The gist
of the argument followed that Jews were trying to subvert the holy

Catholic faith and draw faithful Christians away from their beliefs; therefore their expulsion was critical. These extreme measures against the Jewish religion and race were not new to Europe. Nearly every kingdom and sovereign at one point issued similar decrees. However, this time the sheer number of those who would be displaced or dispossessed was massive beyond belief.

The Jewish population throughout Spain, which exceeded a quarter of a million people, was given a scad four months to convert to Christianity or leave the country. Incongruously, in the name of some pious aspect of fairness, Jews were promised royal protection and security for the effective three-month window before the deadline. They were permitted to take their belongings with them— except of course something of value to the Spanish, such as gold or silver or minted money. The punishment for any Jew who did not convert or leave by the deadline was the pleasure of death, pleasure for the bloodthirsty Spanish that is. Furthermore, the punishment for a non-Jew who sheltered or hid Jews was ostensibly to become a man without a past or a future— the absolute confiscation of all belongings and hereditary privileges.

En mass the Jews conveniently fled to neighboring Portugal. In 1497, at Spain's behest, the Portuguese expelled them just the same. The entire peninsula would be a homogamous parcel of Heaven, or so they expected. By 1500, the Inquisition was burning brightly and the rest of Europe was awash with immigrant Sephardic Jews. Initially, they went mostly to France, Sardinia, Holland, Sicily, and Lithuania. Two centuries later the burning was still bright, if not brighter on the fuel of Jewish flesh. This continuing lot of wandering people, generation after generation, would include the Shelomo family en route to Poland-Lithuania, as it would be known by then.

Another couple centuries, years before the Spanish expulsion of the Jews, the English did just the same themselves, supposedly stemming from the timeworn issue of usury practices. Edward I passed the Statute of Jewry, which made usury illegal and suspiciously linked it to blasphemy. Coincidentally, and yet again conveniently, for the royal confers, those merely accused of such were readily stripped of all possessions, property, and accumulated riches. The Statue of Jewry said in part:

- Usury was outlawed in every form.

- Creditors of Jews were no longer liable for certain debts.
- Jews were not allowed to live outside certain cities and towns.
- Any Jew above the age of seven had to wear a yellow badge of felt on his or her outer clothing, six inches by three inches.
- All Jews from the age of 12 on had to pay a special tax of three pence annually.
- Christians were forbidden to live among Jews.
- Jews were licensed to buy farmland to make their living for the next 15 years.
- Jews could thenceforth make a living in England only as merchants, farmers, craftsmen or soldiers.

However, by 1290, this statue was considered less than sufficient to control Jews from ceasing their financial practices. Consequently, Edward issued his all-encompassing Edict of Expulsion.

***

In 1656 Amsterdam was the financial center of the western world and the richest nation on the face of the earth. This was due in part to the scattering of Jews by the Spanish in 1492, which led many of them to settle in the Netherlands. For their part, 1656 saw Spain and Portugal in a deep spiraling decline. Looking out past that event horizon, they're till of self-induced Heaven spoilt into a noisome swath of an embattled, rot, and bankrupt realm.

Respectably, Lord Protector Oliver Cromwell examined the fundamental difference in the fortunes of the disparate nations. As Spain was once overflowing in wealth and was now an old man, bent and stooped, with the spilling of devalued coinage from its silk-lined pockets and clinging to untenable power— the Netherlands, once simple impoverished subjects of the Roman Empire, were now indubitably rich— astonishingly so! In his assiduous study, the Lord Protector noted one undeniable difference between the nations: the presence of a healthy

Jewish population. Thereupon, Cromwell invited and permitted re-entrance of European Jews onto his sovereign island. However, these Jews were not entirely the same. They were not Sephardic; searching for safe passage, as was the case in 1492. Instead they were Ashkenazi Jews from Germanic states, Jews like those living in the Judengasses, seeking improved social conditions from those in their anti-Semitic discriminatory home countries. History and irony are never far apart, and unfortunately, in time, the Ashkenazi Jews would realize that for their efforts and travel that they would not find such comfort on the sovereign island. Nevertheless, for the time being they came in small manageable waves and by 1690, a humble synagogue in London was constructed. Within thirty years, a great synagogue would be erected and it would remain the cultural, spiritual, and social epicenter of all Jewish activity in England for the following eighty years, including the day in which Hayim Shelomo entered.

***

The extremely dignified ward of Aldgate stood as the historic entry to the Whitechapel, the inner suburban section of London. This area of London, known as the City, London's financial center, was where Jews settled both before the expulsion and after the resettlement. Britain's oldest manufacturing company, the firm and foundry of Lester and Pack, established in 1570, was housed in the rowdy and oft-dangerous playground for the rugged industrious and sometimes darker side of human nature. Settled in a heterogeneous urban social compact, the mostly Anglos, German, and Jewish, residents of the east end were the deep-set working class. From a cornucopia of sweaty manufacturing enterprises, they settled into a loose social compact of live hard, work hard, play hard, and let the next in line do the same. At Lester and Pack, relatively recently, they had cast a one ton bell inscribe with part of Leviticus 25:10, "Proclaim liberty throughout all the land unto all the inhabitants thereof." The mainly copper tocsin was to be used as a simple town chime for the colonial city of Philadelphia. It was commissioned and paid for by the Province of Pennsylvania in the far-off Americas. Serendipitously, the foundry where the symbol of liberty was cast was but a healthy walk down the street to the Synagogue, Duke's Place, where all of London's Jews assembled, including in 1772, one who felt the least of them: Hayim Shelomo.

***

As it was yet another cloudy and wet morning, Hayim purposefully stepped into the main room of Duke's Place. It was not only a shul, but also the community's center and its heart— and it was already known throughout the world. So, it wasn't Hayim's first entry, but it also wasn't Shabbat nor did he have pending business. It was merely a Tuesday, just like any other Tuesday. All that made this average weekday unique in the events of history was that each recorded day of time comes only once, and that once in all lifetimes was the singular record of Tuesday, June 23, 1772, and that by virtue of measurement, it would never be that same date, ever again. For Hayim, he had already been in London for nearly half a year when the unrepeatable day came to fruition. Having experienced his own self-imposed expulsion from Poland for the second time, he arrived in England wearing his entire worth sewn into his coat.

Reminiscent of his first escape, he disappeared from Warsaw in the middle of the night. By the following day his back was to the interior destruction of the Rothschild Bank he had started. The Russians and the Crown Guards collectively arrived and ripped the mansion apart, similar to violently extracting feathers from an eiderdown. Every manager, cashier, maid, and general employee, all unaware of the full extent of Hayim's activities were questioned in a brutal manner that teetered on torture. All that made the brutality remotely tolerable was the individual envelops that each came to find. Left for them by Hayim, they contained, what was for the general wage earner, a life's fortune. Despite the blessing, no sooner than they became aware of Hayim's sudden departure that the full might of authority entered and tore down the wallpaper and turned over the furniture, as they stood. The officials shouted and jeered for the "Jew!" But at best, they were only talking to a spirit. By the light of that morning Hayim had already paid for safe passage on the old salt trail that brought him to an inn in Żary.

The Russians and the Royal Guards were wildly accusing him of being the financier of the plot against the King. Something, in actuality, before hand, he knew virtually nothing of, except for a forgotten slip of Casimir's tongue. There was no incriminating evidence that lead to their suspicions, only the sadist blood-letting induced information by those captured and rumored to hear of a "friendly Warsaw Jew" to the Bar.

King Stanisław August Poniatowski may have escaped his inept captors but the incident reversed the fortunes of Poland beyond his capacity to control events. To the wolves past the door and already pacing in the corridors of power— the Russians that is, and equally to their distant brethren, the panting canines of Prussia and Austria, Poland was now ripe for systematic disemboweling. Like packs that stalk their pray, this had been in the making through backdoor high-level diplomatic channels for two years. The rub of it all was an attempt by Prussia and Austria to preserve the eastern European balance of power in the face of increasing Russian expansion and domination. For financially bankrupt and bleeding Russia, still engaged in war against the Ottoman Empire for dominance on the Black Sea, it was an opportunity to gain an undisputed territorial victory without the further cost of firing a shot. During the start of 1772, Russia was clearly winning the majority of battles against the Turks and were on the verge of complete victory; which had the shuddering and rippling effect of creating great anxiety among Frederick the Great and Austria's aging empress, Maria Theresa. Russian dominance on the Black Sea would make it the single most strategically powerful empire since the heyday of Rome. Diplomats from both empires approached Catherine in Russia two years before with the idea of carving up the weak ineffective state of Poland in a bid to have a sweeping bloodless conquest. For any one of them to advance on an absolute acquisition of Polish territory would constitute armed Polish resistance and hostile opposition by one another. In collusion, there would only be resistance by the Poles and they were little more than toy soldiers to the imperial powers of these great nations. Russia's all-but-certain victory over the increasingly failing Turkish army rather suddenly brought the issue to a heated application after years of slow discussions. Prussia and Austria offered to give Russia the largest slice of the Polish pie if she gave up her conquests in the Black Sea area. Seeing the beauty of the name "Russia" spread out in wider block letters across a further western expanse over the map of Europe was too inspiring for Catherine's ego to pass up. She greedily accepted the deal.

For King Poniatowski and his subjects, the Commonwealth lost 733,000 square miles, which constituted twenty-three percent of her former territory and nearly 5,000,000 of her fellow citizens. Prussia took the least, but economically best, area; Austria acquired the most heavily populated areas, whilst Russia took the largest but least important to anyone but the size-is-all-that-matters Russians. To give this international crime some legality, the foreign powers forced the Sejm to ratify the partition as though a man willingly giving his arms and legs to a pack of wolves that his heart may still beat. His heart was exposed, undefended, and would eventually succumb to their appetite, too.

Nevertheless, for the time being, Stanisław was still the king of the uneaten part of the Polish cookie and there was unfinished business in the name of justice. Just as the Rothschild bank was being ransacked, plundered, and defaced, an all out effort to locate the man officials suspected to be the real ring leader, Casimir Pulaski, was well under way. The monastery at Jasna Góra was violently invaded, and though many confederates fled in the melee, all were captured. To the chagrin of the Russians and the Polish crown, Casimir was not present among them. Unbeknownst to anyone, the general, after departing Hayim's company, spirited on horseback into Prussian Silesia where he took refuge en route to Dresden. As for Jan Kuźma, Walenty Łukawski, John Strawinski, Father Marek Jandołowicz and Adam and Michał Krasiński, and those who disorderly took part in the King's abduction and alleged assassination attempt, their fates varied.

The majority of those captured sang like canaries but couldn't hold a harmonious tune. What they knew among them was often fragmented and contradictory, between both the facts of the Bar and the conspiracy to abduct the King. It was the King's own account of the affair that brought the brunt of the indictments upon Walenty Łukawski, John Strawinski, Jan Kuźma, and Casimir Pulaski in absentia. The Sejm tried them, as regicides. In the trial, John Strawinski begged for his life but refused to implicate any of his fellow confederates or provide further detail of their operation. On the other hand, Walenty Łukawski spoke proudly, openly, and honestly of his involvement and disdain for "Offender To the World," his Russian-controlled King, as he brazenly called Poniatowski.

"It was of my brain that such ideas germinate and sprout and grow into action!" he pompously proclaimed.
Furthermore, he calmly opened the full breath of his testimony by reading a Confederate poem, which prophetically served as a manifesto to action:

> "Without God, virtue, dumbass Stanisław
> Is not too much— Drain the arrow of God to the
> apostle,

It was killed, this offender to the world.
With his miserable self he settled the Polish throne
boldly...
...Let it be wiped off the serpent's head."

However, with some eye to a lifetime in prison instead of execution, he claimed that the idea of regicide was reconsidered for a less violent option to the same ends. Instead, they sought to perform a "drowning of iron in blood," and merely have the King dethroned. When asked who made the final decision, Łukawski admitted taking it to Casimir. The Sejm gasped and wrung their hands in the most desirous of sweat to now capture him alive rather than "good enough" dead. With Łukawski under examination, the line of questioning followed as to inquire as to Casimir's response to the notion of kidnapping the King. Łukawski coolly testified that he met the general in Czestochowa and informed him about the possibility of the ambitious plan—

"...it spoke to him, personally," Łukawski said.
The bomb though, was that apart from the political motives at stake, even higher to the hot-blooded Pulaski was the adoration of a certain woman. He was under the spell of Frances Krasinski, so said Łukawski, and in passion pledged her the King's crowned head on the birthday of her husband. This might have plainly been heroic proof of which man was really worthy of her eternal affection.

The Sejm was outraged at the star defendant who wasn't there to defend himself. Even the King's emotions swung to such a degree against Pulaski, that he sought clemency for the man who plotted his dethronement, and all the men involved. However, it was to no avail. Despite Stanisław's pleas to spare their lives, the king had no authority to grant clemency for those sentenced by the Sejm. In all, thirty of those of low-level influence in the Bar, who knew nothing, knew little, or simply were guilty by association, plus Walenty Łukawski, John Strawinski, and Casimir Pulaski were sentenced as followed:

"Infamously Casimir Pulaski, John Strawinski and
Walenty Łukawski, and those involved in the
crime against our Royal Majesty should not only
be deprived of the honor and worship, but also
their bodies as a tool for ignominious crimes to be

subjected to cruel punishments must, therefore, even for so great a crime on punishment a lot bigger and tougher they deserve, for insertion of the Royal Majesty in our judgment, condemn all accused to include those escaped, to death by decapitation, hanged, drawn and quartered and after a time left to be blown away by the wind."

***

On an unanticipated and bitter morning the death trumpets blew quietly before the full light of sunrise. It was subsequently decided that the accomplices should be shown some mercy, as to also make the punishment of the star perpetrators as emphasized as possible. Therefore, at dawn, with little fanfare, the common thirty were routinely hanged until their necks broke, their breathing stopped, and they dangled to the delight of a scavenging murder of crows. The winged flocks had all day and night to gnaw at slivers of suspended skin and flesh, and the occasional avian ambrosial delight of mucous membrane. By contrast, the next morning saw the square packed with the revelry of more than 20,000 awe-struck spectators in a festive carnival gathering. The music! The Sunday bests! Rousing vendors! Beer! Pickled cucumbers! Kielbasa! Toys and wares for the children! But finally, the hour came, and the trumpets gloriously sounded three times! Once for Strawinski. Once for Łukawski. And once for Pulaski. Casimir though, of course, was not present. By that time, under the assumed name of Korwin he had already met with the leaders of the Generality in Strassburg and assured them that he would take part in the war between Turkey and Russia. Dashing as ever, Casimir fled but he wasn't interested in escape. He was a calvary man, through and through — blood did not run hotter, the will to fight was never in anyone stronger; he divinely — or wickedly, commended his spirit to the gods of war, and on that particular morning he was busily taking residence in Paris preparing for a return to the battlefield.

With the blare of the brass horns, Strawinski and Łukawski, were dragged on wooden stretchers, naked, sweating profusely, with their hands tied behind their backs, into the middle of the square where two scaffolds were erected. They were raised onto the platform and their necks slipped into individual nooses. To the roar of the crowd, two hooded men ascended up the stairs and stood over the criminals with the ominous distinction of being the embodiment of death in the living flesh. These executioners were to work in tandem, that each criminal would equitably receive punishment simultaneously.

All the while, standing front and center, placed ahead of the crowd, dually as either moral support or further penalty for his sins, was Marianna Łukawski. She saw to it that she stood upright, courageously in support of her husband. The state saw to it that she stood prominently, that her husband may feel an emotional and metaphorical gut wrenching pain at seeing her see him, while that is he suffered a literal gut wrenching pain.

Marianna and Walenty's eyes met— the love, the unreachable expanse, the braided devoir of two hearts… then— the shout of, "Rozpocząć!" sent the crows, with the taste of human still smeared and smattered around their beaks, into flight! The levers were wrenched; the ratchets spun; and the trapdoors sprang open! Marianna husband's body jerked and fell; dead weight— swinging from the ligature. His eyes went about swelling, protruding, and slowly bulging out of their sockets until the whites actually reflected the glare of the sun. Concurrently, she burst into a gasp that exuded every ounce of air in her body and became transfixed into a paralyzed primal stare. Her eyes welled wet with tears that flowed unceasingly but never did she take her gaze from his.

Łukawski and Strawinski were hanging, but so in a manner that they were desperately touching their tippy-toes to the platform that was snapped back into place from below. You sensed they were as fish out of water— instinctually flailing about the beach. It was all in the name of spectacles and the spectacular! There they hung, sufficiently enough to inflict great pain but not to actually die. To see them: the weight of their bodies suspended by the strength of the muscles in their fracturing necks— one-by-one the spinal bones between the shoulders and head giving way and splintering, making their gasping for air all the more frenzied. Then, the real crossroads of entertainment, justice, and savagery began!

Each executioner reached into a wooded box on the platform and pulled out a sharp knife that glinted in the sun. Without further ado, they went about slicing off the men's genitals, making for a torrent of gushing blood! The pain, was so sharp the same men who could barely draw breaths let out bloodcurdling piteous screams! But the best was yet to come!

The purveyors of this gruesome capital exhibition quickly reached back into that innocuous looking wooden boxes and brought out an instrument of the most prized horror! The Belgian disemboweling tool! Its ability was perfectly measured in its descriptive name. Łukawski's bowels spilled out before his feet while his heart continued to beat and his brain continued to compute. The executioner lit the entrails on fire and to the thrill of the spectators, the justice of Łukawski's own horror and the somatic smoke that wafted above them was poetic! Eviscerated, Łukawski and Strawinski, weeped in prayer as they begged for the mercy of death to come upon them — but that angel was excruciatingly slow to arrive.

Walenty looked down at his dissected body; blood everywhere, the skin of his stomach nothing more than two flaps of thin blubber. Yet, through it all, he was still breathing, writhing in pain, conscious, and distinctively alive — as people are as a base matter of cause for the effects of those conditions. For some in the crowd, startled beyond belief, the question of "what more" in the name of justice was immediately consumed with the reality of what was next.

The two men were brought down and their trembling heads laid across chopping blocks. Marianna, stared straight on as her husband's head succumbed to the dull edge of a heavy axe, swung high; and instead of splicing the neck, fractured it beyond what the hanging had done. She cringed and almost fainted as the executioner had to hack away from the shoulder up like a bovine slaughter, and eventually tear the head off swinging and twisting the sinew until the man was truly decapitated. As the blade shattered his neck, shockingly Łukawski's eyes and mouth popped open! Both the extra ocular and mandible muscles stiffened to such that he looked in perpetual shock while they struggled to excise his skull from the rest of his body. Breathless, sickened, and grief-stricken to say the least, officials held her head upright and her eyes open in the direction of his body being quartered to the roaring of the crowd. The moment became too much for the newly christened widow and her nervous system went into shock. Her body stopped producing adrenaline in response to the sudden form of emotional stress and her organs simply shut down. Those on the scene tried to save her, but she perished just the same as her husband: eyes wide open.

For his part, Father Marek Jandołowicz was taken prisoner by the Russians as an enemy of the state and died after six years in their infernal custody. The Krasiński brothers appeared to quietly distance themselves from the Bar and politics all together. Their appearances were deceiving but effective.

The last to be sentenced for the abduction of the King was Jan Kuźma. His testimony betrayed any indication of intelligent forethought on his part. He mainly wept and apologized to Stanisław, who passionately wept along with him. The Sejm was prepared to execute the idiot along with Łukawski and Strawinski. However, as the public came to despise Strawinski, Łukawski, and Casimir, they grew to see Kuźma as patriotic, even to a degree swashbuckling, and held a profound sympathy for him. Ultimately, the Sejm conceded to his popularity and questionable heroism and decided that Jan Kuźma would simply be sentenced to exile for life. He was promptly sent to the Papal States. The King, still in his gratitude transmitted a monthly salary to him. In a twist of fate as sweet as a man marrying the widow of his brother whom he slain, Kuźma's life was forevermore made better than it had ever been.

Casimir and Hayim had left the melee of Poland behind. Irretrievably, all Casimir had left to fight for was revenge. His cause, as either an alliance, a coalition, or even a movement, was condemned and disbanded. The Bar Confederation, which initiated the conditions and served as the catalyst for the Russo-Turkish War, was no more. The war itself, however, still raged. If only he could join a campaign— engage, contend, agitate, and enter the fray of combat on the Turkish side— for Casimir personally extracting a price through the barter of spilt Russian blood was a pleasure second to none! So it was, he was therefore in Paris, pacing carefully his impatient tread within the flat-footed world of idle luxury. By birth, he was a noble himself. But in Paris, he chose to reside among the average Parisians, who lived in abject poverty, among narrow, crooked streets with open sewers running down the middle. Crowded with starving beggars and homeless families, Paris appeared to him as surely the most wrenched reality incorporated into the world. His ability to compare was slight, as he never saw of the Judengasse or similar Jewish ghettos. However, at that stage in his life, impoverished lice-ridden conditions, battlefield camps, dark musty hideouts, and desperate charges on horseback, were more comfortable than the luxuriating soirées he frequently attended at the palace of Versailles, as a welcome guest of King Louis XVI and his queen, Marie Antoinette.

For his part, Hayim formulated his way to England embarking from the Port of Hamburg after arriving in the free and Hanseatic city stringently cloaked in the dangerous travel of night for little over a month. The journey was spent taxed to paying full price for horses, protection, and lodging. Caution, speed, and secrecy were the order of the hour, for his life was once again in danger until he reached safe harbor. Far and close enough to those ends he decided was Hamburg.

***

The decision to traverse on the northward route instead returning straight to Frankfurt was based mostly on practical factors. To start, Hamburg was the shorter of the two routes and a defense against being tenaciously followed by the Russians. Another consideration was Austrian cooperation with the Russians which would have lead to his arrest if they knew where he was, assuming he arrived in Frankfurt, where he had come from. Personally and emotionally, Hayim was loathed to return to the Judengasse. He was aware that Meyer had already greased the machinery of his own escape and was able to move out of the ghetto and into a mansion among the highest of Frankfurtian and Lutheran society. Yet, that feat was reserved for a capital mass of power that probably no other Jew in the world had obtained. As for himself, it would have been likely that to stay any length of time there would have subjected him to taking residence in the Judengasse again and he not only despised the conditions but shuddered at the abstract concept of going backwards in life.

As the year readied to turn, Hayim was settled into living quarters in Neustadt. He felt a modicum of safety and immediately went about contacting Meyer. However, taking no chances, he had a furtive letter passed through local banking channels that dealt regularly with the house of Rothschild. The brief message read:

> "Accounts tallied. Please attend hastily. Presence
> of person required. Wish to discuss closure of
> unsettled affair. - Sincerely, Gone But Not
> Forgotten."

The moment Meyer read it, he expelled a sigh of relief; to know for certain that Hayim had escaped the most personal of harm, unlike Łukawski and Strawinski.

Through foreign agents, like little spies for a budding financial military, Rothschild kept tabs on continental affairs. He already knew of

Poland's forthcoming official demise. What he didn't know was Hayim's whereabouts, the government seizure of the bank, and the secret Hayim was keeping. In his indelible low-key style, he reached Hamburg two weeks later, and upon arrival in the evening, he quietly supped with Hayim in his employee's very humble living quarters. After the perfunctory salutations, not a second of time, or a movement of the muscle was wasted. Per usual, it was all business—

"All the ledgers survived with me," Hayim said.

"The money?" Meyer asked.

"As I sent word, we were profitable," Hayim began.

"Why could you never get the Russians? Are you aware of the size of their debt? Since the shekel, no one has carried such a burden."

"The English service their needs," Hayim said, knowing he wasn't directly answering the question.

"Yes, I know. All the good money is in England, is it?" Meyer started to turn the crank of his short sarcastic disposition.

"Our money is cheaper," Hayim said dryly, almost defensively.

"That it is. So, then why, tell me, did the Russians continue to use the English when between them was better than good money, but the best money?"

This was the most embarrassing moment for Hayim since he came home with the blood on his shirt and his father and mother questioning him as to why. He hesitated, and hesitated some more, before finally he crossed the room to a chest atop a table— clearly there in anticipation of the moment which had arrived. Maybe Hayim had already played out this conversation in his head, and here the moment came when he would start his explanation, similar to the long walk home from Noah's in which he feared his life would never be the same again. He opened the chest. It laid with bullion and atop the bullion scatters of paper notes and rare coins.

"I recovered everything in the vault," Hayim said.
Meyer smiled.

"But I have more to tell," Hayim continued, nary a smile.

Hayim spent the evening in great detail of his activity in Poland, his personal tragedy, and his admission that he spent the bank's capital, otherwise Mayer's money, in supporting the futile and failed Bar Confederation—

"How much did this cost me," Meyer asked with an even temper.

"Nothing," Hayim said. "It was about fifty-thousand pound sterling. You will see, it is kept recorded to the last solidus."

Hayim handed him the ledger he had shown Casimir. However, Meyer was a bit confused —

"So then you have the money?" Meyer asked.

"No, sir. You have the money."

***

As Hayim explained, he left behind the full breadth of his earnings saved since he was in the employe of de Neufville. Through his own trading, speculation, and salary, he had come to possess riches in slight excess of that amount.

"Where is it," Meyer asked in wondrous excitement, not at the money, but at the foresight and cleverness in which Hayim exhibited.

"The back courtyard."

"We have moved and there was — "

"I placed it within the strongbox, I was permitted to access," Hayim said.

The mood lightened, so that Hayim made a joke of things.

"Why how many strong boxes do you have in your courtyard?"

"Never you mind," Meyer said with a twitch of a smile at the edge of his lips.

"Look under your wealth in the one I speak, so there you will find my paltry affluence. Which is now fully yours."

As it turned out, Hayim knew the whole time that he was spending his own fortune, which he never expected to pay divides. It was his own blood money. Meyer chose not to personally hold the unauthorized activities against Hayim. However, though the capital was paid in full, the inability to capture the Russian Crown's business cost Meyer money, which was something he could not tolerate. Ultimately, on the basis of principle alone, the two would have to part company. Though, it was more than principle. Meyer believed it was time for Hayim to be his own man. Still, he extended to his former employee an invitation to return to Frankfurt; Meyer could pay for the assurance of his perpetual freedom from Russian or Polish designs. However, even if Hayim could live in luxury among the Rothschild's and thereby avoid a return to the Judengasse, he felt their time had passed, both professionally and personally. Besides, Gutlé was pregnant again and Meyer was convinced that the child was to be a boy. As was now his fate, time and time again, the time had come for Hayim to move on and they spent the rest of the night in conversation about it.

In the wee hours of the morning, Hayim was tired and he spoke rather solemnly when he said—

"Where should I go?"

"You are a banker, follow the market," Meyer told him.

"If Frankfurt is closed, Poland is dead, Russian is indebted, and Amsterdam in collapse—"

"Then, as I see it, you have two choices only, do you see as I see?"

"It is late, it is early, it is always the same, I can see nothing at this hour over the gloom," Hayim said.

"You have but two choices," Meyer repeated, unswayed by the emotion of Hayim's soulful expression.

"And what, say you, are those choices?"

"Well you must know or your instincts lead you safely while your mind dithered—"

"My mind dithered, not. On the contrary, it focused amply on the servicing of my safety," Hayim replied.

"Understood," Meyer relented. "As I see it, your choices are before you— where we sit or across that channel."

***

Hayim arrived in London aboard a Hanseatic ship, over-stuffed with salt beef and pork, sauerkraut, and dried anchovies. Furthermore, he was wearing an old, beat up coat. The coat was threadbare, ugly, and indicated that the likes of the owner was not well to do. In the characteristic fashion that marked Meyer as always a step ahead, he calculated Hayim's means as it was left to him, and what remained he had Gutlé personally sow gold coins into the ratty coat. The garment was presented to Hayim in Hamburg, the coat practically being a receipt. Thus, as much as Hayim was a wayfarer, he wore a significant amount of money on his back. This is how he arrived on English soil.

Half-a-year later on what appeared to be any-old Tuesday, he was in the Duke's Place Synagogue and being providentially handed a piece of paper by Rabbi Schiff. Reminiscent of his grandfather braving the conditions to bestow upon him the prayer book with the address in Amsterdam, this was just as fateful.

The exchange began with a sentence from Hayim, in which he uttered, but shyly did not want to own—

"Rabbi, I am troubled," he said.

The exchange concluded with Hayim peering down at lettering in both, Hebrew he could not read, and in English in which it said:

"Franks. Shearith Israel."

"What you seek, my son, you might be able to find in America. In London, you will only be a Jew," the rabbi said.

***

XII
INDEFATIGABLE

"The most fortunate of us, in our journey through life, frequently meet with calamities and misfortunes which may greatly afflict us; and, to fortify our minds against the attacks of these calamities and misfortunes should be one of the principal studies and endeavors of our lives."

Thomas Jefferson

Aug. 1772
London, England

Elka,
Dear cousin, before I relinquish this ink to the subsumable properties of parchment, forgive me in advance for any untoward expression in which my self-conscious dialogue might unexpectedly convey; and of course for my consistently tardy dispatch. I write you less the serenade of standard fare, the congenial report of comings and goings and the enchanting pursuit of inspiring perspective. I suspect you have aged as such that the more distressing information that marks the vicissitudes of the human experience can pass through your discernment without disruption of your true spirit. Let me take the time to mark that ever since your first post I received in Frankfurt, the one of the pastel portrait of you and I— I have delighted in your winsome character, exceptional kindness, deep curiosity, vivacious attitude, and burgeoning sophistication. I luxuriate in your tidings and sincerely bewail that I have not been as attentive as you deserve since our last correspondence. Further, worry not by what I next inscribe. Pray for my inner being and ethereal

soul, but of your own concern, I beg, that if you must be troubled, to do so more of the dandelions than my following sentence. I fear I am a creature dispossessed of light, in need of absolution. In as such, I thank the masterminding angels of fate that yours is a youth quietly fulfilled and a heart untouched by fire. I learned at the age you now possess that life is a painfully passionate and serious thing. Be grateful to be so blessed, even if at times it seems to you that you may not be so.

Dear cousin, you are acutely aware, I have not sent word since I informed you of my embarkation to Leszno twenty-four months ago. It seems impossible for every second since that time for one to be prepossessed, but I so have. Now, I compose this from the loathsome and vile bowels of a cargo vessel bound from the Port of London to the colonies of America. It is cold, wet, overrun with rats and unlit except for my tiny flame. I am a lone soul taking this trip as a passenger; though as such for hire, as I have acted on my own behalf to offer my services in return for this condition beset upon me. I will refrain from horrifying you still further, which I surely could and am almost tempted for the pleasure of ghoulish amusement. In preference, I acknowledge you adjudge it ever-so titillating that I seem to travel the known well-mapped world. I impress upon you the concept of: distance— that there is far more earth unknown to me than I have traveled or will in time be able to travel to. So said, I arrived in the city of London, the country of England, following uttermost calamity and the painful path of tragedy. Now, I write from the position of being in employe to this vessel that I might not waist the slightest of riches still sewed into my mackinaw.

First and foremost, I would be woefully remiss to not inquire of your studies? Please, as only intervals away from your responsibilities permit, make me aware of your siblings and your parents' welfare? By His grace, the years given to me in Amsterdam, companied by you and family, have been the most cheerful years of my existence. Furthermore, think not that I don't study your words well. You spoke last of love, but I implore you to beware of romance. Beware that it does not derail you of God, family, country, right decisions, and true self. Now, forgive me if I have soused you in unnecessary fear— mine is a world of precaution to defeat the paragons of best intentions.

I will not render you in suspense. I did successfully reach Leszno. My dearest— father, mother, and sister, are beyond us now. I believe they have been so since our ally. I hope you will understand as I close this passage prematurely.

What do you know of world affairs? Poland has been partitioned. Moscow is beset with plague. Many-many dead. I am sure you have awareness of the prodigy Mozart? I am a witness, as such in Salzburg. And, to my understanding, the English have claimed New Holland. I concern if the English assume a majority of world power, that the world will innately be a more dangerous place. The English are intelligent, and industrious, and can turn wood into paper, sand into glass, and air into chemistry better than most, if not all others. But unlike the Dutch or the French, their righteousness is often leveled in kind by unforewarned might. They don't treat people well, I am trying to say. Now, I bring you up-to-date on my affairs, as they do directly involve the world.

I know when you think of me, you often associate affluence with said thought. Admittedly, as you are aware, I am retained for the presumed expertise of economics and finance— plainly, by the standard of most I was moneyed, and by the measure of many, I surely was deficient. Let me take the time to caution of you of the blind pursuit of wealth. Such a diversion is petty in its scope and unyielding in its expense of time. Further, it is believed that fortune is a noble achievement. I assure you, the only noble achievement is unfettered forgiveness. Surely, few seek to deprive themselves of riches. I pray you deprive yourself of nothing, for all things are exactly of equal value, made of the same natural elements; therein with this understanding in your heart, no mistake can ever be made you. It is recorded that the love of money is the root of all kinds of evil. I declare, too complex in its nature is that record. I proclaim, the love of anything other than God, is the root of all kinds evil, especially the love of self as though innately separate from God, akin to an adolescent denying the true patronage of its parents. And, if I am in actuality an expert at fiscal and monetary sciences— I teach on to you: to abandon all lines of worldly reasoning of wherewithal. Money is merely a medium of exchange; a currency of the concept of possibility; a product of the art of human consciousness in which the order of things is critical to individual equilibrium. Wealth, in and of itself is a notion, free of evil until the idea of self-worth is interjected into its purpose. Now, for as I was relating— I assure you at the stroke of this word, by any calculation, I am quite poor. Hopefully that is not more horrifying to you than the rats sniffing around me. If you are as you were, I know it is not. For some, I know it would be. I made great efforts to assist the cause of country in Poland, which I am afraid was not much of a cause of virtue.

I am sure you are wondering how much finance of mine was yielded. Poland is partitioned, so, in discrete answer: I suppose not nearly enough. I suggest there is nothing else of good cheer to add to this event and so if I may, I shall follow another line correspondence.

Hereby, I humbly return— you aver you are in love? Of all the sights I have beheld, the visage of endearment is the least of my worldliness. Oh, the clouds, the sky, the stars— and it is amazingly love which is the most various and artistic of natural perspectives. Be with me a day at temple or about an affair, you'd laugh as I do, to see that to have never married affords me a special place in the sympathies of maids and a mischievous admiration among gentlemen. I do not regret that I am emotionally of my own accord and though I have never wed, I have ventured a time or two with some interest of the heart, be it to the park or a formal occasion. Natheless, I have not been entrusted and consigned to a lasting love or for that matter a courtship. Again, I caution you of passion or dalliances, but I declare: do not spare yourself the invitation to truly love. Love deeply, my cousin! If you are to love; love so deeply that the concept of above and below are asunder in your wake and in your presence all that is left is a mystical transcendence that seeks no change whatsoever, in even the simplest arrangement of the hairs on the object of your affection's head. This model of love I profess is not an impetuous besottedness or a purely material intimacy. I admit to not be acquainted with love but I have seen it, and often it is tangled in a weave of self-interest and the knot pulled so taut that it constricts and fractures the easily-broken heart. Love deeply! Love as deeply as you can, Elka! The love I speak of is so lofty, and maybe that is why I am devoid of partnership— but this changeless essence is a salvation from the shifting tides of duality. Nothing can compare to this love. Nothing can defile this love. This type of love is beyond devotion for it encompasses the whole of romance and renders it just a portion of the union. This love, in all its glory, is the transfiguring death of self.

This is how I once loved He That Is.

Enough, yes? I will save your curiosity from its likely needling. I have storied you in many a tale of what Poland is like. And, through the letters from Frankfurt, alone, you could probably fool a travel writer, by our missives. So, London, I assume you are wondering as well.

Now, it might be advisable to read this less a stomach full of herring. You, who are a girl, will now read words better suited for a boy. But either skip ahead or test your sensibilities hereof. Here I begin—
In all my peregrination, London was the most unique setting in strangely some of the most remarkable ways. It seemed the public appetite for capital punishment was never satiated; nearly a criminal a day was left dangling in a square! Now, I exaggerate, but not wildly! Mired in fog, soaked in rain, crime and criminals know no bounds in London, and suicide is almost as common as a breath of fresh air! Now, can you believe that? Believe it, for it is overwhelmingly true! I venture you will not as such come upon these tidbits in travel guides, no?

Eight months was the length of time I availed myself of the city. I intended upon arrival to make it the last of my travels. It is curious, that England speaks in loud tones of banning the institution of slavery while yet discriminates against us Jews with a mannered disposition meant not to insult but made patently clear. Are the negro now higher on the social strata than the Jew? We are each human, to this I agree. Is it evil to enslave another? To this I doubt. At times more than others. But in practicality, to what degree can a Negro support his welfare, when even the Jew can barely support his own in a society set against his advancement? Will negroes fair worse, less than the beggar, lower than the criminal, confined to be altogether: dispossessed and forsaken? This, my dear— unsavory as it may appear, these are the ways to all the ends of the world. This may be too philosophical, I know. Our conversations are usually rooted in facts of interest or trifling amusement. Lest, I return, in our usual good cheer and favor—

Now what else can I tell you in a word or two? I know, I shall read to you, by writing to you from the news of London, itself.

A very Strange Beast called a Rhynoceros, lately brought from the East Indies, being the first that ever was in England, is daily to be seen at the Bell Savage Inn on Ludgate-Hill, from Nine a Clock in the Morning till Eight at Night. All Persons born in the Country of Northampton are desired to take Notice, That there will be held a Country Feast on the 13th day of November next, at Merchant-Taylors-Hall, for the promoting of Mutual Society and Charity.

Can anything be more amusing? I think not, myself. The English I observed to be an uncommon and good people, within the ranks of their own; not much for expressing their emotions as say the French or as intolerant and self-depreciating as the Dutch, nor as serious, organized, or authoritarian as many are in Berlin or Frankfurt, but they are most interesting and ambitious as a whole. I regress—

I suppose this an apt opportunity to educate you in a way in which I need not do so, but I feel compelled. Your adulthood approaches and with it comes a new set of longings, just as learning to walk brought its own rush of fresh aspirations. Of my own desire, I wish to bestow upon you the expectation that the world is a garden of basic human equality. It is not. The world and life therein is made of interconnected interests, personalities, perspectives, and objectives— aggravated by ignorance, prejudice, hate, and evil. The Jewish race, as you are well aware, has been persecuted since time immemorial. Ours continues to persist in a faithful and facile exercise of hope. Hope, as you like. I hope as well, but in addition to optimism, I wonder "how," endlessly. I tell truly, as much as I wish not to tell you truly, that the world itself is a problem— a problem from Hell.

I landed upon the docks carrying with me letters of honor and known accomplishments— let me state for the record the names and number of firms which derided me as unfit because I, as you do, course with the blood of Abraham—

1. Child and Co.
2. John Drummond and Co.
3. Brown and Collinson

4.   Welch and Rogers
5.   Smith and Payne
6.   Croft, Hart, Blackwell, Pall Mall
7.   Robert Child and Co.
8.   Bland and Barnett
9.   Chambers, Franks, Hercy, and Birch
10.   Gines and Atkinson
11.   Lee and Aytons

I could go on, maybe ten, or twenty more! Save
you, I shall, from boredom but up and down the
streets of pecuniary commerce— Fleet,
Lombard— they wanted my knowledge and skill,
even often whispering for my advice, but rejected
my labor at the cost of my Semitic presence. How
is this to be overcome? I am recoiled to the same
question and dilemma, which caused me to act
impetuously fourteen years ago; an act for which
my family has perished. I have made no progress;
at times I submit to the disposition that my
spiritual and intellectual rudder is a ruined
instrument. Whoa! We are pitching and rolling— I
pray not another night of storm! Excuse the... —
— — —more— — — —cribbed penmanship—
— — — —we pitch and roll— — — —
to my point, my safe passage
— — — — — — — — — — —as I write— — — —
— — — —is underwritten— — — — — — — — — —
—
— — — — — — — — — — — — — — — — — —by
my own labor. As unfortunate as I feel, the
opportunity may be deemed the most fortune of
my English circumstances, for it is expensive to
cross the ocean.
— — — — — — — — — — —Whoa!
It seemed we just pitched so far as to almost be
sideways and I had to catch the candle sliding
away from me! Of necessity, I will course to
shorten my divulgence. England, I return— I

applaud they outlawed slavery but they did not outlaw prejudice. But who is to say you can legislate man's heart? I go now, onward, forward, to the new world. I must continue to go anywhere and everywhere, for I am without a home. I am indefatigable. God gives me nothing. I am like a horse in which he merely replaces the shoes that I might carry on further still with no personal direction of my own taste. Mine is a life of loss. Mine is a purpose unknown. Mine is a grief that couldn't be understood. Mine is reciting psalm 22, night after night.

Dear cousin, dear Elka, I guess what is different about me now is that the facade and fantasy of divine purpose or greater meaning is stripped of my considerations. Am I wandering in the desert? Yes, I suppose. Is my strength and character tested? Yes, I suppose. Without certainty, the diabolic hypothesis of randomness and porous luck prey upon the mind. It is our human instinct to try to make rationale sense of everything—even if our rational is the Will of God. This, and not the thin nature of our covering skin is the flaw of the human design. These postulations will kill us in spirit and initiative long before the body has lost its elasticity and power.

With God's blessing, I shall arrive in the Americas in several weeks time. I shalt not know what I will find until I find it. Thereby, I assume you wonder why I simply do not return to Amsterdam? I have given Amsterdam all I have to give it and seek nothing more from its gentle grace. From this hour on, my objective is unambitious. To be able to live and work in peace is all I desire. If there is meaning in that, I need not know. Ultimately, I live for God and country but I have no country, and at present— I do not wholly understand the

wisdom of God. Let me not doubt my feelings or
deny my thoughts. Both are oft like seeds upon
the wind. In time they will shift. Thereby, dear
Elka, let not your heart be ill at ease for me. I said
God gives me nothing, that is the disposition, for I
cannot refute that over all things he gives me
strength, even when I wish for far less.

Uncle, Hayim

***

XIII
TRAVAIL

"People and nations are forged in the fires of adversity." *John Adams*

Seagulls had been circling the ship for some time. That meant only one thing: land was not far away. The slack of the nautical rope — the burn of sedulous littoral anxieties. Ship hands started up the lookout — their sunburnt scaly skin — orange in patches, sloughing in others. Then —

"Land Ho!"

"Land Ho, Captain!"

Off the port bow lay their final destination in sight.

"Land Ahoy!"

Hayim came rushing up and out of the frigate's cabin! Land? Land?

"Plenty of scope!" Captain Jennings bellowed!

"All standing!"

To Hayim those words meant nothing, he wasn't indentured as a hands-on sailor — more a matelot in trade for passage as an comptroller — a sea-sick one at that. Since the vessel's embarkation at the Port of London, he'd been constantly dizzy, nauseous, and green around the gills. Now, he stood, on the soggy deck — God willing, the drawing of his dead horse done.

"Shelomo, take the rope!" Jennings bellowed over the harking gulls and pattering rain of their droppings.

Hayim stood mouth agape; wondering for a second if there was another "Shelomo" on the crew. Rope? His head was rolling with the irregular reeling of the ship and as during the entire voyage, his stomach was biliously slushing where he stood.

"Don't just stand there, man; look alive!" The Captain shouted as he threw the end of a thick hemp. Hayim fumbled with it; before finally grasping cord with dire strain.

"Now PULL!"

Hayim managed to help steady more than he actually pulled, as fifty other crewman — well experienced in the block and tackle hauled in the beautiful fifth-rate.

"Is that all you got, you hawsepiper?" the Captain cried out with a dastardly chuckle. "I said, 'pull!'"

Hayim contemptuously spit in his hands and rubbed them together. With determination, he wrapped the thick cord once around his arm and put all his weight into it; leaning backward at an odd angle and digging in! He tugged and pulled until he saw spots in his vision and the satisfaction of that first sail finally lowering.

In port, the ship was overrun with a swarm of activity; the colonial raw materials returned home converted into hats, linen, and coats — loaded with flour, corn, biscuits, and other goods bound quickly for the West Indies. This wasn't a slave ship that traversed the Triangle Trade. It was a private mercantile outfitted by cooperating livery companies, courtesy of the Royal Navy. Hayim never knew how lucky he was to land with but only a queasy stomach, and not the typical travelers' contagions: Ship Fever, otherwise known as typhus, or dysentery, smallpox, and scurvy, among others. He was blessed to be on a vessel, so deftly commanded by Captain Jennings, that it wasn't lost at sea or boarded by pirates.

Amid the marshaled flesh and bone into a lever of the imperium machinery of commerce, Hayim Shelomo, at the age of thirty-two was hunched over singularly spilling his guts into the Atlantic. Boggs approached and amusedly wrapped an arm around his vomiting shipmate.

"Welcome to the colonies, Mr. Shelomo," he jeered.

***

Hayim began the trip in the middle of the night three and half weeks before. He could not sleep, as abound on the street was an illumination. A frenzy; a celebration, for what, of what, he knew not. Of all the places he had ever seen, been, inhabited, and took residence, London he felt the least connected to and rarely concerned himself with external activities. The Judengasse, which he would not trade for London, still brought about a greater feeling of intrinsic connection than the damp, foggy, outpost in the north Atlantic.

Amid the raucous, it was between night and morning — another grievous night that had followed so many while he was in London. He held in his hand the paper, which the rabbi had given him. Many aspects of his body, his spirit, and his soul felt intangibly exhausted. There was a sense within him that he was running in place, that all he learned, had risen into, and held as the foundation of his identity was somehow at odds with the Will of God. Hayim was exceedingly religious and over the months he combatted this well of displaced emotion with greater religiosity. Jewish law penetrated every aspect and part of his life. It was the true clock he lived by. But it wasn't enough. He was drifting from losing heart to losing faith, though he had yet to reach that darkest hour, as he placed the paper with the name of the congregation in his prayer book, and he prayed.

His disciplines afforded him a coterie of the solemn invocations of Jewish literary liturgies. He had repeated each day of his life, and as the human mind is wont to do, his wanted to know what it was all for. He was as far beyond the standard calls for clarity, peace, possession, and presence. Now, save the youthful enthusiasm of tomorrow being a better day, that more goodness was to come then the bad upon one, he spoke intimately to God as he had never truly done.

עליו טרפה שדעתו כך כל אני למה ... אלוהים ,אבא?
("Father, God… why am I so bereft?")

Yes, he was a religious man, from youth, by parental training, by the warmth in his heart.

רע עשיתי מה ... אלוהים ,אבא?
("Father, God… what have I done wrong?")

However, the depth of his knowledge of the word of God, and the classical organization of prayer restricted his heartfelt communication, as it does many men of the cloth, the clergy, or the church.

אבד צריכים הם כי לכם יש מתיקות מה ...רק האשמה ,אני ...אלוהים ,אבא?
("Father, God… am I, solely to blame… what sweetness is there to You that they should have perished?")

Sometimes, a man on a desert island who doesn't know the words of Moses— but he hears the Lord more clearly and profoundly than does a quorum in dedicated devotion.

‎אבא, אלוהים ... למה אתה נמצא ולכן הצורך להעניש אותי?

("Father, God... why have You found so necessary to punish me?")

Hayim questioned the wisdom of the Infinite; his life possessed of nothing in the world of wont or value.

‎אבא, אלוהים ... היא דברים בשם ומרמא מביא גאולה בנמצא?

("Father, God... is deliverance forthcoming?")

His person devoid of companionship or intimacy.

‎אבא, אלוהים ... מהי המטרה של הידיים שלי, אם כל אני אם שלוחצים יש סתם הפך האבל?

("Father, God... what is the purpose of my hands, if all I ever touched has merely turned to grief?")

His efforts perverted into other's greed and the depth of loss. He listened for God. That is what was so different about this prayer. He spoke in whispered imagination...

‎אלוהים, אבא

("Father, God...")

‎אלוהים, אבא

("Father, God...")

‎אלוהים, אבא

("Father, God...")

‎אני רוצה לדעת את הלב. אני רוצה לדעת מה אתה חושב- אתה מה אתה עצמך הם הרגשה

("I want to know Your heart. I want to know what You are thinking— what You, Yourself are feeling.")

...and then fell silent in voice and mind. Nothing of the miraculous occurred.

‎אלוהים, אבא

("Father, God...")

‎אלוהים, אבא

_____

172

("Father, God...")

אלוהים, אבא

("Father, God...")

אלוהים, אבא

("Father, God...")

אלוהים, אבא

("Father, God...")

אלוהים, אבא

("Father, God...")

He came out of prayer, his eyes swollen with still lingering uncertainty and his aural facility devoid of the deep resonant or dulcet voice of God. Even below, on the street, the revelry still had life, but the personal silence rung like a mild buzzing that drowned out anything he could otherwise hear or feel.

His coat, the one Gutlé fashioned for him, hung on a rack on the wall. It caught his attention in a way it never did before, in the type that the mind and the eye are in concert and every detail appears brightly. For as dispossessed as Hayim had recently felt, he suddenly came under the sensation of a calm grounded feeling. He drew down the coat and without a second conscious thought, slowly unstitched a gold piece.

***

The next day, wearing the coat, carrying his satchel and dragging his trunk, Hayim meandered about the docks at the Port of London. He was amid the world's largest industrial base, a massive infrastructure of dockyards, food stores and equipment warehouses, all funded by a generous nation that saw its future as dependent on the seas. Already smarting because he felt so unwelcome in the country, he went about with his cap on and head down. He feared that as a Jew obtaining passage might prove to be impossible or cost prohibitive. Possessed with a measure of that calm grounded feeling, he made his way up and down the various docks, watching and listening, waiting for his intuition to hone in on what might be a favorable situation. There was nothing to indicate which ships were embarking or where they were going. Or for that matter, which vessels had just returned to sea that is unless the cargo was presently being unloaded. For all Hayim knew, there wouldn't be a ship leaving port for the colonies on that day. Forcing him to inquire daily with a shipping company on the schedule of departures, or simply venture back day after day.

In an English hymn to adversity, London fog shrouded the atmosphere. Hayim walked mile upon mile, down, across, and by hundreds of ships moored in the river. In an English hymn to wisdom and melancholy, not a single person minded him the slightest attention or concern. High-grade anthracite coal burned — copper smelted. Boilers and tanks bubbled, boiled, and vaporized the rolling liquid of sperm oil from blankets of blubber all along the docks. In an English hymn to the milder influence of heaven, it continually rained. Hayim, hated London. He inquired about several shipping companies but not all, yet of the ones he solicited, none were outfitted with a scheduled departure. A second consideration was to probe the Royal Navy. However, approaching the officials of all officialdom was fraught with more unexpected danger than assured reward, and he avoided them at all cost. The drudgery required was merely to ask every ship — one-by-one — of their issuance. If his luck held out, he'd hear of a vessel launching westward and take it upon himself to bribe passage. Rabbi Schiff had directed him to board and land in New York. However, he was prepared to take a longer route if necessitated by conditions. Nova Scotia, Boston, Philadelphia, any port that got him close enough to New York that he might reach it without further ado. This was an accepted possibility. Luckily though, his intuition gave him the courage to ask one particularly brawny sailor where the ship he was loading was heading.

"…What is it ya ask?" the sailor shouted back.

"I say, where are you bound?" Hayim shouted forward!

"What's ya askin' me?"

"I say, where do you sail next?"

"We sail next? Tell me, eh, where've sailed from, fella?"

Other sailors on the dock laughed with the coarse man. Hayim realized that the long distance shouting was not endearing him to clear communication and that he would have to venture forward and face the sailor rather intimately. He walked down the dock, as always he had come to do, expected the worse, when—

"Where's ya want go, fella?" the sailor said as he rolled his barrel up to toward Hayim who was approaching. Hayim knew by his slightly sarcastic tone and choice address of "fella" that there was a little dig in his words, and thus he couldn't necessarily be trusted. After some consideration, and with his head kept down, Hayim responded—

"New York."

The sailor wondered why he didn't raise his eyes— curious it was. So, the seaman looked down at him a bit suspiciously before he shrugged off any idea of harm coming from the shy little man.

"This ship here, we sail for the Gold Coast. A sailor, ya? Ya don't want to come with us, do ya? Come with us for some adventure?" he said kiddingly.

It was common for young men to make their way to the docks and ask around about joining a fleet. Many were runaways, some debtors, and a few foolhardy adventures. The sailor could tell straightaway that Hayim didn't look like the type but he joked of the part.

"So why's ya want to go to New York, bloody, who wants to go there? It's the ends of the earth I here." the sailor cried out.

Hayim wasn't comfortable with the trifling nature of their exchange, and—

"Thank you," he said; turned and started to walk away.

The sailor whirled him back around, a brawny and tough piece of man.

"Hey's, tells me why ya wants to goes to New York's?" he said.

Hayim wasn't about to argue or confront the man but he needed to gracefully find a way out of the line of interest. The best way he knew how was to money. He drew a English pound and raised it in line with his gaze.

"I have reasons," Hayim said.

The sailor snatched the money!

"That's a very good reason. And, I'm a collector of reasons."

"I don't have anymore," Hayim said.

The sailor waited a moment, a slight standoff, but the brawny man backed down.

"Well, I'll tell you, there's only one ship goin' that's way, and girl's over there," he pointed to a tall mast. "And me brother's on it. His name is Boggs. But I say, you look rather unseaworthy for passage, that is unless you have a few more reasons" he ended with a chuckle and a ripe smile. Hayim flashed the gold piece unsewn the night before. It made the expected impression—

"I's see clearly now's, my own eyes tells me of your utter sea worthiness."

Hayim approached the ship pointed out to'em. It was a fifth-rate ship of the line sloop. Men were rushing on and off the vessel loading cargo with great speed, strength, and sweat. Hayim spotted a peculiar fella who looked to be the closet in appearance to the sailor who directed him to his brother. Hayim took a deep breath and confidently shouted out—

"Boggs?!"

Not a man stopped— not a one. They all continued scurrying about, charging their load as though a mindless social function focused exclusively on the task at hand.

"Boggs!" he shouted again!

This time, the gentleman Hayim spied as the best candidate to be the sailor's brother stopped. His brother was rolling a barrel, but he was carrying a crate. The fella gruffly shouted back!

"Yeah?!"

Now, it was Hayim who quickly approached. Boggs was a brute of a man in contrast to the merely brawny frame of his sibling. However their faces were surely from the same stock.

"I inquire, is it your vessel en route to New York?"

"What's that accent?"

"I've word you're sailing to the colonies?"

"I dunno? Who wants to know? Who's word, speak with the captain," he said, seeking to rid himself of the inconvenience Hayim presented. "Captain!" he shouted.

Captain Jennings was a rather slovenly looking man jammed into a captain's dress jacket with epaulettes. He looked, felt, seemed, and smelled to Hayim more like a bloke that was in his second career— his first being a pirate.

"Who's the dog-hearted?" Captain Jennings said with a laugh, a scowl, and a hiccup all at the same time.

"I dunno, captain," said Boggs. "But he's got a funny accent."

"My name is Hayim."

"You're not English, are you?" Boggs said.

"You're a Jew?" the captain asserted.

"I never heard no one speak like that," Boggs continued.

"I want to travel aboard your ship. I'm prepared to render a fair for passage."

With that Hayim cut to the chase and offered up his gold piece. Just as Boggs was impressed, Captain Jennings laughed.

"We don't take passengers or stowaways. This is a merchant vessel," Jennings said.

"Are ya's funny Welsh?" Boggs said curiously. "How'd ya know me names?"

"He's a Jew," Jennings said.

"He knew me name," Boggs said.

"You're brother," Hayim said.

"Ya know me brother?"

"You're no English Jew," Jennings said, somewhat cautiously. "Ya runnin' from the law, or somethin?"

"No, on the contrary."

"What 'contrary?'"

"How ya know me brother?"

"Ya isn't in troubles with anyone, is ya?"

"I'm prepared to pay you."

"We don't know, no Jews, no Jew peoples or they's family."

"He asked him on the docks or somethin', don't be so daft," Jennings chided Boggs.

Hayim held out the gold piece. Captain Jennings laughed again, spittle flew as he did, and said—

"That there's not enough of those for ya to be carried on board with us."

The two men stood there, staring eye-to-eye. Jennings broke it off, slapping Boggs—

"Get back to your duties," Jennings shouted at him, more in good measure of authority, rather than anger.

Boggs quickly picked up his crate.

"Captain, what are these?" Boggs asked

Across the wooden crate was painted: "porcelaine." The good captain looked at it and scratched his head in uncertainty.

"Just toss it among," Captain Jennings said.

"You rather not, it's fragile," Hayim spoke up.

"You can read — ?" Jennings asked.

"Word in French."

"Thought ya said, ah, you're a Jew?" Boggs interjected.

"He can be a French Jew, ya harpy" Jennings scoldingly said.

"Polish."

"From Poland? Where's Poland? I know it's far," Boggs said.

"What'd you say your name is?" Jennings asked.

"Hayim. Hayim Shelomo."

"And you can read this? Tell me, can you read these?"

With that, Captain Jennings showed him the Bill of Exchange. It was a document pages thick. The majority of it was written in English but their were French, Hanseatic, and Dutch goods listed in their native language. Hayim was able to read through it with ease. Bestowing the unexpected knowledge on Captain Jennings seemed to do something for the captain. It gave him a sense of power he didn't possess before, and his natural inclination was to retain the means of that power.

"Maybe, upon a second consideration, we could make to accommodate ya," Captain Jennings uttered with a grin.

***

In 1772, the average journey across the Atlantic from England varied depending upon the embarkation port, time of year, and if the gales cooperated. All this considered, the average span of time for the full crossing was within two weeks to a month. However, life and work at sea was in stark contrast to an occupation and life on land. Hayim was brought on as the ship's comptroller. This made him a full-fledged crewmember, though without being tasked anything greater than his accounting obligations for passage. They ate a diet of salt meat, hard biscuit, and sauerkraut; no different than the ferries Hayim took into London. For many of the penurious crewmembers, the ship's diet was superior to their own when docked at home. This was supplemented with limitless supplies of beer and limited nips of rum. They were well fed and given a sufficient ninety minutes a day to consume their rations. It was an organized, well-ordered ship. Yet, for Hayim, it felt like a dizzy descent into indisposition. He proved to be unfit for oceanic travel. Though not his first marine expedition, the travel from Hamburg to London was a case of multiple ferries in what were primarily calm seas. This was an adventure; now not one of epic portions, mind you, but of the occasionally nominal storms. To the well-seasoned crew, they were underwhelmed by the tempests. However, Hayim— the salty soaking wet conditions, sleepless disgorging nights, diarrhea, lice, fleas, rats, molding hardtack, and the flat beer was more than his shocked system was able to absorb. After two days aboard ship, he found himself constantly in a state of discomfort over what became three and half more weeks. Nonetheless, he would muster the indefatigable strength to perform his duties admirably, yet all the while dribbling traces of ejected matter from his stomach down his chin.

***

Hayim was spilling his guts into the Atlantic with Boggs armed wrapped around him, jeeringly showing him a sailor's hospitality, when he said—

"Welcome to the colonies, Mr. Shelomo. How do you say, "America," in any one of those languages of yours?"

Boggs lifted Hayim's head up by his hair and dropped him back into prostration before breaking into hysterical laughter and callously walking away carrying the crate of "porcelaine." Eventually, Hayim gathered himself, wiped his mouth clean and made his way to disembark. He carried his ever-present trunk and satchel; and prepared to walk the gangplank to more comfortable and lively strides on stable footing.

"Shelomo!" Captain Jennings shouted so loud that even the birds exploded back into the air! Exasperated but respectful, Hayim stopped and turned—

"Wait! We have unfinished business, don't we, you's and I?" His relatively weak accountant held his belongings closely and looked across the stern into the wild over-amused eyes of his captain. He couldn't imagine what more could be necessitated of him. In his capacity as purser he had performed in excess of all that was required— inventoried and labeled every wretched item and crate on board; painstakingly balanced the books, and calculated taxes down to the last shilling— all while the ship pitched and yawed upon the raging sea! In his mind, he had more than paid for his passage to the new world.

The captain exuded confidence as the muscled behemoth strolled up to him. Then, without saying a word, reached into his jacket pocket— unbuttoned almost to his waist, and cupped a few large coins. He pressed his enormously callused hand— hard as seashells, into Hayim's yielding palm—

"Some money for old rope," he said. "Thanks to you, this is going to be the easiest delivery exchange I've ever had as captain." Hayim was never afraid but he was relieved. He appreciated the acknowledgement and tender but in truth, he personally loathed nearly everything about the man standing before him: his brashness; his rudeness; his ill temperedness, ill manneredness, and despicable sarcasm. The broker, who once held no grievance against royal courts that slighted him, had grown tired in his soul and impatient with the world. None of this showed on the outside, but within, Hayim was failing to a weariness stemming from a disillusionment of purpose, like living under a twenty-four hour midnight, straining a gratitude for God.

When it came to Captain Jennings, merchant sailors, the Royal Navy, and the great wide-open sea, he had seen and heard all he wanted and was glad to be rid of them all. Nonetheless, gratefully, Hayim placed the silver pieces in his pocket. Then, he hobbled down the gangplank to the bustling pier below. His grueling trip was over. In twelve years, he had gone from Leszno, to Amsterdam, to Frankfurt, to Warsaw, to Hamburg, then across the channel to London, and finally to New York. He may have been the most traveled Jew in the world, and yet, after 6000 miles, he was still a man without a country; without a family; and without a home.

***

Time seemed to have been manipulated and deluded, that his circadian rhythms were in wreckage and he had no real barometer of existence, only existing. What had been months since he brought the full measure of his pain to Father God, the memory of all that time was compressed so tightly that everything that had happened since seemed like it had to have happened only yesterday — one incredibly long God-given day. Continuing...

...After a short distance trudging down Broad Street —
his mind is spinning —
his stomach whirling —
his equilibrium teetering —

His body reflexed to vomit! He bent over — but mustered the fortitude to hold it in. His eyes watered. The skin of his hand crinkled and his knees wobbled.

לא

("No!")

לא

("No!")

לא

("No!")

He thinks and begs his internal biology. He's almost made it. Wherever it is to, he's had to have almost arrived, yet again.

אלוהים, אבא

("Father, God...")

אלוהים, אבא

("Father, God…")

כוח לי תן

("Give me strength")

***

The earth, manifest in its geologically densest: eighteenth century New York crust, was flecked in natural patches of freshly fallen snow; and on wobbly knees, qualmish faith, queasy stomach, and the glory of God, Hayim came to his first intersection at Pearl. To him all the streets and their names might as well have been the same.

אלוהים, אבא

("Father, God…")

Weary, but he felt the strength of his mind rise as the water level of a dry lake, resurrected with life. From where he stood, Hayim decided to step into a yellowish brick constructed Georgian building that reminded him of those in Amsterdam, and in particular, the de Neufville brothers banking house.

It was a popular tavern. Fraunces Tavern. So popular, that every geometrically square table designed to seat four was accommodating no less than six. Long tables pressed with chairs one after another filled-in the remaining space, and they too were overrun. Beer flowed! Voices bellowed! The fireplace roared, and suddenly — in another collapsing of time, space, and circumstance, Hayim was unexpectedly ushered in!

"Comin' in out the cold to warm up a wee mite?"
Hayim was still absorbing the accent and deciphering the question when the man introduced himself —
"Samuel Fraunces! Welcome to me place."
In one fell swoop Samuel crammed his guest at a table and instantly returned with a cup of rum. Of course Hayim didn't know anyone at the juncture in which he was seated, and they did nothing more than glance at his presence while their bantering pitched and swayed over him just as the sea had done against him.
Everything was dizzying.
The rum —

"The King, I say— that bracket-faced, beetle-browed ensign bearer!"
Drunkards spiritedly tumbling over themselves and one another—
"Who wants to be English— look-look my arse— you see a stamp? I say, with no stamp, how'd they know I'm still officially English!"
Bellows of laughter! Bellows to the fire! To be hospitably welcomed but known to no one. The domestic heat and the welkin cold. The warm soothing, nip of alcohol through the blood and the correspondingly bitter chill in the drop of body temperature. It was a dizzying affair from all angles— not to mention that the patron's words, perspective, and directives were in striking contrast to what he knew, understood, and remembered from the mother country. He listened— what else could he do? And he listened— engaged in the noise of volleying conversations— these were the disgruntled voices and complaints of a colony.

While in London, two things out of the ordinary monopolized Hayim's time— searching for employment and bettering his English skills. Of the two, he found his talent for languages acute as ever with English. Without Elka or the family in his mists, as was the case in Amsterdam, he had no one to practice the subtle nuance of the language with. At temple, Yiddish or Hebrew were the language of choice and speaking English was even frowned upon. So it was the papers that he turned to for ordinary style conversation. He read them voraciously and aloud to himself in an effort to perfect his tongue and expand his vocabulary. This course of study led him to be exceptionally familiar with the English point of view in regard to the stewing bitterness amid the American colonies. He was unequivocally informed and versed, much more so than many Englishmen themselves. For he read the same articles in a repeated and disciplined manner until he could recite them verbatim. A majority of the publishing favored the internal pro-British attitude of the English government. Ironically, with the passage of time and geography, there he was, across the sea, seated with his ears peppered by grieved assaults in a variety of temperaments, ranging from cordial to rollicking, but all anti-British.

What came across, as the most shocking aspect of the grousing pioneers was that these subjects were surprisingly belligerent and indeed ungrateful? Among the high to low that wailed against the being forced to pay more for imports from countries other than the one providing for them.

They complained that their commerce was restricted and taxed! They decried western lands closed to them! Who was the King, they questioned, to require stamps and subvert their own currency? From the most benign to most fanciful accusations echoed about the room in a din of clanking, reeling, and jeremiads! This was the proverbial: other side of the coin. For Hayim who had just come from the prevailing opposite perspective, he wondered, didn't these people realize that they were indebted to the King and the nation that protected them, purveyed their culture, and provided them with manufacturing goods? They want representation they say, but they are no different than many in England— not all are represented in Parliament— these seats they decry— what seats are there for Liverpool, Manchester, Birmingham, there are no seats! They protest inequity as a child does to the parent— yet they are the child, and still the apple of the parent's eyes, the jewel in the English crown. In his hearing, they burned from this passion— these people seemed to be utter extremists. Hayim, like most people, never knew life or government without a monarchy— an unfettered and unorganized concept indeed! Was it not the system of power but the men in power of the system that corrupted the fate of populations? Rule without a king? Hath the king simply been benevolent, just, and fair. This New York— this America— and some, right there in the open, even talked of independence, and still others, of revolution! Incredible! Yet, in many aspects it reminded him of the folly of the Bar Confederation.

Samuel Fraunces reappeared to attend to his new patron. With the luxuriant of liquor and the warmth of fire, Hayim was apt to speak and in his heavily accented English asked the proprietor—

"Good man, can you say with certainty, the direction in which the Jewish section resides?"
Fraunces looked quizzically at him. Instinctively, Hayim concerned himself, that as a Jew, such averted eyes might lead to him being asked to leave or worse yet— roughed up. However, Fraunces coolly responded—

"Come again?"

"Which way to the Jewish district— the alley."

"Ah, come again, I can't say I know what you mean, me boy?" as Fraunces could easily say being a wee bit from twice Hayim's age.

"I say, where do the Jewish people reside?" Hayim pressed over the noise.

"This is New York, we all reside in New York!"

Hayim had to scratch his head.

"Say, what are you looking for?"

"A synagogue," Hayim thought and finally said.

"Like me church?"

"Yes, like a church!"

"There are all sorts of churches — all bits of churches around!" Fraunces assured him.

"But this one would have a star, a special star — six points" Hayim removed his grandfather's precious siddur from the satchel and showed Fraunces just what he meant.

"Ahhh…" Fraunces soughed.

***

Look upon our affliction and plead our cause and redeem us speedily for your name's sake, for you are a mighty redeemer. Blessed are you, O Lord, the redeemer of Israel.

It was before sundown and Hayim stepped into a small wooden building among the most pastoral scenery he had seen since leaving Poland. Exhausted, he crept forward, further and further up the aisle, until he nearly collapsed at the ark. Finally, he was in the Shearith Israel.

אלוהים אבא תודה

("Thank you, Father God.")

So tired was he, he tried to pray but the words stuck in his heart would not come to his mind. He remained knelt in contemplation, at one with his God as is a child falling asleep in its mother's arms. Suddenly, he heard the sound of footsteps. He was too tired from the travail, too spent to turn —

"Good evening," a voice spoke.

Hayim kept his head bowed. The salutation simply echoed and rolled over his consciousness, not resonating as someone addressing him but sounding ethereal in nature.

"Good evening," the voice spoke again.

With the second calling, the greeting rang in the fashion of an alarm. Hayim cocked his head around. Standing before him was a rather slender and serious looking man with a flowing beard, surely less his age. The man was Gershom Mendes Seixas.

***

XIV
GOD

"Here is my creed. I believe in one God, the Creator of the Universe. That he governs it by His Providence. That He ought to be worshipped."

Benjamin Franklin

אלוהים אבא
אלוהים אבא
אלוהים אבא

.אחד יהוה אלהינו יהוה ישראל ,לשמוע
Hear, All Israel, The Lord is our God, The Lord is One.

שלמה חיים בעלי צער
(Hayim, Son of Shelomo)

***

XV
COMMUNION

"The doctrine of divine providence is very full and complete in the sacred oracles. It extends not only to things which we may think of great moment, and therefore worthy of notice, but to things the most indifferent and inconsiderable"
John Witherspoon

As the sunset, a chilly night bloomed, and the two men broke bread at Seixas' home. The rotating spherical orientation… betoken in a paramnesian illusionary figment of warped time and space impacted by a body of uncertainty and faithlessness— aptly described mind you, but more simply understood: Hayim's ever-so-unconscious temporal compression, <u>CEASED</u>. The surreal psyche unmooring of his bearings was a mash of hollow: memories, travel, travail, tragedy, sorrow, sadness, incidents, accidents, and a deep-set impression of worthlessness. Everything that seemed: sped up, outside of his grasp, held locked within, disjointed, and woven together— suddenly all dissipated into a poised praise and calm landing. Within the man-made edifice of the Shearith Israel— a tear escaped him, but it had not drifted conscious emotion behind. It came instinctually from the confines of his own weary spirit— moved for his own physical well-being and safe harbor.

He was in the Lord's house— it was who he was, pained or overjoyed… and, he whispered faithfully in expedited gratitude— "Hear, Israel, the Lord is our God, the Lord is One." The life or death notion of the plight was over.

He had reached the destination bestowed upon him, as he had done so many inglorious times before. This hour of resurrection and light— prevailing in untied knots and a rabble of butterflies migrating— this inner sensation that had onset within him— aptly described mind you, or more simply symbolized: as akin to free-falling from a great dreamed height, and landing safely asleep under the covers. America warmly welcomed him, similar to how he was received in Amsterdam, many-many years (almost lifetimes) before.

***

Seixas was a native colonist and five years Hayim's junior. He made an immediate impression upon Hayim that reminded the well-traveled man of his first meeting with a then youthful Meyer Rothschild. The pattern consistently repeated itself in which providence associated Hayim with individuals younger than his own budding self. Seated across the table from one another, Seixas held in hand the paper Rabbi Schiff had vested in Hayim. He, too, couldn't read the Hebrew scrawled on the vellum but was well aware and excitedly pointed to the congregation's name and that of Franks!

"Did the rabbi tell you much of the Franks family?" Seixas warmly asked Hayim.

"Very little we spoke," Hayim said with a defensive sense of embarrassment. "Mostly to seek them— to seek out Shearith Israel."

"Well, you've successfully completed that task, haven't you?" Seixas was very relaxed just as Hayim was understandably tense. The host looked over the note, quite interested and titillatingly mystified.

"Hmmm... then, if I may: what's your purpose— say your— your, over arching purpose, in coming here— such an amazing distance?" Even though Hayim knew English, he wasn't entirely sure of what Seixas was asking or more, why he was asking him as such. The confusion must have appeared on his face but Seixas made a point of qualifying himself, hurrying to comfort Hayim—

"Please, don't get me wrong, this is asked among welcome!"

As much as Hayim was relaxed, comfortable, and securely on dry land, he was also naturally cautious, guarded, and feeling uncharacteristically vulnerable. It wasn't that he was expecting to receive any antagonistic behavior from his guest, however, he knew he was at the whim of Seixas— and if for any reason the man's whim opposed his personal presence, literally he would be out in the winter cold. Therefore, he was keen to carefully speak. Seixas handed him back the epistle from Rabbi Schiff and after supping his soup, spoke excitedly—

"May I inquire, when you were in London, did you happen to attend the Bevis Marks Synagogue?"

Hayim calculatingly held his response; scrutinizingly examining Seixas' anticipation of his response. The banker, broker, agent, believed he had learned from years of negotiating transactions and terms that analyzing the visage of another in suspense will likely unlock the secrets of their fundamental nature. He had successfully dealt with callous and cynical ministers, self-possessed royalty, and shrewd marketeers. In Seixas' beaming face, "trust" continually came to mind, but his mannerism remained careful.

"I know it is— on the west side— it's founded on a Sephardic congregation—

"I was on the east side."

"Oh," Seixas exhaled disappointedly.

Hayim had eaten very little, except for portions of bread and a larger than usual share of water. Seixas acted the good host and poured him another cup.

"I hope you don't mind my prying."

"No, it is nice to be interested in," Hayim graciously allotted him. Seixas carried on, partaking in a bit of the food on his plate. But he couldn't help but excite himself to learn more about his guest.

"Why would it be that you left England? I often hear the most exciting things— often, I say, when many speak of it— I mean beyond the political class."

Hayim mused before he concluded his answer—

"One could deem it not suitable for my particular abilities."

"I see, I see… and what particular abilities are those?"

"By trade I am a broker."

"A broker!"

Seixas broke out in self-amused laughter of familiarity, which drew Hayim to wonder if he said something accidentally funny.

"The banking business? Well, you won't find a more active market here than in England. There, I understand it that they need brokers by the handful— from India to the West Indies they seem to be speculating on the price of even the next hour in the following minute. Oh, I've come to examine that money and it's position of dominance is never in sufficient quantity for English, at least as I observe them."

"Is that so? Well, I have observed positions on monies from every angle of nations— and universally, it often appears to be exactly the same."

"What sameness is that?"

"Covetousness."

Seixas was impressed, even feeling a bit over his head with Hayim. He slowly nodded his head as he said—

"You're very smart, aren't you? You're obviously well-traveled— you understand finance and man's willfulness for it. Rabbi Schiff was—"

"How do you speculate—" Hayim cut him off. "Well, how do you and the others of the colony differ, that is if you see the English the way you do in relationship to finance?"

Seixas laughed. Now he felt slightly tested or again, over his head, that no matter what his opinion or observation was, Hayim would have a stronger position. Nevertheless—

"Surely, I could be wrong, but I believe we differ in tremendous human strides. We are a people of principle, before we are a people of profit! The English, as I have seen, are a people of profit in which principle is thereof defined."

Again, Hayim was surprised to encounter an anti-English sentiment just as he discerned in the pub.

"Might I ask and receive a wholly honest answer?"

"Of course," Seixas said.

Hayim paused for an extraordinary length, just to gather the full annunciation of his question and then he let it rip—

"Do you hate the English?"

An evening full of laughter as Seixas just had to chuckle, and the chuckle quickly elevated into laughter.

"Do I sound as such? I say, maybe I do by the words I use. But no, I do not hate. I merely wish."

"Wish for what?"

"Freedom. As a child does when it is old enough, from it's parents. I wish for an independent nation."

Seixas was another of those whom Hayim found confounding. However, his respect for the man brought him to interest in the furor, and it brought up a heightened intimacy in which he decidedly spoke more freely.

"I see. Yes, I think I see," Hayim said.

"And what do you see?"

"Mostly — discontent," Hayim, said.

"Very easy, I say, to see among, some of us."

"But you do not hate the English, per se?"

"It is simply time to be free— freedom— instead of used as mechanism and arms of commerce. Do you know that they have banned slavery?"

"Yes," Hayim said.

"But do you know what they don't ban? Their own export. They flood us with this muddle of humanity or morality —"

"Are you for the abolition?" Hayim asked.

"I believe in the full expansive definition of the word 'freedom,' Seixas said with conviction.

A long silence, marked by the sound of the wind blowing outside marked the passage of time in the moment between them. Hayim threw off his wary nature and continued the thread of conversation —

"Then… now, I will tell you truly," Hayim said before pausing yet again.

"Yes?"

"I will tell you truly if you want to know."

"Yes. What is it that I may know?" Seixas said.

"I hate the English," Hayim said boldly.

Seixas stared back in a mild sense of shock and Hayim coolly peeled off a piece of bread.

"I left England because they would not even enslave me. There is little in the way of opportunities for our people in their institutions of finance."

"Why, that is strange to hear; for the Franks come from, as I understand it— one of the most prominent banking families in all of our mother country."

"Well, I found it to be a closed society. That is why Rabbi Schiff gave me direction to come upon these shores. Excuse my forwardness, but do you know the Franks? Are they in your congregation?"
Hayim appeared somewhat worried, somewhat weary, as he couldn't shake fear. Seixas couldn't shake being amused and laughed with a certain air of glory.

"Worry not my friend, worry not, you have most certainly arrived," Seixas said.

***

There was something extraordinary about Seixas, something Hayim had never experienced in another individual. He was inherently peaceful. He radiated a calm, leisurely confidence, and congenial pleasantness— a nature that mimicked nature itself. Hayim found himself comfortable and comforted under the man's roof, in the man's country. Off the tenterhooks of peril and jeopardy this was without question an auspicious landing.

Gershom Mendes Seixas was twenty-seven years old on the day he met Hayim Shelomo and already he had been the minister of his congregation for six years. He was born with a unique significance, that he was a first generation American Jew. His father Isaac Mendes Seixas, was a Portuguese converso whose family, like Hayim's had to flee to London after Isaac's father was accused, in 1725, of secretly continuing to practice his ancient faith. In 1730, Isaac left London for New York, where in 1741 he did something culturally remarkable; he married Rachel Levy, an Ashkenazic Jew. Their intermarriage represented a symbolizing blending and eventual diminishing of distinctions between the two Jewish cultures. They themselves were not aware of this, but their son Seixas would in time embody a unique characteristic that distinguished American Jewry from the more socially stratified Jewish communities of the Old World. As he and Hayim spoke, Hayim knew he was speaking to a Jew, but there was a freshness, a newness, that marked him with an incredible quality of reinvigoration among the Jewish type.
Seixas grew up surrounded in affluence and as a result of the New York Jewish community at the time no more than three hundred or so, among anglo's as well.

Both sides of his family were among the successful bankers and merchants who characterized elite Jewish society in the colonies. However, Seixas was drawn to a higher calling than the accumulation of wealth. Early on, he chose a very different path for his life and answered the call to God.

As Seixas began his course of study, there were no more than 2,000 Jews scattered throughout the British Colonies, and of those, one hundred were in the New York congregation. There were other congregations, including Newport, Philadelphia, Richmond, Charleston, and Savannah, but none of them had an ordained rabbi. Cantors, known by the title "Hazzan" led the worships. So, there were no elders, resources, schools, or formal training. The majority of Seixas' education in his religion was self-taught. He learned from what he could from the few books, which were available in English about Jewish thought and history, but he also read extensively in general philosophy, history and the classics. He was well rounded in his study of human nature even more than Jewish doctrine.

Joseph Pinto was the resident Hazzan at Shearith Israel. He, too, was young, twenty-nine. He was Dutch, from Amsterdam, but at the time he took the position, he had come from London on recommendation. He was something of a talmid chacham and it was from Pinto that Seixas learned the Torah. In 1766, Pinto informed the congregation that was leaving for Europe to visit family. The truth was that he was secretly taking the position of chazan of the Sephardi community in Hamburg. Two years later when he hadn't returned, the Shearith Israel was left with a vacuum. Seixas, only twenty-two at the time, enthusiastically applied for the position as religious functionary. However, the congregation was considering various foreign candidates, with an eye toward someone slightly more aged. Nevertheless, Seixas presented himself to the leaders of the Shearith Israel. In the summer of 1768 the Trustees of the synagogue were justly proud that one of their own native sons had achieved such distinction, and they were evidently impressed with his complete educational set. Thereof, on July 3, 1768, they unanimously appointed Seixas as Hazzan. He was licensed by the New York State Legislature as a "Minister of Religion," with legal authorization to perform all clergy functions such as marriages and funerals.

***

Hayim and Seixas retired from their repast and the two men were lounged, but for a lack of a better term, before a quaint fire. Seixas sat without rocking in a rocking chair, nibbling on the middle colony deliquesce of dedicated tobacco; Hayim faced him, angled in the leeway between upright and slouched in one of those stout chairs carved in the curt lines of Puritan taste. From the outside in, it was a common and handsome two story traditional of the period. However, inside, it was more impecunious and under-furnished than the area accommodated.

"If you wish, you may retire here for the night," Seixas offered. "However, I insist," he concluded.
Hayim stared back without a word but a faint enough smile of appreciation.

"You may stay as long as you like," Seixas gladly added.

"Have you no companionship?" Hayim asked.

"A wife?" Seixas delighted and joked. "With an appearance like mine?"
On the contrary, Seixas had a youthful handsomeness with piercing blue eyes and like Hayim, straight jet-black hair. Hayim certainly didn't see anything wrong with Seixas' countenance and though he laughed along with him, something in his heart felt emptier than it had since his return to Leszno.

"For we both have no companionship," Hayim said with a somewhat self-effacing and reflective scoff.

"No, neither of us," Seixas returned with admitted laughter. However, Hayim wasn't laughing anymore. He quickly resolved into a meditation on the fire and unlike any other time in his life, spoke fluently as though addressing an Athenian dialogue.

"What is a man and his life without a wife and a family of his own?"

"Oh, one day, I intend to wed," Seixas said assuredly. "I might say to if you are keen to keep a secret that I have my eye on someone most beautiful. Oh she is beautiful, of first heart, and then of gaze. Her name is Elkalah. Elkalah Cohen. Maybe one day I shall marry her. And if so, I hope to have the biggest and most beautiful family about us."
Hayim was listening but continued to stare into the flames, before he looked back far enough that the two men made eye contact—

"You assure me, you know the Franks?"

"Yes, of course. Why would you question as such?"

"I've just come a long way, more than crossing the seas, I've come a long way and I have little grasp of what— ultimately for," Hayim said after a long delay.

"Are you suggesting a loss of faith?"

Seixas' guest withdrew from the line of questioning and drifted into another stream of thought—

"In some manner, would you say that you, or I, or we, are but half a man— living only a portion of life?"

"Well that is certainly a mouthful, I must say, but under what context do you derive your assertion?"

"That we have no companionship," Hayim said.

Seixas certainly never considered himself in such a deprived manner. The unusual question left the noise of the room to be consumed by the crackling of fire, and the mood to turn eerie— for which Hayim felt responsible and shamed of.

"I don't mean to be a gadfly!" Hayim said, embarrassed with a little burst of counter energy.

"You are welcome and accepted, notwithstanding a thing!"

Seixas offered him tobacco but Hayim declined. Then, on second thought, he wanted to touch it, smell it— hold it.

"If you are from Poland, where did you learn to speak English? I mean, in England, I suppose, yes?" Seixas asked.

"Yes."

"As queer as your accent is, you speak it well— quite well. And— if any, what other languages do you speak?"

"Oh, many, for I have traveled extensively," Hayim said, somewhat dismissively.

"And what is your first language?"

"Polish—" but Hayim quickly corrected himself, as though establishing is personal identity! "Yiddish! — Do you speak Hebrew?"

"No. But I sing it!" Seixas proclaimed. "Yiddish. Polish? And what other languages?"

"Well, I do not speak Hebrew, a word or two here or there, but not as well as I would like, so I will say that I don't."

"Singing it is well enough! God hears in all tempos," Seixas said with lightheartedness.

"I speak Polish, Russian, Italian, German, Spanish, and French."

"Besides English and Yiddish?"

"Yes," Hayim said.

"Say something in German, if you will."

Hayim thought for a moment, and in a peculiar way, both smiled and frowned as he said—

"Das meer ist salzig."

"What did you say?" Seixas asked, ever-so-amused.

"The sea is salty."

The hazzan laughed.

"I have heard German before, but I have not understood a word of it," Seixas said. "My, speak in Russian if you will. I have never heard Russian!"

"Yest' krysha nad golovoĭ."

"What an amazing sound! But now what was it that you've said?"

"There is a roof over my head."

"Yes! And I hope it does not leak!"

"Mam nadzieję, że to nie deszcz!" Hayim burst forward.

"What was it you said now— Russian?"

"Polish! I said, I hope it does not rain!"

They laughed together. It was a moment of bonding— of unconditional friendship forged. For Hayim, he hadn't spent more than a casual hour with any one person in relaxed conversation in years. He himself did not realize or consider that fact, but the muscles of his body relaxed and he enjoyed the communion of friendship.

***

"You say, again, there is no ghetto?" Hayim uttered in true disbelief.

"As I told you before, there are no places like pens for pigs in which Jews are herded and forced to live," Seixas rejoined, naively amused. "Is there such a thing in England, for if there is, I have not heard of it?"

Hayim marveled at the man's ignorance and naiveté. Instead of merely answering his question in good taste, Hayim played with his response and toyed with words—

"There are not so many of us in residency— there is no reason for a Jew to traverse the North Sea or the English Channel, there you can't be a Jew and be English— not by law— now my good fellow, did you know that?"

"No, my good fellow, I did not."

"But you're English, aren't you?" Hayim said shrewdly.

"I am colonist! I am a citizen of the crown."

"You're not a citizen, I just told you. You're a Jew! That makes you at best a subject and at worse... a light that darkness intends to extinguish."

Even in the relaxed state and manner, it appeared the sum of Hayim's experiences, were resting in a perlocution of frustration on the tip of his tongue. No more was he wide-eyed and making his way in the snow. Neither was he ambitious nor reinventing the monetary system. Nor was he a confident representative of naked financial enterprise. Furthermore, he was anything but a child straining to be taken seriously or an employee under priority. He sat there in the most intimate setting he had with a man of equal stature ever in his life. Hayim Shelomo had seen at least half of the world and he now had a whole opinion on it. For his part, Seixas understood Hayim's point, both spiritually and in terms of the political, besides the raw nature of fact— and it personally penetrated him to his core, adding to an already radical motivating force that churned in Seixas' psyche.

"What would you say our people's community is like in London?" Seixas asked.

"There is a small band of Sephardi, as you know, but it is dominated by Ashkenazi," Hayim said. "It is the same in Hamburg, Frankfurt—"

"You lived there?"

Hayim nodded.

"I see. We are both Sephardi, you and I. Well, I am of both, but this is a Sephardic congregation," Seixas said solemnly. "I'll tell you— they arrived here over a hundred years ago— coming they did, from Brazil." Even the annunciation of "Brazil," to hear someone say "Brazil" sounded utterly exotic to Hayim and his interest suddenly transfixed on Seixas' account.

"Twenty-three of them to be exact. Before that they were crypto's, mostly from Spain— well Portugal, too, and some originally from— well the names I don't know— of those scattered islands closely around. By the time they reached the port of Recife, all together they were more than twenty-three, a handful more."

It was cold and getting colder. Seixas momentarily withheld his narrative to stoke the fire and pour Hayim, and himself, cups of brewed cider in aid to their body temperatures, and then he continued —

"They reached New Holland — that's what they called Brazil, then, and they were able to erect a synagogue — they were settled, rather peaceably under the Dutch — till — well do you know of André Vidal de Negreiros?"

"No," Hayim said.

"Well," Seixas said before resigning into a somber exasperation instead of continuing on that narrative line. "The Portuguese gained control, and they had to abandon everything. Many of them accepted passage to Amsterdam, others to further reaches into ports of the Dutch West India Company, and a group of twenty-three settled here, when it was New Netherlands, the last stop before, you could say, the old Netherlands. And, so, here we are, today."

"'Today?'" Hayim said.

"Today."

With that the story was over. In truth he spoke it so fast that Hayim didn't comprehend it in full, though he understood the basic premise and Hayim too, exhaled in an exasperated sigh; drank his cider —

"3,000 years and we still wander deserts," Hayim ruminated.

"Yes, I suppose," Seixas, added.

"Why do you think we, the Jewish people — why are we so despised, rabbi?"

"Oh, know that I am not ordained. No, I am not. There is no one here to act to ordain me. I am in fact a hazzan, but I act as a rabbi. But "why," you ask?"

Hayim appeared to lean into the shadow of the light's fire and from within a growl in his stomach, he said —

"'Why?' I have seen much and everywhere I have ever been, the Jew is loathed, put upon, detested, ridiculed, cheated, herded, and yet tolerated, as personal gain will admit. Why, in truth — hazzan — or rabbi, do you suppose the world operates in tandem against us?"

"You ask one of the more profound questions, of course."

"I yearn for a profound answer — a profound solution — a profound change in circumstance."

"I will tell you, that I believe the solution is in this nation, if it is to be one. This will be a new —"

"The solution is entirely divorced of the cause! Before you utter the solution, convince me of the cause!" Hayim forcefully rebutted.

Seixas was a bit taken aback, but again, he was a calm individual that did not worry himself with the emotions of others.

"Yes, this is so. But you want why's, and cause, and reasons. Well, I may disappoint you, but there is no good reason. There are just reasons." Now Seixas was slightly cautious, due to Hayim's small burst of emotion. They stared into each other's eyes and Hayim sought to reasonably reassure him.

"Then let us examine these reasons, shall we? We are men of mind."

"Yes, we are men of mind," Seixas agreed. "You have seen much as you have recounted — "

"And more," Hayim interjected!

"Why do you believe it is the case that we are — "

"An abomination! You see things through the eyes of words in books and the course of history! Words and books and prayers — they are," he started excitedly but calmed in remorse and respect. "Excuse me... I know of this hate, it bears the order of my life."

"There can be no offense between us. I pity you, I commend you, and I sympathize with you, but there is no good reason for any of us, as men, as people, as God's creatures, to hate."

"What of the hate of those who hate you?"

"That, too, is without just reason. Be not prejudice against the prejudice, Hayim, nor hateful against those you hate — or angry with those angry at you. Tell me then, tell me true, if you have had occasion to bare this burden, why do you surmise the world hates us to the extreme? Don't ask me, tell me."

Hayim was incredible still and Seixas waited. Then —

"I will tell you. I will tell you what I know, from here, to here, to here," Hayim said between gnashed teeth, pointing to his head, then his heart — to the bottom of his feet. "As we so comfortably speak, the Jews of Poland are being expelled to the Pale of Settlement."

Clearly, Seixas' expression spoke that he didn't know anything about that or even what or where it was.

"And I can assure you the same will happen in greater Warsaw in due time. Name me, if you will, the first place that we as a people were first expelled?"

"Why, you could say the holy land, of course, or maybe Carthage, followed by Alexandria," the hazzan said.

"When?"

"Carthage? Roughly 250 AD."

"1,500 years. And since then! Italy! France! Bavaria! England! Austria! Spain! Netherlands! Prussia! Portugal! Lithuania! Worms! Vienna! Kiev! Naples! Mainz! And where not in the world— where not? Tell me where not?! The causes here are of no cause but mere excuse! If one takes away the cause, then these persecutions should not exist."

"You are saying that the cause is not the reason?"

"It is a veil— a justification! Just an excuse! They say we are too wealthy. I have known more poor Jews, in great swaths of humanity than I have of wealthy Jews in small courts and merchant professions! What of the wealthy Gentile? Is he too wealthy? Are they more numerous than the peasant? Absurdity abounds in this justification. I assure you on good account, which the number of Jews in abject poverty, begging for the tiniest of morsels is in a more extravagant number! They hate us— or so they said because we profess to be God's people. Well so don't they! All that bound together in groups and armies that have persecuted us, considered themselves charter members of the Will and linage of God, or their persecution bares no justice in their own distorted rationale. So it is we who are different? I beg you and them to consider that we are all different, all the same! They hate us for even being the objects of hate by which we are supposedly the cause of such hatred. You merely have been born of your mother's womb and your father's seed, and you have spent your time reading in books, studying in papers— I do not yearn to demean or offend, but what object made you subject to being despised for causing the contempt?"

Hayim waited, but Seixas gave no answer, just as Hayim suspected.

"Is it because we killed their Christ? It was not we. We are not the erectors of crucifixes nor were we the judge and jury of his guilt. It is convenient— it absolves them of their own hand soaked in blood. You see, we— we Jews are hated in paradoxes. The scorn for being lazy and inferior, but, for also being wealthy, industrious, and successful in finance. But that is nothing to the scorn for keeping to ourselves, or the paradoxical murdering of us, if we assimilate into their society!"

Seixas took a deep breath. He was moved by Hayim's thoughtfulness and the passion of his diatribe. However, he made no case for the actual answer and Seixas called him on it.

"I respect your worldliness. But I might add, that we are the light of the world, and in our laws, are man's true morality. Our morality is the direct gift of God most seen among the peoples of the world. But if everything you say is true, and I do not doubt that it is, then what is the true cause of this passionate disinclination toward us? You have not answered that question, my friend, I respectfully repeat— you have not answered your own question."

"My friend," Seixas said. In that moment, a brotherhood between them solidified. Hayim had Yankel, the farmer, members of his extended family, including Elka, de Neufville, Rothschild, and many others who befriended him through the years. Though, less the spirit of need, orchestration of business, drama of danger, condition of service, and the circumstance of family, did he ever have a deep friendship? With hearing, "my friend," said so freely and sincerely, his heart buckled under the weight of his own loneliness and esteemed Gershom Seixas as his most trusted friend.

"Let me tell you true," Hayim said. "For you are my friend, and I want you to know what I know."

"Yes," said Seixas in subtle agreement and kind acknowledgement.

"The answer you claim I denied you— I deny you no longer," Hayim said. "The answer: because it serves a purpose. Because it serves a purpose."

"What purpose is that, what purpose does it serve, stretched out over thousands of years? What purpose is there in hating, enslaving, defiling, and suppressing a people for thousands of years?"

"We, the Jews— we, serve the purpose of being a politically expedient entity— how do I say in English: scapegoats— we are the to fail— default scapegoats— yes, to deflect responsibility— any responsibility, in an aim to control the masses."

The two stared at one another, just staring....

"Say so if you like, I neither agree nor do I disagree, but I can say with certainty, not so in these Americas. You may call me a subject, but it won't be forever. America, Hayim, is different, it is very different" Seixas said with his patented spirit of conviction.

The host stood and quickly crossed to a box on a shelf that seemed to be for safekeepings. Then Seixas fumbled around and finally found what he was looking for, a key! He crossed again to the other side of what seemed to be an enormous room in the light of it being without much in the way of furnishings. He came to a trunk, which he pulled a bit from the wall to allow for the cover to swing all the way open. Then, he followed that exercise with an almost reverent turning of the key. With the expectancy of a father at the birthing labor of his child, he unfurled a wide swath of parchment— a broadside, and handed it to Hayim. Out of respect, and with an assumption that it was the Torah, Hayim accepted it with the same reverence as he read it aloud—

"Thursday afternoon, November 5, 1772. The True-born Sons of Liberty, are desired to meet at Fraunces Tavern at 12:00 o'clock, THIS DAY, to discuss resistance by Committees of Correspondence."

"Now His Majesty seeks to try His subjects no longer on the soil for which the crime is alleged, but under his nose in which he sneezes," Seixas said with contempt— a contempt that mirrored Hayim's.

"Hayim, as one Jew to another, I tell you— this is a new and different land, a new and different place! I don't know why it is and I don't why it has taken so long— but I believe that this loam is chosen and on it the creator placed us and all these people here to be a new people, a new government, a new society that does more than tolerate religion, but celebrates the individual above their collective heritage! Everywhere you have gone, you have been a Jew. Here, you will find, that you are first a man, and then a Jew, if you so wish. I believe we are at the birth of a new star, the glory of many promises, and it will be at the severing of our dependance from the British Crown."

Every word Seixas said burned in his eyes. As a matter-of-fact, the hazzan could have said nothing at all, but gazed in that expression and Hayim would have known every word his pupils represented. His words were alarm bells, and an ushering of angels of sorts. Poland was the land of milk and honey, or so said his father, but now he wondered if it was really just a shelter from the sun?

The host took his broadside back and with the same careful consideration in which he exhibited it, he locked it into the trunk, all the while speaking—

"It's late. I won't keep you from sleep any longer, but you can rest knowing you're not in fear to leave. Leave not until you're good and ready— spring, summer!"
Seixas' back was to Hayim and he couldn't see him warmly smiling. Finally, the good man turned, and said—

"Tomorrow you will come with me to dinner and meet in my opinion, a very great man. And— I assure you, his name will be Franks."

***

XVI

THE SIDDUR

"The law of nature and the law of revelation are both Divine: they flow, though in different channels, from the same adorable source. It is indeed preposterous to separate them from each other." James Wilson

Unquestionably, the siddur is the most read, handled and beloved Hebrew text next to the Bible. The ubiquitousness Semitic prayer books have steadily evolved from their original inception by Amram ben Sheshna. Amram possessed an exceptionally analytical and legal mind, but as the head of the Sura Academy, the foremost Yeshiva in Babylon, his heart was firmly rooted in the faith. In time, his rabbinical efforts brought him to be recognized and honored with the distinction and title of Gaon— honorable sage.

In ancient times, Jewish prayer services consisted primarily of reading the Torah, the five books of Moses and the Nevi'im, the book of prophets. The wheel of progress slowly began to churn in approximately 850 AD when Amram arranged these inceptive prayer services into a systematic code, a complete liturgy for the faithful— designed for both use in Temple and personally at home. This ritual arrangement was known as the Siddur Rab Amram. The word "siddur" means order or arrangement. The prayers in the siddur were arrayed to closely follow the order of sacrifices in Temple. For it was prayer in a synagogue, that came to take the place of sacrifices after the Temple. Amram's siddur set a uniformed standard for the procedure of these prayers and the compositions of new prayers themselves— which in time would serve as the modern foundation of all Jewish liturgies.

However, the siddur is more than just a prayer book. When properly understood, it is revealed as a vast repository of the Jewish faith. It is a record of the great victories and tragic defeats Israel has experienced during her long, beautiful, but brutal and tragic history. It is a testimony to the aspirations and hopes of the Jewish people for all time and it provides guidance into daily Jewish living and all lifecycle events in the calendar. It is for study as well as prayer; moral instruction and ethical guidance as well as personal pleas— therein, duties and rights are equally emphasized among the pages. These prayer books reside in a dimension of timelessness as a living tome and a true inspiration of divinity. Yet, maybe above all other considerations, the siddur provides a record of Israel's relationship with God, and that of the possessor of the book. By the time Hayim held his grandfather's prayer book— at what was his first break of twinkling dawn light in the new world, his recently strained relationship with God was fettled.

The book he held— stitched with the six-pointed star, was bound in a ragged tanned calfskin; tattered at all the edges and scribbled in the margins through almost every page. The Hebrew from the heart and hand of the grandfather, and his father before him, and like was his father before him— and even his father before who preceded them all. Hayim was illiterate to their worship and veneration, and devotion. He could not read a single word that was written, though of the prayers, he knew all of them by heart, word for word.

This hour was reserved for God. He had slept enough— the old type of sleep, in which his eyes involuntarily closed and everything in dense matter was absolutely forgotten to dream-state. But he unexpectedly woke, just as the first particle of dawn energized into a visible spectrum. His first and only thought was "Yahweh." And, Hayim Shelomo, comforted by the grace of a stranger, Gershom Mendes Seixas, thousands of miles from any location he might be able to conceive as home, penitently felt chastened, ashamed, and appreciative to his God.

"Father, God," he said quietly aloud, in a euphonious tone. "Thank you... not for what you have done for me— Father, God... nor where I find myself in safety and kindness... nor the favorable outcome of my passage... but thank you, Father God, for your patience of me." He held his eyes closed and his hands pressed upon the siddur, essentially squeezing the hand of God. "If you further trust upon me your will, Father, God— it shall be done."

***

XVII

DESTINY

"There is a destiny which has the control of our actions, not to be resisted by the strongest efforts of human nature." George Washington

"You're wishing to understand what this says, yes?" Moses Franks said with a bellow of laughter, turning his gaze from Seixas to Hayim.

"Precisely! What does it say, my friend?" Seixas implored him. Moses Franks was holding in his hands the bit of parchment Rabbi Schiff had written on for Hayim to carry with him in passage to the colonies. Most of what was scribbled was done in Hebrew. However, at the bottom the rabbi wrote in English for Hayim to be able to read and remember— and this consisted of merely the name of the congregation and that of "Franks." Moses Franks was relishing a grin. With his audience waiting, he nonchalantly revealed the answer.

"What can I say, it is a letter of recommendation, of passage— you could say, of proof. Oh, it recounts a little story of my grandfather— and his fortune in a lottery— it appears of a ticket he shared with Moses Hart. I assume you know who Mr. Hart is? He speaks a bit here of his great synagogue."

"A story, tell us the story, father," a young boy seated among them excitedly said.

"No, I'm afraid it's not story time," Franks declared rather dismissively. "I'm trying to make clear that the good rabbi is merely assuring any Frank that handles this commendation— as I presently— that the question of character— of which the rabbi knows our character... and is sending to us a gent of the same quality, of character that is," Franks fumbled through saying as he continued to glance and transcribe. "And it is that you do not read Hebrew?"

"That is all, but there is so much script!" Seixas said.

"Well yes-yes, that appears to be about, the most of what it says," he rather coyly remarked.

Still grinning, Franks went about and folded the paper as though it was personally his own; going so far as to coolly place it in his coat pocket. Hayim found this action quite strange, as it was his from Rabbi Schiff. Yet, he knew he did not necessarily need it anymore and so he dismissed the curious conduct.

"Again, my honored guest, I ask, you do not speak Hebrew?"

"Would you believe it, he speaks a multitude of tongues, but ironically, no, he doesn't," Seixas enthusiastically jumped in and unsolicitedly spoke for Hayim.

"But you keep your Hebrew name? Interesting."

"For so it is my name," Hayim said evermore confused by Franks' indisputably sagely authority.

"And you've never had found occasion to anglicize it?" Franks continued.

"Moses, Hayim is not from London!

"I thought I was made to understand —"

"No, he was an immigrant. He had only been there approximately a year. A year, is that correct?" Seixas asked Hayim.

"Eight months, post my arrival from Poland."

"Where's Poland," the young boy spoke again, out of turn.

"Isaac, you're place, thankfully at times, is not to ask questions," Franks said very low in his breath, gently reprimanding his son.

"Yes, father."

"Now, where was I, well you see, my grandfather's name at birth was Naphtali Hirsch! Yes, Poland, how exotic," Franks suddenly made sure to mention, as not to appear to be so rude, what his guest had said. "So, too my grandmother, she was born Sarah Phila, until it was anglicized to Abigail. Oh, the beauty of becoming English!" he ended with a laugh. Isaac, the young boy laughed along with him, as to communion with his father. But they were the only two in laughter.

"Interesting," Seixas said, though he had no idea why this was a topic of conversation from Franks.

"What I am trying to convey is that it is common in this language to simplify our Hebrew names."

"Yes, yes it is," Seixas, said, now understanding where Franks was leading his monologue.

"So I am a Franks, as my grandfather became— Abraham. Abraham Franks, was the chosen derivative of his name. And you, you are Hayim Shelomo, yes?"

"Truly. I am, the Son of Shelomo," Hayim said rather proudly.

"Well, I impart upon you, that people prefer monikers that are easy to sound, to remember, and fit in the diction of their language. You are my guest and my hospitality is paramount to my personal opinion, but may I make a discourteous suggestion?"

"'Discourteous'?" Hayim said, clearly unsure what it meant.

"Moses, you don't mean to be ill-mannered," Seixas requited, being cordially stuck between the two.

"On the contrary. But I acknowledge my instinct here is impolite."

"Please speak openly, speak what you intended to say. This is your home, I am but a guest, and even as a guest, I assume I am free to disagree or depart," so said Hayim.

"Certainly," said Franks. "Well then— first, are you intending to travel back to Europe—"

"Back? To Europe?"

"Yes, to leave us permanently?"

"I have just arrived!"

"Permanently?"

"At least until I return to dust." said Hayim.
Everyone had a laugh, and finally—

"Fair enough." said Franks. "Then you are now forevermore, Haym Salomon, not Hayim Shelomo. Haym Salomon!"

Just as the sound penetrated Hayim's hearing, he heard the name as one can feel the wind. Something came over him; he didn't just hear it— he felt it, and it felt uncommonly refreshing.

***

It was already the second hour of the evening, the topics had ranged from the financial markets and the credit crisis, to public finance, colonial administration, mercantile policy, and Franks "good friend," Samuel Adams and the new found Committee of Correspondence. What hadn't been discussed directly was: revolution. However, the topic made it's way into the conversation and Franks and Seixas engaged in a mutual appreciation society of one another's similar positions— though it was odd that Moses would disagree and yet easily concede to Seixas' patriotic point of view. Hayim was still staring down at his plate, cutting his beef as Franks' laughter came to a slow ceasing. The guest hesitated for a moment, then calmly took a bite and chewed the tasty serrated and cooked flesh—

"Excuse me, but dare I opine, wouldn't it be wise to reflect on the dangers inherent in sudden and violet innovation of government? I have come from a country that is gradually losing its governance and I wonder if good government contains within itself the means for legal and legitimate change."

"Hayim, are you suggesting that revolution is illegitimate?" Seixas asked.

"Legitimacy will be made by the winners if war were to break out," Hayim said.

"How astute!" Franks delighted!

"Nonetheless, these are the conversations of learned men. I am a simple man."
His humbleness was amusing if not convincing. Hayim turned his head back to his plate and while his guests waited for me. Turning his eyes up, he saw the spotlight was still on and the stage was all his—

"It is true— I am essentially a man of practical finance as is a farmer intrinsically a man of practical real estate."

Franks was doubly amused and impressed. Around him at the large formal table sat his daughter Rachel— all of ten, and her older brother of two additional years, Isaac. The setting was a matter of full blown opulence and Moses Franks was a full blown bear of a man; gregarious to say the least.

By the time of this meal, Moses was already fifty-five years old. He wasn't so much fat as he was just exceptionally full-figured and thick. Large he hovered, in every way. They say some carry their heart on their sleeve, well Moses Franks carried his soul on his jacket like a dollop of spilled gravy and he wore a mask of generosity and goodwill over his venal intentions which endued him with a genius advantage to see into the inscrutable motives of others. As unappetizing or unappealing as the dollop may have sounded, he was impeccable in fashion, manners, and presentation. Endowed with a deep baritone for a voice, every word he said carried like thunder and struck the ear like lightening. At all times he sweat profusely — even if it was -20 below zero. Yet, it made him seem stylish, especially that he continuously dabbed his handkerchief with a suave flair. Most notably of all his idiosyncrasies was that he never stopped speaking — exaggerating, but just barely, even as he slept. He carried on conversations aloud just the same as others snore. Heaven be helped the hour he is called, for no room, home, mansion, building, or plot of land was ever vast enough to comfortably engirdle him. It seemed that his personality more than his girth extracted the majority of oxygen in any given space he occupied.

He was the son of Jacob Franks and Abigail Levy. His father was an exceptionally prosperous merchant in New York, having arrived from London in the late 1720's. By Moses' teens, they were one of the most prominent Jewish families, both of England and the colonies, on par with the Van Dam's, Beekman's, and DeLancey's. So wealthy and well connected were they that his grandfather, Abraham was an intimate of King George and nine years before had loaned the monarch the most valuable jewels in his crown for the coronation. Not to mention, a further eight years before, he arranged for the transportation of a Lester and Pack bell on the family ship Myrtilla for the colonial city of Philadelphia. As London seemed closed to Hayim, for the Jewish Franks success there ostensibly came easily.

He was also the brother of David Franks of Philadelphia. From there two integrated their merchant endeavors moored to the family interests in London, all the way up to King George. David was a staunch Loyalist and his wife and children fierce Loyalists.

The Franks were not only in America but well established in Canada where Moses and David's brother, Heartsy, moved the family from Philadelphia. David's loyalist position made the more religious branch of the Franks uncomfortable. David S. Franks, was also conscious to use the "S," in announcing himself, as not to be confused with his uncle. Further, his loyalties favored the colonial position.

It could be said that the Franks were a very serious-minded, educated, driven, and talented family, from top to bottom. Their learning and accomplishments were extensive. To a man and a woman, they lived life like worker bees, always pushing forward, producing more, looking to the future. Reared and instilled with initiative, they were divinely blessed with supreme superlative luck. Good fortune seemed to be their pedigree. Abraham Franks, the family patriarch was the twelfth and therefore last of the original twelve Jewish brokers admitted into the London stock exchange, which established a maximum quota of just twelve Jewish men that was still in effect. As luck would have it, his bother Isaac happened to win a £20,000 pound lottery, which he entered into with Moses Hart, the founder of Duke's Place Synagogue, the same synagogue, which Rabbi Schiff gave Hayim direction to his destiny. As the story goes, the two young men shared their winnings but Isaac was able to promptly double his money by marrying up, to the daughter of his friend and lottery partner, Moses Hart. The Franks' brothers and Hart family, Sephardic and Ashkenazi Jews alike, combined their wealthy, interest, and influence to dominate English Jewry. The brothers Franks collectively succeeded in establishing a powerful reach of enterprises in London, eventually stretching to Philadelphia. Each succeeding generation excelled in their chosen profession, and when Abraham Franks' son, Jacob, arrived in New York, he went about taking the Jewish community by the old preverbal storm.

Jacob found the Jews in New York colony to be a second-class group among the various religious communities. He set about purchasing a cemetery and infused the fledging Shearith Israel congregation with money and life. Being the importer of the best goods from London at the cheapest price, his business expanded rapidly as Moses and his siblings grew. He sold among other things: nails, spikes, spades, shovels, rods, frying pans, anvils, vices, and small guns. Though he made his fortune in the colonies, he was English to the bone, and a loyalist through and through.

At home, between he and Abigail, they produced Moses and eight siblings. Abigail Franks was a most colorful woman. She ran the house, not with an iron fist, but an iron tongue. She was opinionated, outspoken, and dominated every aspect of the family's life by her tastes and expectations. Though mots interestingly, above all, she detested organized religion. This in ironic coincidence and fact that her husband, was for a time the Shearith parnas. Little Moses had the privilege of being her favorite son; nevertheless, it was childhood of strict observance, classical education, and the arts. You could say, Moses and his brothers and sisters were born into a liberal arts college and spent everyday in the classroom — so was their childhood rearing. You could also say, though it would be as true as mentioning that the sky is blue, that Moses Franks wouldn't hurt a fly, even if you asked him to. However, the human heart was the least of his concerns — at best maybe a rook to sacrifice. Money, not morality was the principle commerce of his concern.

***

"Father, if we're finished, I'll clear the table," Rachel said.

"Shall we take it to the drawing room?" Franks asked his guests.

"Yes, and I shall clear the table!" Rachel redoubled her effort.

"Good then," her father said.

"Does anyone want tea?" asked Rachel.

"Rachel, my dear, are you sure you're finished with your meal?" Franks then kindly said to his daughter.

However, in point of fact, Rachel's plate was still full. Not only was she the last to sit, but also she spent the meal dutifully attending to each occurring need of the guests. Her mother had tragically passed away five years earlier from pneumonia and almost since then, she took it upon herself to embody the role of wife or woman of the home, without complaint or second thought. She may have only been ten years old, but as it is commonly said, she seemed much older, especially in the course of tending to things. Regardless of the fact that she hadn't eaten more than a few bites, Rachel quickly set about removing the dishes from the table and preparing the drawing room for further conversation.

"Oh Father," she responded and went about cheerfully clearing the table.

The men and the children gathered amid the drawing room, a plush setting awash mainly in brocade velvet powder blues. Aglow by a picturesque fire brought aflame by young Isaac, it was a warm soothing setting. Franks played the flute while Hayim slid his finger across volume after volume of books, pamphlets, and articles shelved against a wall that was from floor to ceiling decorated in tomes: Vergil, Jean-Jacques Rousseau, Horace, Justinian, Voltaire, Nepos, Beccaria, Caesar, Tacitus, Lucretius, Eutropius, Phaedrus, Herodotus, Thucydides, and Plato, Polybius, Aristotle, and Cicero. Subjects of Latin, logic, rhetoric, as well as arithmetic, geometry, astronomy, and music. Even though there were but five people in the room, the large oil painting of Sarah Franks that hung over the mantel gave the impression that she was impassively taking in the conversation. Per usual, Rachel was busily pouring cups of English tea when her father, silent for all of a minute broke into an impassioned exploration!

"Please, if you find something of interest," Franks freely offered to Hayim.

Then returned to his beloved instrument. He was playing the second violin part of Handel's baroque "Hallelujah."

In particular, two of the articles crept forward under Hayim's fascination. The Spirit of the Laws, by Charles-Louis de Secondat, baron de La Brède et de Montesquieu, and John Locke's, Two Treatises on Government. The former described checks and balances on government by dividing the functions of power between three separate branches to protect liberty. In the latter, Hayim would later hear for the first time the phrase: "Life, Liberty, and property." These were the works of classical liberalism, that in short time, would enlighten Hayim on the path that man must pursue for God and country.

***

As Moses played the violin, Seixas spoke over it in asking him aloud —

"Moses, would you accompany me in inviting Hayim to join our congregation?"

"Wonderful idea!"

"Hayim, we'd like you to extend an invitation to you to join on congregation," Seixas said, shouting over the music!

Be it his fascination with the literary titles or the beautiful sound of the music, Hayim didn't seem to hear him.

"Hayim, I said we'd very much like you to join on congregation," Seixas said raising his voice!

Yet, still Hayim didn't respond. His entire attention was fixated upon a passage from Two Treatises on Government:

> "If man in the state of nature be so free, as has
> been said; if he be absolute lord of his own person
> and possessions, equal to the greatest, and subject
> to no body, why will he part with his freedom?
> Why will he give up this empire, and subject
> himself to the dominion and control of any other
> power? To which it is obvious to answer, that
> though in the state of nature he hath such a right,
> yet the enjoyment of it is very uncertain, and
> constantly exposed to the invasion of others: for
> all being kings as much as he, every man his
> equal, and the greater part no strict observers of
> equity and justice, the enjoyment of the property
> he has in this state is very unsafe, very unsecure.
> This makes him willing to quit a condition, which,
> however free, is full of fears and continual
> dangers: and it is not without reason, that he seeks
> out, and is willing to join in society with others,
> who are already united, or have a mind to unite,
> for the mutual preservation of their lives, liberties
> and estates, which I call by the general name,
> property."

Young Rachel approached him and kindly tugged on his jacket. Hayim swung around and wildly looked to Moses—

"Have you read this?"

"Why, yes, of course!"

"I'd like, very much to read this."

"Be free," Moses said.

"Hayim, sir, they are asking you of your desire or willingness to become part of our congregation," Rachel cutely said, a few tugs more.

He was surprised by the question and taken with Rachel's dutiful demeanor, as he once remembered Elka.

"Yes, Hayim, we'd be honored if you were to join the congregation!"

"No, it would be my honor," he said.

Even though Hayim said as such, his eyes glared at the book.

"Then it is settled!" Seixas said.

Rachel beamed and her father sent a musical rift through the room— a sound of celebration.

"Wait!" Hayim exclaimed! "I'm sorry, but what is the tax?"

Franks roared with laughter!

"You are a banker for sure! A man always with money on his mind!" Franks boisterously declared.

"I am a man without sufficient means, that is what I am," Hayim said in somewhat defense of himself.

"Never-the-mind, it will be adjusted to your welfare," Seixas assured him.

"Tell us another story," young Isaac requested.

"Yes, you already told us of the kings and queens, what other stories do you have to share?" Rachel chimed in.

Seixas was reveling in the enchantment the Franks were taking in Hayim. It was the same delight he enjoyed in his company.

"Stories! Stories! Who wants to hear stories! Tell us stories not, I declare! Tell us of truly yourself!" Franks bellowed.

Hayim hadn't been the captivating focus of a group or family since Amsterdam, and he, too, delighted in the atmosphere of sober family and friends.

"Well, let me recount— what have I not already told you? I'm come from Poland."

"And your family?" Franks asked.

"Spanish, like us!" Seixas said.

"Portuguese," Hayim corrected him.

"Yes, we know all that, tell us a story, something of adventure!" Isaac implored.

Again, this reminded him of his warm and meaningful relationship with Elka, which was, of age, personally, the closest experience to his heart.

"He's traveled far and wide, I must say— and speaks many languages!" said Seixas.

Suddenly, an operatic tone of voices speaking at almost the same time, one after the other — over one another filled the room —

"So you've said," Franks remarked.

"What places have you been to?" asked Isaac.

"What languages do you speak?" asked Rachel.

"He's already spoken of that," Franks said, in a somewhat playful battle with his children. "More of importance, what plans do you have for your welfare and success?"

Hayim held up his hands to quiet the barrage. He'd heard each and every question and one-by-one, he labored in which order to answer them.

"Well-well, to answer you, I have been to many places and lived in many countries," Hayim said, directing his words to the children.

Then, he paced in a tight circle and mused on how to answer Moses.

"Mr. Franks, I am not for certain of my intentions, that my welfare is accounted for, except to eventually ply my trade."

"As a broker?" Moses asked.

"Yes," Hayim said. "However, until then, I was considering... dry foods."

"'Dry foods'," Seixas chimed.

"What have you for money?" Franks cut to the quick and straightforwardly asked Hayim.

"With all due respect, but a portion that might suit me to start."

"Just a portion?"

"Well, how much capital does one need to commence a dry foods store?" Seixas entered fully into the exchange.

"If my portion is in inadequate, I will venture to endow myself until such time that I can proceed," Hayim said.

"Doing what?"

"Whatever anyone will ask of me. So I did in London."

"Odd jobs?"

"If I am so fortune," Hayim humbly replied.

Moses Franks was impressed. Hayim clearly appeared to him to be a man of process over outcome, and he knew this was the type of man that could stand the unforeseen darkness and still walk into the light.

"Of course-of course," Franks commented.

"I will do as much as necessary, to assist you, Hayim," Seixas added.

"No need-no need. If it is dry foods, there is already much we can do to bring your fruit to bear."

"Would you, Moses?" asked Seixas.

"Of course-of course," Franks said, taking out of the piece of paper he had placed in his pocket and holding it up. "Just as Rabbi Schiff requested."

Rachel took the piece of folded paper from her father's hand and unraveled it. She could read Hebrew and unsolicited, she began to translate and read it aloud—

"Let this portion of this correspondence serve as a personal request to anyone of the Franks family to endow Hayim Shelomo with the requisite aid which will allow him to endeavor the disciplines of his unprecedented talents. - Sincerely, Rabbi David Tevele Schiff, London," Now, Hayim really knew what was actually written in Hebrew and his true indebtedness to the rabbi.

***

XVIII
AWAKENING

"Is life so dear or peace so sweet as to be purchased at the price of chains and slavery? Forbid it, Almighty God. I know not what course others may take, but as for me, give me liberty or give me death!" Patrick Henry

To the Inhabitants of the Province of the Massachusetts-Bay.

MY DEAR COUNTRYMEN,

AWAKE! — Awake, my countrymen, and, by a regular & legal opposition, defeat the designs of those who enslave us and our posterity... shall you, the descendants of Britain, born in a Land of Light, and reared in the Bosom of Liberty — shall you commence cowards, at a time when reason calls so loud for your magnanimity?... This is your duty, your burden, your indispensable duty. Ages remote, mortals yet unborn, will bless your generous efforts, and revere the memory of the saviors of their country....

I exhort you to instruct your representatives against promoting by any ways of means whatsoever, the operation of this grievous and burdensome law. Acquaint them fully with your sentiments of the matter... They are clothed with power... to be faithful guardians of the liberties of their country.... Happy, thrice happy should I be, to have it in my power to congratulate my countrymen, on so memorable a deliverance;

whilst I left the enemies of truth and liberty to
humble themselves in sackcloth and ashes.

With a combined teaspoon of copperas and tannic acid, a pinch of gum
arabic, and a pint of rain or distilled water, this was the battle cry sounded
and pressed in sable shade spread across the weekly rag linen of the
Boston-Gazette, October 7, 1765. In twenty-three more days, what was
commonly referred to as the Stamp Act was poised to come into effect.
The North American Colonies were Britain's prized possession, arguably
the center of their imperial majesty, and in way of commerce, their most
trusted principle-trading partner. By 1772, Sixty percent of British overseas
trade was Americanized and the American colonies had long been a vital
source of trade for their mother country. In spite of that, following the
Seven Years' War— the same global hostilities that served as the backdrop
of Hayim's successful stint with de Neufville, relations between Britain
and her prized possessions began to fray. The conclusion of the conflict
marked the victory of the British Empire, as well as the start of their
reputation as one of the most powerful countries in the world. Popularly
and locally the Seven Years' War was known as the French and Indian
War, it was the North American Theater of the warfare. Britain would
eventually defeat France, however, the conflict of war was not without
significant cost and blood-red sacrifice.

The lives that were lost, the ships and supplies that were destroyed, and
the damage that was laid, were the cause of unprecedented financial
wounds upon the austere empire. Subsequently, Parliament decided to
change an aspect in their rule, to redirect the administration by collecting
more proceeds from the colonies to cover for war debts and military assets.

From Parliament to people on the street, triumph and victory over
their arch rivals in the Seven Years' War was soon muted by the realization
of an immense increase in the national debt, leading to strong anxieties
about bankruptcy. The financial crisis spurred fears at the rising costs in
both money and blood to support the American colonies, in particular the
additional cost incurred by their possible expansion, which the Americans
were haughtily clamoring for.

In the mists of fighting the Algonquin, Mohawk, and Shawnee Indians, along with the French, the British lost one of their allies on the battlefield, the Cherokee. Again, the British were on the hook to defend the Americans in what became the Cherokee War. Lasting two years, it expanded the scale of the British theater of war and expediently added to the cost of conquest. Following the ceasing of all hostilities, in the British Parliament, they already conceded that it would be difficult to halt the disorderly tide of colonial expansion, and at the projected cost of future indian wars, they had to find a counterbalance. As for the colonists, who now were considering themselves, "Americans," the atmosphere of laissez-faire prosperity during the Seven Years War gave way to a post-war period of increased economic depression. The goodwill, patriarchal link, and cooperative mood in the American colonies towards Britain quickly began to transform into an overripe fruit hankering to fall from the tree. Political consciousness was the new enlightenment, and it was evident amongst the colonists.

It was against this background, that on February 13, 1765, the Chancellor of the Exchequer presented a Bill to the House of Commons at the instigation of the Prime Minster, entitled with a length of name for the ages: "A Bill for granting certain Stamp Duties, and other Duties, in the British Colonies and Plantations in America; and for applying the Same towards further defraying the Expenses of defending, protecting, and securing such Colonies and Plantations."

The American Stamp Duties Bill was devised as a measure not only to raise revenue in both the North American colonies and the West Indian plantations towards the cost of defending these areas during the war, but also to make them more directly responsible for bearing the burden of the overall increased cost of supporting them. The provisions of the bill were quite unremarkable and merely required certain goods to bear a revenue stamp, similar to those already used in Great Britain, and for which a fee was payable to the government for such "stamping." The proposed legislation sought to impose duties on all legal and official papers, such as deeds, wills and ship's papers, as well as on pamphlets, newspapers, dice and playing cards. It was expected that the measure would rise upward to £100,000.

The bill met with little real opposition in the House of Commons, and although several petitions were received against its provisions, these were swiftly rejected. The Commons passed the bill with some minor amendments on February, 27, 1765, and the following day it was sent up to the House of Lords, where it prompted even less debate. The Lords agreed to the proposal without amendment on March 8, and it ultimately received Royal Assent by commission, as George III was ill and unable to attend Parliament, on March 22, 1765. The bill read as follows:

> 1765 American Stamp Act: 5 George III, c. 12. "An Act for granting and applying certain Stamp Duties, and other Duties, in the British Colonies and Plantations in America, towards further defraying the Expenses of defending, protecting and securing the same; and for amending such Parts of the several Acts of Parliament relating to the Trade and Revenues of the said Colonies and Plantations, as direct the Manner of determining and recovering the Penalties and Forfeitures therein mentioned."

When the Act received Royal Assent, the standard formula of words used for granting assent to Supply Bills was written across the top in Anglo-Norman French: "Le Roy remercie ses bons Sujets, accepte leur Benevolence, et ainsi le veult" (The King thanks his good subjects, accepts their benevolence, and wishes it thus).

**

Hayim Shelomo entered Fraunces' Tavern for his second time in three days. Accompanied by Seixas, the meeting of the Sons of Liberty was already underway and heated. Tobacco smoke clouded the air from one end of the tavern to the other— to such a degree that little more than figures of men could be seen. It was chiefly a rude and undigested mass. Men were assembled to discuss politics. These men were primarily from the mercantile class— artisans, traders, lawyers and local politicians. In whole, they were neither the upper echelons of the social rung, nor the least fortunate of classes. Though, at the time it would not have meant anything to Hayim, but flitted around like the brightest objects in the sky were: Marinus Willett, John Lamb, and Isaac Sears. The topic du jour was the HMS Gaspée and shadow governments; the superseding of the colonial legislature and royal officials, and hotly— open revolt against the British Colonial Government, the Crown, and Parliament. Where others would have been aghast at some of their notions, these men were underwhelmed by their own schemes and devices. It was well known that British authorities kept a watchful eye on the activities of these rabble-rousers and those alike across the colonies, especially in New York. The smug loyalists derided them as the Sons of Violence, instead of the Sons of Liberty. They were known as the most rowdy, dangerous, and proactive of all the Sons of Liberty, for not all demonstrations they undertook were peaceful. In May 1766, the New York Sons, some of the same men in the room, interrupted the opening night performance at a new theater by shouting, "Liberty!" and forcing the audience into the street. Wigs and other signs of class distinction were taken from the theatergoers. The building was pulled down and the resulting jumble of wood was used for a great bonfire! However, by 1772, the political group had come of age by over the years having absorbed all the local resistance to British rule that propagated from the fomenting opposition to the Stamp Act. From the Boston Caucus Club to the Loyal Nine, they promulgated into a well coordinated and functioning underground partisan resistance movement. Individually they referred to themselves as "Whigs." They weren't related to the British Whig party but they took their name from the parties overarching definitions of parliamentary power and constitutional government superseding monarchial authority. For their part, they purely opposed the King's right to power over them. Collectively, they were widely known as: "The Sons of Liberty."

***

In 1765, as the cry went out across the Massachusetts-Bay, the British government was confounded by the attitude and vehement opposition of the colonists. December 1765, the London Gazette, ran the following:

> The riotous behavior of the people in Boston is remarkable. I would have been less surprised by their behavior if we had taxed their beer, because everyone drinks beer. But the Stamp Act is a tax on none of the necessities of life.
>
> It does not affect the poor. And even a poor person can afford this little amount of money. The tax on newspapers only affects the rich— common people do not purchase newspapers. Isn't it surprising, then, that the mob in Boston has begun to riot against this tax even before it has officially gone into effect?

This was the cultural and political standstill, the mindsets, and the schism between the crown and an influential portion of her subjects. Mr. George Grenville, during his brief administration as Prime Minister, adopted the ill-fated plan for replenishing the exhausted treasury of Great Britain, that is: the Stamp Act. It had been often proposed before, but rejected by every preceding minister. However, in this great time of national financial crisis and need, it was poised to become law. As previously stated, the bill met with little real opposition in the House of Commons; the "real" and "opposition" aspect was to be embodied in the form of a man: Colonel Isaac Barré.

Isaac Barré was an Irish solider and politician who served with admirable distinction in the Seven Years' War. He strongly opposed the pending legislation and from the tread of his experience down to the fire in his belly, he indignantly replied to the charge of ingratitude, leveled upon him by Charles Townsend. The man who also paternalistically labeled the Americans, as "children planted by our care, nourished by our indulgence, and protected by our arms."

"They planted by your care?" said Colonel Barré on the floor of the House of Common. "No! Your oppressions planted them in America. They fled from your tyranny to a then uncultivated and inhospitable country, where they exposed themselves to almost all the hardships to which human nature is liable; and, among others, to the cruelties of a savage foe, the most subtle, and, I will take it upon me to say, the most formidable of any people on earth; and yet, actuated by principles of true English liberty, they met all hardships with pleasure, compared with those they suffered in their native land from the hands of those who should have been their friends. They nourished by your indulgence? They grew by your neglect of them! As soon as you began to care about them, that care was exercised in sending persons to rule them, who were, perhaps, the deputies of deputies to some members of this House— sent to spy out their liberties, to misrepresent their actions, and to prey upon them; men whose behavior on many Occasions has caused the Blood of those Sons of Liberty to recoil within them; men promoted to the highest seats of justice; some of whom, to my knowledge, were glad, by going to a foreign country, to escape being brought to the bar of a court of justice in their own. They protected by your arms? They have nobly taken up arms in your defense; have exerted a valor, amid their constant and laborious industry, for the defense of a country whose frontier was drenched in blood, while its interior yielded all its little savings to your emolument. And— believe me— remember I this day told you so— that same spirit of freedom which actuated that people at first, will accompany them still. But prudence forbids me to say more. God knows I do not, at this time, speak from motives of party heat. What I deliver are the genuine sentiments of my heart. However superior to me in general knowledge and experience the respectable body of this House may be, I claim to know more of America than most of you, having seen and been conversant with that country. The people are, I believe, as truly loyal as any subjects the King has; but a people jealous of their liberties, and who will vindicate them, if they should ever be violated— but the subject is too delicate and I will say no more."

The lower house of Parliament was in shock and the prophetic warning that was issued was so in vain. For his effort, Isaac Barré, on behalf of the Colonies, liberty, and in his estimation the good of England, was promptly dispensed to the tower of London. However, the most lasting effect of his speech was the description of the young daring Americans as "Sons of Liberty." It was from the printing of his speech in Colonial papers that the separate motley names of Whig clubs would eventually derive their iconic moniker. Before the speech and universal adoption of the name, the Sons sprung from a group in Boston know as the Union Club. All along the eastern seaboard, similar groups came to fruition in vehement response to the Stamp Act. These local organizations were not necessarily well received by the general Colonial population, often considered more to be ruffian mettlesome agitators than some kind of lionhearted defenders of life, liberty, and the pursuit of happiness.

Nonetheless, by the winter of 1772, the germinating seeds of revolution were a sprout just breathing the open air, but strong in their long deep roots: The French and Indian War, The Sugar Act, The Stamp Act, Townsend Acts, and the Boston Massacre. And more recently, yet another incident served to anchor the sagacious planet securely into the insurgent fertile soil.

***

The second week of June 1772, the same time that across the Atlantic, Hayim Shelomo was rapidly reaching the conclusion that England had nothing to offer him; in Rhode Island, June 10, was a day that would live in infamy.

Lieutenant William Duddington, of Her Majesty's Ship Gaspee, was charged with patrolling the waters of Narragansett Bay, off the colony of Rhode Island. Duddington had earned a reputation as an overzealous enforcer; boarding and detaining vessels and confiscating cargoes, often without charge, and without recourse for merchants whose goods were impounded. Losses were mounting and it was widely believed that these harassments were directed specifically at members of the Sons of Liberty. The ninth of June was yet another day of revenue collection for Duddington, but for the Colonists, it was the anticipated moment of reckoning.

Rhode Island was already branded with a reputation for trade smuggling with enemies; and a local vessel named Hannah, out of Newport, was under way to Providence when its captain mischievously baited the HMS Gaspee and led Duddington into shallow waters near Warwick. The Gaspee predictably ran aground. News of the grounding quickly reached Providence. Thereafter, a party of fifty-five, led by a man named John Brown, planned an attack on the ship. The following evening they surrounded and boarded Her Majesty's possession, wounding Duddington and capturing the entire crew. All were hauled ashore and abandoned, to watch as the Gaspee was promptly looted and then ebulliently burned.

The boldness of this attack was even more remarkable in that none of the attackers made any effort to hide their identities. Duddington and the British crew were able to readily point out most of the participants. However, this did them little good because the local courts, too, were antagonistic toward the Royal Navy and the British dictates. Rather than attempt to prosecute the attackers, charges were actually brought against Lt. Duddington for illegally seizing goods. When this news reached Parliament, there was outrage. A special commission, under the authority of the vice-admiralty courts was sent to apprehend the perpetrators of the entire affair, and to haul them back to England for trial. Though the identities of the offenders were widely known, the investigation was fruitless. No arrest was ever made. But a further outrage was ablaze. The idea of bringing Colonists under criminal charge and tried outside of the Colony for a crime alleged to be committed in the Colony was a reach of injustice to the Sons of Liberty that they wouldn't readily forgive.

***

The men of the tavern spoke in rousing and shrieking voices. The din of conversation emulated brawls with words, ideas, and opinions thrown instead of fists. Much of the dialogue was above Hayim's head, and some to fast for his English to comprehend — ranging from the case of Calvin, the Articles of Capitulation, various edicts, antiquated laws, and legal case study that he was unaware of.

Suddenly, vapors from the mantle of tobacco smoke parted and curled in rolling casts of shifting veils. From the rear of the room to the front, it continually wafted through the air in the rifted manner. The haze was being rent by the forward pace of one: Alexander McDougall. His footsteps trod in onward and escalated motion as he perched himself upon a table. This act, of standing on the table, intimated an official-type seriousness that brought a slow hush to the hall of people. Hayim stood in the back with Seixas. He watched with eager anticipation as all noise descended to a deafly silence. Then... McDougall opened his mouth, unfurled his tongue, and roared like the king of the jungle —

"My fellows, see me, if you will, see me stand here and look into my eyes, be so brave as to ask yourselves, 'what are all the riches, the luxuries, and even the conveniences of life compared with that liberty where with God and nature have set us free, with that inestimable jewel which is the basis of all other employments?'"

The tavern's patrons responded in agreement with an overflowing enthusiasm! McDougall, fiery and audacious, was the New York Son's unelected, unspecified, and unmitigated leader. Interestingly, of all the men in the room, he had most suffered by the courage of his convictions.

***

Alexander, born in 1731, was a simple Scottish milkman's son; but in the year of our Lord, 1734, unbeknownst to him, his life would forever be claimed by providence. Colonel Cosby, Governor of the Province of New York and New Jersey, by and with the advice and assent of his Council, published a printed advertisement encouraging the Resort of Protestants from Europe to settle upon the Northern Frontier of the his New York Province. His advertisement glowingly promised each family two hundred acres of unimproved land out of 100,000 acres purchased from the Iroquois Indians — without any fee or expenses whatsoever. However, the charge of nothing did include a little something, that was but a small fee for surveying the land and liable only to the King's Quit Rent of one shilling and nine pence farthing per hundred acres. So, maybe a little something. Nonetheless, these settlements would at that time have been of the utmost utility to the province and these proposals were looked upon as so advantageous, that they could not fail to have the desired effect upon prospective immigrants. And mightily they had the proper effect, indeed.

By 1737, these advertisements and proposals found their way into the hands of Captain Lauchlin Campbell of the island of Islay. Lauchlin was, if anything, enterprising. He braved the seas and arrived in Philadelphia. Ever since the bitter persecution of Presbyterians during the periods of episcopal rule in the latter half of the seventeenth century, there was money to be made in relocated Scots. Scottish emigration to the new world had been steady for a hundred years and while in Pennsylvania, Lauchlin rejected many considerable offers that were made him. He then proceeded to New York, where, though Governor Cosby was deceased, the new governor George Clarke, assured him that no part of the lands were as yet granted. To be sure, Lauchlin made his way 200 miles north to visit the lands in questions and was kindly received by the Indians. On his return to New York he received the most solemn promises that he should have a thousand acres for every family that he brought over, and that each family should have according to their number from five hundred to one hundred and fifty acres. However, strangely, the governor declined to make any grant until the families arrived. That was as he explained, because according to the constitution of that government, the names of the settlers were to be recorded in the grant. Fair enough, and Lauchlin conceded.

Captain Lauchlin Campbell accordingly returned to Islay, and brought from the islands at a very large expense, his own family and thirty other families, making in all, one hundred and fifty-three souls, including the McDougall family.

Alexander McDougall measurably stood atop the table — a forty year old man, a crowd pleaser; proudly crowing, energetic and excitable. If anyone ever looked the part of a colonial leader, a composite of the erudite continental man, it was McDougall. He had the comely appearance of a rugged strapping man — broad shoulders, a muscular neck, and a well-proportioned head. Though, when he wasn't speaking in excitable rants, he pattered out his communications with a slight stutter. Still, he was tough, as tough as Scots and sailors come. The crowd wanted more — more from their captain! But he wasn't a captain by rank. That's what his enemies called him, those who derided his snappy, "vulgar," flamboyant dress. In good society, he was subtly shunned for he was viewed as opinionated, flashy, and a tavern owner who freely drank as much as he served. He found his true calling in the Sons of Liberty — his hatred for the British was in platelets of his bones, marinated into the marrow, and seeped into the soul.

"Are you as I am?" McDougall shouted! "Little do they suppose but for I, and you, and all of us — that we reserve the honor of giving impulse to the mighty political revolution — that on this day, in this our slop-shop — is an unstoppable gathering of strength before our Heaven-born power over the corruption of courts and the tyranny of kings — which at our rightful decision we shall ground into power!"

The patrons screamed in scatters! "VERILY - VERILY!" The full multitude shouted in rhythm to clanking their steins! Beer slouched and spilled! "Black Sam," as good-old Samuel Fraunces' was nicknamed, hastily refilled the steins and kept a mental tabulation that exceedingly rose in profits as McDougall maintained whipping them up!

"The Mother Country?" McDougall hollered! "Mother we are not children anymore!"
They cheered hoarsely! Galvanized and frenzied, his audience shouted back in streams and heaps of defiance and grievances: Immunity for corrupt and abusive British officers! Oppression of political protesters! Restrictions to free trade! Forced quartering! However few of the men in the room had ever truly suffered by the courage of their convictions! To the Betrayed Inhabitants of the City and Colony of New York began:

My dear fellow-citizens and countrymen,

In a day when the minions of tyranny and despotism in the mother country and the colonies, are indefatigable in laying every snare that their malevolent and corrupt hearts can suggest, to enslave a free people, when this unfortunate country has been striving under many disadvantages for three years past, to preserve their freedom; which to an Englishman is as dear as his life, – when the merchants of this city and the capital towns on the continent, have nobly and cheerfully sacrificed their private interest to the public good, rather than to promote the designs of the enemies of our happy constitution: It might justly be expected, that in this day of constitutional light, the representatives of this colony would not be so hardy, nor be so lost to all sense of duty to their constituents, (especially after the laudable example of the colonies of Massachusetts Bay and South Carolina before them) as to betray the trust committed to them.

Signed, "A Son of Liberty," On December 16, 1769, this anonymous broadside caused an uproar in New York City. It went on to directly attack and denounced the money scheme as a deception, a covering cloak for their evil. It was the issuing of bills of credit, on the security of the province, to the amount of $700,000, to be loaned to the people, and the interest to be applied to defraying the expenses of, ostensibly, the colonial government, but in reality, for maintaining troops in the province — otherwise, a monster bank without checks. Further, the broadside went on to astutely declare that evidently the proposition to grant supplies to the troops unqualifiedly was an acknowledgment of the right to exact such subsidies, and a virtual approval of all the revenue acts; and that the scheme was intended to divide and distract the colonies! The castigating polemic directed the attention of the Assembly to the patriotic attitude of the other colonies, and exhorted them to imitate their example. It hinted at a corrupt coalition between the unapologetic acting-governor Cadwallader Colden, and the ever-powerful royalist DeLancey clan. The affixed seditious averments called upon the Assembly to repudiate the act concocted by this combination. It closed with a summons of the inhabitants to a meeting in The Fields, on the outskirts of town, the very next day. Presumably, a gathering, to express their views and to instruct their representatives in the Assembly to oppose the measure; and in case they should refuse, to send notice thereof to every Assembly in America, and to publish their names to the world!

The very next day, no less than fourteen hundred people congregated around the Liberty-Pole, where they were harangued, by a Son of Liberty, John Lamb— in the radical forceful violent parlance the New York Sons were known for. Lamb, a well-to-do merchant, a fluent speaker, and prolific writer, was thirty-four years of age as he swayed the multitude by his eloquence and logic.

By unanimous vote they condemned the action of the Assembly in passing obnoxious bills. Their sentiments were embodied in a communication to that House, which was borne by a committee of seven leading Sons of Liberty, namely: Isaac Sears, Caspar Wistar, Jacob Van Zandt, Samuel Broome, Erasmus Williams, James Varick, and of course, the fire starter: Alexander McDougall. But the authorities were done with dear Mr. McDougall.

When the obnoxious handbill was read by, the Speaker, Mr. DeLancey of the New York Assembly, moved that the sense of the House should be taken "whether the said paper was not an infamous and scandalous libel." The vote was taken. Twenty of the DeLancey influenced Assembly voted the same mind as the Speaker, and only one member voted "Nay." That singular member was Philip Schuyler. He unexpectedly and boldly faced the rising storm, and by his solitary vote rebuked, in a most emphatic manner, the cowardice of his peers with whom he had stood shoulder-to-shoulder in former trials. Philip Schuyler was beginning to find his direction in his providential call to liberty.

The assembly then vigorously set about ferreting out the author of the broadside. They authorized the lieutenant governor to offer a reward of $500 for the discovery of the offending author. The most obvious suspect was John Lamb. He was savagely dragged in before the House and cited as the miscreant, but was soon discharged. Following the trail of evidence, the printer of the handbill, when discovered, was brought to the bar, when the frightened man gave the name of Alexander McDougall as the author.

McDougall was violently taken before the House, where he would make no acknowledgment and refused to post bail. Immediately, he was indicted for libel and cast into prison, where he remained fourteen weeks until arraigned for trial— much of his time spent crudely carving a deep reminder of his presence in wall. At the arraignment he made a intellectual spectacle of the hearing. First, he fearlessly pleaded "Not guilty," and still refused to post bail. Then he stuttered through his first few words until he rose his speech into a vast propriety, and awed and astonished many who wished him ill, and added to his roster of friends, some on the court, including fatefully, Mr. Schuyler.

Several months afterward he was again brought before the House, when he was defended, by George Clinton, an active member of that body. Faced with the question whether he was the author of the broadside audaciously signed "A Son of Liberty," McDougall replied—

"You have declared the words and paper they have been printed on to be a libel. How can I answer, for also I am under prosecution in the Supreme Court— in all righteousness of justice, which surely you are interested, do you not agree that it would be an infraction of said justice to punish twice for one offense? Yet, I do not deny the authority of this body to punish me for a breach of privilege when no cognizance was taken of it, in another court."

"You are in contempt!" DeLancey shouted!

"So be it! I rejoice!" he shouted to the rafters!

"In prison you shall have the opportunity to take up said rejoice!" DeLancey angrily responded.

"Well then, let me rejoice further that I am the first to suffer for liberty since the commencement of our glorious struggle."
DeLancey promptly ordered McDougall to prison where he instantly became a celebrity martyr. He was the unqualified man of the people, the Jonah in the mouth of the whale. Eighty days in jail. All the while ladies of distinction visited him. Popular songs were written in his honor. Emblematic swords cast and worn in his name. "McDougall" was on everyone's lips.

***

"I am a son of liberty!" McDougall returned to shouting across the tavern! "Is this a state to be rested in, when our all is at a stake? No, my countrymen, rouse! Imitate the noble example of the friends of liberty in England; who rather than be enslaved, contend for their right with king, lords and commons. And will you suffer your liberties to be torn from you, by your representatives?"
Hayim was undoubtedly impressed by this man, from his words to the fact that he held the crowd in the palm of his hand and continued to grip tighter and tighter! McDougall was emphatically a "man of the people." He thoroughly sympathized with those classes in society— the workingmen and women— who were generally weak in social and political influence. Without any of the spirit of a demagogue, he was a popular figure, because the people saw that his whole soul was enlisted in his efforts in their behalf, and like every really earnest man, the utterances of his convictions carried with them great weight. For Hayim, unlike in Poland and with the Bar, there seemed to be a spirited underpinning of a religious enthrallment to the Colonists cause of liberty, as embodied in McDougall rousing the crowd still further! They were not merely an old hapless social order seeking a restoration on the bloody tip of a sword. All of this impressed and moved him to be intrigued, to understand more, that he too, might be as certain of man's rightful relationship with governance. Mesmerized, Hayim made his way closer to the man.

"To what other influence than the deserting of the American cause," McDougall continued his brilliant tirade. "Can the ministry attribute so pusillanimous a conduct, as this is of the Assembly; so repugnant and subversive of all the means we have used, and opposition that has been made by this and the other colonies, to the tyrannical conduct of the British Parliament! to no other. Can there be a more ridiculous farce to impose on the people than for the Assembly to vote their thanks to be given to the merchants for entering into an agreement not to import goods from Britain, until the revenue acts should be repealed, while they at the same time counteract it by countenancing British acts, and complying with ministerial requisitions, incompatible with our freedom? Surely they cannot!"

McDougall exhaled of the last of his spitting breath and looked down to see a face he'd never seen before staring up at him. The face was Hayim's. Gripped in his own excitement, he shouted down—

"And what say you, of what I've said?"

Hayim was speechless. Seixas appeared. His was a face that Alexander knew well—

"He has come of my invitation, his opinions are not complete," Seixas said in gentle protection of Hayim from the rowdy nature of the evening.

Nevertheless, McDougall jumped down from the table and lifted Hayim on top of it in his place.

"So, say you?" McDougall in raucous enjoyment loudly needled the visitant.

All eyes were on Hayim. The steins were pounding and someone yelled—

"Speak your name!"

Hayim stood there, a bit frightened, put upon, and surrounded by a hostile and drunken crowd. Yet, he also had an awakening. Hundreds of calls for his name filled the air to capacity until no other sound could be heard. Finally, he courageously stood up as straight as he could and spoke—

"My name is Haym— Haym Salomon," he said. "And unfortunately, I am not, one of you, a Son of Liberty. But… I am liberty's son!"

XIX
"CONCORD HYMN"

"Objects of the most stupendous magnitude, and measure in which the lives and liberties of millions yet unborn are intimately interested, are now before us. We are in the very midst of a revolution the most complete, unexpected and remarkable of any in the history of nations." John Adams

By the rude bridge that arched the flood,
Their flag to April's breeze unfurled,
Here, once the embattled farmers stood,
And fired the shot heard round the world.

The foe long since in silence slept;
Alike the conqueror silent sleeps;
And Time the ruined bridge has swept
Down the dark stream which seaward creeps.

On this green bank, by this soft stream,
We set to-day a votive stone;
That memory may their deed redeem,
When, like our sires, our sons are gone.

Spirit, that made those spirits dare,
To die, and leave their children free,
Bid Time and Nature gently spare
The shaft we raise to them and thee.

Ralph Waldo Emerson

(July 4, 1837)

***

"And fired the shot heard around the world."

XX

REVOLUTION

"The Revolution was effected before the War commenced. The Revolution was in the minds and hearts of the people; a change in their religious sentiments of their duties and obligations… this radical change in the principles, opinions, sentiments, and affections of the people, was the real American Revolution."

John Adams

4:58 am, the sun began to rise— April 18th, throughout the Middlesex county of New England— 1775. Shortly thereafter, drizzle and light rain fell from the seraphic shores of Heaven and cascaded downward through the divine realms and almighty atmospheres onto that geographical coordinate of the earth. It continued to shower without cease through the overcast hours of daylight.

At 6:30 pm, the solar star set and on the variable winds veering from the northeast to the south, the clouds gradually parted. Presumably, the Gods of Hadad and Adad abandoned their connate powers of precipitation and the night rode into a clear pleasant evening. Then, the Spirit of the Lord stirred and rose in a stormy squall— a blustery chill— a downward western wind that would amplify and carry every sound into all those who had ears!

"The British are coming! The British are coming!"

***

A grey-haired maltster, Samuel Adams and his compatriot, the always fashionable merchant— or smuggler as the British would claim, John Hancock, were wanted men at the footling behest of the King of England. In mid-April of 1775, ahead of the British expedition to apprehend them, they were secreted away in the parsonage of Rev. Jonas Clarke in Lexington, Massachusetts; en route to Philadelphia and the Second Continental Congress, with the express notion of engaging in the act of drafting a declaration respecting the sovereign aspirations and intentions of the imposed upon North American Colony. King George had demanded that these men, in particular, be detained, immediately, and the execution of the said vexed and irritated imperial instruction laid in the pugnacious hands of General Thomas Gage.

General Thomas Gage was the British Military Governor of Massachusetts and the commander in chief of British forces. He had the doomed honor of replacing Thomas Hutchinson, who ineptly served in the same bureaucratic capacity— officially denominated: The Governor of the Province of Massachusetts Bay for roughly five years following the arrival of his predecessor. Boston born, Thomas Hutchinson was at heart an historian, man of the letters, a chap of words, a dandy of delicate care— with an indefensible nature to defend the more exquisite matter of man's mind. He petitioned to be recalled from office at the same time the Whigs and the Colonists were actively in operation to remove him from his lofty perch. The Whigs issued their effort through Parliamentary debate while the Colonists used a triumphantly more colorful expression of their distain— a mob ransacked his home and commandeered into their possession all articles of monetary value and for good measure, ripped away the finishings and toppled the house's cupola. In June of 1774, Hutchinson was gladly replaced with a man ready for a fight. General Gage entered into office loaded for bear and released a proclamation to the Colonists that could not be dismissed as an idle threat.

BY HIS EXCELLENCY

The Hon. Thomas Gage, Esq; Governor, and Commander in Chief in and over his Majesty's Province of Massachusetts-Bay, a Vice Admiral of the same.

A PROCLAMATION.

...In this exigency of complicated calamities, I avail myself of the last effort within the bounds of my duty, to spare the effusion of blood; to offer, and I do hereby in his Majesty's name, offer and promise, his most gracious pardon in all who shall forthwith lay down their arms, and return to the duties of peaceable subjects, excepting only from the benefit of such pardon, Samuel Adams and John Hancock, whose offenses are of too flagitious a nature to admit of any other consideration about that of punishments.

And to the end that no person within the limits of this proffered mercy, may plead ignorance of the consequences of refusing it, I by these presents proclaim not only the persons above-named and excepted, but also all their adherents, associates and abettors, meaning to comprehend in those terms, all and every person, and persons of what class, denomination or description soever, who have appeared in arms against the King's government, and shall not lay down the same as afore-mentioned, and likewise all such as shall so take arms after the date hereof, or who shall in any-wise protects or conceal such offenders, or assist them with money, provision, cattle, arms, ammunition, carriages, or any other necessary for subsistence or offense; or shall hold secret correspondence with them by letter, message, signal, or otherwise, to be rebels and traitors, and as such as to be treated.

And whereas, during the continuance of the present unnatural rebellion, justice cannot be administered by the common law of the land, the course whereof has, for a longtime past, been violently impeded, and wholly interrupted; from whence results a necessity for using and exercising the law martial; I have therefore thought fit, by the authority vested in me, by the Royal Charter to this province, to publish, and I do hereby publish, proclaim and order the use and exercise of the law martial, within and throughout this province, for so long time as the present unhappy occasion shall necessarily require; whereof all persons are hereby required to take notice, and govern themselves, as well to maintain order and regularity among the peaceable inhabitants of the province, as to resist, encounter, and subdue the Rebels and Traitors above-described by such as shall be called upon those purposes.

To these inevitable, but I trust salutary measures, it is a far more pleasing part of my duty, to add the assurances of protection and support, to all who in so trying a crisis, shall manifest their allegiance to the King, and affection to the parent state. So that such persons as may have been intimidated to quit their habitations in the course of this alarm, may return to their respective callings and professions; and stand distinct and separate from the parricides of the constitution, till God in his Mercy shall restore to his creatures, in this distracted land, that system of happiness from which they have been seduced, the religion of peace, and liberty founded upon law.

GIVEN at BOSTON, this Twelfth Day of June, in the Fifteenth Year of the Reign of his Majesty GEORGE the Third, by the Grace of GOD, of Great Britain, France and Ireland, KING, Defender of the Faith, & Annoque Domini, 1775.

By His Excellency's Command,
Tho's Flucker, Secr'y.

Tho's Gage.

GOD SAVE THE KING

This proclamation was versified in many parts of the colonies, and in various instances, published as a ballad, that the law could be easily remembered and even sounds more friendly to the ears. Over and above Gage's blazon pronouncement, his arrival and ascendancy to a near dictatorship over the American Colonies and unequivocal dictatorship over the Massachusetts Bay Colony came neatly disposed with new and far-reaching powers of fiat in the form of the force of law consolidated in the Intolerable Acts. The view and the impetus of the sponsoring British were summed upon tidily by the Prime Minister Lord North to his King. "The Americans have tarred and feathered your subjects, plundered your merchants, burnt your ships, denied all obedience to your laws and authority; yet so clement and so long forbearing has our conduct been that it is incumbent on us now to take a different course. Whatever may be the consequences, we must risk something; if we do not, all is over." These new sets of laws were the most restrictive and heavy-handed the English ever enforced by the Colonists.

They basically encompassed five new coercive acts. 1) The Administration of Justice Act. The Act allowed for trials of accused royal officials to have their venue moved to another colony or even to Great Britain. 2) The Boston Port Act. It was a direct response to the action of the Boston Tea Party. The Act closed the port of that city until the East India Company had been reimbursed in full. 3) The Quartering Act. This Act allowed for British Soldiers to be housed in any unoccupied building. 4) The Quebec Act. It extended the boundaries of the British Province of Quebec— outside of the Thirteen Colonies, south to the Ohio River and west to the Mississippi, wherein it transferred western land claims by the colonies to a non-representative government. 5) The Massachusetts Government Act. This gem of legislative jargon brought Massachusetts under the direct control of the governor or the King. There was no longer to be local government bodies in the colony. Instantly, this made the activities of men like Adams and Hancock dangerously outside of the law.

***

Three days prior to April 18th, General Gage was ruminating over the latest and greatest of the administrative directives he had received from London. It had been an extraordinarily tense tenure since he was commissioned— he fearlessly held the bull by the horns; grasped the tiger by the tail; and by February, order over the colonies had spiraled out of his tenuous control. The portent began with John Hancock and Dr. Joseph Warren leading the colony to engage in defensive preparations for a state of war. Upon the disquieting news reaching Parliament eight days into the future, the body hurriedly declared the Massachusetts Bay Colony to be in an insolent state of rebellion. This declaration did less than sit well in any of the colonies— as a matter of fact; it went over like a lead ballon weighed down with anvils. The overarching result was that every colony came to attention and hastily convened to decide if they would follow in Massachusetts' footsteps and prepare themselves in a defensive position for war. From the tip of the Bay Colony on the border with Canada to the southern most hectare of Georgia, which bordered on coveted Spanish territory, the thirteen colonies were metaphorically no less than wasps ready to defend their poked and disturbed hive.

Six weeks later, in shadow of the dissolved House of Burgesses, enclosed in a white steepled church, by the name of the Virginia Convention, it was to be discussed and ultimately voted on if the Colony of Virginia would constitute an army and send troops in the event of a war set upon them, or looking through the other side of the looking glass: a war of revolution. Was the lion intent on attacking the lamb to defend its territory or was the lamb artfully dressing in wolves's clothing and itching for a fight?

There was Thomas Jefferson, one of the richest and maybe most respected man in the colony was among the congregated, and they talked of defying the king. George Washington, the military man, and undisputedly the wealthiest landowner in all of Virginia was in attendance, and they passed scathing resolutions condemning Lord Dunmore. James Madison, the young intellectual protégé of Jefferson was present, and they announced that the people of Virginia were ready to protect themselves "against every species of despotism." Edmund Randolph, a man who embodied the perfect pitch of humility with the profoundly disreputable character of a politician was too gathered, to the right of Washington, and they collectively spoke of possible military preparations and issues. John Blair, the London educated American listened as fiery sermons of taxation without representation were delivered. George Mason, the career politician, likewise was present in St. John's Church as they questioned the truest and most fundamental role of government in the lives of men. James McClurg, the physician, answered to a roll and rocked in his chair as Peyton Randolph, the best legal mind in the country was chosen president. It was a day in the which the feast of enkindled and earnest thought was consumed in glorious God-inspired gluttony— a day of sunlight and divine influence extended into an evening in which Locke, Hobbs, Cicero, and many of antiquity and the Enlightenment were quoted as though bolts of fabric tossed to unravel! However, as the sun finally sank in its set, a lawyer, known for his brilliant oratory skills had heard enough and stepped to the pulpit of the alter.

Patrick Henry knew all the immaculate compositions and publications on the great thinkers whom they all so deeply admired; men who considered the unalienable rights and self-evident nature of man, government, and God as a second trinity. Yet, he came to the front of the church before his 120 fellow Virginians with his heart filled with the deceased but unforgettable persona of Reverend Samuel Davies. The Reverend had once said, "Whatever be your place, imbibe and cherish a public spirit. Serve your generation." He was the light of the Great Awakening that served as the beacon for the postulation that this assembly of colonies should break free of her begetter and miraculously become a nation under God. With those feelings in his overflowing heart by the solution of his simmering blood, the thirty-eight year old Mr. Henry started his words in eloquence and ended them in shattering thunder!

> Mr. President: No man thinks more highly than I
> do of the patriotism, as well as abilities, of the very
> worthy gentlemen who have just addressed the
> House. But different men often see the same
> subject in different lights; and, therefore, I hope it
> will not be thought disrespectful to those
> gentlemen if, entertaining as I do, opinions of a
> character very opposite to theirs, I shall speak
> forth my sentiments freely, and without reserve.
> This is no time for ceremony. The question before
> the House is one of awful moment to this country.
> For my own part, I consider it as nothing less than
> a question of freedom or slavery; and in
> proportion to the magnitude of the subject ought
> to be the freedom of the debate. It is only in this
> way that we can hope to arrive at truth, and fulfill
> the great responsibility, which we hold to God
> and our country. Should I keep back my opinions

at such a time, through fear of giving offense, I should consider myself as guilty of treason towards my country, and of an act of disloyalty toward the majesty of heaven, which I revere above all earthly kings.

Mr. President, it is natural to man to indulge in the illusions of hope. We are apt to shut our eyes against a painful truth, and listen to the song of that siren till she transforms us into beasts. Is this the part of wise men, engaged in a great and arduous struggle for liberty? Are we disposed to be of the number of those who, having eyes, see not, and, having ears, hear not, the things, which so nearly concern their temporal salvation? For my part, whatever anguish of spirit it may cost, I am willing to know the whole truth; to know the worst, and to provide for it...

...Gentlemen may cry, Peace, Peace but there is no peace. The war is actually begun! The next gale that sweeps from the north will bring to our ears the clash of resounding arms! Our brethren are already in the field! Why stand we here idle? What is it that gentlemen wish? What would they have? Is life so dear, or peace so sweet, as to be purchased at the price of chains and slavery? Forbid it, Almighty God! I know not what course others may take; but as for me, give me liberty or give me death!

With Henry's last breath exhausted in the dour word, "Death," his fellow patriots were roused to chant and roister in response — "Give me liberty or give me death! - Give me liberty or give me death!"

***

243

General Gage's principle concern in April of 1775 was Massachusetts suppressed and not Virginia, dead or liberated. However, he was the commanding officer of all standing British troops, and insurgency in another colony was of issue to him, but not as preeminently as Massachusetts. That latest and greatest order called upon him to take into custody Adams and Hancock and, to further seize and destroy the rebel's military stores at Concord. The latter this was a directive connected to the February declaration of the British Parliament that the Colony of Massachusetts was found to be in open rebellion. The decree was contemptuously laden with obsequious temerity that authorized British troops to kill the violent rebels— the fallen savagery of an Englishman killing Englishman.

The General, as a military man, and an officer of the Crown dutifully sought to enforce any of the military orders given him. He was a military man, first and foremost, but not least and all. Regardless of the bluster of his opening proclamation, personally he was a gentleman of moderate political persuasions and compassionate toward patriot sympathies. His psyche was cast in the nonconformist liberal mold of an Englishman who believed all Englishman, even in dissent carried a God-given sacredness, which was to be tolerated. That effectively, it was the English nature and a Christian fundamental, in the spirit of liberty, to expand in mind, consciousness, and ideals. Not to mention, everyday he wantonly went home to a beautiful wife, who was an American. He met her in Albany while fighting in the French and Indian War. Though a military officer of great regard and glory, Gage was an irremediable romantic and he irresolutely worshipped her.

Ultimately, the General's administrative praxis and leniency toward political groups such as the Sons of Liberty heaped criticism upon him and unintentionally played a hand in their ability to exponentially grow safe from the meddlesome harassment of royal authorities. The juncture of 1774-1775 in their metamorphosis was critical. That transmuted from primarily being ideological political ruffians opposing Parliamentary dictates with local protests such as the Boston Tea Party to well-armed militia-minded groups with a saber rattling undertone of war. For Gage, his straddling of tough talk with calm action had evidently placed his career, and ostensibly, his neck, both on the line.

To accomplish the task at hand, Gage assembled the flanking units, including Light Infantry and Grenadiers, from his Boston Garrison.

He placed Lieutenant Colonel Francis Smith and Marine Major John Pitcairn in charge of the operation. He also composed a relief column under the command of Lord Hugh Percy to leave six hours after the main column. In an attempt at cagy secrecy, he did not tell his officers his plan until the very last minute. Yet, the unforeseen problem with his security measures laid in the fact that Boston had become nothing less than a glass fishbowl. All rebel eyes were watching to see the British' next action, and whenever the garrison committed to an action, the Americans knew their every move. One more thing about the fishbowl— one of the fishes was Gage's aforementioned beautiful wife, Margaret Kemble. As mentioned, she was a native colonist with inherently deeply divided loyalties.

Gage's effort to keep his troop movements a secret stemmed primarily from humiliation many months before then it did tactical advantage. With pressure from London mounting and tension between the Colonists and British Troops on the rise, Gage committed to a proactive approach to governing the rebel military ability that could match their sentiment. In the event of a full scale rebellion, he needed to ensure that troops would be able to secure the colony with relative ease, so to avoid an actual battle. Thereupon, the orders went out to confiscate weapons that the Colonists had been storing throughout the countryside, in what was the worst kept secret in the Americas.

Several parties of British troops had been sent up the coast to confiscate ammunition in Salem and surrounding communities. In both of those cases, the silversmith, Paul Revere and other riders who were members of the Sons of Liberty, alerted the townspeople of the movement of British troops well before the troops reached their destinations. Not surprisingly, the munitions were successfully hidden and Gage and his army were thoroughly humiliated. Well, on the night of April 18th, history was set to repeat itself.

***

Without mincing words, Dr. Joseph Warren was a troublemaker. By his patrician patriot colleagues he was duly appointed President of the illegally convened Massachusetts Provincial Congress. The King had expressly outlawed local governing bodies in Massachusetts, and the American Colonists notably respected the mandate by simply erecting a new one, anyway. Furthermore and quite significantly, in April 1775, he and Dr. Benjamin Church were the two key members of the Committee of

Correspondence left in the anxious and jumpy city of Boston. Oh, and of consideration, Dr. Warren was quietly having an affair with a married woman— Mrs. General Thomas Gage.

During the drizzling afternoon rain of April 18th, the British troops stationed in the anxious and jumpy city, were mobilized for the long-planned raid on nearby Concord. As predictably as night follows the day and death follows life, before nightfall, word of mouth had spread and knowledge of the mobilization was universal throughout Boston. It was also known that they would be taking a route through Lexington. Everyone— from the Americans to the British had been anxiously waiting this day to come, the tempest in the teapot would now be lifted of its lid. Toward the end of the afternoon, Dr. Warren clandestinely received a patient who asserted a desperate need for his care. The young woman was clenched in a frantic quality of character; not trembling, but ready to burst. She was a chambermaid for an influential British family and she complained of dropsy in her lower extremities. As the good doctor pressed his thumb to her seemingly healthy flesh, she lowered her lips and whispered into his ear… words of treason.

The fortuitously feigned dropsy disseminated to Warren additional information about Gage's troop movements and preparations to arrest Adams and Hancock. The American call to action, which had long been in place, was simple and by this examination, triggered. Warren and Church convened with the thirty year-old tanner and shoe maker, William Dawes and Paul Revere, who was a generation older than his counterpart. These two men were to be the chief messengers to advance the intentions of the British to the Colonists. Warren, Church, Dawes, and Revere were all part of "The Mechanics." It was a group of thirty men in Boston who watched every move the British made. They had contingency plans on top of contingency plans and Warren and Church also informed others, relying similar tasks. Nonetheless, it was William Dawes and Paul Revere who were to make the fated midnight rides.

***

"…We have little time," Warren said. "Dawes you will go one way, and Revere you will go another."

"How is it we proceed?" Revere asked excitedly.

As it was, the game silversmith was the polar opposite of Dawes in their dispositions. Revere could hardly contain his excitement and similarly his contempt for the British. While Dawes, was humble, matter-of-fact, and still tracing an odor of effluents. He waited patiently for the orders and by the grace of God; he hoped he could carry them out as expected.

"I fear our caution may be less than unrestrained," said Church.

"And why should it be?" Revere countered in a hiss.

"How many are on foot?" Dawes asked.

"I report as many as might add to a thousand."

"A thousand!" Revere nearly shouted.

"Verily, we must not trifle. We are best served to carry out the warning but not to engage," said Church.

"I am not afraid to engage the enemy," shrieked Revere.

"They too are English, not the enemy," Church asserted.

"I am an American, I spit on those who deny me otherwise," Revere derided him.

Warren motioned his guests to extinguish their conflagrations and he calmly served them tea in a matter of meditation before his final instruction.

"Dawes, you are to ride, as quickly and as far as Lexington, and bring there due awareness to Hancock and Adams. Revere, you will meet him as such, but first arrange for another rider to be patient across the Charles that certainty may be upon us as the General's chosen route.

"I know just the fellow." Revere said.

"He is to hang but lanterns from the Old North Church. One if by land… and two if by sea."

Per Warren's instructions, around 8:00 o'clock Revere arrived at a modest Bostonian house where he aroused his sleeping friend Robert Newman. Robert was the sexton of the North Church. As it was late for an unannounced call and the Newman household rented quarters to British Soldiers, who could have still been present, Revere couldn't simply knock. He was forced to pelt Newman's bedroom window with individual pebbles, like a forlorn lover come calling to win back his love. Finally, Newman raised the window —

"Revere?"

"Newman— the church!" Revere whispered up as loud as he could. "Meet me at the church, double time!"

Then a beam of light burst from behind Robert and silhouetted him into a panic! Revere jettisoned away! "Robert?" his father said opening the door. A British Solider just happened to walk behind and past the man, clearly in more a staged hurry than would normally be expected so late at night.

"Yes, Father?" Newman said.

"I though I heard voices?"

"Oh, I guess I was just talking to myself."

"With the window open?"

"Oh, well, yes-yes… with the window open."

His father intuitively questioned his son's answers but by then he also knew he was keeping something to himself which might be difficult to ply at such a strange hour. Resolved to revisit it tomorrow, he slowly closed the door. Newman pretended to go back to sleep until he was able to sneak out of the house undetected by his family or the officers.

Within an hour, Newman arrived at the Old North Church where Revere was waiting on tenterhooks. He didn't come alone, assuming that it was a matter of grave importance, he brought with him two friends: John Pulling and Thomas Bernard. As night grew on, the temperature was rapidly dropping. However, with the adrenaline racing through the boys, they were sweating in anticipation.

"Get the lanterns!" Revere instructed.

"The lanterns? Newman said.

"Quickly!"

"They're marching?" Newman said.

Bursting through the church doors, the four rushed up the stairs into the belfry!

"You're going to operate the signal?" Newman turned to Revere and asked.

"No. You are!" Revere replied.

Newman was shocked, even momentarily overwhelmed if not also proud!

"Now listen well, when you see the British march, and assuredly they will be marching, hang this lantern aloft as the signal light—"

"Yes-yes!"

Revere interrupted Newman's eagerness, with a silent hush.

"With this lantern, one, if by land—"

"Yes, 'one if by land,'" Newman said.

Revere was perturbed at the second interruption but continued and held up the second lamp—

"Two—"

"Two—" Newman repeated.

"If by sea." Revere said.

"Yes."

"Yes," he said with a fighting spirit! "And, I will be on the opposite shore, sure to see them glow— ready to ride and spread the alarm— the alarm to take arms!"

***

At exactly 10:00 o'clock on the night of April 18th, 1775, the destiny of mankind, the fortune and fate of human nature, and the highest Will of Almighty God was set into unstoppable motion. From Boston, William Dawes, with his heart beating in his knotted stomach, took the well-trodden land route out of the city. Lieutenant-Colonel Smith, assisted by Major Pitcairn, and Brigadier General Percy confidently stirred and lead eight hundred British troops silently marching to the foot of the Common, where they secretly embarked in boats. And, like a bat out of hell, with the wind at his back, Paul Revere galloped to the river's edge where he surreptitiously jumped into a waiting shell boat, which would ferry him across the Charles River. In sixty seconds 10:00 o'clock April 18th had elapsed and splendidly passed into divine decree! Dawes, panicky, whipped his horse to press on, to drive and glide through the city! And a good thing, too— as he passed through the Boston Neck and into Roxbury, the military was sealing off the town, posthaste. Smith, Pitcairn, and Percy crossed into Cambridge, when textured layers of luck and bad luck fell upon them. Percy overheard one of a group of citizens says, "The British will miss their mark." "What mark?" inquired Percy. "The cannon at Concord," was the reply. Percy hastened to inform Gage, who immediately issued orders to his guards not to allow any person to leave the city that night. Posthaste, that went about sealing the entrances in and out. However, it was too late, and Revere reached Charlestown; where he stopped and turned to see just how many lanterns were going to glow.

Across the span of the banks and shimmering currents of the Charles River, the silvery-darkness of clouded moonlight irradiated the night into strange half casts of grey tints that projected the landscape in lineations of stark sight and sightlessness. The British troops landed on the Cambridge side of the water stripped in these delineations of clouded and unclouded night, forgoing their own lanterns for the element of surprise. Dutifully, Newman hung out his two lanterns, and the anxiously watching Revere, sprung into a saddle on the back of a fleet horse owned by Deacon Larkin, and hurried across Charlestown Neck! At the end of the isthmus he was confronted by two British soldiers, who attempted to arrest him. With the skill of a cavalryman, he yanked the horse and turned the beast back toward Charlestown, and soon reached the Medford road, where he was able to conclude his narrow escape.

Midnight struck, and ushered in on a dawn of darkness: April 19th, 1775 — a day that would mark the new history of the world upon the backs of those seeking to reach Concord. As the new day began, Revere rode up to Clarke's house in Lexington, which was well guarded by Sergeant Monroe and his men.

"I must see— speak— open— Mr. Hancock—" he said trying to catch his breath.

"I'm quite sorry, but the family have just retired," said the sergeant, "And I am directed not to allow them to be disturbed by any noise."

"Noise!" exclaimed Revere. "You'll have noise enough before long; the Regulars are coming out! I tell you— the British are coming!"
With that the sergeant gave way and allowed him to knock at the door. First, he had to catch his breath. Then, he knocked. Mr. Clarke opened a window on the door, and inquired—

"Who— bothers, I say, who is there?"

"I want to see Mr. Hancock! I must see Mr. Hancock!"

"My, it is late, and I prefer not to admit strangers into my house so late at night," Clarke replied.
Hancock, abed but not asleep, recognizing the voice of the messenger, called out—

"Revere?"
He was brought in from out of the cold and story of impending peril was soon told. Before long, the whole household was astir. Dawes, who went exclusively by land, suddenly arrived. With the first task completed, the patriots, quickly refreshed themselves, they rode swiftly toward Concord. They screamed themselves horse—

"The British are coming! The British are coming!"

Fortuitously, the wind carried their cries and every inhabitant between Medford and Lexington was energetically aroused! And as luck would have it, en route they were overtaken by Dr. Samuel Prescott. He had been engaged in wooing a young woman in Lexington, and he joined them in their patriotic errand—

"The British are coming! The British are coming!"

Revere was riding ahead of Dawes and Prescott when he was suddenly and unexpectedly, surrounded by some keen British officers. They made quick work of taking two of the three Americans prisoner. Prescott dashed over a stonewall by the nimble ability of his fresher horse, and escaped. He continued to Concord for his life and his country. The whole way he sounded the alarm—

"The British are coming! The British are coming!"

In the middle hours of the morning, sometime after two and before three, Revere and Dawes were under close quarters being thoroughly questioned concerning Hancock and Adams. They were peppered with questions, insults, and veiled threats. Yet, they consistently provided nothing more than a steady stream of evasive answers. Ultimately unsatisfied with their cooperation, the Red Coats threatened them with the business end of a blunderbuss. It was not a veiled threat. However, for Revere and Dawes, they began their evening risking their lives for their country and to them that would have been a good place as any to die for it. In fact, Revere mocked them in the face of their threat, and told his captors that men from all reaches were out arousing the country in every direction! The British believed they had to be bluffing and were incensed by their impertinence— whereupon, one of the soldiers pulled back the hammer of his flintlock just to see how willing they truly were to die for fruitless insolence—

"Let me squeeze hard enough," the solider said as he oscillated between whom he was aiming at. "And you my fella or you my fella, are dead."

Then he burst into laughter that was quickly accompanied by his comrade-in-arms, when suddenly a church-bell was heard; then another… and another. Dawes uncharacteristically spoke with authority and distain—

"The bells are ringing— the town is alarmed— you are dead men. Congratulations, my fellas, you are now dead men."

The frightened officers left their prisoners, and immediately fled toward Boston!

Since midnight on the 19th of April the British column, consisting of approximately 900 troops left Boston, crossed the Charles River, and were marching towards Concord. They came to learn that the entire countryside had been alerted to their presence, and rebel militia had been deployed to meet them.

Until this time there was no armed resistance to the British that had resulted in loss of British life. Several months earlier, Gage had attempted to destroy military arms at Salem and met with resistance but no shots were fired, and the British retreated without completing their objective. Lexington Militia Captain John Parker had heard of the events at Salem, and collected his men on Lexington Green to face the British column.

At the break dawn, Smith's advanced parties under the command of Major Pitcairn arrived at Lexington Green to see a group of armed Militia in formation across the Green. Pitcairn ordered the militia, led by John Parker, to be surrounded and disarmed. In response Parker ordered his men to disperse. Then—

BANG!

A shot rang out. No one really knows who fired first, but the British, hearing the shot, fired upon the small group of militia, killing eight, and wounding ten more. The militia broke ranks and retreated into the woods to avoid anymore of the well-trained British fire.

However, the shot, which was fired in Lexington, Massachusetts Bay Colony was manifestly heard around the world. For the American Revolution, a call to liberty had irreversibly begun.

***

XXI

REBIRTH

"Before any man can be considered as a member of civil society he must be considered as a subject to the governor of the universe." James Madison

The newly christened Haym Salomon did not join the Sons of Liberty on that rollicking renaissance day in 1772, nor did he in 1773, 1774, or 1775. However, he held them in an esteem that he never beheld for the Polish Noble's Bar Confederation. Nevertheless, he departed that meeting of hard-drinking ideological hooligans and settled into the humdrum existence of an uncomplicated proprietor of a dry goods store. Life was simple; easy. Moses Franks, through his family, made good on his offer, in spades. He arranged for Haym to acquire his full inventory below wholesale cost. The lucky man would enthusiastically unstitch every coin in the coat Gutlé sewed for him and with the means, proudly opened a store on 222 Broad Street in New York City. To walk into his humble emporium was to be overwhelmed at the stupendously diverse variety of goods. Broadcloths, maple syrups, bath coating, quilts, duffels, paint, fine and strong shoes and stockings, deerskins, check and white shirts, glasswares, dish wares, Irish linens, osnaburgs, bohea tea, pearl barley, rum, medicines, the best Florence oil in quart bottles, cloves and cinnamon, English bacon in sides by the box, best indigo and sundry other goods. Likewise the best of gunpowder tea of the first quality, two desks and book cases, twisted chairs, two arm dittoes, a washing stand, a ladies dressing and writing table, all of the best mahogany, and a bedstead with green silk curtains, all offered for sale just a cut of margin below the going market rate— surely just as his mentor Meyer would have done.

Further still, he operated a manageable one-man distillery in the back and sold his own crafted spirits. About New York, he was much sought after to translate for appreciative immigrants and servicing professionals— such as doctors and lawyers, with the majority of the immigrants being German. It was a warmhearted and fulfilling community-structured life. He was a quiet member of the Shearith Israel and at home privately steeped in his culture and Judaism. He was free, unhindered and unhampered, and he sought a kind of invisibility, not unlike the private man nobody knew. God came first; washed thoroughly in his ethos, Haym then presented himself. Publicly, he was surrounded by, friends and friendship. Many of the New York Sons of Liberty took him into confidence and shopped almost exclusively at his store, especially for an afternoon nip or two. Tragically, he had no family of his own, but the Franks acted to some degree as an extended one. Seixas was undoubtedly his best of best friend. And, into the bargain from that night in Samuel Fraunces' tavern, Samuel became a frequent intimate. But of the most contrasting of styles, salty boisterous McDougall would become a constant companion, and another best friend. After so many years of untold misery, Haym Salomon felt a peace of mind— a sense of deliverance. He was reborn. The newly spelled and pronounced identity "Haym Salomon" represented that rebirth and in every insistence in which he was called upon, he was reborn again. In point of fact, America could have been Leszno, as Leszno could have been Amsterdam, and so on— nothing but places, defining spirits and mood in a given area which one makes their fortune or not. "Home," is where the heart is. Thereupon, it was in America, where his freedom appeared to be all encompassing to his nature and privilege, and unquestionably he rested his mind, spirit, and his soul in the center of his own heart. The history of man and government since chiefdoms, tribes, and the presence of Alulim, has been humanly rooted in the engineering of Political Law. In the theory of Natural Law, Political Law was and is the arbitrary legal statutes made by rulers, kings, queens, czars, councils, szlachtas, imperial and democratic bodies. They are edicts, decrees, dictums, ordinances, and enactments that are conceived and written by individuals. These laws, be them for better or for worse, are subject to the whims of the individuals who wrote them and the future selfsame individuals who will inevitably follow in their same position of political power which ordains their right to draft laws over the society.

Naturally, these whims are just as likely t[...]
season, or political influence, as anything else the de[...]
imparts. The devised laws of man-given political station[...]
holiness are unpredictable and constantly changing, and in[...]
purpose— right or wrong in the eye of the beholder, that inten[...]
the balance of one thing over another or give legitimacy where it o[...]
is absent. However, Natural Law isn't written, it is revealed;
acknowledged as the inherent and unchangeable reality of the universe.
Contrastingly, Natural Law is rooted in the single constituent of the
Divinity of God. To recognize Natural Law is to concede it is preeminent
to all man's political laws— above the deity of the king, the power of the
legislature, the changing tastes and whims of ministries— they are no less
than immortal truths in the face of tyranny. They are the eternal
unchanging moral principles of human regard and conduct which stand
demonstratively as a primary set of rights bestowed upon us all by an
unprejudiced nature or creator.

The essence of Natural Law is that individuals, regardless of any
factor or variable WHATSOEVER are endowed with certain and
fundamental rights as human beings, in relationship to all other human
beings and mechanisms, bodies, and authorities created by them. These
fundamental rights cannot be forfeited or taken away by mortal man or
self-righteousness divinity, for they come from the godhead, and if not
God, but the simple humanity of nature itself. These are "inalienable
rights." What are these inalienable rights? John Locke in his Two Treatises
of Government wrote that political society existed for the sake of
protecting "property," which he defined as a person's "life, liberty, and
estate." He went on to further give definition in A Letter Concerning
Toleration, he wrote that the magistrate's power was limited to preserving
a person's "civil interest," which he described as "life, liberty, health, and
indolency of body; and the possession of outward things." John Locke,
Father of Classical Liberalism, modern philosopher of law and ideology, in
his Essay Concerning Human Understanding, declared that "the highest
perfection of intellectual nature lies in a careful and constant pursuit of
true and solid happiness." These are the inalienable birthrights of man, the
human creature that the theory of Natural Law states no person, king, or
system of government can amend; these rights are beyond the reach of
mortal men and women, and cannot for even a second be stripped in any
just cause. The foundation of the social and political equality of men is
rooted in the unchanging, unalterable law of nature. Self-evident are these

greement, beyond consensus, beyond
f the Son ship.

had been reading. These were the
tions of the Sons of Liberty. And, every
ıst as he did when he was a child, he
Natural Law before a Shabbat candle
ҁ. As 1772, '73, and '74 turned on the
private hours where spent in the study of
ery book Moses Franks had at his disposal
on the subject. Surprisingly, ꞁlike the majority of the aristocratic rebels
that made up the brain-trust of the revolution— Jefferson, Madison,
Adams, his favorite author was not Locke or Hobbs, but a Catholic: St.
Thomas Aquinas. Aquinas grounded his theory of Natural Law in the
notion of God as Eternal Law. In asking whether there is an eternal law, he
begins by stating a general definition of all law: Law is a dictate of reason
from the ruler for the community he rules, and that all rulers are to rule for
the sake of the governed. This dictate of reason is first and foremost within
the reason or intellect of the ruler. It is the idea of what should be done to
insure the well ordered functioning of whatever community the ruler has
care for. Since he has elsewhere shown that God rules the world with his
reason, Aquinas concluded that God has in His intellect an idea by which
He governs the world.

This idea, in God, for the governance of things is the eternal law. Next,
Aquinas asked whether there is in man a natural law. First, he makes a
distinction: A law is not only in the reason of a ruler, but may also be in the
thing that is ruled. In the case of the Eternal Law, the things of creation
that are ruled by that Law have it imprinted on them through their nature
or essence. Since things act according to their nature, they derive their
proper acts and ends according to the law that is written into their nature.
Everything in nature, insofar as they reflect the order by which God directs
them through their nature for their own benefit, reflects the Eternal Law in
their own natures. He said that the Natural Law, as applied to the case of
human beings, requires greater precision because of the fact that they have
reason and free will.

It is the nature of humans to act freely by being inclined toward proper acts and end. That is, human beings must exercise their natural reason to discover what is best for them in order to achieve the end to which their nature inclines. The natural inclination of humans to achieve their proper end through reason and free will is the natural law. According to Aquinas, the Natural Law is defined by humans' participation in the Eternal Law, through reason and will. In applying this universal notion of Natural Law to the human person, one first must decide what it is that God has ordained human nature to be inclined toward. Since each thing has a nature given it by God, and each thing has a natural end, so there is a fulfillment to human activity of living. When a person discovers by reason what the purpose of living is, he or she discover what his or her natural end is. Accepting the medieval dictum "happiness is what all desire," a person is happy when he or she achieves this natural end.

Of course during those years, Haym was well aware of all the dramatic events happening about him in his newly adopted home. He didn't attend any further Sons of Liberty meetings but virtually every discussion in his store, with his friends, even in casual conversation were concerning storm clouds of war. In those years: The Boston Tea Party, Dunmore's War, the Intolerable Acts, the first Continental Congress, the Powder Alarm, Annapolis Tea Party, the Greenwich Tea Party, the Second Continental Congress, and the latest news of the Battle of Lexington and Concord— he was isolated, a lowly dry goods merchant, and not a party to any of these events. For the first time in his own life, he was outside of the storm— dry and content. But with the shot heard around the world, the war had begun, and events were bound to overtake him and sweep him directly into the tempest.

***

May of 1775 and Haym closed the shop for the evening. He locked the door and turned to light one of his Shabbat candles. Suddenly, there was a loud sound at the entrance. The sound was greater than a knock but slightly less than a pounding. He ambled over and without any concern or fear, as he once noticed how people attended to visitors in Amsterdam, he freely opened the door. Standing in the pouring rain was Alexander McDougall.

"Come in, my friend," said Haym.

McDougall knew to go straight to a false bookshelf to find a bottle of whiskey that probably still had his salvia on the lip. McDougall had clearly already been drinking but was far from drunk. He had come from a meeting of the New York Provincial Congress, but by way of Fraunces'. He arrived at the store with his shirttails crumpled and hanging lower than his jacket— dripping wet at the bottoms. Haym knew exactly what that meant, and he brought out another bottle and lit the lamp.

"It rains, hard— rains out there," McDougall said.

"Sit. It is dry in here," Haym said with a comical tinge. "Sit." McDougall plainly took a seat at the table, which was beside him, which he was already leaning on with one hand. In actuality, it was an item for sale and not where Haym usually sat with him. Nonetheless, Haym, the always tolerant host, carried with him the lamp and an additional bottle of whiskey to the other side of the room and accommodated his friend by taking a seat across from him.

"Where are you coming from, Alexander?"

"An assembly of the congress," he said, and then burped.

"Straight?"

"No, first… well you know where!"

"I hear they're calling you "The Wilkes of America."

"More rightly— I call Wilkes, the McDougall of England!" Haym laughed as McDougall drank.

"Let me tell you a story."

"A story?"

"A true story! A scottish story!"

"I don't mind."

Then, McDougall changed his focus and was very serious but unnerved.

"This— look at me, my friend— this is the Promised Land," McDougall began. "We must not— not now, question ourselves, our motives, nor our resolve. Some, I hear, in Philadelphia— have you been to Philadelphia?"

"No, I can't say I have."

"It doesn't compare to New York! More flies in summer! More flies!" he blurted before darkly growing serious again. "I hear of there— at the Continental Congress, some— some so I hear— have won the day and they have drafted a parchment unworthy of wiping the shit that comes out of an American's arse! They want to sue for peace. Fie! Did we not prevail in Concord? Liberty for peace! Fie and fie again! I hold these men in contempt! I know— yes I know who they are! Dickinson! A shitten fool if

I've ever seen one! God's teeth, and I'm sure on his bloody bleeding heart he twisted their minds with fear— even Jefferson, I understand! But I also know who cannot be swayed! Adams! Our good friend, the Lord's friend, John Adams! He stands without a quake in his boots. Petition the King! Piss! I would hand him not an olive branch but instead lift the trunk of the tree and commit an act of violence so grand, that our Almighty might smile on my handiwork."

He poured himself another glass and drank. He drank unlike a drunkard indulging and more as a seaman determined to brace himself for the voyage ahead.

"Haym, I have talked long this day, and we of New York are prepared... at present we have four companies of volunteers, but—"
Haym was listening, but in the meantime, he had rose and in his own workaholic manner, fixed things among shelves as McDougall spoke.

"But what?"
McDougall drank.

"Four companies at the ready and why are we of New York, not to your preference?

"Our sensibilities are to preparation but our hearts are still loyalist," he said frankly and somewhat embarrassingly."
Haym turned and they looked square at one another, until McDougall lightened the mood—

"You haven't heard my story. I have yet to tell you my story," McDougall said

"That is right, I have yet to hear a story as you so promised."

"I did not promise. No. I offered."

"And I excepted."

"Sit down, then, sit down."
Haym would rather have used the time to accomplish something worthwhile, while listening, but as was his good nature, he respectfully answered the request.

"Salomon, do you believe in fate?"

"I know in God," Haym said after musing if it was a riddle or something. "I need believe in nothing."

"Does your God rule the universe?"

"Of course."

"Would you say man has free will?"

"Of course."

"And has your God briefed you on all the incalculable possibilities that your free will avails you at every commencement of the moment?"

"I am to limited a vassal," he said with slight amusement.

"Then the word 'fate,' accounts for something to you," McDougall asserted.

Haym could not honestly dispute his terms.

"Do you know who the holy are about us in life? The bastards! Yes! It is the bastards that are the holiest of the holy," McDougall pronounced.

Haym guffawed at the suggestion but was also fascinated in the realm of the notion.

"You see, it is the bastard that undermines the good man, and causes him to go beyond himself. Without the bastard, an oblivious tool of the perverted free will— the ignorant afterthought of God's recalibration, the good man would not move from his seat but sit contentedly in blissful callow praise of the Lord. But you know, I am a sailor, and as a sailor, I have acquainted knowledge that the Lord cannot be properly praised without the expansion of erudition."

Haym remained silent, unsure of what McDougall was driving at; but McDougall was still driving—

"You know, from the earliest age I can remember, I remember with my ears better than my eyes. And I hear in my memory like someone yellin' into a copper pipe plumbed into your ear— I hear the sound of the sea. It's beating; it's never-stopping rhythm— the waters of the North Atlantic pulsating on my shores of my Islay. Oh, to say that I love— is not my wife first, or my children above her, but it is to say before them: the sea. Is it that you've ever heard of a fellow by the name of Campbell— Captain Lauchlin Campbell?

"No."

"Well… come when I was of the age of six, we was livin' in a black-house. Not a Negro mind you, it's kind of stone-and-peat walled cottage, a bit of timber and thatched-straw for a roof. Me father was a tenant on two farms. Then one day this fellow come around, this captain and he tells me dad about the Colonies. Beautiful he says. Free he says. Open he says. Now where's we were, we didn't get no problems with the English in London, and their designs of domination, but me dad thought that in New York where's he was told there was unlimited parcels for a pittance, that he'd be his own man.

Think, to be your own man. So we embarked. Me father had never traveled the sea, his hands as familiar with worms as are mine now with fish. Now, you's get sick at sea— I's gets well. But forgive me if too much I digress, but it was a long, cold, and harrowing journey— but all eighty-three families, togethers, we made it. You sees, each family paid for a number of acres. But when we's disembarked and traveled upwards on the soles of our feet about untamed land, to promise of our expectations, we were roundly chased off, like mice in a cupboard. Seems they said, the deed the government of New York gave this poor captain was resold and in's the time it took for him to sail back to Islay and accumulate us onto colonial shores, greeds gots the best of the governor. We's left our homes and suddenly had no homes or roofs, but the sky. Me father, with me mother, found refuge, where, even I, am too embarrassed and haunted to utter. Captain Campbell protested his innocence, but that is not much to eat on, and so me father set about and became a milkman. Imagine if you might, a farmer who thought he'd have his own farm, but instead, he was a milkman in strange land. Bastards.

"'Bastards?'" questioned Haym. "Less say, what happened to the captain?"

"He died, pennilessly of ill-repute."

"Yes. And... you site bastards."

"For which I am who I am, and we are where we are, in the service to fate that is incomprehensible, with all due respect, to 'vassals' such as... we."

Haym felt the poke of McDougall's intellectual little needle but nevertheless he could not resist the urge to rearrange the merchandise on a few of the shelfs, instead of partaking in a full recognition of McDougall presence.

"Join us!" bellowed McDougall! "Now is the time! Join us!"

"Join who? The congress?"

"The Sons! Join us; the Sons of Liberty!"

"I am honored—"

"Pribbling!"

Cutoff and suddenly insulted; Haym turned— not taking it well. He stopped his rearranging of jars and approached McDougall without so much rage, but with definite fire in his eyes.

"Say not what you said. Say it not. I do not succumb to piddling aspersions of my character. You know of the sea and I know of the land. Pray that I am wrong but I assure you that rhapsody will only take your cause so far before it is drowned in enthusiastic bloodshed. Accept my honored with honor. You remember in your ear the sound of the waves. I remember with my being, Poland. If you could see what I saw and know what you will now know — the scale of the armed protest was so embarrassingly small considering the size of the nation and the might of the enemy that in retrospect my memory has treated them as but a godlessly reckless strained effort than a true rebellion! I fear the same may be said for the American cause of self-determination."

McDougall, by now, his brain disinfected in liquor, had heard Haym talk so many times before but never with such a finely stated defense of himself and it almost left the drunken man speechless.

"Participate. I say it better to die an American than live an Englishman."

"Say nothing at all," Haym said in an attempt to bring the conversation to a close.

"The revolution has already begun! I suggest to you, a way of tripling your income! Triple it, I say! Cause be your cause first and still cause the same of all those of us who cause of higher virtue! The fort at Ticonderoga has been taken for arms! Massachusetts has moved on it and they are prepared to fight! New Hampshire prepared to fight! Connecticut prepared to fight! Sell your provisions there! A captive audience awaits! Nothing, I proclaim shall be left on these shelves to rearrange!"

***

In Boston, George Washington led Massachusetts Militiamen in a siege of the city. Following the Battle of Lexington and Concord the militia that was sounded to action by Dawes and Revere's cries immediately banded together to cutoff and isolate Gage and the British from being resupplied by the sea or able to march into further battle. It was war.

The Continental Congress that was adopting the Olive Branch Petition asking the King to rescind the Intolerable Acts in exchange for the Colonists' vowed loyalty and return to the fold, at the same time was splicing the razor's edge. They unanimously elected George Washington as its Commander-in-Chief against British aggression and as the Colonial forces continued to gather around Boston during the siege, they soon came upon a disquieting reality. They did not have the munitions or cannon to carry out a successful siege or any stalwart military operations.

Fort Ticonderoga, which was located on Lake Champlain, instantaneously became an objective for its stores of munitions and the strategic position of control that it held over the waterways to Canada. As a result, expeditions were immediately planned to capture the fort. Benedict Arnold, a captain in Connecticut's Militia proposed the capture of Ticonderoga and Crown Point, and the plan was approved by none other than Dr. Joseph Warren, chairman of the Committee of Safety. Thereafter, Arnold was commissioned as a colonel by the Provincial Congress of Massachusetts and directed to raise 400 troops in the western counties and surprise the forts. The same scheme had been entertained in Connecticut, and troops from that colony and from Berkshire, with a number of "Green Mountain Boys," had already started for the lakes under command of Colonel Ethan Allen. Allen was made colonel of an armed force known as the "Green Mountain Boys," raised in order to protect holders of land granted by New Hampshire. In the clash of territorial claims, this prior act was disputed by the Province of New York and served as cause for New York's Governor, William Tyron, to declare Allen an outlaw, and offered £120 for his capture.

Marching north, Arnold met up with Allen and sought to claim command of all forces. However, he was flatly refused and all he could do was to bitterly join Allen's expedition as a volunteer. Though, the intrigue of power would not cease at Arnold's yielding volunteerism. A few days later, Arnold and fifty of his own men boldly captured Fort St. Jean in Quebec. For his heroic action and leadership, Massachusetts asked Connecticut to put him in command of these posts, but Connecticut preferred Allen. When Arnold learned of Allen's final push toward Ticonderoga was underway, he left his men behind and hurried to catch up with Allen and the glory capturing the fort offered.

On May 9, Benedict Arnold arrived in Castleton, forty miles from the fort where he met up with Allen and his Green Mountain Boys. He haughtily insisted that he was taking command of the entire operation, based on his orders and commission from the Massachusetts Committee of Safety. Again, many of the Green Mountain Boys objected, insisting that they would go home rather than serve under anyone but Allen. Allen, wise to Arnold's vainglorious desires but most concern with the success of the expedition, worked out an agreement in which Arnold was given joint command of the operation.

Before the break of dawn, the following day, most of the British soldiers garrisoned were fast asleep as the rival Patriots stood on the edge of the fort and contemplated their next move. As the light of dawn emerged, fearful of losing the element of surprise and faced with only one sentry on duty at the southern gate, Allen and Arnold attacked!

Easily the militia overtook the single sentry and stampeded into the fort! The two leaders charged up the stairs into the officer's quarters! Allen kicked open the door, and shouted —

"In the name of the Great Jehovah and the Continental Congress, come out there, you damned old rats!"

So it was that the old dilapidated fort, was captured by the Americans, with but one errant shot fired. The spoil consisted only of two British Officers and fifty men. Yet, still it possessed a large stock of artillery. From the victory 100 cannon would make their way to Boston to support the siege. And before the month was over, the Green Mountain Boys were buying everything that a dry goods merchant named Haym Salomon had to offer. Shortly thereafter, Haym was once again, reborn, a fairly wealthy man.

***

XXII

WHELMED

"We must all hang together, or, assuredly, we shall all hang separately."
Benjamin Franklin

The sweltering summer of 1776 enraged and engulfed the skies with fire and the American consciousness with the prerogative of eternal self-determination. "We hold these truths to be self-evident, that all men are created equal, that they are endowed by their Creator with certain unalienable Rights, that among these are Life, Liberty and the pursuit of Happiness." So were the words that emblazoned the colonial path into a confraternity of peoples predominantly bent on a life lived in liberty over the kingly generosity of a life lived freely. And with war, for some solemnly and heroically comes death, and for others profits. So it was for Haym. There were not enough wagons or enough supplies to satisfy the insatiable at Fort Ticonderoga. Between his fortune and ability to acquire items cheaply by way of the Franks, and in turn, to sell them at impressive bargains— no solider, indian, or outfit went without his supply. Flush, he returned to New York and promptly moved his dry goods store to a larger location at 245 Broad Street. He ceased his distilling of whiskey, which he abhorred at any account, and fulfilled his personal ambition with the ensign operation of his own brokerage. However, before the sweltering summer reached it's zenith and smoke filled the air, that wasn't all he was engaged in.

***

A man tried by fate, Eustace was a general born Placidas under the Roman emperor Trajan. On one rather momentous afternoon, during a hunting excursion near Tivoli, in the deftly portent of supernatural encounters, his path crossed a stag with a crucifix glowing between its antlers, whereupon an empyrean voice prophesied that he was to suffer for Christ. As might be expected after being miraculously spoken to in Greek by a glowing deer; he and his entire family instantly converted to Christianity and were baptized. Promptly, he took the converted name of Eustachius.

After their conversion, tribulations, catastrophe, and various wicked disasters befell the family. Tried by fate, Eustachius was stripped of his property and position. To add insult to injury, his wife and children, were unceremoniously carried off by the Imperial Romans. However, his faith to Christ was unshaken, and only deepened. Undaunted, he was finally restored to his former position and reunited with his family. Now, tried by men, he refused to sacrifice to the gods, and was seized upon. Threatened with the choice between faith in Christ or the mortal life of his family, Eustachius, held his hand out to his wife and children and told them to come. Obediently, and without fear, they stood behind him; whereupon he thundered—

"Together, we live in Christ," he said.

In Christ they lived, together in death they roasted inside a brass bull.

Eight miles square. Centered between the British, the Spanish, and the French. Scorched by a Caribbean sun. The Island of St. Eustatius lay undefended by the Dutch. It was the richest island in the world. Per capita, a greater percentage of Jews lived, free of any restrictions or prejudice, than anywhere else in the world. It may have been the smallest swath of heaven anywhere on earth. And in the summer of 1776, a copy of the Declaration of Independence had traveled to the freewheeling island. Subsequently, a ship carrying a translated version to Amsterdam, was intercepted by the British. A letter accompanied the copy of the subversive document and both were confiscated and rerouted to London. It was assumed that the letter was seditious, because it appeared to be written in some secret code. The letter that needed to be deciphered was in a written Hebrew script— American Jews were simply communicating with their Dutch brethren around the world.

***

Haym was also a man tried by fate. He returned to New York City permanently in the spring of 1776. His fortune, he knew, was due to his friends— connections, favor looked upon him. There was no quid pro quo or implied sense of debt. However, the atmosphere and attitudes were such that emotions and tensions were running as high as a rabbit in a foxhole. What was incumbent upon him was to openly take a side and participate in any proactive way suggested of him or be looked upon as an ingrate and maybe worse, a loyalist. Still, he resisted all invitations to joining the Sons of Liberty, but when Seixas and Franks approached him about utilizing the store as a clearinghouse for some matériel, he was hesitant to resist. Though he would have rather not involved his own welfare, it seemed the least he could do.

Under direct command of the Dutch West India Company, the Dutch Government, in Amsterdam declared their small island of St. Eustatius in the leeward group of the West Indies a free open port. Due to the fact that the Dutch were neutral, the island couldn't rightfully or morally be attacked by their European rivals. In short time, St. Eustatius became the principal depot for the transshipment of goods to and from the American colonies. Neutrality permitted a triangle of various suppliers and purchasers in Europe, in particular— the Amsterdam based firm Isaac Moses and Company— to ship cargo directly to St. Eustatius or to the English, French, Spanish or Danish islands in the West Indies for transshipment to neutral islands which circumvented interference from Britain's navy.

At the time, the island was of some importance for sugar cultivation and also home to a Jewish settlement, mainly merchants and plantation owners. Since the island sold arms and ammunition to anyone willing to pay, it was one of the ways the rebellious thirteen colonies could obtain weaponry before the war. Once the war began, this light flow of traffic had to rapidly expand for the Americans to have any chance of defeating the British.

***

The little inlets of water into land— singular individual harbors— slips as they were called throughout Manhattan, could be traced back to the days of New Amsterdam. The waterfront of the East River was swampy, and the area around it was covered by high tides. The Dutch, the inveterate artists of nature that they were, filled in those marshy swamp-ridden areas. In the art of their exquisite efforts and the ordained purpose of practicality, they left a few arms of the river reaching into the land to shelter ships being unloaded. At the Whitehall Slip, adjoining the Battery, at the bottom of Whitehall Street, stood the Fighting Cock Tavern.

It was a tavern of exceptional ill-repute. The name spoke volumes but was insufficient to communicate the alehouses' entire story. The tavern was a magnet for the immigrants who were not of standing order, religiously speaking that is. The clientele were mostly Baptists and

Methodists who arrived from the east end of London. It may be presumed they were attracted to America by the illustrious promise of freedom of religion. However, this hardly accorded with the traditions they brought to the Fighting Cock Tavern. Those who frequented the establishment were generally addicted to drinking, gaming, horse racing, wrestling, sex, and of course, cock fighting.

In the early morning hours of September 21st, before the seraphs of goodness wake and the black-hearted fiends of wickedness sleep, somewhere in the activities of these debaucheries, a fire was set — accidentally or purposefully. In little time, the flames would esuriently engulf a third of the city that was once New Amsterdam. Before the last ember smoldered into a thin vaporizing trail of smoke, over 500 buildings would burn to ashes in the incredibly hot inferno. For a time, as the sun broke the black into blue, the British soldiers attempted to extinguish the flames, but with sabotaged equipment — it was an impossibility that even English doggedness could not overcome. And, among the buildings that were charred into a state of carbon, was a popular dry goods store at 245 Broad Street.

***

Haym had grossed a small fortune selling and trading provisions to the Army and to the soldiers in Lake Champlain. He arrived one of a few different merchant-traders. One was a dry goods proprietor from upper New York who dealt mainly in pelts. Another was a dealer who sold many of the same items that Haym did — rice, tea, iron, and guns, but did not possess the same advantage of having acquired his items so far below cost. Not to mention Haym had another secret weapon that enticed customers — he traded currency! In direct competition with "the Jew," the second dry goods merchant lasted only a month before the only goods traded and sold were from either Haym or the pelt dealer. It was a 90-10 split when it came to sales, but that wasn't enough of a monopoly for Haym. His financial instincts were lethal. He was a friendly — even kindly fellow, but a ruthless businessman and competitor. Haym shrewdly offered to buy all of the man's pelts, that is on a discounted rate based on volume he was acquiring. The man joyously sold his furs and considered himself rich! Rich is a relative concept, and Haym, who didn't consider himself "rich," stood as the single merchant for all of the Fort's needs.

From the shop to the fort, Haym was primarily able to conduct his affairs and build his Lilliputian empire by the graciousness of the Franks. Moses' father, Jacob, was arguably, New York's most successful merchant. With the advantage of the family merchandise in England, family owned ships crossing the Atlantic, and Royal commissions, his power to set prices was beyond standard market leverage. They were the most powerful Jewish clan in the Colonies. At one time, Moses' father Jacob, was the king's fiscal agent, similar to the position that Meyer had held with Prince Wilhelm. As the royal agent for the Northern Colonies, he distributed royal revenues to governors, ships, soldiers, and others who had dealings with the government, including loggers entitled to bounties on pine for the Royal Navy. In turn, he was able to supply Haym with cast-off merchandise, supplemental inventory, and remnants of products sold in bulk, and every-day essentials at a price that made anything beyond giving it away, a profit for the nascent shop owner. This generous arrangement was not going to last forever, but it was something through the patronage of Moses that Haym would be able to exploit until he had saved enough to start his aspiring brokerage firm.

While at Fort Ticonderoga, Haym held many a British Brown Bess' and French Charlevilles. These were traditional long flintlock rifles. Around the colonies, the British guns were predominate. However, the French Charleville flintlocks were quite common. But now, in the glow of midnight lamplight, in his hands he held a Dutch Liège. It was lighter than the British armaments and mechanically simpler than the typical French carbine. Clearly, it was built on lightweight stocks with slender wrists and fine lines. A beautiful appliance for the death of a living organism.

He had just received a shipment from St. Eustatius — and the wooden cargo boxes were stenciled with "Isaac Moses & Co." In his new building, he had a significantly larger storage capacity and alone, two-by-two, he began to carry the inventory of munitions into the storeroom.

***

By the final day of summer 1776 — lower Manhattan burned in a conflagration of air, spark, fuel, and unparalleled events. The first of these events began with arguably the most inflammatory tract in the whole of human history:

> Some writers have so confounded society with government, as to leave little or no distinction between them; whereas they are not only different, but have different origins. Society is produced by our wants, and government by our wickedness; the former promotes our happiness positively by uniting our affections, the latter negatively by restraining our vices. The one encourages intercourse, the other creates distinctions. The first is a patron, the last a punisher…

The literary arsonist was none other than a professional corsetiere and expert agitator named Thomas Paine, and his tract was unpretentiously entitled, Common Sense. At the time of the circulation of the thin little pamphlet, many, even in the intellectual circles of the independence movement, were divided as to the most proper course of action to achieve their aims. As Englishmen, they didn't want to cease being Englishmen. Yet, as Americans, they didn't want to sublimate their Americanism to English volition.

General George Washington, as much, if not more, was a metaphysical leader of men, just as he was the general of the American cause. He had spent months maddeningly camped outside of Boston wriggling the combination to the lock that would reveal the riddle of how to take Boston from the besieged British. He was low on men, morale, money, armaments, and answers. He attacked at Breed's Hill, and was repelled. Recruits were leaving in droves. The ones who didn't, were moved by Washington's tireless emotional appeals, and remained out of guilt or daft inspiration. Then came Paine's words. They brought a clarity and focus to the soldiers' libertarian purpose that exponentially raised the spirit of the men. With that newfound élan and cannons from Fort Ticonderoga, Washington and the Americans took Dorchester Hill and watched as General Howe and his professional army retreated out of Boston. The score between Washington and Howe was 1-1.

Events continued to unfurl at a rapid refractory pace. England declared all commerce and trade with the Colonies closed — forbidden — an act of war! Outside of the Colonies, the least pleased about the development were the European trading partners. Naturally, the British left the shipping ports open to their own goods but closed to all other

270

traffic. Thus, what couldn't readily go to America, readily headed south to St. Eustatius, where if there was money and will, there was always a way.

Trade and commerce was the heart of the American psyche and the British action simply exacerbated the acrimony. All across the Colonies, patriots easily expelled the Royal governors and suppressed the loyalists. Each colony erected and elected its own representation. The Colonies of Rhode Island, followed by North Carolina went so far as to declare their own independence from King George. The Second Continental Congress had hastily drafted the "Declaration of the Causes and Necessity of Taking Up Arms," which accompanied their Olive Branch Petition of a year earlier in hopes of avoiding war. These documents outlined their self-serving positions and by the summer of 1776, they were still discussing a peaceful resolution through diplomatic channels when the Americans' minds profoundly changed.

> "When in the Course of human events, it becomes necessary for one people to dissolve the political bands which have connected them with another, and to assume among the powers of the earth, the separate and equal station to which the Laws of Nature and of Nature's God entitle them, a decent respect to the opinions of mankind requires that they should declare the causes which impel them to the separation."

Thus was their opening salvo to the most eloquent text on the plight of the human spirit, articulating itself to already be free. The nation ceased vacillating or being divided in its providential cause. Americans were Englishmen no longer.

The Bourbon monarch, Louise XVI pledged a million louis d'ors, munitions, and matériel. Charles III of Spain followed suit. The British would stand for this betide no more. It was a colonial civil war that had the potential of being yet another world war, as was the Seven Year's War only thirteen years before. George rejected the Colonists Olive Branch straight out of hand; going so far as refusing to even read it. Under no circumstance was such a sovereign who viewed himself the most powerful of all the world's sovereigns going to acknowledge the independence of his simple subjects. He was going to punish them, even if it had to be all the way to hell. His reply to the Olive Branch Petition was the standard lyrical fare over the rhythmic pounding of war drums.

> Whereas many of our subjects in divers parts of
> our Colonies and Plantations in North America,
> misled by dangerous and ill designing men, and
> forgetting the allegiance which they owe to the
> power that has protected and supported them...
> ...have at length proceeded to open and avowed
> rebellion, by arraying themselves in a hostile
> manner, to withstand the execution of the law,
> and traitorously preparing, ordering and levying
> war against us...
> ...And whereas, there is reason to apprehend that
> such rebellion hath been much promoted and
> encouraged by the traitorous correspondence,
> counsels and comfort of divers wicked and
> desperate persons within this realm...
> God save the King

The British began their full-scale operation of war. Washington knew the geographical prize Howe would endeavor first: New York. A last minute peace conference attended by John Adams and Benjamin Franklin proved fruitless. Washington, even if unprepared, was prepared to take the fight to Howe. The American forces were prepared, even if they were unprepared to engage in the fight. Fight he did, at Brooklyn Heights. Unprepared as they were, the Americans were decisively defeated at Long Island. New York was evacuated to the very prepared and undeniably superior British forces. Howe 2 - Washington 1.

***

"...did you receive the—" Seixas said, cutting off his own words.
"Receive what?" Haym somewhat innocently asked.
Seixas stared mightily at him, until Haym concerned himself with the stationary and courtly manner in which Seixas was carrying himself. Haym was abuzz, busying himself with multiplying, adding, subtracting and dividing numbers across multiple ledgers. Seixas stood majestically in

his humorless disposition. Haym quickly knew exactly what the hazzan was asking.

"Yes. I am in possession."

"Well."

There was a long restlessness between them. Haym's voracious appetite for mathematics was suddenly curbed and though it was the middle of the day, he felt fraught with nervous tension. After that, therefore because of it, he peeked around his own blind corners, and posthaste, settled about closing and locking the shop. An element of the emotional memory of the Rothschild Bank in Warsaw played upon his sense of equilibrium. He wanted very much to feel different, to feel how he felt before he received the shipments. The innocence in his Americanism was dashed.

It wasn't running from the Russians in Poland to Amsterdam. It wasn't the infernal discomfort of the Judengasse, and it wasn't the displacement of London. Yet, the overwhelming feeling of being an active part in the enterprise of other's ideals, conventions, and campaigns was hauntingly familiar. However, as he consistently did, he suppressed the emotional memory and deftly rose to the occasion expected of him.

"What do I do now?" Haym asked.

"Speak not," Seixas replied.

The words stopped. But Haym was nervous, and he desperately wanted to speak of it.

"Where—?"

"Speak not," Seixas hushed him.

Haym was annoyed, discombobulated, like an insect trapped in a glass jar—

"It is only us," Haym assured him.

Then, a knock came to the door! They froze. Knock-knock— Knock-knock— Knock-knock— it was incessant. Finally—

"Haym, are you in there? It's me, Rachel!"

They exhaled and breathed a palliated sigh of relief. Haym opened the door and Rachel Franks, now a pretty fourteen year-old girl, entered with easy familiarity. She had blossomed into a comely young woman. She was as dutiful and forceful as ever. Her motherly instincts and people pleasing skills were matched into an agreeable personality.

"Oh, hello Rabbi," she said. "Why was the door locked?" she asked, suddenly realizing it had been.

Haym could have very well have told her a fib, but instead—

"I was speaking on private matters with the rabbi."

"Oh," said Rachel, unbothered. "My father has sent me to invite you to sup with us. My uncle, my grandfather, will be in attendance, and also the rabbi—"

"Yes, I came about to invite him also," Seixas said.

"So, shall I tell me father you will be in attendance?"

"Yes, like it or not, you shall see my smiling face."

She smiled—

"I'd like it."

They smiled at one another. It was an innocent smile but it wasn't without Rachel's obvious maturing sensibilities. Haym mussed her head and sent her off more the child he met her as then the woman she was quickly becoming.

Haym and Seixas were alone again— the door of the store left open. Before Haym could bring down the sunlight and bring up the over-ripe mysterious aura of the cloak and dagger, Seixas severed the solid air—

"Now for your curiosity," Seixas said. "Is this a dry goods shop?"

"Yea," Haym said, patiently playing along.

"And do you sell ammunition?"

"Yea."

"And do you sell guns for that ammunition?"

"Yea."

"That's all the information you need to know. The inventory will move by itself— like it has legs."

Haym astutely got the point just as a customer entered.

"Good afternoon, sirs! I need a washboard!"

***

Outside of the fifty-six men who signed the Declaration of Independence on July 4th, 1776, that summer was dominated by three names: George Washington, William Howe, and Nathan Hale. Subordinate to those towering figures co-oped by history, Captain James Cook set off from London for yet another voyage to the South Pacific, Australia, and the uncharted Antarctic region. The famed wonder, Mozart, a mere twenty years old and at the height of his powers, premiered his exquisite Serenade No. 7 for the wedding of Marie Elisabeth Haffner. In Russia, Catherine II personally oversaw the interactions between the fledging American Colonies with an eye to undermine the British Empire at every turn of the screw. In Morocco, Sultan Mohammed III took the extraordinary step of recognizing the American nation when the British failed to fulfill their promise of aid to buttress his siege of the Spanish at Melilla. In Poland, King Stanisław August Poniatowski led the horse to water in an attempt to codify the nations perviously uncodified laws. As expected, some things never change and the horse didn't drink. Let it be noted, that the span between the vernal and the autumnal equinoctial points of 1776 was not a time for the unarmed, the unwilling, the unprepared, or the fainthearted.

General George Washington just might have been the tallest man in the war. At a good measure, he was a strapping 6′3, and appeared to stand even taller from the height of "General," — looking up at him, that is, from a lower size and rank. He was born in the Colonies, a Virginian. He descended from an old and titled family in Lancashire, England, and was the eldest child of his father, by Mary Ball, his second wife. He received a common English education, and upon that, a naturally thoughtful and right-conditioned mind. Truth and justice were the cardinal virtues of his character, and propitious self-promotion his foremost vice of personality. At fourteen, he wished to enter the navy, but yielded to the discouraging persuasions of his mother; landlocked, by the time George was seventeen, he was one of the most accomplished land surveyors in Virginia.

His military career began at the potent age of nineteen and at the humble rank of General's adjutant. However, he soon resigned his commission to accompany an invalid half-brother to the West Indies. Two years later, when the French turned their designs in a meridional direction and began to build forts southward of Lake Erie, he was sent by the royal governor of Virginia, to demand a cessation of such hostile movements. He performed the delicate diplomatic mission with great aplomb; and so highly were his services esteemed, that when, in 1755, General Edward Braddock, commander-in-chief of the British armed forces for the thirteen colonies in the French and Indian War came to drive the French from the vicinity of the Ohio, Washington was chosen to be his principal aid. In a fateful skirmish in the southern end of the Pennsylvania Colony, Braddock was defeated and killed, and his entire army only escaped utter destruction through the skill and valor of Colonel Washington, who heroically directed their retreat. Washington continued in active military service until the close of 1758, when he resigned his commission, and retired to private life.

With the refined requiescence of a fish flopping on the beach, he quietly pursued the business of a farmer. That was until he heard the "shot heard round the world!" Washington dusted-off and pressed his old uniform, and by the unanimous voice of his compatriots he was chosen commander-in-chief of the army of freemen which had gathered spontaneously around Boston. He was also the only individual present immodestly wearing a uniform and intimating a desire for the prestige and the post.

General William Howe was two and half years older than his American rival. Born in Twickenham, he was the illegitimate uncle of King George III, the crowned head opposing the Colonists effort to be free. Howe, like Gage before him, whom he replaced after the debacle at Concord, was a Whig, and sympathetic to the Colonists' aspirations. However, for him, eternal glory lay in whipping the Colonists into shame, just deserts, and surrender!

Howe entered the army at seventeen by purchasing a cornet's commission in the Dragoons of the Duke of Cumberland and cut his teeth in the War of the Austrian Succession. Stationed in the Low Countries at Flanders, he distinguished himself as a burgeoning cavalryman. In Scotland he gloriously engaged in opposing the Bonnie Prince Charles from regaining the Scottish throne. Howe was a complete military man. His hands bloody, his vision of the battlefield, stereoscopic; his mind nimble— with a tremendous storehouse of courage to execute daring.

Advancement in the ranks, again sent him abroad. Like many in the Revolution hierarchy, he saw time in the French and Indian War. He fought bravely, but undistinguished. He returned to England without abandoning his military service— and with the domineering assistance of his mother, he was duly elected a Member of Parliament. As tensions rose between Britain and the colonies, Howe continued to steadily rise through the ranks, and came to be widely regarded as one of the best officers in the army.

He arrived in Boston a month after the "shot heard round the world," decorated as a Major General. Immediately upon landing, he roused a fighting spirit and led the trapped and embarrassed Bostonian British on the attack. This would be the hallmark of Howe's command— attack! Attack! Attack! And, in the summer of 1776, just as Washington expected— having lost Boston, Howe and his troops began the battle for New York.

Nathan Hale was a brilliant young mind waiting to happen—however tragedy alternatively transpired. Nathan hailed from a prosperous and successful farming family. He was a student of higher learning and attended Yale College, where he excelled academically as well as in the arts— and in particular, the drama of theater. Finishing at the top of his class, he was exceptionally handsome, exuberant, carefree, learned, and serious-minded; by all auguries of youth, Nathan Hale's future appeared very bright.

After graduation, at the tender age of eighteen, he probably intended to become a Christian minister, as his older brother did. But, as was almost a custom of the time, he began his active life as a teacher in the public schools. As the news of Lexington and Concord reached his home of New London, Connecticut, a town meeting was called. At this meeting, the young man, not yet even of age, was one of the speakers. "Let us march immediately," he said, "and never lay down our arms until we obtain our independence!" He assembled at his school as usual the next day, but only to take leave of his scholars. He gave them earnest counsel, prayed with them, shook each by hand, and then bade them farewell.

Immediately, he was given a commission as a First Lieutenant in the Seventh Connecticut regiment. The first duty assigned to the regiment was in the neighborhood of New London, where they were to drill until discipline assuredly fell upon them more than the enthusiasm, which infected them. Then, on September 14th, 1775, they were ordered by Washington to Cambridge. There they were placed on the left wing of his army and made their camp at the foot of Winter Hill. This was the post, which commanded the passage from Charlestown, one of the only two roads by which the English could march out from Boston. Here they remained until the summer of 1776.

***

As the fire burned, Haym was still in the city. Many inhabitants had left New York with Howe's imminent capture and eventual occupation. Those that remained and woke to the light, heat, and cacophony of the blaze, were cautious not to loiter about the streets or lift a helpful finger. However, one such brave and foolish man was Peter Roome. He was an active member of the city's sterling volunteer fire department. Excluding himself, every other member had evacuated the city when Washington abandoned it to Howe days before. Peter, bless his heart, couldn't watch the world burn without taking action. Lionhearted, he rushed into the dawning street and with his own bucket, did all that could in the face of an unimaginable inferno. Howe's men, fell upon him, and credulously assumed him guilty of having a hand in the blaze, though he was tirelessly expending an effort to extinguish it. They savagely beat him until his body surrendered to sin of the flesh and his soul answered the call of heaven. This though, was not to be unexpected. The British were rightfully over-suspicious of any colonist. Since February, flash mob violence against Loyalists had been a common occurrence. Throngs of patriot colonists with politics and fever running high through their nerves and loins were not beyond rounding up suspected Loyalists and stripping them bare while pummeling them with sticks and rods. However, this, too wasn't without cause. The citizenry of the city were clearly divided over who they were supporting. Those who supported the British while Washington held the city were often brazen in their aid and comfort. Around this time the provincial congress appointed a "Committee to Detect Conspiracies," which uncovered an astonishing plot to assassinate George Washington. Two dozen New Yorkers, including Loyalist Mayor David Mathews, were taken into custody. Thus, once the British had taken the city — a city they believed was their property by right, it wasn't safe for any patriot to show their face. Everyone was a suspect, a betrayer of the King, a backstabber, a double-crosser, a turncoat, a collaborator, a mole, a fink, a rat, a Judas, a quisling little deserter. And, Peter Roome, a member of the well-known Patriot swayed Volunteer Fire Department, defied the sensibilities of his fellow New Yorkers and revealed himself in harm's way. Sure, the British could have recognized his bravery, but as the fire jumped from rooftop to rooftop and buildings disintegrated in a matter of minutes, they were already looking for their "suspected" patriot arsonist amid the sweeping flames conflagration. The Red Coats were quickly organized into an ad hoc fire department but they soon discovered that the church bells to sound the alarm were missing; and fire buckets lacked handles or were inexplicably punctured with holes in their bottoms — presumably by the Volunteer Fire Department.

Even though it was before dawn, Haym was already at the dry goods store shelving bottles of Ayer's Sarsaparilla. He hadn't fled the city. As a matter of fact, six months ago he was returning while many were leaving. By the time the fire broke out and the embers were flitting on the stream of hot dry winds, he intended to ride out the glowing pyre. But, as the brightness approached and lit the darkness of night into a blindness of smoke and flames, he gave way to reality and withdrew to the synagogue. From the safe distance, the majority of the congregation was present and they watched the sun compete with the light and heat of the inferno. Seixas ended his prayer session and drew a deep breath. Then, without warning, he went about collecting the scrolls and carting them right in front of a suddenly shocked and upset congregation. He met their shock and horror in a dire tone of his own—

"New York is lost! We must escape with our lives," he said. The sat about with their mouth's agape.

"I implore you, today— today if you can!" he said. "How many other congregations have left the city? We are one of the few, and now, by the flames that rise above us, see that God is saying it is time." He looked down at his new wife who was virtually grasping his feet looking up—

"To your families far away, to your in-laws, your uncles, aunts, friends, anywhere, but this ground we so cherish! To stay here, is to surely be seen as an enemy. They— the dogs of war, will kill their enemies." No one present was aware that Peter Roome was dead, but chills ran down many spines. After a few moments of heads turning, there was nothing else to do but bid one another farewell. Of all the worry and tears, Haym was the coolest and least moved. Seixas though, was concerned for him and approached. Haym was standing with all of the ledgers from the store safely in his arms.

"We are going to Strafford— in Connecticut, to her father's— I know you have no one here, and I welcome you to come with us," he said to his friend. Elkalah Cohen was now Seixas' wife and she nodded her head in approval. However, Haym stared at them a bit more resolute than Seixas may have expected—

"My home and my store are here," Haym said.

"Your store is burning! And your home will soon burn, too!"

"He can stay with us," Franks suddenly interjected.

"Seixas looked incredulous, my friends, we cannot chance the trust of their goodwill to stay," he said. Then through his teeth, he sibilated, "And we can't advance our cause, dead— or worse, from New York."

"Has anyone employed your merchandise as of today?" Franks whispered into Haym's ear.

"Agents of the Continental's have been prompt— they come the same day in the month until I am stocked."

"You should not stay here," Seixas said to Haym.

"I intend to stay—" said Franks.

"And neither should you," he responded to Franks.

"We will stay until the last moment," Franks asserted; something that pleased his daughter Rachel.

Rachel stood near in the conversation, pretending to be looking in her prayer books but her ears were listening intently.

"I am not any agent of organization or registry which indicts my character against the British," Haym said.

"Suttling at Ticonderoga—"

"And I'll "suttle" for them here if they step into my store," Haym said.

"Traitor," Seixas accused him.

"Then logic would state I would otherwise have to flee."

"Which by all rights you should!" Seixas raised his tone.

"I will stand in protest alone," Haym defended himself. "But I will not flee!"

Seixas sneered, upset at his friend, which that alone upset him. Franks, Elkalah, and Rachel were entwined in the tension and the most was uncomfortable just as much as it was pressing. Above all, Seixas wanted to save his friend and could not understand his obstinate orientation...

"They will break you—"

"I've heard that before, Haym said after scoffing. "I'm not running."

"You're a Jew— they will have no mercy and only suspicions!"

"Seixas, my friend... I am grateful— your consternation. But understand that I have fled my whole life. I flee no more," Haym said sincerely and resolutely.

***

Once Washington had captured Boston, Howe and his modest force set sail for Halifax, Nova Scotia. There he would lick his wounds and devise his counterattack. Washington wasted no time in his fortifying of Boston and marching out of the city. He suspected that Howe would regroup and set his sights squarely on North America's biggest prize, New York. Indeed, Washington was correct.

With Boston behind them, Washington drove his army through spontaneous celebrations that adored them with glory all the way south to

New York; whereupon the glory ended and he positioned the Continental troops on the hills back of Brooklyn on Long Island. It was there, from March until late June, they waited.

The wait waned when a massive British war fleet arrived in New York Harbor on June 29th and landed on Staten Island on the 3rd of July. Of course, the following day in Philadelphia, the Continental Congress, comported itself in a way no body or group of people have ever done in the whole of human history. They righteously declared Independence from their ruling nation.

Nevertheless, the British disembarked a retinue that consisted of thirty battleships with 1200 cannon, 30,000 soldiers, 10,000 of which were Hessians, 10,000 sailors, and 300 supply ships, under the command of General William Howe and his brother Admiral Lord Richard Howe. Washington and his farm boy army watched them impressively spread out below their heights to a final tally of 32,000 armed troops.

Despite overwhelming superior forces, in the name of civility and bloodless victory, Howe decided to employ a little statesmanship and diplomacy before blasting the Americans into overpowering submission. He wrote to Washington, offering pardon to all persons who should desist from rebellion; he addressed the letter to "George Washington, Esq.," and sent it under the flag of truce. The messenger was told there was no one in the army with that title. A week later another messenger came with a paper addressed as "George Washington, Esq. etc. etc." This time he was received; and when Washington declined to receive the letter, the messenger explained that "etc. etc." meant everything. "Indeed," said Washington, "they might mean anything." He was determined that Howe should recognize him as a commander in chief of the Continental Army, and not treat him as a leader of rebels. The stage was set and Howe was obliged to employ total war.

Washington had built batteries on Manhattan and Long Island to prevent the British fleet from penetrating past New York. Of his 18,000 men Washington had positioned around 10,000 in fortifications on Brooklyn Heights, facing the sea and inland, to defend the approach to Manhattan. This force was commanded by the old Major General, Israel Putnam. Part of the American force held the fortified area along the coast while the main body had taken up positions along the high ground inland. It was only a matter of time, and that matter concluded on August 22nd when the British force confidently landed on Long Island to the South of the American fortifications.

It was a spectacle of power; as the British were adorned with red coats and headgear of bearskin caps, small caps or tricorne hats depending on whether the troops were grenadiers, light infantry or battalion company men. The Americans were still dressed as best they could, for the most part, whatever was in each man's closet when he enlisted. Both sides were armed with muskets and guns. The more-well-to-do Pennsylvania regiments carried rifled weapons. Washington was staring into the collective might of: The Queen's Royal Lancers, the 17th Light Dragoons, the 4th, 5th, 10th, 22nd, 27th, 28th, 33rd, 37th, 38th, 42nd, 43rd, 44th, 45th, 49th, 52nd, 53rd, and 63rd, divisions of foot, a battalion of grenadiers, light infantry, and the 1st, 2nd, and 3rd Foot Guards. To add to the armed humanity, reinforcements began to arrive from Britain and Major General Clinton returned from his abortive foray to Charleston, South Carolina. You could say that the weight of the world was set against the virtuous patriot band of militia defending their homes and their ideals of humanity. Or you could say the traitorous ragtag army of rebels lead by a wealthy Virginian ex-British officer was in over the heads.

Finally, on 26th of August the main body of the British troops marched northeast along the line of high ground held by the Americans to begin their attack. Information revealed to the British that the most northern of the three roads across the high ground was not guarded. Howe personally lead his troops over the road and was enabled to attack the left American division commanded by John Sullivan in the flank and rear while Hessian troops attacked in front. Routed, Sullivan's troops were forced to leave their positions in runnels of blood and checkered patterns of human shells and retreat behind the main Brooklyn fortifications.

On the right of the American position, Clinton had attacked with a smaller force. William Alexander, who claimed the disputed and dubious title of "Earl of Stirling," fought bravely, and his men resisted for a considerable time until the British appeared in their rear from the other flank. Eventually, out flanked and out numbered, facing their own massacre, they fell back to the fortified line. Washington brought reinforcements from New York but with the increasing threat from the Royal Navy he withdrew from Brooklyn and eventually the city itself. Inexplicably, Howe failed to interfere with the withdrawal more than once, losing the opportunity to capture Washington and much of the Continental Army.

When the gunpowder cleared, the British suffered no more than 400 casualties while the Americans lost over 10% of their fighting force. By the time Washington skillfully fought his way backwards to Delaware, as he had done in the French and Indian War, a larger majority of his army gave up the fight and deserted. However, one who didn't lose hope or abandoned the cause was Nathan Hale, on the contrary, he was standing tall! While the army retreated, Hale volunteered to enter the British lines on Long Island to procure information; or simply put: to spy.

For the time being the Continental Army was roundly defeated and New York was insufferably lost. Howe 2 - Washington 1. The only question left for Washington's retreating army was, should they depart cataclysmically burning Howe's prize to the ground?

***

Nathanael Greene's nickname was "The Fighting Quaker." His patriot originated military career began on the qualities of enthusiasm, love of country, and grit. Despite that tenuous commencement, by the Battle of Long Island, Washington had promoted him into the rank of a Major General. As they were making preparations to concede the city, Nathanael officially presented his general with a one-size-fits all solution to many of their pressing problems, namely the loss of a valuable piece of geography and psychology, New York.

"…and what are you proposing, Major Greene?" Washington asked.

"Dear General, sir, proposing no. I have nothing to propose. However, I do have a suggestion," he said.

"And what might that be?"

"Let it burn… let it burn, sir."

"Let what burn, Major?"

"New York," he said after a hard swallow. "I would burn the city and the suburbs, burn them to the ground."

"Do I detect the timbre of madness? What do you mean?" Washington said, flabbergasted.

"I say, General, if we are forced to give them the apple, let us not give it to them in edible condition."

It was an incredibly reckless suggestion. Yet, intensely smart. It also had been bandied around among some of the officers, but no one wanted to say it aloud. Washington considered the recommendation and did not deny the possible value in it. As a matter of fact, he loved the idea! To him, it represented the best military option in the face of retreat!

Without losing another minute, he rushed Greene to Congress for their input. At the same time, Nathan Hale received his approval from General Washington and began what was planned as a four-day mission.

In the hours of twinkling and chirping hours of twilight, he set out with his childhood friend, Sergeant Stephen Hempstead. They boarded a small dinghy called the Schuyler, and it quietly floated them to Long Island. For Hempstead, that was as far as he was ordered to go. The two friends knew the danger involved and that if misfortune came upon Hale, surely, they would never see each other again.

Nathan stepped off the boat with a certain unneeded air, pomp, and circumstance. He was tall and lanky with self-crowning majestic pretension. Spies are generally low-key individuals, intent on blending into the crowd. Hale was just the opposite. He was a spy that brought grace to the character, if the character of espionage needed one. He didn't intend to merely blend in. He intended to be a magnet— or a flame by which the moths were compelled to come. Nevertheless, as he stepped ashore, he clutched his Yale diploma, ready to play the theatrical role of a Dutch schoolmaster wandering about in search of employment. Maybe it sounds ill-conceived or half-baked, but it was September and his less than brilliant disguise, was to him, altogether brilliant.

As he walked from the shore toward town, his mission was on track. His strategy was simple; pretend to be a benign Dutch schoolmaster with Tory leanings. As Long Island was primarily populated from Dutch as far back as when New York was New Amsterdam. Under this winsome proposition of delightful panache and intelligence, he would head straight for Brooklyn and work his way into Howe's camps along the shores of the East River on the Long Island side. Once there, he would causally take up conversations with soldiers and civilians, and with any luck, gain an understanding of Howe's troop strength and short-term plans. From there, he planned to draw maps, keep detailed notes, and get a feel for how the British viewed the war. Subsequently, once he accomplished this nearly impossible feat for yet a mere Dutch schoolmaster, he was to cross back to New York and meet up with his Connecticut Officer, Captain Pond— once again reverting back to his true pompous identity: Nathan Hale, spy extraordinaire!

Well, phase one of the plan of moseying into the army and ingratiating himself proved more significantly difficult then he assumed. Too many sentries, too many questions, though the Dutch schoolmaster wiggled and wormed his way out of every cross looking eye. To approximate the plan, he traveled from Huntington to Flushing, and somewhat cleverly improvised. Hale spent his few appointed days and nights in taverns talking to patrons, looking for drunkards and loose-lipped grunts to support what he talked up as Howe's eventual drubbing of the Americans! He laid it on thick! "I pity the rebels as I do a pig to slaughter!" "I drink to his majesty, my king!" "Washington is a fool; long live Howe!" Generally, he made a jackass out of himself, but it was moderately effective.

Everything Nathan did was tactical but beyond his perception, luck served him more than his wits. Many an opportunity passed in which he could have been stopped and questioned by the numerous sentries the British had about the island or kicked in the teeth for being so loud by a tavern owner. But luck appeared to be on his side, and unarguably, he succeeded at avoiding both and ultimately was able to obtain information, draw maps, and accumulate copious notes. For all of Nathan Hale's self-importance, success was within his pocket.

Phase two of the mission was the return and relaying the information to Washington. Unbeknownst to Hale, while he was gone, Washington, who was already forced to retreat to Harlem, took it upon himself to fall back even further, across the Hudson to New Jersey. However, the General made a critical error in this excursion. A force of 1,800 fighting men he left in Manhattan, he put under the hesitant command of General Putnam. This was an unmitigated mistake. The old fart didn't have the nerve to stand his ground against the withering British cannon fire and he flatly disobeyed Washington's orders. Directing Colonel Lesher to jettison the garrison, he constructed a full retreat, effectively abandoning lower Manhattan to Howe, lock, stock, and barrel.

The fire, the blaze, the combustion, the phlogiston, the white-hot inferno that started at the Fighting Cocks Tavern raged all morning, all day, and into the night, until it consumed a quarter of the erected pine New York had to offer. Without doubt, the blaze created bedlam. True or false, Peter Roome wasn't the only reported story of homicide. The British caught one woman cutting the hemp rope handles of fire buckets and as the account goes, if they couldn't throw water on the blaze, they'd fight fire with her flammable flesh and bones. Unsurprisingly, the fire only grew higher and hotter. It was so hot that by the afternoon, the Red Coats scrapped their angry, crazed efforts and let it burn. They concentrated instead on rounding up suspects. They claimed most everyone they apprehended was carrying matches. However that was not uncommon. Lieutenant Frederick Mackenzie, a British fusilier, wrote in his journal, "When I got there the fire had got to such a head. There seemed to be no hope of stopping it— and those who were present did no more than look on and lament the misfortune. From the variety of circumstances that occurred… beyond doubt… designedly set on fire." He went on to record that as the fire raged, many soldiers caught civilians torching buildings that had somehow luckily escaped the original flames. "Many were detected with matches and combustibles under their clothes." On the other side of the tribulation, Washington received his answer from Congress on the plan to set the city aflame ahead of the British occupation. It was terse, "It should in no event be damaged." Washington was not going to defy the men who entrusted their lives, fortune, and liberty to him, and the stratagem was cast off. However, crossing the Hudson, Washington and Greene could see in the distance, the fire incinerating the British spoil. They couldn't help but gleefully smile that their wish seemed to be so providentially fulfilled; but who can say "how?"

***

As the various pounds of blushed flesh were weighed and debased and ravenous pleasures of corporeal existence were imbued into self-induced conscious oblivion at the Fighting Cocks, Nathan Hale arrived back onto the shores of New York at Whitehall and made his first stop, the above cited tavern. Inside, he struck up a conversation with a rather unique and strange gentlemen, Robert Rogers. Immediately one could tell he was a natural leader by the thick lines in his leathery face. He had recently returned to the Colonies to serve the British, and Howe in particular. He had been in the British military employee for years. He was head of the famed Rogers' Rangers, was an independent company of colonial militia attached to the British Army during the French and Indian War. There was one problem though; scandal often seemed to beget him.

With the nickname, "The White Devil," and an innate understanding of Indians, combined with his hard drinking, constant gambling, and roguish ways, he found himself on the unappreciated end of General Gage's opinions. Gage perceived him as immoral, wild, and difficult. Further, he believed his allegiance to enriching himself superseded the Crown. Gage had him exiled to Canada and brought up on trumped up charges. To the general's extreme disappointment, Rogers was exonerated. However, in the meantime, he wasted away in a solitary life among the Indians. He was a man that was nothing without war to occupy his time and his mind. So, when Howe took command from Gage, he fervently answered a call that rang only in his ears.

Hale continued his dumb Dutch schoolmaster routine but a grifter knows a false imitation. Hale gave away too much and Rogers knew he was a spy. In the standard British practice of sting operations, he invited Nathan to breakfast the following day. As they departed the tavern, Hale stayed back and Rogers tried to keep an eye on him. Then, the fire broke out.

The great fire lasted less than twenty-four hours. By the next morning, the city was chocked in a smoldering haze as Rogers and other officers waited for Hale to arrive— that is if he was going to take the bait. The plan was uncomplicated. They would talk to him and thereby assess if he was a spy behind enemy lines. They didn't know if Hale was gullible enough to appear or was already making his way back to the Continental Army. Rogers was using the opportunity to place himself in the good graces of the British and he was most nervous of all. But as promised, Hale happily arrived at Rogers' quarters expecting to discuss troop movements and to be the one who cleverly left with the infiltrated espionage that only a majestic hero could obtain. Surprised, he left arrested, and was soon intimately acquainted with a noose and an apple tree.

Among pinning Hale with the accusation of spying— which wasn't hard to determine by the hastily scribbled notes and indecorous maps of Long Island, they accused him of being the arsonist who had started the fire. He denied it but to them it was obvious. There was no way for Washington or the Continental Army to save him. At the time, they didn't know where he was or what had happened to him. As a matter of fact, Captain Pond was risking his own life still waiting for Nathan to meet him at the rendezvous point near Huntington.

Before sundown, the soldiers marched a head-up Nathan Hale out to Rutger's orchard where they had erected a simple scaffold surrounded an apple tree. Around the orchard, among the houses and about the road, Loyalists jeered at Hale, asking him of his expectations of hell, that is, among the more divisive insults. Hale sought to answer each and every catcall and taunt by his former dynamic of the instructor teaching the pupil! The British sought to stifle him. However, he was as energetic and slippery a captive as a fish in the hand. The solider brought him to the ground and roughed him up a bit, and then they shackled his legs in chains and moved the proceeding along.

Provost Marshall William Cunningham, the man in charge of all prisoners and prisons for the British was presiding over a little fire he was stoking of Nathan's gathered intelligence and personal missives. He read to himself the last of the correspondence, a letter he assured Hale that would get to his Mother and his friend Miss Adams.

"I wish to be useful and every kind of service,
necessary to the public good, become honorable
by being necessary. If the exigencies of my
country demands a peculiar service, its claims to
the performance of that service are imperious."

He threw it, too, into the small fire. Finally, Nathan was assisted in his ascend up the scaffold and under the noose tied and waiting to thick and study branch of the tree. They lifted him onto some apple carts and unceremoniously slipped the noose around his neck.

The soldiers looked to Cunningham, who, for reasons unknown was quite reserved on this day, far from the man of his moniker, "Bloody Bill." He was prepared for the outcome to quickly consume its place in the past and gave them the signal to let him hang. Just as they were about to, Cunningham stood up—

"Have you any last words?" the Provost Marshall asked?
Hale stood as firm as he could, acting with pride that the twisted fibers hung around his neck, and said—

"I only regret that I have but one life to give for my country."
The eyes both stared into the other. Hale's expanded with pride as Cunningham's contracted with disgust!

"Let it hang!" Cunningham screamed at the top of his lungs!
He bellowed so deep and loud that it seemed that the earth just about shook. Then, the soldiers kicked the crates clean from under his feet, in the process breaking them from the center— apples slipped out and tumbled

down the stairs in a rush of cascading fruit! Nathan Hale's body fell the few feet needed to separate him from the mortal soul's definition of "Life." While Nathan gurgled, chocked, and manifestly expired — Haym Salomon was in but only a fairly better condition.

***

XXIII
LOVE

"The most important consequence of marriage is, that the husband and the wife become in law only one person... upon this principle of union, almost all the other legal consequences of marriage depend. This principle, sublime and refined, deserves to be viewed and examined on every side."   James Wilson

It was pitch dark at high noon, and he quivered in jerks of pain and heat exhaustion, pressed into the corner, half-naked, arrayed in strips of tattered clothing, which represented his remaining dress. This was Haym Salomon in the aspersed darkness of human construction. There were four distinct sounds he could hear, which weaved in waves of song into a full symphony of horror. The melodic pattering of hungry rats— he could even feel them brush upon his skin or sprint up his arm; but still he could not see them. The excruciating metronomic plop-plop-plop of distance dripping water. The curious staccato sniffling of those gnawing rats, which at times he heard in the clearest sound directly outside of his eardrum; before he'd shake and flail his body free of them, and the rhythmic clomping noise of boots upon the wooden floors above. Plus, there was a smell... a grotesque sweetness, like an overripe fruit emitting a pungent odor, which attracts legions of flies. He was in the dungeon of the Livingston Sugar-house prison on Crown Street.

Suddenly, a creek of iron and wood, and a beam of light perforated the oubliette. To the seeing eye: Haym was cobbled in the corner, sweating to death and fending off the numerous rodents that scurried about him. Two uniformed Lobster Backs hurriedly grabbed him and at Sergeant Walley's insistence—

"Stand him up!"

In the blindness of Haym's adaptation he felt, more than he saw— two hands forcibly grip his shoulders and raise him off the hard pack earthen-floor. They stood him up, as straight as his loose folding body could stand. He was bleeding from a large deep cut over his eye and the imprint of a musket butt was impressed upon the side of his head. He was profusely bleeding. The stream of gore cascaded down and forked— one part dribbled into his eye, while the other continued downward across his cheek and into his mouth, where he tasted his own spilled blood.

"Stand him straight up!" Walley yelled.

His hands were bound and he himself had little balance. Ever-so-slightly he turned and his backside revealed the bloody nature of the horror of flagellation. They caned him raw and his flesh rose in pustules and welts that oozed over his already blood stained back. It was the reason why the rats were so attracted to him.

"Are you Haym Salomon?"

Haym didn't answer; his eyes were still acclimating to the light and his equilibrium to the jarring posture.

"I said, 'Are you Haym Salomon?'"

"Yea."

"So, then, you're a Hebrew?"

"No, but I am a Jew!" he unexpectedly screamed in defiance, as if scalded by a hot poker.

BAM— and a solider struck him for the outburst and Haym crumpled half way to the ground in the arms of the other Red Coat. At the same moment, Provost Marshall William Cunningham entered making swift steps and sharp turns.

"Stand him up!" Walley yelled!

They held Haym up for the Marshall. He looked Haym over and with a rather disgusted eye and a frothy sibilation he spoke—

"Mr. Salomon, I presume," the Marshall said.

With blood painting his eyelid and soaking the inside of his left eyeball, the mess that Haym was, fearlessly held his stare to the Marshall and said nothing. That was fine to Cunningham, he would expect nothing less of someone he considered a dog. A dog because he was a rebel and not because a Jew.

"You, are an enemy of the Crown, are you not?" Cunningham said.

"Speak up," Walley threatened him.

"It is I that bleeds, not the Crown," Haym said in somewhat of a hazy delivery.

"You bleed because you have acted against the Crown," Cunningham asserted.

"I have acted only in the course of the Will of God," Haym in turn insisted.

"Yes-yes, that's what all men who oppose the normal state of affairs say in their defense. Now, tell me, did you start the fire?"

"The fire?"

"Well, of course you didn't. We know who did, and he's dead, or maybe he didn't but he was a spy nonetheless— and even better— he's very dead. But you, Mr. Salmon, you were supplying guns to the rebellion."

"My sir, I am a broker."

"You sir, are a saboteur!" Cunningham shouted at him. "We have confessions from captured men, who confess—"

"As you flogged them," Haym interrupted.

"As we gave them just deserts," Cunningham said with a chuckle before he retuned to his ever-so-serious nature. "We have, I assure you, on good word, that you distributed guns from your place of business for the army of Washington."

"I sell dry goods, and… among them arms."

"Oh, I see, you sell dry goods, and you sell arms. Do you have a record of these purchases?"

"I cannot be sure of which purchases you speak."

"Then let me ask you, do you keep a record of all your purchases?" he said after a quick thought.

Haym hesitated, and Cunningham beat him to the punch—

"Surely, we can go through all of your records and ascertain the purchases I speak of, yes?"

"My store has been consumed in flames."

"Oh, how convenient."

"Yea," Haym finally brought himself to say, somewhere between sarcasm and exhaustion.

"Well, it's a lie! I know it's a lie! You know it's a lie! I asked these men before I let them dangle— I asked them if they had record of their transactions with you.

And do you know what they told me? That it was an arrangement, an understanding," Cunningham said. "You welcomed contraband into your shop in which you allowed a third party to take possession. And you knew where they were going, because you, Haym Salomon are a dastard, Son of Liberty!"

"I swear I am not."

"Oh, but you are. Do you think we know not who is who in our colonies?"

"I have never been a Son—"

"Marinus Willett! Alexander McDougall! John Lamb! Moses Franks! Gershom Seixas! Are they Sons of Liberty? And, are they your friends? And if you lie, let me show you what we do to liars... head to toe."

Haym remained quiet until Walley violently shoved him —

"Speak up!"

"Yea," Haym said meekly.

"But you're not a Son of Liberty? Now, how is that?"

"I am not a Son! I tell you and I have told you!"

"Well then... you're a spy?"

"No!"

"Well," Cunningham said, "Maybe you'll be so lucky."

Haym stared at Cunningham; his eye blinked and splattered blood, which landed on the marshall's cheek. Cunningham wiped it away in disgust, and turned to Walley —

"Throw him in with the others for now. Soon, I will decide if he is better to the Crown, dead or alive."

***

Escorted out of the dungeon, Haym found himself thrown into the general lot of prisoners on the first floor, which was merely a warehouse of open space. It served as something akin to a holding area or pen, until each man was processed, in what was decided to be their fate. Prisoners could wait for months in that collecting sea of humanity, while five floors rose above them in which ten men a piece occupied small rooms as their permanent cells.

The Livingston Sugarhouse, was a dilapidated abandoned building; abandoned because its roof leaked too badly for repair. From the outside, it was a dark stone structure, five stories in height, with small deep windows like portholes, giving it the somber appearance of a prison. Each story was divided into two apartments. A large, barred door opened upon Crown Street, and from another, on the southeast side, a stairway led to gloomy cellars, and dungeons. Around the whole building was a passage a few feet wide, and there, day and night, British and Hessian sentinels patrolled. The whole edifice was inclosed by a wooden fence nine feet in high.

On this first floor, 500 men in wounded, sick, or other dire conditions were crammed together, including Haym. Every other day, they were tossed rations, similar to throwing slop over the fence to pigs. When this took place, the madness and confusion was breathtaking in its primal devolution of mankind. The prisoners would fall upon the food like mana from heaven— old biscuits, broken, and in crumbs, mostly molded, and some crawling with maggots. And, every other day between those days, they received their ration of protein; pork— an irony that was lost on the British. The pork was also unsparingly tossed over in round raw slabs, which they would tear and fight over, like possessed animals. Unbeknownst to the starving rebels who carried the day to win their share of pork, they were filling their stomachs with more than meat, but parasites. What water they were given to wash down the feasts or hydrate in the sweltering heat was given the royal treatment. It came expressly from used chamber pots that had serviced the intestinal relief of the officers and soldiers. Haym was not immune; there was no corner to wait in some meditative dignity. There was kind of an unorganized but orderly shuffle. Except for the men who fell moaning in one spot, men dawdled about hour to hour in circles of eight. To almost a man, below their feet and dripping from their chins or running down their legs was blood, pus, vomit, urine, or feces in any number combinations. A racket of diarrhea, coughing, and spitting up, were measured cadences, like songbirds, in the echoing din. Smallpox, dysentery, typhus and yellow fever were of epidemic proportions, but the British didn't care. A common practice among the suffering prisoners was to dare the guards to kill them. Direct murder stood against good English conscientiousness. However, each morning, corpses in a monstrous state of rigor mortis were dragged out, thrown into wagons like logs, and then pitched into a large hole. In a brief time, the naked bodies would be exposed because of the weather conditions and afterwards consumed by swine and other wild animals. Adding to the insufferable conditions were the flies buzzing about. They learned to make quick strike meals of the prisoner's flesh. In the fading September humidity, the stench of the Sugarhouse reminded Haym of the Judengasse, but improbably worse. In the want of exercise and fresh air, under the throes of suffocating summer heat, every knothole, gap, and slit of those strong walls were filled with human heads, face above face, seeking a portion of the external air. Inside, there were only two small windows on each end of the room and being a sugarhouse, it served to increase the air temperature by twenty degrees and the humidity to 100 percent. Seven to ten men died a night and to wake in the morning amid the destitution and still be alive was to inevitably find a dead body or two squirming in internal animation by burrowing rats that had chewed through the soft emaciated tissue of the abdomen; and horseflies exploiting the body as a source of food and depositing eggs into their wide open mouths. During its prevalence the prisoners were marched out in companies of twenty, to breathe the fresh air for half an hour, while those within divided themselves into parties of six each, and there alternately enjoyed the privilege of standing ten minutes at the windows. They had no seats, and their beds of straw were filled with vermin. They might have exchanged this horrid tenement for the comfortable quarters of a British soldier by enlisting in the king's service, but very few would thus yield their principles. In their virtue they preferred to be among the dozen bodies, which were daily carried out in those carts and cast into the ditches and morasses beyond the city limits. When the population swelled beyond prison capacity, sheds, stables, and other outhouses received hundreds of captures, who exceedingly suffered even more terribly from cold and hunger during the winter. Few lived to recite their experience of horror of Livingston. Damned in hell are the men who oversaw the sinful enterprise.

In a twist of irony, Haym, in the company of 500, was not alone. Isaac Franks, at only seventeen, enlisted in Colonel Lesher's regiment, New York Volunteers, and served with it in the battle of Long Island; two weeks before the fire, he was captured and taken prison, requisitioned among the inhumanity on the first floor of the Livingston Sugar-house. They found one another somewhere, sometime, in the daily dawdling shuffle. Together, they both survived the horror of the conditions, the flies, the rats, the pork, the biscuits, the maggots, the corpses, the beatings, the cheap rum, and the piss laced water, for two weeks, before the angelic presence of Rachel Franks arrived.

***

Moses Franks knew something was wrong. He hadn't heard from Haym since the congregation disbanded the morning of the fire. The Shearith Israel was for now, no more. Franks' world was changing rapidly beyond his normal capacity to control through wealth, status, and connections. He was also gravely concerned about his son Isaac, who he learned was captured at Long Island but knew not of his fate. The Franks family as a whole was a deeply divided but still personally close clan and Franks worried that both the British and American spies were watching his every move.

He sent servants to Haym's residence on Wall Street. Miraculously, the structure had escaped the flames. They reported back the best and the worst, that the house stood, but Haym was nowhere to be found. Franks, fearing the worst, had his servants remove everything of value from the house and bring it to his own. Next, he personally made a trip to each of the buildings the British commandeered throughout the city and reduced into infernal prisons. At the time, the Red Coats had about 4,000 Continental soldiers incarcerated, all in conditions similar or worse to what Haym and Isaac were experiencing at the Livingston Sugarhouse.

He carried his girth from one prison to another; the Sugarhouse was the last prison Franks visited. He inquired and learned that both his son and Haym were in custody. Hastily, he met with Cunningham, who would not accept his straightforward bribes to release them. As a matter of fact, he threatened Moses with imprisonment himself for suggesting such a foul transaction. Franks was undaunted and he returned home, devising a plan inspired by Gutlé Rothschild.

Rachel spent every waking hour of eight straight days designing, spinning, and sewing two coats lined with secret compartments containing pound sterlings in gold guineas. One for Isaac and one for Haym. Burning the candle at both ends, she labored over the assignment with a determination that can only be found in love.

When the articles were ready, Franks outfitted her with shillings and two pound sterling in her hand for the ready. Then, after the second most heartfelt entreatment he ever made to God — the first being when his wife died and the right care of the children was passed to him, he prayed that He protect her and spare him the judgement for calling her on to provide the duty.

Rachel set off for the hellward paradise of the Sugarhouse. Armed with the directive to avoid Cunningham, she arrived like Aesop's Little Match-Seller. Her feet were bare, her head uncovered and she heaped a heavy basket, which she courageously showed no strain in carrying. Rachel brought a remarkable innocence to every aspect of her posture, words, and movements. However, she wasn't innocent, she knew that she was there to bribe certain men to release her brother and Haym. Upon making her way one Spanish bit at a time past the Hessian guards, she reached a Red Coat. He asked her of her business and she asked to see the man who answered to Provost Marshall Cunningham. The Red Coat was not inclined to take her seriously, but she offered him a bribe — a shilling.

For guards who made no more than eight pence a year, before taxes and the obligatory cost of army supplied rations, the shilling represented a tax free year and a half of salary, more money than they would be able to accumulate and save in three years of service. Her persuasive efforts were richly rewarded and she received a coveted audience with Captain Walley.

Ushered past the first floor to offices on the second, she took a seat in a small, hot, room that reeked of fermented fruit and was overrun with flies.

"…What brings you here, little girl?"

"Nothing, but that I have provisions."

"Provisions? For who?" he asked, looking at her, noticing how pretty she was— young but pretty. "For me?"

"No, for my brother and our family friend. But I have for you something else."

Walley was partially deflated and uninterested, but curious as to what was for him.

"And what might that be?" he said.

She held up a shiny pound sterling, the face of George III purposely facing her and not him. As an officer, Walley made a decent amount more than the Regulars but before him was a considerable little jackpot.

"Little girl—"

"My name is Rachel," she said sweetly.

"Yes, Rachel. Do you expect me to receive your offer, or should I say, 'bribe,' and release your brother and family friend?"

His tone and manner suggested that he might not be as easy to impress as the Hessians and the guards and she felt that she had to think fast.

"No. That would be against your duty and your honor. What is a man who turns his back on his honor and his duty? He is a coward to his self."

With this he was utterly impressed and attracted to her. He reached forward across his table and placed her coin in his hand. He weighed it up and down. It felt real, but he wasn't taking any chances. Walley, went to a low shelf and brought back a scale that he placed between them. He weighed the piece and it was genuine. His respect and attraction for her, rose even more.

"Might I question, what you have in the basket, little girl— Rachel."

"Just some coats and a few jars of jam," she said innocently, hoping he wouldn't inquire further.

"Coats?"

"To keep them warm."

"Warm, do you not feel the heat upon you now?"

"But soon it will be winter, unless that is if you release them."
Walley laughed — she was astute, almost a refreshing air to the adult seriousness of war.

"I am afraid to tell you, that I don't have the power —"
Rachel reached forward for the coin as she said —

"Should I speak with another?"
Walley grabbed her arm and stopped her —

"No, I assure you that no one above myself will even entertain a conversation that requires scales."

"I promise you that I can come everyday and bring them provisions, and have something for your scale," she said.

***

First, Rachel tended to her brother. He was placed alone in a small bucket room that served as his cell. Old wooden buckets, with dried syrup hanging over their rims hung on the wall. The walls themselves were covered in similarly thick lines of the viscid sweetness and ants were numerous in their numbers.

Isaac had been there longer than Haym but he was still fit, undismayed in his youthful resolve to fight. He appreciated his sister's arrival but wasn't overly thrilled. To some degree he was embarrassed. Every fiber of his being intended to continue to fight. He was a prisoner that was sure no prison could hold him. However, the bread and jam, his sister brought him was warmly welcomed by his body and palette.

She gave him his coat but when she asked him to put it on, he admitted that his arm was broken. She set it and with the tablecloth that lined the bottom of her basket, she made a sling. Then she placed into his pockets more of the shillings her father had given her. Isaac inquired about the Continental Army and of Washington. Rachel wasn't abreast of anything military. Nonetheless, she promised to come tomorrow and tell him everything she learned.

She left her brother in good spirit and good health considering the conditions he endured. A Hessian guard led her down into the basement, but instead of the dungeon, Haym was confided to a boiling room. Even with a candle lit, it was dark. She entered the room to see Haym lying face down on a bed of straw laid over the floor. It soothed his backside that it was exposed and untouched. The two were left alone and she immediately tended to his medical care. Rachel bargained for some clean water and bandages and immediately set about healing him.

***

Under the horror of the microscope, the disease Consumption is a red-hooked shaped bacteria. The disease was called "consumption" because it maliciously consumed the afflicted. The symptoms were as tell-tale as the rooster crowing of the hour— the flushed cheeks, the bright eyes, fever, night sweats, weakness, loss of appetite, and most of all, the cough. The horror of the telltale cough— each one, the insufflate toll of death ahead of the church bell.

"Ay, thou art for the grave; thy glances shine/Too brightly to shine long; another Spring/Shall deck her for men's eyes— but not for thine— Sealed in a sleep which knows no wakening/The fields for thee have no medicinal leaf, /And the vexed ore no mineral of power;/And they who love thee wait in anxious grief/Till the slow plague shall bring the final hour. /Glide softly to thy rest then; Death should come/Gently, to one of gentle mould like thee, /As light winds wandering through groves of bloom/Detach the delicate blossom from the tree. /Close thy sweet eyes, calmly, and without pain;/And we will trust in God to see thee yet again." These words by William Cullen Bryant spoke romantically of Consumption. The eighteenth century was no different to the mortal coil, everybody was going to die, but most were going to do so on the red hook. It took more people in the Americas than other disease but did so in a disproportionate nature. It affected the poor more often than the wealthy, females more than males, and people of all ages. Anyone could be a victim, but it was especially prevalent among young adults; cruelly it would strike down those in the prime of their lives.

Nobody knew why, or how it was contracted. It was thought that it might be a vaguely environmental, "something in the air"; but more likely caused by the victim's own constitution, either physiologically, psychologically, or both. It was not believed to be contagious as the Black Death, so those suffering from the disease were not avoided. Recommended steps toward prevention included fresh air, a wholesome diet, exercise, and healthy manual labor. But, in fact, it is an air born disease, which settles in the lungs. The perfect environments are those of squalor— bad damp air, rotten food, and crowded conditions. Once contracted, it could lie dormant in its host, giving no indication that they are marked for death; until one day they cough their telltale insufflation. Besides smallpox, dysentery, typhus and yellow fever, the first floor of the Livingston Sugarhouse was rampant with hacking coughs of Consumption. It hung in the air— smaller and more numerous than the particles of dust.

***

"…My mother used to make me coats," said Haym.

"She did?" Rachel said, as she poured him a bowl of soup she made especially for him and Isaac.

Haym wasn't wearing the coat but he was covered in a shawl she had knitted for him. It was November, and the heat, the flies, and the ants were gone. As a matter of fact, it was nearly teeth-chattering cold. There was no fire or source of heat in the boiling room, just the soup, which was almost still at a boil when she arrived that day. Had they been still processing syrup in the dwelling it would have been a warm habitat, but the Sugarhouse now was a prison only. The privilege of fire, heat, and warmth, was reserved for officers and the soldiers only. All the prisoners, on each and every floor went without basic need for warmth and the horror of the death rate increased by two fold.

Rachel had spent everyday, including the Sabbath, visiting her brother and Haym. She came with fresh food, clean clothes, and of course her pound sterling for Walley, who went so far as to tell her she did not have to afford the guards financial interest.

"When did your mother make your coats?"

"Oh, she used to make them every year," Haym said.

"Does she still make them?"

Haym fell silent and uneasy; gripping the side of his bowl for both heat and comfort. Rachel realized that she must be dead and she was slightly embarrassed, but oddly, not put off, quite the opposite—

"We're different, you and me," she said.

"Oh? How's that?"

"I speak my words, you hide yours," she said bluntly just as she lit another candle to illuminate the room.

"Is that so?"

"Yes. You're inside out, I'd say."

She removed the shawl and in the fashion of a nurse, examined the progress of her handiwork across his backside.

"'Inside out?'I'm no such thing. Ask me anything, what do you want to know?" he said somewhat playfully.

"Tell me about your first love— yeah, all about her."

Haym hesitated and mused. She began removing bandages, which brought pinpricks of pain, combined with the realization and sensation that the almost unbearable pain had expired.

"What was her name?" Rachel put forth.

"Ilana."

"Ilana?"

"It is Polish-Jewish!"

"Why, I've never heard such a name. What was she like?"

"She was—"

"How old were you?"

"Oh, I'd say about eight!"

"Eight? I don't mean eight! I mean a girl you wanted to marry!"

All the while they spoke, in soothing circular motions, she salved his scars with a beeswax ointment. Between the cool relief spread over the scars on his back and the warm feeling over his hands and into his mouth, he felt an emotional eclipse of comfort and reassurance that he hadn't known since the last coat his mother, Rebekah, had sewn and placed across his shoulders.

"Well, come on, who was it?" Rachel prodded him.

"I have never wanted to marry."

"And why not?"

"Because I have not found the right... woman."

"And what makes the 'right woman,' for you?" she laughed.

"One who doesn't ask a lot of questions of me," he said playfully. They laughed together.

"Well, who would want to marry you, anyway? An old man like you," she playfully roused him back.

There was a good quality of nature about her, a fine easygoing character, an appropriately talkative manner, and an unusually pretty way in which she went about the charge of tasks. He felt a kinship with her, similar to his relationship with Elka. However, Elka was much younger and flitted about as the girl she was. Rachel was grounded— beside him. In fact, she had been at his side for almost two months. Fifty-five straight days they had been in each other's company and if it wasn't for her and her father, he believed death would have become him by then. Instead, he was in the horror of darkness but consoled by the tiny lamp of light he was afforded and the shining beam of radiance that Rachel Franks inherently was.

"Do you have a beau?" he dared to ask.

She blushed.

"Com'on, you ask me of my interest to marriage, and I ask you," he said.

She blushed more, her high cheekbones glowed pink and her tawny turquoise sprinkled eyes turned away in abashed high water. He motioned the suggestion to "drop it." But she gathered herself and said very lady-like—

"No. I don't."

Haym was surprised, even slightly enraptured by this elevated proportion of maturity. Yet, he didn't prey upon her, but jocularly kidded around instead.

"And why not? Don't you fancy someone, or does no one fancy you," he playfully poked— relieving any tension between them to bringing their conversation back to a dueling match of wits.

"A lot of boys fancy me, I'll have you know!"

"So you say!"

She was flabbergasted and amused.

"I'll have you know, that I don't fancy boys! They're just boys."

***

Toward the end of 1775, the situation of England was betwixt and between grave. The opponents in Parliament to the action of the ministry were numerous, and comprised some of the foremost men in that body and the military position of the country was still worse. Twenty-eight thousand sailors and fifty thousand soldiers had been asked for; but these were insufficient for the purposes required, and a bill enabling the king to call out the militia, to use in America, was precipitately passed.

Yet the need of soldiers was immediate, and application was made to various Continental powers, among them Holland, where a so-called Scottish brigade had existed since early in the seventeenth century. But

Holland refused the use of this body, except for employment across the continent. This offer would not suffice or solve the English predicament. George III graciously declined, for he had, indeed, obtained assistance from another quarter. Contracts had been made for the enlistment of soldiers in some of the petty German states. These were in part secret, but open negotiations were carried on with the Duke of Brunswick and the Landgrave of Hesse-Cassel. The subjects of these magnates were bought like so many cattle, it being arranged with the duke that every soldier killed should be paid for at the rate of the levy-money, and that three wounded should be reckoned as one killed. An annual subsidy was to be paid.

The German troops obtained in this discreditable manner numbered seventeen thousand men. Of these, Hesse-Cassel supplied twelve thousand, and Brunswick and other petty states the remainder. The affair was a disgraceful one on both sides, and aroused indignation throughout Europe. Frederick the Great, a man not over-scrupulous in his own measures, viewed it as an abominable traffic in human lives, and whenever any of these hirelings passed through his territory he levied on them the usual toll for cattle, saying that they had been sold as such.

Many in England entertained a similar feeling; yet the treaties were ratified by large majorities in Parliament, and these disgracefully obtained troops were shipped to America. There the proceeding was viewed with the utmost indignation, and served to increase the bitterness and determination of the colonists, whose rebellious energy was greatly added to by the means thus taken to overcome it, and particularly by the measures employed to bring the Indians into the conflict in support of the British cause. Such was the state of affairs in America and England in the period at which the Hessians arrived.   The majority of the guards at the Sugarhouse were Hessians, as were a large number in the New York Colony occupied by Howe. The one thing the English neglected to consider in this mercenary traffic was the language barrier. Less than five percent of the Officers in the British Army could speak German. Even fewer of the Hessians could speak English.

***

It was fairly easy to bribe any of the guards at the Sugarhouse. However, as Rachel learned, depending on rank, they were only willing to accommodate so far. With the money Rachel supplied Isaac, he was able to acquire fresh meat, water, milk, hot cordials, and peas. The peas were to fight scurvy— everyone in the Sugarhouse was afflicted with scurvy. He bought as much peas, water, meat, milk, and cordials as he could, to increase his strength, accelerate the healing of his arm, and keep warm. Then, he sprung his escape.

As the calendar evolved from November to December, the snow started to fall and Isaac gave his sister a note to relay to Haym. It read simply: "You speak German, no?" Haym replied in kind and Rachel delivered the note the next day to her brother. With that, Isaac wrote a final one to Haym outlining his request. Haym read it and was aghast at the audacity but he wasn't going to refuse the brave young man.

The following night, as the sun fell to evening, a Hessian guard looked into the boiling room where Haym sat at a small table. Anticipating the guard's arrival, Haym had already placed under the lamplight, three shimmering gold guineas. The profile of the king reflected off the light with the seeming brightness of a distant sun glowing out of our galaxy. The Hessian guard could not miss this unexpected enticement. Haym cooly unfurled his words in German and made him an offer to the lowly impoverished solider that was impossible to decline.

When Rachel arrived the next day, she spirited the commodity made in exchange for the pound sterling. It only cost Haym one, as the other two were reserved as the promise for further fleeting discipleship down the line. She wonderfully bestowed upon her brother a blue wool uniform coat as worn by the Hessians. Accompanying the clandestine delivered was a note. The note from Haym to Isaac consisted of a phonetic dialogue in German.

That night, when a Hessian guard approached and did his duty to peer into the bucket room, he was amazed to see Isaac Franks adorned in a Hessian coat with two pound sterling worth of coins held in each of his hands; just waiting for the man's eyes to fall upon them. Once the men's eyes made contact between the iron-barred square, Isaac rushed to the door and carefully read his phonetic German as best he could. It was almost unintelligible to the Hessian, but he understood enough that in exchange for the fortune before him, he was to unlock the door and walk away in ignorance.

The Hessian was cautious and unsure. But as his fingers grasped one end of the coins and Isaac held firmly to the other end — the feel of the money, the possibility it procured in fantasies throughout his mind; and all that opportunity, for nothing more than just looking the other way upon one lowly solider who meant so little in the overall value of the rebels' effort, was simply too appealing to turn down.

He twisted the key and quickly unlocked the door. Isaac relinquished his grip on the gold coins and dashed out of the bucket room — make for the opposite direction, then the solider carried himself away!

The patriot had two floors to negotiate and a well-guarded exit. From a distance, he looked like a Hessian, but up close the coat wasn't enough to fool anyone. He considered this and made a daring decision. At the end of the corridor was a glassless window. It was a cloudy sky making for an extremely dark night. Below the window the first snowfall of the year had created a foot of cushion over the ground. If he could squeeze his body through the space, he could jump. Furthermore, if he could sustain the landing without breaking a leg or disturbing the horses, he might be able to make himself free. This he decided was the best means of escape. However, there was one more "if." If he could only be quick enough before another guard passed through the corridors.

Just then, he heard the clomping sound of alternating boot steps. More than one guard climbing the stairs. There was no time to take stock, whatsoever. He leapt onto the windowsill and contorted his body as though shimmying like a fish and let his body drop in the particular manner of a sack of potatoes!

The rush against the air, the pressure of gravity, and the butterflies that fluttered in his stomach and — BAM! He crashed to the ground before he could finish his thought of it all. The snow did little to soften the fall. He seemed to fall on his side and after wincing for a few moments with the air in his body having escaped him, he rose in no harm. He was at the back of the building and no guard appeared before him. He could see the grey shadows of them and their rifles extending beyond the corners. Yet, he knew from the window that ahead, over the fence, lie a rubble-filled lot, due in thanks to the fire. However, there was no practical way to scale the fence. Darkness be friend.

Isaac spotted an empty jug of rum. He buttoned his coat to the lapel and clutched the jug into his hands. Then, he took a deep breath and turned the corner to face the guards. He played it off like he was the most drunken of sentries! He stumbled, fell, arose, spoke gibberish, and as they laughed he walked out beyond the fence. It appeared as comical to the Hessians as they'd ever seen. Even the wandering out beyond the fence — they laughed as they waited for him to stumble back into the fold. He was already long gone before they realized, maybe he wasn't one of them after all.

Free of the prison grounds, Isaac followed down the streets, keeping in the shadows, but it was touch and go, as he turned uptown. Soon the clouds parted and a full moon appeared. It seemed to light the night into shade of dusk. The gentle breeze died into a doldrum. The snow on the ground crusted over and thereupon, a person walking could be heard a great distance. He saw soldiers everywhere and often had to crawl along his stomach to avoid being discovered. Often dogs snarled and howled as he passed. But by sheer determination and luck, he reached the river and escaped to New Jersey in a leaky skiff with one paddle. By the morning, incredibly, he had rejoined Washington's army. He was well received and rewarded. Washington raised his rank and importance, owing to him as a confidant— an aide-to-camp.

***

Isaac's escape didn't sound unbridled alarm bells. The Hessian guards were not going make mention and the Red Coats could not effectively communicate with them, which conveniently allowed the Hessians to play dumb. Everyone had been on the take for one thing or another since Rachel arrived. Between Haym and Isaac, guards flocked to attend to them more like waiters or concierges; for at any given request, there was an impressive amount of money to be made. Once Isaac's escape came to the sergeant's attention, he waited patiently for Rachel like a snake in the grass.

"...You have not visited us for four days," Walley said sounding rather disappointed.
He sat across from her just as they first met. She carried in her arm a basket and across her face a smile, but she was freighted by his tone. At that point, she didn't know if her brother had been successful in his escape, or, God forbid, he was dead. Further disconcerting to her was that Walley

seemed more dispassionate but attentive than normal— a man with something sinister on his mind.

"I have had a cold, and my father said it is best that I not be out in the snow," Rachel said with her best most innocent voice.
At the same time she dropped her guinea on his scale. He glanced at it, then to her.

"You might be surprised to learn that your brother is no longer a prisoner— might be, I say."

"You're releasing him?"
Walley slid his coin off the scale and into his pocket and walked around the table, pressing his nose into the space of swirling blond hairs between her cheek and her ear, and said in a rum scented come-hither voice—

"He released himself, my dear."
A chill went up her spine.

"I do say, you smell as fresh as fallen English snow."
And he held his nose in her face, his masculinity swelled. However, he controlled his urges; stepped back and walked around his desk.

"I shall go now and see Mr. Salomon, if I may."

"You may not."
Instantly, she trembled inside but was doing her best to disguise it.

"How do you suppose I make up for the time spent missing you?"
She placed her hand into her pocket. It trembled. Rachel fought every nerve of fear and forced that hand to remain still as she pulled out another guinea and laid it upon the table. The sergeant was mildly pleased.

"I don't know how he got away. Would you?"

"No, of course not."

"Of course not."
He dabbled a moment with the scales, tipping them back and fourth, before he looked her in the eye with a deep gaze and with a sudden guffaw—

"Do you ever think of me?"

"Pardon me?"

"I said, 'Do you ever think of me—' beyond our short encounters that is?"
She was frozen to her seat, too startled to think clearly and too scared to speak.

"Don't be afraid of me," he said self-amused. "Those who call me barbarous are practically the same children who pulled the wings of butterflies. I say, if a man deserves a caning, he deserves a caning."

Silence followed… and as he sat smiling at her, she jostled her eyes around to every other meaningless item in the room.

"Yes. Sergeant, if you don't mind —"

"Yes, Rachel, I do mind," he interrupted her.

Taken somewhat by surprise, her internal trembling intensified. He came across the desk; bent to one knee and leaned his face into hers. She tried to turn away but was too afraid to be brusque about it and he simply angled his face to hers.

"How old are you now, Rachel?"

"The same as I was…" she said with a slight quiver in her lip. "Fourteen."

"Do you know what my most favorite thing is… about little girls? It is to see them grow from running to walking."

He gently directed her gaze to his —

"Do you still run, little Rachel, or do you walk now?"

She was ready to cry; tears welling in her eyes. She felt trapped, overwhelmed, nothing in her arsenal of wit could defend her from his advance.

"I say you are beautiful, you don't resemble a Semite at all."

He seemed to be waiting for an answer but she remained silent, concentrating on suppressing a show of fear.

"You can say thank you," he said.

"Thank you," she said, humiliated.

"I'm Irish. Damn, if I ever saw a Hebrew in me Ireland."

He brushed her thin auburn hair from her forehead and as their skin met, the first tear escaped her eyes and ran down her cheek.

"Oh Rachel, no need to weep. I don't know how your brother escaped. But I have many drunkards under my command and I wouldn't doubt that their lack of temperance had a hand in it," he said. Then he whispered — "You smell delicious."

She was ready to burst into full flowing tears, when Captain Corne entered.

"Sergeant, the Provost is here and he's demanding your company."

Walley nodded and the Captain exited closing the door. He turned his attention back to Rachel and with a slow pivot of his head —

"Go! Take your provisions to Mr. Salomon, but from this point on, what once cost you one honorarium, now costs you two. Understood?"

———

308

He was curt, but curt was the best he could muster, when metaphorically, he truly wanted to bite hard and draw blood.

"Yes," she said.

Haym received her in tears and happy news. There was little he knew he could do to Walley. At least not now, not outwardly, not personally. But he vowed to himself to effectuate a plan that would effect the man drastically. Less the warmth of a fire on a cold day, for the first time between them, he held her as she cried the few remaining tears she had held in under the assault. Despite that, she was thrilled to know her brother had escaped and she couldn't wait to tell her father! Yet, Rachel was unwound; all of the human emotion, from positive to negative was overcoming like a ship taking on water. She couldn't hold back either of her tears, those of fear and those of joy. Nestled in his arms and under his chin, she turned and looked up to Haym, and with a quiver in her lip said —

"I love you."

***

XXIV
CONTENTEDNESS

"Patriotism is as much a virtue as justice, and is as necessary for the support of societies as natural affection is for the support of families."   *Benjamin Rush*

Philadelphia, 1 January 1777.

Sir,

I was honored with your favor of yesterday by Mr. Howell, late last night, and, ever solicitous to comply with your requisitions, I am up very early this morning to despatch a supply of fifty thousand dollars to your Excellency. You will receive that sum with this letter; but it will not be got away so early as I could wish, for none concerned in this movement, except myself, are up. I shall rouse them immediately. It gives me great pleasure that you have engaged the troops to continue, and if further occasional supplies of money are necessary, you may depend on my exertions either in a public or private capacity. The year 1776 is over. I am heartily glad of it, and hope you nor America will ever be plagued with such another. Let us accept the success at Trenton as a presage of future fortunate events; and under that impression, I do most sincerely wish you a successful campaign in 1777, to crown you with immortal honors, in reward of the dangers and fatigues of war; and that you may, for many, many years after, enjoy the sweets of peace and domestic happiness, in reward of your social virtues. With sincere esteem and regard, I ever am, Sir,

Your obedient servant,
Robert Morris

Robert Morris is arguably the most significant man in the life of Haym Salomon, only after his father; and in the success of the American Revolution, only after George Washington. At the start of 1777, Morris was busily supporting his best friend, George Washington by going so far as to personally participate in the financing of the army in their war against the British.

In the predawn half-light, the beating drums and peeling bells summoned between dozens of militiamen to the town green at Lexington. As they lined up in battle formation, the distant sound of marching feet and shouted orders further alerted them to the Redcoats' impending arrival. Soon the British column emerged through the morning fog. General Pitcairn, on horseback, could hear the anxious rustle of armed men in the trajectory of his march forward. In all decisions of his mind, he was going to be painstakingly careful. This was not a war, just a rebellion, and battle was to be the last resort.

"Men! Load your weapons!" he yelled as loud as he could, partly to scare the militia. The concert of synchronized loaded weapons made marital music. "But on no account fire or even attempt it, without order! Now march!" he screamed!

They proceed at double time in double ranks. Pitcairn looked into the eyes of his drummer and nodded. With that the drummer rolled, rattled, and beat out the Call-to-Arms! The farmers and townspeople of Lexington, the part of society that opposed the status quo of British rule, could hear the dynamics of the rat-a-tat-tat and they tumbled out of bed, ran off the farms, and stumbled out of the taverns!

The militia quickly grew to it's full strength of seventy-seven, of which thirty-eight were in ranks. Pitcairn arrived on the commons and the two forces stared into one another's eyes. John Parker was in ad hoc command of the defending militia mob. He lined them single file, parallel with the horizon, almost akin to a children's game. It amounted to a suicidal dare to Pitcairn to try and pass through them. As the British continued their advance— one fluid organized step at a time, it quickly dawned on each militiamen that whatever four, five, ten, twenty bayonets to a man, they were staring at what might be cause to an untimely demise.

"Stand your ground. Don't fire unless fired upon. But if they want to have a war, let it begin here!" Parker defiantly shouted!

Pitcairn, with no other options, as it would have been suicidal to advance around the men to Concord and leave a hostile force at his back, detached two parties and further advanced toward Parker and his rebels.

"Disperse, ye rebels, disperse! Lay down your arms, you dammed rebels, and disperse or you are all dead men!" Pitcairn cried out in warning over the Lexington bells that were still tolling and the drums that beat with an increasingly stentorian announcement... as he advanced closer... and closer, to those opposing his wake.

At times, the fighting spirit and the fighting itself cannot be reconciled in the constitution of a man and most of the rebels were already scrambling to get out of the way! At that instant, a shot rang out— echoing through and into the heavens; supernally broadcast around the world. Who fired first? The British? The Rebels? No one knew for sure. But in a rapid succession of reports, more shots were fired and when the white smoke of dark black of the propellant cleared, eight militiamen lay dead or dying. It was these eight men that changed the course of Robert Morris' English loyalty to patriot outrage.

The news of the April 19th "massacre" at Lexington, as it was evocatively described by the colonists, reached Philadelphia four days after its occurrence. Morris in the festive company of a large party was celebrating St. George's Day. The news was received with the greatest surprise and appall. The tables, at which they were dining, were immediately deserted. Only a few in the party, among whom was Mr. Morris, remained. To these, indeed to all, who had been present, it was evident that the die was cast— that Lexington was an event, which must lead to a final separation from the aggressive murderous British government.

"Let it take place," Morris lamented.

From that moment on, he cordially entered into all the measures, which seemed the most likely to affect the object.

Born a Liverpudlian, at thirteen his father voyaged the family across the sea to Oxford, Maryland. Nonetheless, Morris', roots, youth, memories, and sense of self were enmeshed in his English identity— though he was now looking out over the wide open spaces of opportunities the Colonies embodied, that he would never be going home again. Indubitably, after apprenticing for four years with a busy shipping company, at the age of 20, he became a junior partner in a large banking and importing firm in Philadelphia. Born of modest means, in an ensuing manner, money was the least of his needs but the whole of his concerns.

Only three year later, young, hungry, aggressive, Robert Morris entered into a partnership with Thomas Willing. Together they established the firm of Willing, Morris, and Company, which became one of the most successful businesses in the American colonies. The firm purchased ships to transport their goods, selling grains and household products in Maryland and Virginia, exporting flour and lumber to Europe, and importing sugar, dry goods, and molasses. In a stroke of risk for reward, the two dipped their big toes into the lucrative but volatile slave trade. It was only meant to be a side business, an experiment to see if they could prosper in the field as they had done so brilliantly in their other ventures. Both being of means, and as was the standard, each owned a couple of slaves for domestic duties and the trade was a natural extension of the shipping business.

Well, anything and everything that could go wrong did so in spades. The ship they sent to buy West Africans was seized by French raiders and the plantation they bought in Louisiana, was expropriated by the Spanish. The best they could do was organize auctions of the 500 or so slaves recently imported into Philadelphia from the Sephardic Jewish businessmen of Rhode Island looking for new markets to invade. This, too, was not a success and by all accounts Morris and Willing lost money and abandoned trading in the dark pigments of flesh. Nonetheless, their regular shipping operations grew to global proportions and without question, Willing, Morris, and Company was Philadelphia's most powerful and prosperous enterprise.

By the age of thirty-five, with a fortune already accumulated, he married Mary White, fifteen years younger than he. Immediately, he sought to make up for his lost time and monopolize hers by working on a family. Before January 1st, 1776 they already had five beautiful children and the oversimplified domestic bliss that is the rival of every superficial man.

It could go without saying, but Morris was a strict churchgoer and deeply god-fearing man. He was also personally highly ambitious, a man for which enough was never exactly enough and to the best of his understanding, life was equally divided between a secular earth and a future heaven. Examining his career and his successes, it seems it would be obvious to note that he was highly ambitious, but it wasn't business that ignited his fancy— it was the intrigue and passion of politics, and before April 23rd, 1775, Robert Morris was a devout Loyalist. However, in 1765, he joined in the opposition to the Stamp Act; anything that taxed his interest he was naturally opposed to. Yet, it didn't curb his allegiance to the Crown. That fatefully was severed at Lexington.

On November 3rd, 1775, Morris was elected, by the legislature of Pennsylvania, a delegate to the second congress to meet in Philadelphia. He was also appointed a member of the committee for fitting out a naval armament, and specially commissioned to negotiate bills of exchange for Congress; to borrow money for the marine committee, and to manage the fiscal concerns of Congress on other occasions.

Early in 1776, to add to his responsibilities, he was given a special commission by congress, with the authority to negotiate bills of exchange, and to solicit money by other means for the operation of the war— a tall task indeed. His first idea was to form lotteries about the colonies. It was a failed idea and once the figures were tallied, accounted for a zero sum. As July rolled around, Morris was present at the 2nd Continental Congress. He was one of the few that voted against the Declaration of Independence, because as he saw it, "it was an improper time." However, upon the adoption of the explicit statement committed to parchment, he proudly signed it.

In late 1776, with the Continental Army in a state of severe deprivation because of a shortage of capital and the failure of several of the colonies in paying for the war, Morris loaned $10,000 of his own money to the government. This money provisioned the desperate troops, who went on to win the Battle of Trenton where Washington heroically crossed the Delaware.

Washington was the general of the military forces but Morris was the single financial instrument of providence that found means to provide for Washington. Congress had relied on domestic borrowing early in the war to supplant, and in some cases, retire the Continental Currency. In 1777, with the sales of Loan Office Certificates lagging and France committing only to secret grants of aid, Congress teetered on insolvency. They moved to entice more creditors by paying interest on domestic loans in bills drawn against the French funds. Morris was betting on indignation, disgust, anger, and lawsuits. He thought he knew exactly how to use the potential bitterness of creditors to tip the scales. He would get exactly the outrage he wanted. All that was left was to pull the strings of the hidden emotion that accompanies the world of high finance.

***

On July 6th, 1777, Rachel Franks and Haym Salomon were married in a simple unembellished ceremony officiated by the hazzan Abraham I. Abrahams. Circumstances forced the nuptials to be held at Moses' home; for Seixas had barred the doors of the Shearith Israel and was himself was still in Connecticut. Though the house was palatial, Rachel requested a low-key and solemn affair in respect to the financial troubles the country faced and the rivers of blood being spilled. Haym's ketubah, the marriage contract, which spelled out how he was going to provide for Rachel, used words that were modest in language and expectation. However, as he saw Moses as the example he was obliged to live up to, he had exceedingly more opulent designs.

Time flies when you're free and it had already been six months since Haym was paroled from the Livingston Sugarhouse. Released in January, he spent the remaining previous months incarcerated, wallowing in a desire to cause pain, hurt, injury, distress, misfortune, or some other devastating trauma to Sergeant Walley. He wasn't alone in that fantastical fantasizing violent aspiration. The good sergeant was one of the 20th Regiment of Irish traitors in the British service — he came with a mean streak and bottomless moral. For every prisoner — to a man, colonial farm boys, he was the most barbarous and cruel embodiment of authority they had ever seen. From the rotten and poisoned food to the canings, there was no sheer hell he would not visit upon the prisoners with the august arrogance and glowing pride of power. If the hands of fate had impassionately afforded Haym the opportunity to strike and kill the fiend, it would have been hard for him to resist a savoring ingestion of vengeance — though he knew such an opportunity preyed upon would have cost him the balance of his life. So… he had to devise a more cleaver plan; more subversive in nature, which would leave his hands unsullied and Walley professionally bloodied.

Haym provided himself an audience with the sadistic sergeant by standard means, the pound sterling. Walley feared a confrontation, unsure what the crafty, untrustworthy, dirty Jew wanted.

As Haym sat in the same seat in which Rachel did; Walley stood gripping a cane, a clear display of power and, for good measure, in case Haym foolishly considered acting on something more than speaking. They stared at one another— Walley's eyes sharp and threatening; Haym, as a tact, held his focus softly and harmless. Not a word had yet been spoken and the sergeant turned over an hourglass.

"Do not waste words," Walley said. "The sands trickle."

"I can be of value," Haym quickly responded.

"Why you have been of great value so far," Walley laughed.

"It would be of value to you to have a voice which can speak for you."

"How can you speak for me?" Walley said shaking the hourglass as if it would make it move faster.

"The Hessians," Haym said.

Upon hearing the word, he immediately understood the worth of the suggestion— the hourglass slipped out of his hand and crashed to the floor!

"Yes, 'the Hessians,'" he mused.

There was an irresistible quality to the offer, a quenching of the thirst for power. Walley, twisted the plantar of his boot over the spilled sand and broken glass, grinding them into the wooden floor. Then he dabbled with his scale as he mused…

"…I don't ask for much," Haym said. "A desk for writing. Two more oil lamps, and a pardon."

"'A pardon?'" Walley laughed. "If you're servicing the prison, surely it would be counter productive to have you exit."

"Due consideration in a timely manner," Haym said.

"Your pardon is not my proviso."

"I appeal to you honor. Those whom you have the ear of, speak of worth of my service and thou suggest my freedom."

Walley didn't want to show it, but he desperately wanted what Haym had to offer. Soon the boiler room was furnished with a writing desk and one additional oil lamp. The Salomon trap was set.

For the next month and a half, Haym spent whole portions of his day in the company of officers relaying translated orders to the German soldiers. Haym's presence had an immediate effect on the Hessian morale and output. Almost instantaneously, the sergeant had a well-run prison, which gave rise to less drunkenness and fewer escapes. Haym became so renown, he was released to the custody of General von Heister, the commander of the Hessian mercenaries, who did not speak English, and he was taken into the field to communicate with entire divisions. Soon, everyone in the British army around New York knew who the "Jewish" translator was.

What Walley and the British didn't know or realize is that between British orders, Haym was indoctrinating the Hessians as only he could do. He spoke to Hesse-Kassel's soldiers one-on-one; every chance afforded him and secretly coordinated cabals. He was sharing his own story. He told them to abandoned their posts and return home or take advantage of the generous land grants being offered by the Americans! He inspiringly read them the Declaration of Independence and rallied them to the aspiring heights of freedom. He spoke in soliloquies of how they were being used as little more than Negro slaves! As a matter of fact, he went so far as to rail against the absolute monarchies and dictatorial governments of Europe. He articulated republicanism, democracy, representative government, and human rights. He wasn't fiery, but sharp and to the point in defining the true palladiums of liberty. He told of the princes, kings, and queens he had met in his travels. He recollected accounts of the corruption of Sejm and the Russians. He gained converts by the day and one among them was himself. Of all the things he decided he had to do if he survived being jailed, was to join the Sons of Liberty.

Haym's propaganda campaign was wondrously successful and the Sugarhouse mercenaries were filled with a spirit of dissatisfaction and desertion. Haym was a prisoner but with the continuing help of the Hessians, a savior to many. Often the German sentries looked the other way as Haym ushered many back to freedom beyond the grounds. At the same time, his organization of the Hessians and their efficiency as needed for the British increased substantially. After little more than two months, Haym was pardoned. However, he had one parting gift for the good sergeant, which was more sadistic than anything Walley could conceive.

On his way out, he convinced the Hessians that Walley was cursing them, catching those who deserted and secretly caning them to death, going so far as to ground their meat and bones into the food he served them. None of this was true. But for his own safety, Sergeant Walley had to be transferred out of New York before he was killed by his own Hessian mob.

At the same time that Haym was undermining Walley and the British authority, Rachel came less frequently as Haym was better provided for and often engaged in his prison service. Her amorous confession had taken him by surprise and for the time being he deferred from acting upon it. However, Rachel honestly announced her love for the man that was more than twice her age of fifteen, to her father. He didn't openly object but promised her that he would speak with Haym one day soon. Whence the day came the night of his release.

"...So you'll agree to stay?" Franks asked Haym.
They were in the drawing room; quintessential, Rachel's mother looked down on them. Franks ended his question by quietly placing his well-played violin to his side.

"Be it not of an inconvenience," Haym replied.

"What inconvenience?"

"My gratitude is eternal," Haym expressed.

"You need not —"

"It is Moses. Be not for you would I have had a business — be not for you, I would not have the means I have acquired — and if not for you I most assuredly would be dead, by now consumed, digested, and deposited about the earth through the intestines of a swine."
Moses was only slightly moved but truly appreciative of the appreciation. Isaac was Moses' son but if Moses had not married so late in life and sired beyond his best years, he imagined his son would be as Haym.

"I must speak to you," Moses said.

"I pledge you anything," said Haym.

"Worry not, but I need nothing and that which could sustain me further is little in your possession," Moses said. "But it seems that my daughter proclaims an never dying love for you."
Haym was silent, even nervous.

"She is but still a child, or so my eyes perceive," Moses continued.

"I perceive a preciousness beyond the precious," Haym said.

"You do?" Moses said softly.

"I love her also," said Haym. "I know I am more of age and the world, but it is those qualities that make me sure of my heart."

"I see," Franks said. "I see... and it makes me glad."

It made him glad all right. Moses was carefully constructing his escape. Though it was his liberal mindedness that sparked the flames of Haym's philosophical approach to the nature of government and man, Moses himself was secretly a duplicitous greedy marketeer. He and his brother ventured into the open conflict between their home country and

318

it's rebellious colonies with less political convictions than they had ambitious capital exploits. Before the war, Moses was the sedentary brains of a large syndicate that fueled the British army. There was nothing immoral about his practices. However, as when the war began, he used his influence to quietly outfit both armies.

Between Moses and David they divided the territories. Moses supplied Canada, the American Colonies, the Caribbean, and every army along the Ohio and Mississippi rivers. David, who was centered in Philadelphia supplied Pennsylvania, New Jersey, Virginia, and the Southern Colonies. As mentioned, Franks' family was appointed Royal Purveyors by the King before the French and Indian War, but Moses and David, the son's of Jacob, keenly used their position to further discount their own imports to such a degree that their volume was massive. This is what allowed Moses to give Haym goods so cheaply but in turn proved useful in having a constant ready-made buyer who could serve as a front for arms purchases outside of London. Likewise, the brothers canvassed Jewish Merchants all over the colonies and created a vast network of partnerships, which engaged in a holistic number of ventures, big and small. Phenomenal amounts of capital was earned and occasionally lost, routinely as day after day— engorging them in greater and greater wealth. The war though, placed them on a collision course with vested interests beyond money— governments that demanded loyalty over profit and rightly saw attrition of the enemy as a tacit of victory. This reality would not only curb the market for earnings but also make them traitors to one side or the other. David, as the King's registered agent in Philadelphia could not openly abandoned his position without being branded a traitor by the British. The best he could do was to greedily straddle his commerce on both sides of the fence and hope that the British contained enough control that he was not taken in due course. However, Moses knew it was only a matter of time before either side arrested them on the measure of caution or worse, treason. And, he was right, David was imprisoned by the United Colonies as a security threat, even though he supplied Washington's army. Thereupon, Moses was prepared to make his escape to England as soon as he secured his young unsuspecting daughter's well being.

The Sejm rejected Casimir Pulaski's plea from Marseilles to reenter Poland by apathetically ignoring it all together. He drafted the desperate dispatch from debtor's prison. He was twenty-seven, but a very lonely and weather-beaten seven years into his adulthood. For he was an exile, imprisoned in the most horrid and ghastly conditions the French could muster. Days and nights he spent in the redolence of the stench of death and the slowly dying. The moans and cries of broken bodies. The jaunty breaking and pulverizing of those bodies by ruthless perverted warders. The hours of sleep he spent in a standing posture, be it for his will only that he had the requisite strength to find rest while commandeering his own weight. The untenable option was to rest his head on red worm and mice infested rotten straw. He endured starvation by neglect and masticated his small rations of meat in his wine to prolong tricking his body into thinking it was being fed. Yet, he had friends in France, Polish expatriates who still hailed him a hero— a man of the people! They wrote letters back to Poland detailing his conditions and fate. Money poured in and after six months imprisoned, he walked out into the street, gaunt and weary, but with the devil left confounded at his back.

Though Casimir begged to return to Poland, it was only a ploy to be released from prison. He had no great desire to return to Warsaw. By 1777 in the face of the partition, the Polish-Lithuanian army was reduced to a scant 10,000 troops. There was no place for Casimir, just as there was no place in the army for his friend and compatriot Tadeusz Kościuszko. There were very few options open to Casimir. One was to follow in the path of Kościuszko and return to Dresden to join either the Saxon court or the Elector's army. For Kościuszko though, such was a failed venture and he was reduced to returning to Paris where the two men last convened in spirited company. Casimir was a man of war and he needed war as necessarily as the body needs water, every three days or so.

While in France, Kościuszko caught the national fervor for America and support of the emergent country over the English. Kościuszko was not a man of war, but he was a man of vigor and action, and without a second thought, emigrated to the nation and offered his services to the Revolutionary cause. Presenting himself to Congress in June of 1776, he was allowed to serve as a volunteer. However, as fighting intensified and the flames of New York were fanned, Kościuszko's educated talent, was tapped by Washington and he was made the chief engineer for the Continental Army. His first task was to sure up the fortification in all-important Philadelphia. He constructed the New Jersey fort of Billingsport and fortified the banks of the Delaware against a possible British crossing. He was invaluable to Washington and by 1777 he was attached to the Northern Army under Major General Horatio Gates where he directed the construction of several forts and military camps along the Canadian border.

For his failed part, Casimir was still stuck in Marseilles, but on his way to Paris. While in Paris he found the French had as little regard for him as the Poles and he received permission to go to America where there was the good graces of war. The American ambassador, Benjamin Franklin was told of his heroic exploits for the Polish cause of liberty — or so it was defined, and he requested the calvary officer's company.

Franklin sagaciously read the Declaration of Independence to Casimir, annunciating every word to tip of the most glistening height of its epitome — proud he was. Every man who signed it he honored by full name and colony. At Franklin's breath the Declaration sounded in its timelessness — applying to the human condition through eternity because it was a document devoted to maintaining and proclaiming the freedom and liberty of the individual. It's brilliance spoke of being the greatest set of words of liberty and freedom every written by human beings. In all the fibers and threads of his being, Casimir Pulaski was stirred even more profoundly than he was at Podolia, where he sought to save the fatherland. He said unto Franklin that he had never heard something that sounded so sweet to his ear and his heart, even sweeter than cannon fire and the intimacy of a woman. Franklin expressed that the floundering nation need a man like him more than they knew, and he outfitted the Polish general with a letter of recommendation addressed to Washington.

On June 6th, 1777 Casimir boarded the ship Massachusetts from Nantes to America. He landed in the United State at Marblehead near Boston. After a short stay in Boston, he reported at the headquarters of the commander-in-chief of the Continental Army, George Washington. He was at the Moland House near Philadelphia, where he was auspiciously entertaining the likes of another Frenchman, Gilbert du Motier, marquis de Lafayette. Casimir presented his letter from Franklin and offered his services. Washington knew an officer when he saw one and he named Casimir the general of the nonexistent cavalry.

***

By the middle of the year of Our Lord 1777, upon the hearing of Benedict Arnold's approach, the British withdrew from Fort Stanwix in New York and Howe landed his troops at Head of Elk, Maryland. As

Washington wintered in Morristown on the laurels of his victory at Princeton, Arnold, as maybe the Continental's most tactically adept leader, had the British on the retreat even with snow still on the ground. However, there were as many gains for the Americans as 1777 progressed, as there were losses. St. Clair surrendered at Fort Ticonderoga and the Red Coats, with the assistance of the Iroquois nation, forced the patriots back at Oriskany, New York. To outside observers, the war appeared to be in a deadlock. However, maybe the most significant development of 1777 was the Congress deciding upon a national flag. They passed a resolution which stated: "Resolved, that the flag of the United States be thirteen strips, alternate read and white; that the union be thirteen stars, white in a blue field, representing a new Constellation."

As for Haym Salomon, the middle of 1777 was as sweet as his life ever was or would ever be. He was content and fulfilled. He owned a beautiful new house. He was blessed with a doting wife. And, as a wedding gift, he acquired for her Anna, an amiable female Negro slave to help with domestic chores along with a strong black buck named Joe. The days of being a dry goods merchant were behind him. He opened up his brokerage firm and settled into a comfortable, stable, and relatively normal life. However, before he married, Haym followed through on his intention of becoming a trueborn Son of Liberty and being a politically proactive patriot on the side of the angels of liberty. The decision would forever catapult his life into a tumult of dire consequences.

***

Morris had been convinced that the key to sweeping policy change was rooted in the public creditors— those speculating and trusting Americans who had purchased the congressional bonds. He fancied it was they that could provide the sort of vocal and local political pressure to which the state legislators would be obliged to respond. He calculated to bring them into one mind, one collective agreement of action— so his gamble and plan was built on. However, the gamble, if unsuccessful cut from both ends of the knife— the solvency of the country and it's ability to pay it's bills and Morris' own substantial holdings in the domestic debt. Yet, he was betting that cutting off interest payments would spur the public creditors into glorious action and have them come running to him, the financial congressional representative, for relief.

It wasn't long after congress' pronouncement of halted interest payments that his strategy sprouted a seedling. Morris' report on French funds was referred to a committee, which concurred with him in favor of ending the drafts on French grants. But Morris still needed the investor uncertainty and fear, followed by outrage. To what end — to harness self-interest to the public weal. What Morris learned in his years of finance, which is often lost on men chasing money for the sake of their own earthly wealth, was a deep intuitive understanding of capital in the jigsaw of finance. It wasn't a mere product of money. To Morris, capital was the great appliance by which society organized itself and pursued its endeavors. Capital must flow freely, as Morris believed; and the bedrock of that flow was unquestioning credit reliability.

Finally understanding the interest payments toward the domestic loans was not unforthcoming by a government struggling to fund an army and win a war; the creditors unleashed their outrage on Congress. The blest administration naturally referred the matter to Morris. Morris brought the creditors together and made an astonishing recommendation. They should sue. He went so far as to confer with their attorneys, whom he recommended, and to direct the language of the complaints with the softest protests of grievance — as not to insult Congress or offend the men who were fighting on their behalf. The result? Congress made Morris responsible for addressing the problem any means he saw fit. This shifted the command of the nation's financial policy from committees and men plagued by regional interests, self-interest, and short-sidedness to a single well-honed pecuniary mind.

Morris would immediately redirect the financial policy. Everyday would be a struggle and a challenge, but by the end, his genius would set into place the United States' principle course of actions on taxation, debts, debt relief, and by the Almighty grace of God, the ultimate financing of the war. The financial envy of the world would be left in the wake of Robert Morris.

***

XXV

FATE

"The only principles of public conduct that are worthy of a gentleman or a man are to sacrifice estate, ease, health, and applause, and even life, to the sacred calls of his country."   James Otis

On July 20th of 1778, Ezekiel Salomon was born into the soft loving arms of his mother Rachel. On August 11th of the same gloomy year, Rachel's husband and Ezekiel's father Haym, was sentenced to death.

***

Fresh from the wounds of Lexington and the enthralled enthusiastic victory of Concord, The Second Continental Congress met on May 10th, 1775 at the State House in Philadelphia. There were several new delegates including: John Hancock, Thomas Jefferson and Benjamin Franklin. While Washington was pointing his cannons down on the British in Boston, President Peyton Randolph convened fifty-six delegates from twelve colonies, as Georgia abstained. Among the numerous resolutions that passed that day, the last of them created was the Committee of Secret Correspondence. It read:

> "Resolved, that a committee… would be appointed for the sole purpose of corresponding with our friends in Great Britain, and other parts of the world, and that they lay their correspondence before Congress when directed."
> ""Resolved, that this Congress will make provision to defray all such expenses as they may arise by carrying on such correspondence, and for the payment of such agents as the said Committee may send on this service."

With those dual resolutions they gave approval to a fifth column of intelligence gathering networks, spy rings, and clandestine operations.

On June 13th, 1777, Abraham Patten was hanged as a spy. A native Brunswick resident, he passed himself off as nothing more than an everyday, run-of-the-mill dry goods merchant. In the fervor of his patriotism, he drafted a letter to Washington saying that he would set off the most tremendous fire this side of the brimstone pit of hell to all the magazines in Brunswick. Furthermore, he would do it in obeisant glory of the revolution by charging the blast on the 4th of June, the King's birthday. The letter was handed for delivery to an English grenadier who had offered to desert for money. Instead, the grenadier delivered the communiqué to Lord Cornwallis. At the gallows, Patten spoke his last words with bloated pride. "I die for liberty, and do it gladly because my cause is just."

The quartet, James Rivington, Robert Townsend, Abraham Woodhull, and an unnamed woman known numerically as "355" constituted the secret operatives called the Culper Ring. The false-hearted, double-dealing, perfidious blemishes on the role of the king's subjects used sophisticated codes, ciphers and secret ink for communications and a series of couriers and whaleboats for transmitting reports. James Rivington was the King's Printer. He owned and operated a coffee house frequented by British soldiers and officers, which became the principal source of intelligence for the ring. One of the choicest pieces of information Rivington was able to obtain was the Royal Navy's signal book. This helped the French fleet to hold back the British ships trying to relieve General Cornwallis at York. Townsend, known by his own ternary assumption of "723," and Abraham Woodhull who went by the alias, "Samuel Culper Sr." specialized in disinformation and answered directly to Washington. As for the unnamed woman, "355," who was she? It is likely she was a beautiful and seductive member of a prominent Tory family. Tracing the missives of the ring, it seems obvious that she was in direct contact with Major André, a British officer — who himself was hanged as spy in conspiracy with Benedict Arnold. Pregnant and ratted out by the rat, Arnold, she was incarcerated in the most irrefutably cruel, savage, barbarous, unpitying, relentless bloodthirsty and blood-soaked, filthy, malignant death factory the unrelenting penal history of civilization had ever known: the brig HMS Jersey. After giving birth, to a son named Robert Townsend, Jr., she fittingly met the fate of all captured spies.

During the occupation of New York, British officers regularly shopped at Hercules Mulligan's clothing store. The big, burly, affable

Irishman was born during the Great Frost and famine of his countrymen. He grew up in a victimized and repressed Northern Ireland by a system of Protestant English rule. The British passed penal laws that restricted an Irishman's right to education, to hold office, to vote, to possess arms, and to own property. In response, the Mulligans, as many others immigrated to America. Hercules root of disgust for England ran as deep as a mesquite. However, he was a gregarious heavy drinker that invited soldiers at a time to join in late night riotousness. Theretofore, he passed on to Washington the plans the British had to capture the general himself and also their planned incursion into Pennsylvania. The oft came under British suspicions, but his affable nature allowed him to persuade and cajole suspicions away from him.

John Honeyman was a butcher and a weaver by trade. He had served the British admirably in the French and Indian War; however, he was sympathetic to the American cause and the enigmatic value of freedom. He promptly presented his genuine services to Washington. The general accepted his call to duty and sent Honeyman to the British as a Tory where he could watch their maneuvers. Posing as a butcher, which in point of fact he was, he learned that the British were preparing a big Christmas celebration at Trenton. By using a ruse, Honeywell allowed himself to be "captured" as a Tory and taken to Washington. The two devised an elaborate "escape" plan and Honeywell returned to the British with a dramatic tale of the great escapades of his escape. He told the British that the Americans were demoralized to attack and that they should proceed with their celebration with no fear of Washington. In drunken revelry, the British were caught by surprise when Washington attacked the day after Christmas. As it was, if not for the excellent and far-reaching work of Honeywell, Washington would have been unable to capture Trenton.

Born a Virginian slave, James Lafayette began his life with the given name Armistead. In his admiration of the great French General Lafayette, he bestowed upon himself his regal identity. However, he could not bestow upon himself his freedom and he was forced to request permission of his master to join his hero and namesake at York. Permission was graciously granted. As a solider in the general's army, LaFayette used LaFayette's indentured status as a shrewd ruse. He sent the Negro across enemy lines to pretend he was an escaped slave and General Cornwallis quickly recruited him as a spy. Then, as planned, Washington forged false orders for a large regiment of colonial soldier replacements. James

Lafayette handed the piece of paper to Cornwallis, telling him he found it lying on the road. Cornwallis never knew that he was tricked into thinking the Americans were stronger than they were. For this bravery and other espionage services during the war, slave James Lafayette, was granted his freedom by a grateful Virginia Legislature following the completion of revolutionary victory.

Intelligence was always on General Washington's mind. On highest orders, General William Heath sent James Bowdoin, a draftsmen, to Canada to collect information about Halifax. Washington wanted detailed information on the British defense works and Howe's reserves on wait in Nova Scotia. Bowdoin brought back detailed plans of Halifax harbor and all the specific military works and information Washington wanted. Armed with knowledge, the general crafted his military strategy against Howe.

Lieutenant Lewis J. Costigin had been captured by the British and sent to New York as a prisoner. As part of a prisoner exchange he was required to take an oath of parol. He accepted his freedom upon the agreement of refraining from exchanging military intelligence. He stayed in New York and disregarded the oath in its entirety, that he may have exacted his revenge. He gathered intelligence on logistics, British commanders, shipping, and troop deployments, all the time acting the role of a harmlessly paroled loyal oath-abiding prisoner.

Like many, in the overused but consistently effective plan, Sergeant Daniel Bissell "deserted" the Continental Army, posed as a Tory, and joined Benedict Arnold's "American Legion." He was able to gather information on British fortifications and detail the British methods of operation before he escaped to American lines.

Dominique L'Eclise was a Canadian intelligence agent for General Schuyler. Detected and caught by the soldiers of the Crown, he was duly imprisoned and had his property swiftly confiscated. Later, he was granted reimbursement by the Continental Congress, as compensation for his contribution to the American cause.

Lydia Darragh was yet another cunning spy in the great coruscating history of espionage. As legend has it, British officers in Philadelphia used a large room on the upper floor of the Darragh house for conferences. Mrs. Darragh would hide in an adjoining closet and take notes on the British military plans. The notes were then transcribed by her husband into a form of shorthand, placed on scraps of paper and Lydia made covered buttons with the paper under the fabric. The buttons were sewn onto the coat of her fourteen year old son who took them to his elder brother; a lieutenant in the Continental Army. From there, the brother would cut off the buttons and transcribe the notes into readable form to present to his officers.

And, then there was Haym Salomon, who was paroled at Livingston, joined the Sons of Liberty, and took to service for his adopted country as an undercover agent. With his wealth, he continued to have guards bribed at all the British run prisons in New York. As of 1777, his artful mischief against the British Crown knew no bounds. However, his luck did.

Aug. 11— Haym's interrogation begat the roaring voice of Provost Marshall Cunningham. Tied to a chair, the Marshall kicked Haym and the chair over. His head slammed to the wood floor and he was left horizontal to ground level. From that point forward, everything to his sight was blurred and upside down. The Provost stood over him screaming every word he spat!

"You dare lie!" Cunningham screamed in spittled regalia! "You dare lie! Embroiled you are— you schemed— so you sought to burn His Majesty's fleet! To destroy His stores! Whose hand was it upon the planks on Mr. Stewart's store? Mr. Stewart, I dare say not!
He turned Haym's hands over, looking for suggestive signs of combustion residue! He found none, yet Haym's hands gave the recent appearance of greater labor than the counting of coins.

"You watched, didn't you, as the conflagration spread to the docks?
Haym was silent. Cunningham bristled.

"And your foreign tongue— a tail for lies— a means to provoke desertion among His ranks! You sir, are in no judgement worthy of your God-given place on this earth! You, sir, I sentence to the gallows and pendent rope! I can only say, may God have mercy on you, for I... shall most certainly not!"

Haym was cast into the squalid steaming hold of the ship which made him but one of about 1,100 prisoners. They were like a hoard of rats enclosed in the dimension of a bird's nest— and ironically, there was no room for even rodents among these rats. At first thought, Haym worried for Rachel and Ezekiel more than himself, until he observed a prisoner across from him. His eyes were glazed and a lunacy seemed to have overcome his attention. Haym watched as the emaciated man sat in his little corner with his shirt in his hands, having removed it from his body — contentedly picking the vermin from the pleats and rapaciously placing them in his mouth. Suddenly, with the sense of specter in his mists, the crazed prisoner snapped his head and looked up to see Haym in a stared state of shock.

"What is your name?" the man said with a certain delirium.

"Haym."

"Perfect," he whispered. "Don't you think?"

Haym was transfixed, fearing he was looking into the flesh of a moiraian mirror hitherto reflecting his own fate.

"What do you see?" the man said with a certain rapture of high-spirited insanity. "And what... do you see?"

Haym gathered himself, and by the breath — approached a further conversation within the temporal confines of standard reality. He wanted facts.

"How long have you been here... my good fellow?"

"As long... long... long, as there has been the observation of God by the quantification of time," he said as though he was a flake of fairy dust fluttering down in the air.

Another, lying on his back, with his gums bleeding, spoke up in logical tones and splattered blood!

"He has been here longer than I, and I seventeen months. Save your breath — he is mad!"

With that, the man accused of madness flailed his skeletal arms and laughed ever-so-hysterically —

"Madness! Madness! Madness is but seen from the lout! His aperture narrowed to the focus of an insect — yet an insect standing in the unseen pastures of eternity. Madness! Madness is but such a small sight of the whole picture!"

Aug. 12 — Haym wasn't able to sleep during the night and he watched the sunrise scale the horizon off the ripples of the ocean. A roll of the prisoners was called. It was something that was done every three months, unless a large acquisition of prisoners should render it necessary more often. The marshall regulations of the ship were read. Of the new regulations in effect, there was one in which Haym listened to with knot in the pit in his stomach. Every captive assayed to the effort of escape should suffer instant death, and should not even be taken aboard alive. He worried that it might mean his usual modus operandi of bribing a guard may be ineffective or just effective enough to get him hung even quicker.

As it was, Haym and a couple of Sons, were captured by Red Coats while coming away from a dock anchored with British vessels. They brought them down to Colonel Buskirk's at Bergen Point, and from there they were sent to General Pigot, who sent them with Captain Van Allen to the Provost Jail. Marked with a reputation for manipulating and bribing guards, Provost Marshall Cunningham alone transferred Haym to the HMS Jersey. As always, Haym was financially outfitted and ready for the worse. With two guineas sewn into his undergarment he was initially not all that concerned about his capture. That was until he was transferred in chains and thrust into the forepeak. Then, he feared, even two gold guineas might not be enough to alter his fate. The next morning proved that fear to be valid.

Aug. 13— Haym and the lot of prisoners received muddy water to quench a thirst made worse by the blistering heat and a biscuit to presume his hunger satisfied. Though he wasn't sufficiently relaxed enough to consume a meal, he peeled open the biscuit to find adult beetles, three millimeters in length, oval in shape, reddish brown in color, with a dense covering of yellowish hairs. He watched others eat of the same and a new pit of sickness enveloped his stomach. Haym had also developed a cough. It only appeared in reoccurring spurts but as it did, he hacked in dry exasperations of air. Come nightfall, the unbolting and unlocking of the chains echoed throughout the hull. Shackled, the prisoner Salomon was paraded up to the quarterdeck by intemperate officers sent to retrieve him. They completed their exercise of instruction with drunken cackles; laughing as though a minion of defrocked curates from the church of darkness. Though Haym was not sure where he was being led, he felt as if he was literally walking away from salvation and beyond past the sanctity of God's reach. Depraved, Cunningham was waiting for him. Soon, Haym found himself on deck fettered by iron to a cannon and his scarred backside exposed to the lacerating propulsion of the whip. Those who had come before Haym— spread eagle, prostrate across the cannon, wailed and shrieked in suffering prayers for mercy so loud that the local women petitioned Howe to prevent further capital punishment upon the ship. They begged that their ears be spared to hear the dreadful unanswered appeals to Heaven, which loosened their faith in the religious promise of

God's rejoinders to man's cry. With each lash, Haym refused to wail or sound more than a murmured grunt.

"Confess your crimes!" Cunningham screamed as the whip was laid to the man.

"I am true-born Son of Liberty!" Haym would only respond with guttural impetus!

"Confess!"

One tailed end of the cat-o'-nine-tails rose over Haym's bleeding back and struck the top of his forehead. A stream of blood rolled down the center of his angular nose and cascaded to the deck.

"Admit your intentions!"

"I am a true-born Son of Liberty!"

"Give me the whip," Cunningham yelled at the Captain administering the punishment. The Provost's mulatto servant took the cat-o'-nine-tails and handed it to his master. Cunningham slowly approached Haym, bent down and looked him deep in the eyes.

"I will not quibble. You will confess," Cunningham said in a seething clench of his teeth and fist.

"I am a true-born Son of Liberty," Haym repeated.

"You are, are you?" Cunningham responded, and then spit in his face! "Do you not see? I have already commended you to death!"

The spit spread across Haym's face like a spider web and hung off his eyelids, nose, hair, and lips in dangling threads.

"This is but an exercise in mercy," Cunningham implored. "I will gladly reconsider your fatal castigation in the light and blood of your confession and pledge of loyalty. Doubt not my sympathy for your soul, I shall go so far as to wrest every ounce of your blood, drop-by-drop, if that's what it will take to save your life," Cunningham contended with the twinkle of an obscene sadistic smile.

"Bloody Bill" Cunningham was not a man to cross or bargain with, as a matter of fact, it is likely the devil himself cringed when he looked into the bowels of Cunningham's soul. Spat out of his mother's loins in a Dublin barracks, he was the son of trumpeter in the Blue Dragoons, and — it is more than likely that he was bottle fed on a rum liqueur other than the breast of his mother's milk. At sixteen he became an assistant to the riding-master of the troop. Soon thereafter, he earned the rank of sergeant, but peace had broken out the previous year and the company was disbanded. True to his nature, he commenced to the business of a scaw-banker, which means that he went about the country enticing mechanics and rustics to ship to America. They sailed on the disingenuous promise of having their fortunes made; and then by dishonest and devious design, he produced their indentures as servants, in consequence of which on their arrival in America they were sold, or at least obliged to serve a term of years to pay for their passage. This business, no doubt, proved a fit apprenticeship for the career of villainy before him. In 1774, he arrived in New York with some indentured servants he had kidnapped in Ireland. He treated those poor creatures so cruelly on the passage that they were set free by sympathetic authorities upon arrival in New York. When Cunningham first appeared in the city he offered himself as a horse-breaker, and insinuated his person into the favor of the British officers by blatant Toryism. However, he soon became obnoxious to the Whigs and ahead of a mob seeking his head, fled to the Asia man-of-war for protection. From thence he went to Boston, where General Gage appointed him Provost Marshal.

Even before Haym was defenseless upon the deck, Cunningham is said to have compassed the death of thousands of prisoners by selling their provisions, exchanging goods for spoiled food, and going so far as to even poison them. To inflict pain seemed to bring Cunningham an almost sexual gratification. He wasn't simply violent; he was freewheeling and murderous in his violence.

Haym was not the first in the midnight of the moon; he was among the three hundredth to satisfy Cunningham's gluttonous thirst for blood. And so it was that he held the whip and paced in a semicircle around his victim; then with howls of untempered aggression he fantastically whipped Haym until his body collapsed and rolled off the cannon! He hung upside down; bleeding and suspended by the iron chain shackles. The deck below him was awash in his essence, more than appeared could still be in his body. But Cunningham wasn't done with him, yet.

"Free him!" he yelled! "Rouse him!"

Haym was unshackled and sal volatile placed under his nose. A jolt animated him; his eyes rolled up to stare at Cunningham.

"Here— paper. Write," he said. "Lest I forget, I well inform you that we visited your house and your home on this afternoon. Be aware that everything, which was yours in worldly possession, is no more of said possession. Now, of myself, I came to understand that you are married and even a father. Well, I assure you no harm came to your quaint family.

Further, you should be pleased to know that I was so gentlemanly as to refrain from having her become indecent and allowed her to keep the clothes on her back and the milk in her breast— though in fact they belong to Our Majesty. But that, I assure you was all she was allowed to retain. Now, I want you to write her and let her know just how you are faring in my care."

Aug. 14— Another prisoner died of smallpox. It was a stormy day and the rain cleared the desk of Haym's blood. Captain Corne visited the ship and observed the wrecked state of affairs to which Haym's body and mind were in condition of.

Aug. 15— Captain Van Zandt ordered all prisoners locked in their cells during the entire length of day to accomplish an accurate headcount. Many prisoners were sickly and lights were ordered out at sundown. Haym slept throughout the day as British civility reigned and nurses formally cleaned, bathed, and dressed him with fresh bandages. At times he was thought to be dead.

Aug. 16— Rachel having received Haym's blood-soaked parchment arrived with her aunt Richa to see her husband. She was turned away and left hysterical. Luckily she wasn't beaten in the process as many wives in past have experienced upon attempting to pay call to their husbands. An influx of new prisoners boarded from the Sugarhouse. Provisions were exceedingly ordinary— pork, peas, and bug infested biscuits.

Aug. 17— Horrid scenes of whipping, two prisoners do not survive more arbitrary British punishment. Haym begins to regain nominal strength. Warm weather. Prisoners supplied with new clothes and sundry articles. Mercy shone down and a prisoner's daughter was allowed to visit her sickly and dying father.

Aug. 18— A stray paper found. The contents intimated that three prisoners had a rope concealed in a bag in order to make their escape. Sergeants examined the whole ship. Random beatings followed. 300 men confined between decks, half Frenchmen. Sergeant was informed there were three more of these vehicles of contagion, which contained a like number of miserable Frenchmen also, who were treated worse, if possible, than Americans. Haym continued to regain physical strength and mental clarity.

Aug. 19— A prisoner from Connecticut exchanged. Another woman arrived to see her sick husband. She was beaten by sentries. Prisoners are allowed on deck for air. Haym's coughing returns, at times blood accompanies, but probably mostly due to beatings. A man diseased with smallpox asks Haym to keep his will.

"Why do you ask me?" whispered Haym.

"For an angel appeared to me," the man said with a weak-rasping voice. "It appeared in a state of vision— I could see it. There, it hovered above me, and there, it sat next to me. I could see it, but I could not see thus in full. A halo of light washed from me all there was to see—"

"Say, you were dreaming—"

"No, I tell you!" said the man, coated with blisters on the back of his neck and dotted around his face said. "The beams and light of this halo stole from me the sight of male or female, but it sat next to me, and it grazed against me, it did! I could feel—"

"What did it feel like," Haym said in disbelief.

"Feel, if you can remember— feel the body temperature of your mother's fluid in the womb—"

"You're telling me something solid—"

"Yes, the solid felt not in pressure but sensation—"

"Pardon me, but this is a dream—"

"No, it was the night," said the man.

He held out his scribbled will, looking around to see who might be watching.

"I tell you, forgive me, but I regretfully decline your request," Haym said. "It doesn't bring me joy, but unless you are called within this week, it is I who will be remembered by you—"

"And where is your will?" the man asked.

"Mine? Mine rests on the flat surface of my tongue. It is to die as I have lived and all that is left of me is memory, that it shall be remembered and followed in example— to live and die for God and country."

Aug. 20— Beef, loaf bread, and butter drawn today. Six tailors brought here from prison ship to work in making clothes for prisoners. They say the people on board are very sickly. Of the three hundred sent on board reduced to one hundred. Remaining prisoners grumble, as it is learned fresh meat was sent in for the prisoners at the order of Howe through negotiation and prisoner exchange agreement with Washington. However, men-of-war confiscate for their own use at the directive of Provost Marshall. Fresh air and fresh water were received. As one prisoner said in passing to Haym, "God's free gift is our tears to salt the tasteless fare."

Aug. 21 — Haym worries himself of the gallows or escape. He sits with his hand jostled down his pant, commiserating with his gold coins. No guard has been kind whatsoever on the Jersey. The odds of a bribe being effective are not high enough to chance the operation. He prays to God through the night.

Aug. 22 — Five or six a day cheating the law and dying before the hangman has his due. They are lowered down the boat like any other item in store. Cunningham called to shore as evidence in a Court of Admiralty for ill treatment of prisoners. He happily escaped justice.

One person alone was admitted on deck at a time, after sunset, which occasioned much filth to run into the hold, and mingled with the bilge water, which was not pumped out while he was aboard, notwithstanding the decks were leaky, and the prisoners begged permission to let in water and pump it out again. Nights hot sweat invite rats to lap the sweetness of the body and make lice feel itchier. Haym's cough increases in frequency and intensity. Another night and he does not sleep— at times curses God..

Aug. 23 — Two men carried out to be hung for desertion, reprieved. Jail exceedingly disagreeable. Malnourished and abused, death as common as common sense. Haym tortures himself through the night in repentance to God.

Aug. 24 — An afternoon of heat so intense all prisoners stripped of their clothes, which also served them well to be rid of vermin, but the sick were eaten up alive, too tired to fight the parasite off. All around Haym, he observed the sickly countenances, and ghastly looks which were truly horrible; some swearing and blaspheming; others crying, praying, and wringing their hands; and stalking about like ghosts; others delirious, raving and storming— all panting for breath; some dead, and corrupting. The air was so foul that at times a lamp could not be kept burning, by reason of which the bodies were not missed until they had been dead ten days. Be it of certain moments, Haym questioned wisdom of the infinite, but then he questioned his own questioning. Cunningham visited Haym's cell and told him that tomorrow he would be transferred to the Provost Prison for his hanging after midnight of the following day. Haym spent the night, unable to sleep, surrendering to God.

Aug. 25— Haym, encased in a half-broken and bludgeoned body, was transferred in chains by escort of Cunningham's hirelings. He arrived at the epitome of perdition known as the "New Jail" Provost Prison— and for a split second, by initial comparison; his memories of the Livingston were fond. If he considered the Sugarhouse a wretched pit, then Provost was rise of eternal damnation. Haym found himself half-naked and sharing a cell with a tired but zealously upbeat Ethan Allen. The space between them was a mere sixteen feet square with no air and no sanitation. However, to Haym's amazement, he was on sacred ground— crudely carved into the wall was the name of his old friend "Alexander McDougall."

The nightmarish infernal regions of purgatory and pandemonium hath have no equal like the New York Provost prison. At the time of Haym's incarceration, in excess of 2,000 prisoners had already gone the way of the flesh by starvation and disease. As meager as the rations were at the Sugarhouse, at the Provost, Cunningham often stopped rations altogether and sold them for his own profit which he niggardly shared among the presiding solider sentries and Hessians. In addition to the above-mentioned obnoxious body count, there were 300 executions without trial. Haym Salomon was to be the next. The "New Jail" was made a provost prison, intended to be where American officers and the most eminent Whigs who fell into the hands of the British were confined. It was the main theatre for the balance of Cunningham's brutal conduct toward the recipients of his sanguine spite. As Walley ran the Sugarhouse in a disordered fashion, Cunningham ran his particular palace with distinct discipline. Everything had a certain unalterable procedure, for example: prisoner arrival. Once a captive or group of internees arrived, they were formally introduced to Cunningham, and their name, age, size, and rank were fittingly recorded. They were then confined in morose cells that hearkened to the last whit of life, or to the equally abominable upper chamber, where the highest officials in captivity were so closely crowded together, that when, at night, they laid down to sleep upon the hard plank floor, they could change position only by all turning over at once, at the words "right" – "left!" Their provisions were inedible and that was by avaricious design. It wasn't beneath ol' Bloody Bill to personally pocket some profit by trade of fresh rations for some rotten pig slop. The rogue would go so far as to confiscate food and treats sent for the prisoners from their friends or the commissariat. These little delicacies brought by relatives or well wishers of the captives seldom reached them, and the brutal Provost Marshall would sometimes devour or destroy such offerings of affection, in the presence of his victims to gratify his unendingly cruel propensities. The Provost was Hell's worst kept secret but its best previsional representation. Wealth, social status or military rank did not immune a single soul. If apprehended and arrested, gentlemen of fortune and education— who had lived in the enjoyment of the luxuries and refined pleasures of elegant social life— found themselves in the New Jail doomed to a miserable scarce-existence of existence, embittered by coarse insults and beatings at the gore soaked hands of Bloody Bill, the bleeding gums of scurvy, the severe fever of smallpox, the pending demise from starvation, the gnawing fat rats with the taste for human flesh, the fulsome congestion of ticks and lice, the stomach pains and delirium of dysentery, the night sweats and the finger clubbing of consumption, the want of palatable comestibles, at any given time fresh air, a cool breeze or a warm fire, reprehensible criminal indifference, and the still most appreciable of the iniquitous cruelties— wholesale slaughter. This greatest fiendish inhuman unholiness was practiced upon the less conspicuous prisoners, and many were hanged in the casting helpless gloom of night— without trial or known cause for the foul murder. The authorized might of the British Empire in administration of military despotism was a fact well known but ignored by the powers that be. War they say is hell. If so, then the British were demonic, and Cunningham, Beelzebub in the garment of human flesh.

Aug. 26— The night grew darker and the scheduled execution grew closer. Allen sat in one corner, rubbing the thick tender scars around his wrists and ankles—

"The day will come— in which we will win the day," he said angrily.

"So thus it might, but… for now it is but the night," Haym calmly responded.

Allen's scars, which he continually gazed, inspected, and rubbed were due to disproportionate suffering. His luck following the capture of Ticonderoga was dismal. He led an ill-fated attack on Montreal, which concluded in the capture of himself and a majority of his small army. General Richard Prescott enchained him aboard the infamous HMS Gaspée, which at the time was anchored in fur-trading outpost. Allen was shown no mercy and for his colonial "rebelliousness," was treated to the second most effective tool of government after taxes: torture. Extraordinarily, Allen and the other captured Green Mountain Boys were placed on the Adamant, a fourth-rate merchant ship bound for England. He and the thirty-three of his "boys" were stuffed in wooden cages and held among the common cargo. For forty days and nights, their ankles and wrists were shackled so tightly that not only was the circulation cut off by the thirty-pound weights, but also the irons cut into their skins— and bled outwardly. During the entire passage, the sailors amused themselves by mercilessly teasing Allen. His uncontrollable and impassioned fires were events of great jest and merriment. They drank and laughed, as Allen would froth at the mouth while he pulled and yanked at his unbreakable chains— but of course to no avail— like a latched dog out of the bites reach! The best Allen could do was return the insults in empty threats of their future to come if he was ever free again. Finally, the ship arrived at Falmouth, England and the prisoners were imprisoned in Pendennis Castle, Cornwall. Deliverance was nowhere to be found and the deplorable treatment of the British captive continued. Ironically, Parliament found itself faced with opposition from within the Romantic Era English society to the military treatment of the North American captives, and a scandal was on their hands. If only the whole of the English population knew of the conditions of captives on North American soil, then the Parliament would have had more than a scandal on it's hands, but a national outrage. As it was, King George decreed that the men should be sent back to America and treated as respectfully as prisoners of war. Allen and his men were put on board the HMS Soledad, which sailed for Cork, Ireland. When the people of Cork learned that the famous Ethan Allen was in port, they took up a collection to provide him and his men with clothing and other supplies. Ireland proved to be too flattering to the Americans and troublesome for the Red Coats, so they sent the Soledad afloat to Canada. Allen and the men were never allowed off the precisely worded, "stinking ship," and disease proceeded to set in, first and foremost of these contagions: scurvy. Fortunately for Allen, his constitution, disposed in his volcanic temperament, was aptly spared. Once in Halifax, Allen and other prisoners were temporarily put ashore, owing to conditions on ship that even the British could not rationalize. The scurvy was so rampant that more bloody teeth littered the deck than were in mouths of men. Once Howe had secured New York, Allen and those of the "Boys" still living were sent on-shore to the British occupied city. Considered an officer and no longer a threat, Allen was given a limited parole. With the financial assistance of his brother Ira, he lived comfortably, if anxious and out of action, until August 1777. He then learned of the death of his young son Joseph due to smallpox. Everything Allen touched seemed to turn to grief but instead of lamenting, he consumed himself in the cause of America with a simmering zeal that rendered his mind absolute. He sought to escape Howe's country and make his way to Philadelphia where the brain trust of New York, Boston, and the better personages of the nation had retreated and assembled. However, he was caught "wandering" beyond the designated confinement of his parole, and placed in solitary confinement at the Provost.

As the night grew darker, Haym, sweat in fear and anticipation. Suddenly, he was visited by the past familiar face of Captain Corne.

"The Marshall has sent me," he said.

Haym rose and stood; his hands clasped the bars.

"He says to tell you to prepare yourself to meet the devil."

Aug. 27/12:30am— Per the usual procedures of an execution, a guard was dispatched from the Provost after midnight to Barrack street behind the prison and the neighborhood of the upper barracks to order the people to shut their window shutters and put out their lights, forbidding them at the same time to look out of their windows and doors on pain of death; after which the unfortunate prisoners were conducted and gagged, just behind the upper barracks, and hung without ceremony. There they were buried in the sound of Cunningham's wretched diabolic laugh. The hour of Haym's demise approached in what felt like minutes into seconds. There appeared to be no means or measure by which to avoid a life lived briefly. Then, a Hessian officer passed the cell. He noticed Haym and remembered him from the Sugarhouse. The young man was ecstatic! It seems his turn never came to receive a shilling bribe and he looked at him as though a prize found. Immediately, he wanted to know if there was anything he could do for the man, anything that would of course render him a twentieth of a pence. It appeared he wasn't even aware of Haym's impending execution. He expected maybe some fresh water or good biscuit would be all that was asked. Haym reached into the under garment of his dirty and tattered pants and wrestled out two of the most beautiful pieces of precious metal the German had ever seen.

"Sind dies Ihre," said Haym in the Hessian's native language. The guard could barely hold his excitement—

"Wenn sie mich frei," Haym coolly concluded.

The Hessian solider didn't hesitate; nothing was going to keep him from the fortune awaiting! He unlocked the cell and in a rush, led Haym up to the enormous attic of the building. Here linens, other beddings, and a host of sundries, which should have been freely distributed to the prisoners, were kept. However, before Haym's possible savior lifted another finger— though it may have been already too late— he employed the time-tested method of biting into the coin to confirm its genuine factor. At the sight of his own indentation, he was impressed, overjoyed, and ready to do anything he could do to commandeer the fate of his benefactor. He quickly went about successively tying the clean unused linens until the length was five stores long. The Provost, unlike the Sugarhouse did not require such an impregnable barrier to surround it. As a matter of fact, the fence around the perimeter was no higher than five feet of spiked timber posts. The Hessian hung the sheet out of one of the west facing windows. It was the only inactive side of the building while Cunningham's sentries were committed to the order of activity on the north side, which prepared for the impending use of the gallows. Haym rappelled down the knotted woven threads until he came close enough to the earth— dropped and landed on his feet! Protected by the age-old cover of darkness, once on the ground, his feet never stopped. Bruised and battered, he struggled to scale the palisade. Remise, he would, in the name of Rachel and their son— and to weigh the yoke of all his burdens, none became lighter than this! He summoned the strength, the mechanism, and the will of His God — and by such courage and call, hoisted himself just high enough, that to tumble was to do so into freedom. Barefoot and free, forsooth he ran through the darkest part of the darkness of the low whining quiet of the empty streets for dearest of desires: the life and love of others.

***

XXVI

PHILADELPHIA, 1778

"If ye love wealth better than liberty, the tranquility of servitude better than the animating contest of freedom, go home from us in peace. We ask not your counsels or arms. Crouch down and lick the hands, which feed you. May your chains set lightly you, and may posterity forget that ye were our countrymen."

Samuel Adams

Voltaire died in Paris. He did so adoring God, loving his friends, relinquishing hate for his enemies, detesting superstition, and on his death bed refusing to renounce Satan— shrewdly, he fashioned it was no time to make new enemies. The metal molybdenum was discovered. The human body contains about 0.07 mg of it per kilogram of weight. It can be found in the liver, the kidneys, the spine, and even the teeth. In high dudgeon, England declared war on France. William Pitt, the last man to lead England in victory over its archenemy, the 1st Earl of Chatham died— in the Kentonian dust, a giant was lost. Also, it began as the coldest year on record and it ended with the finest weather in memory.

Benedict Arnold was in Philadelphia, the de facto center of the world. Washington had made him the commander of the city after the victory at the Battle of White Marsh. The decisive defensive stand would soon mark Howe's exit from the theater of war and the English designs on America's most important stronghold. However high his military rise in the American cause, Arnold's mind was on what he saw as a country headed for ruin. His perspective across the landscape was dire— from the internal fighting in Congress, to the plummeting value of the newly printed currency, and what he saw as the disaffection of the army. But what coerces a man's mind and outlook even greater than the glory of God, but the beauty of woman? Arnold was in love, his heart weaving valentines and his mind fabricating an eternal future on an exquisite eighteen year old from a deeply Loyalist family— Margaret Shippen. To have her, was but to have to side with her. From the Royal Academy in London, the mass of the earth was found to be 6 sextillion, 587 quintillion short tons. Since the Earth is a sphere, the formula $4/3\pi r^3$ was used to find the volume. The volume of the Earth was then considered to be a mere 2.5988×10^{11} miles^3. Subsequently, the density was ascertained by dividing the mass by the volume— $\rho = m/V$. And so it was that Charles Hutton the English mathematician received the Copley medal for his work and calculation of the earth's mass and destiny. This figure included the self-bloated appreciation the French had for themselves.

By the steady stewardship of the upper crust Parisian adoption of Benjamin Franklin, in the quill and ink of written treaty, Louis XVI recognized the United States as a full-fledged backward nation with high ideals. The King's reward was war with England. Oliver Pollock was an Irish born New Orleans businessman— smart, savvy, and creative. He was a man that stood by his convictions down to the sterling pound. However, with the advent of the founding of a new nation and currency, he had a brainchild, the "$," the dollar symbol. For the nation's finances weighed heavy on his mind and Pollock used his own modest fortune to help finance the cause. Appointed by Congress to be the commercial agent of the United States at New Orleans, he was the sole representative of the Union in the Spanish city. He went so far in his belief in the American ideal of independence and liberty that he personally borrowed $70,000 from the Spanish Louisiana Governor Bernardo de Gálvez to finance the American operations in the west.

The single women of Bethlehem, Pennsylvania were of the Protestant Moravian order. They were also figuratively in love. Together, they spent day after day stitching a lustrous crimson silk into a banner for a man they found as strikingly handsome as Jesus Christ: Casimir Pulaski. The designs were beautifully wrought by the needle of their own hands. One side the capitals "U.S." were encircled by the motto "Unitas Virtus fortior"; and on the other side it was embroidered with an all-seeing eye of God in the midsts of the thirteen states of the Union surrounded by the words: "Non alius regit." With permission from Washington to lead his own legion, Casimir was 150 miles away from the needlework, camped in Baltimore organizing his corp of calvary. For the general's part, he was in Philadelphia. The good news was that the French fleet had arrived and they stood stronger than the British at harbor. Also his army had reached its maximum size of 17,000 troops present and fit for duty. However, the usual lack of food and supplies and the troubling breakdowns in discipline and morale demanded Washington's close attention, as did the logistical and political difficulties of planning proper troop dispositions for the coming winter— the fourth straight winter that Washington would not see home or victory on the horizon.

America was a just cause, as even the English Whigs acknowledged. It was the first of its kind, which spoke to the equality of "Men" in meaning "Mankind." Therefore, it is not surprising that a woman appeared from the battlefield smoke of cannon fire to be a hero among the Americans. Mary Hays, better known as "Sergeant Molly" or "Molly Pitcher" was the hero in the Battle of Monmouth. Major General Charles Lee recklessly attacked Clinton and Cornwallis on an extremely hot and humid summer day. Mary bravely followed her husband into the pitched engagement. She spent the morning carrying water but when her husband collapsed from heat exhaustion, Mary took his place at the cannon. For the rest of the day, regardless of heat, incoming, and the fact that she had no military business on the field of battle, Mary continued to "swab and load" the cannon using her husband's rammer! At one point, a British musket ball flew between her legs and tore off the bottom of her skirt! No matter to her, "Well, that could have been worse," she quipped, and went right back to loading the cannon. Mary's cannon protected Washington's rear and by morning the protracted conflict was too much for the British morale and Clinton called for a retreat. After the battle, Washington asked about the woman whom he had seen loading a cannon on the battlefield and in commemoration of her courage, he issued Mary a warrant as a non commissioned officer. Afterwards, she was known as "Sergeant Molly," a nickname that she used for the rest of her life.

In the Highlands on the Hudson, no such valor was on display. Alexander McDougall was as overwrought, drunken, surly, and cantankerous as ever. As a commanding officer stationed in New York he saw his share of battles— but of all it, he was on the losing end. Kicking up dirt, swigging down rum, swearing and fightin' with his own company of men, McDougall had for a time been succumbing to the emotional and intellectual calcification of the better half of his sense of self— a common fate when lubricated in alcohol. Defeat did nothing to humble him but rot away all of his charm. Nonetheless, he fought on in ever-raising insubordinate battle cries though he was relegated to assisting Kościuszko in fortifying a position. Deflating as his talent was from his guise, he made the most of it inflating the morale of others who still gleamed the likeness of mythical and heroic leader to the greater cause of their irreproachable and almost angelic notion of the liberty that was to come from the millstone of their sacrifice.

Fortification of Dorchester Heights, Battle of Long Island, Landing at Kip's Bay, Battle of Harlem Heights, Battle of Fort Washington, Battle of

Brandywine, Battle of the Clouds, Battle of Germantown, and the Battle of White Marsh— Howe 5 - Washington 4. However, Washington was the last man standing. The year before, Howe sent his letter of resignation to London, complaining that he had been inadequately supported in that year's campaigns. He was finally notified in April that his resignation was accepted. He sailed for England and General Clinton took over as the commander-in-chief of the British armies in America— by which time Washington was already giving chase. Washington nil; Clinton nil. Far from the American Revolution, Meyer Rothschild was still in Frankfurt am Main and further still practicing the comprehensive business tactics, which characterized his persona. The year saw the courts remedy a complaint by Danish, Dutch, Swedish, French, and Portuguese merchants in which he was cited for organizing an enterprising combination of Jewish businessmen to undermine competitive bidding for the purchase of damaged cloths publicly sold by the East India Company. Mayer's misadventures for the year weren't without joys, as he and Gutlé brought into the world their fifth child. Likewise, in the Delaware Valley of Pennsylvania, Rembrandt Peale was born. By the age of eighteen he was without question the first great American artist. His legacy would be cast in his iconic portraits of Washington and Jefferson.

In the picturesque mountains of the Papal confines of San Marino, Jan Kuźma was enjoying exile as well as others do vacation. Stipend with a yearly allowance by the borrowed time of the to-be last King of Poland, he luxuriated on his own little farm in wine, women, and the course of the stroke of his great luck not to be in the company of angels. All that the little man could not have was his "home." A supposed small price to pay for raptured oblivion.

John Adams was far from home himself. He was duly in Paris, like all men of truer sophistication and shallow virtues. Though he was the exception of both and was happily diverting his chagrin with an excursion to Amsterdam. An American ambassador, the former lawyer was sent to the French capital to shore up the Union's alliance and explore further possibilities to raise funds for the war effort. Finding both the French and his colleague Franklin to be gracious but insufferably conceited, he took the opportunity to broaden his travels across the continent. It was in Amsterdam, which he struck up a significant and lifelong friendship with a man who was infamous in creating wealth: Leendert Pieter de Neufville. Oh, the ever-so humorous universal agent of God's Will and its bending, twisting tendrils of fate— in conversation between de Neufville and

Adams, the Dutchman spoke fondly of a former associate name Hayim Shelomo. Adams had never heard of the man. De Neufville wondered where the seas of time might have tossed him. "If he was here," de Neufville slyly said, "He'd devise a cleaver practice in which you and your country would be gayly outfitted… and personal advantage, too, might be for the make." De Neufville's eyebrows betrayed his inescapable scheming nature for profit. Little did either de Neufville or Adams know.

Rachel Salomon was in British occupied New York, nursing her fatherless child. Under the roof of her aunt Rich, one of her father's older sisters. They heard the incredible rumor that her husband had unimaginably escaped the gallows. Heaven so she hoped, but where he was, no one knew. By that time, Seixas had moved to Philadelphia and rekindled the congregation under a new name: Holy Community of the Hope of Israel. Astride his own metaphorical horse, he was clamoring for his friend Moses to join him, if only he could safely find his way out of British controlled New York.

If Philadelphia was the center of the world, then Boston was the old forgotten flame. The city was securely in American hands. Robert Newman was there, no longer a sexton but a solider. His friend, Paul Revere whose contributions brought about the start of the American divorce from her mother country was too, in Boston. However, he was in the comforts of his own home. Along with many other invigorated New Englanders, he conversely joined the Massachusetts Regiment and rose to the respectful rank of Lieutenant Colonel, even fighting alongside his beloved son. The life of a Continental solider in the field was confounded with hardship and with Boston secured and fighting in Rhode Island at a standstill, Revere quietly retired; his service left for the golden glow of the ages. King Charles III of Spain and Queen Maria I of Portugal signed the Treaty of El Pardo. It marked the year as a peaceful one between the squabbling Catholics nation. The treaty resolved a long-standing territorial dispute arising from non-observance of the terms of the Treaty of Tordesillas and subsequent treaties to rectify the matter. Finally, there was an equal footing and sense of relief that strife at the southern tip of Portuguese advance into region of the Misiones Orientales on South American soil was resolved and the Spanish–Portuguese War was itself too, closed to the golden glow of the ages.

To the east, the year recorded Stanisław August Poniatowski in St. Petersburg being awarded with a membership in the Academy of Sciences. There was no Academy of Politics, had there been, he would have been greatly rewarded on the recognition of consistent political futility. That while his political cover in the form of Catherine acted as a mediator in the War of Bavarian Succession between the pugnacious German states of Prussia and Austria. Incidentally, Johann Ernst Gotzkowsky, the art dealer, friend of Frederick the Great and Leendert de Neufville, and brain-child of the Seven Year's War, was already dead by the common year, and had been so laying in a Berlin cemetery for three. However, his family was still suffering through the bankruptcy he had left them with— fitting as a microcosm of what his little war had wrought the world with. Every nation that had participated was bankrupt, including England, which sought to raise revenue on the backs of their colonial possession, America. Gotzkowsky's puny little scheme for a covetousness of wealth directly resulted in the major European powers at war again and a group of far and away political rebels citing that men are endowed by their Creator with certain unalienable rights. 365 days 5 hours 49 minutes 12 seconds, in the Gregorian calendar year of our Lord; sequentially labeled the year of 1778.

***

Haym sidestepped the devil and on the wings of careful navigation in the recontextualized chreia which nicely summoned up his life. In an account of the least expensive but most precious tasteless, colorless, odorless, shapeless, indistinct, commodity of them all, it was two weeks before Haym reached safety in Philadelphia. However, he didn't make the trip alone.

Almost too battered, beaten, and broken to make a further escape from the Provost, Haym's initial flight took him as far as his home, where he collapsed from exhaustion and a body unfit to promote an accelerated advance of his muscles. The house itself was ransacked and bare, but not abandoned all together. Rachel was at her aunt's but Anna and Joe, though now for all intensive purposes free, had nowhere to go and remained in the home. Upon the sight of Haym, it was as if they were seeing a shade of the fantastic. Surely, he was dead but obviously he wasn't. They took care of their subscriber with the mercy of human compassion beyond the tether of their inhuman station. Unfortunately, there could be no rest for the enervated consumption of desperation.

As Anna did all she could— soaking Haym's superficial wounds with hot water— Joe bent to his knee and asked the man where he thought the British would first come to look for their fugitive. Haym replied in kind that he expected them to arrive at the door in any given moment. As it had been once before— those in the home were laid to risk by Haym's exploits. Apoplectic, Anna feared for her life. Joe ordered her to go— to run— anywhere, but to escape the house before Cunningham and the British surely arrived! Then, in a remarkable act of courage and heroism, the slave re-enslaved himself and took on the responsibility to carry his master into the starry night as far away as he could. For the next week, Joe and Haym hid by day; and by night they carried themselves as far southwest as Haym's body would take them. Once safely in New Jersey, their pace quickened.

It would be again, as it was before: Gershom Mendes Seixas found Haym in the teetering buoyant balance of half-dead and half-alive; praying at the bimah in the only synagogue in Philadelphia. Neither could believe their luck or the mystifying wisdom of their God.

Upon the sight of one another, they spoke no words of the tongue, but embraced one another in a communion of brotherly commitment. The order and range of their love was unequal to nature's common allegories. Of all the propulsions, movements, crossing traverses, from the constellations, to the particles of dust on the wind, the density, mass, and covering of space across the planet, the paths of the hunters and the hunted, tosses and turns in the sleep of night, visions of love glanced, items bought, things remembered, and yet circumventing the wielding scythe of death, they were unexpectedly together again on God's scheduled timetable. The odds in Heaven must be absolute.

Before they left the shul, Haym asked Seixas to read, to comfort him in the crystalline prose and remembrance of their Creator. He mourned that of all things less the flesh of his love, he had not in his possession his prayer book— only in dithering memory. He wanted to hear the text, the words, the mighty holiness of the erudition of אל.

***

As 1778 hurried to it's measured and predetermined conclusion, Haym and Seixas were busily assembling a network of trusted companions and safe houses, which could deliver Moses, Rachel, and Ezekiel to them in Philadelphia. Seixas introduced Haym to General Washington at his wintering headquarters in Pawling, New York. Seixas insisted that they make the grueling trip in a horseshoe shaped route through Pennsylvania as to safely avoid the British. At the Kane House, they arranged through

Washington and his coterie of intelligence to get Moses and Rachel to Philadelphia by the beginning of the New Year. Washington extended an invitation to Seixas and Haym to remain, rest, and recuperate before the grueling return. They did so for three days in which the men rhapsodized much about the war, their future lives in the event they won and they're ignominious death in the likelihood of their defeat. Further, unarticulated as it was, much desperation had set in and Washington waxed poetically of sending Lafayette back to France to secure financial backing before the Continental Army's last meal was eaten, last stitch of thread unsewn, the last cannon fired, and the last musket ball expended. But of all they uttered, expressed, and conveyed, it was prayer in which their lips grew almost chapped of issuing.

In a last passing gathering, which would augur things to come, Washington introduced Haym to General Rochambeau and the French contingency that had recently joined him. Two armies acting in concert, but not as one. Rochambeau impressed upon Haym the French hopelessness for funds or their further participation could not be guaranteed. In a spirited exchange on the mechanisms of finance, Rochambeau asked Haym when he returned to Philadelphia to pay a visit to Chevalier de la Luzerne, the French minister.

***

Haym, his wife, and his son were reunited to begin 1779. The first night in which the separated husband and wife found themselves in one another's arms, their child was placed between them and the constituent ingredients of love in measure to their physical presence beheld them to a higher state of union than just the somatic admiration of one another. They were a family now and forever in debt to "miracle." Rachel spoke as though no time had ever passed. Her eyes lit, coruscating the minute distance of space between them, which was easily crossed in their warm, breathes upon one another's face. She asked him if he still fondly recalled the day before when they were married— how he subscribed to love her before her father, uncle, and cousins— oh and the beautiful canopy of white and red silk— her long train and how she came downstairs biting her lip to chase away the nervous laughter tickling the rear of her mouth— the wine from which they sipped— the ring which adorned her finger— how she threw the glass upon the pewter plate— and in a hush of emotion:

"We were married," she said. "Do you remember?" Before Haym was even able to bring an answer to his lips— lips that extended across his face and were welded to the emotions in his heart— she asked him if he remembered the morning of the next day, the dawn of the night in which they were presently engrossed, the day in which their son was born—

"Do you remember, this morning… when he was born?"
She breathlessly bloviated in recollection and questioning of his emotional memory— do you remember-do you remember-do you remember— oh, the first moment she held her child— aw, the first gaze in which he beheld his pride? Finally, she started to cry and could not stop crying. Of all else that was spoken that night she apprehensively dared to ask him "How?" How was it that he could still be alive? The world he explained was a classroom, one in which the students are prisoners to lectures of truth and lessons of consequences. And to be deeply loved hallucinates the mind with strength, but that too deeply love fills the character with enduring courage.

Rachel would soon be pregnant, again. Haym took up shop at a single table in the London Coffee House, selling bills of exchange, operating a private pseudo-stock market and, before long he was one of the most well respected men in the community. He did pay that visit to de la Luzerne and took a position as a broker for the French government.

In a year's time Haym would accumulate more money and property than he had ever lost to confiscation by Cunningham in New York. Besides a new house and a new child, he retained Joe's property of flesh, and everything that was— for the most part was again in spades. Everything in Haym's life was steadily improving, except for his health, which in opposition to the entire ascendency, was incrementally descending in condition.

***

As Haym and Rachel stared into one another's eyes and Ezekiel slept cradled between them in their collective arms, Rachel had one other thing for her husband. She rose from the sofa and reached underneath the baby's carriage. In her hand was his siddur. Even more ragged, torn, and worn from tribulation, but of all the things Cunningham took from them, it was this, which she had found the artfulness to save. Haym's heart melted; never in history was a man so besotted and in love with a woman, who was so deserving of the uncompromising devotion and idolization.

The Salomon family was reunited but the Franks family was permanently divided. Moses did not accompany Rachel. As Haym and Seixas learned, their friend surrendered his spirit to the Loyalist cause. He left for London and joined the firm of securities firm of Colebrooke and Nesbitt. Moses became a sore of disappointment for them. A vast majority of Jews supported the revolution but Moses' opportunities for self-advancement and greater social status won his heart. With his knowledge of the North American networks and his brother released from prison, he worked as the first leg of providing the British army in war with provisions, arms, and political parliamentary encouragement. With one of his conspiring letters of business interests to Moses intercepted by the Americans, David would find himself on trial by the "radicals" and face guilt by association. Rachel Salomon, with her brother fighting bravely beside Washington, no longer had her family of youth. At sixteen, she was all alone, but for Haym.

***

"I sent for Haym Salomon."   *Robert Morris*

"...I need— let me rephrase that— if this country is to be a legitimate nation, a proud upright example of what men can do without being collared by the diamond-studded dog leash of imperial power, I say, it needs— it requires— it demands— a man like you, Mr. Salomon," Robert Morris said rather frankly to the man sitting across from him as he stood. "Now, let me spare as many words as I may— I also wish to assure your sensibilities that the rumors— you may have heard— in particular from the likes of the foulmouth— Paine and others, he less a foulmouth, but ignorant nonetheless— are founded on a misrepresentation of my character and sheer ignorance of the complicated vestiges of finance— which of course you are intimately familiar with."
Morris took an extraordinarily long pause in which he expected Haym to respond positively to his assertion— something akin to a gentlemanly acknowledgement; but no such response was forthcoming. Finally—
"Let me also comport myself to report that I was given allowances by the Congress of my right to continue business as it pleased and provide for the culture and welfare of mine and my family's essential well being." Still, Haym simply remained silent, softly staring back; he blinked his eyes but lent no further indication of his perspective or acceptance of Morris' protestation. Needless to say, this didn't sit well with the country's Superintendent of Finance.
"I say, you have— have you heard the rumors?" Morris interrupted himself and asked as if antagonized into doing so.
"Of which rumors do you speak?" Haym inquired.
"Surely you do not mean to toy? I have made very little money in my transactions on behalf of this nation! Balanced between what I myself have contributed in purchases of notes and even personal loans, my personal financial acumen, I assure you, has been less than stellar! Regardless of what that skin-trader Laurens or that windbag Paine

cackles— I do not inflate my fees— and what if I did— though I don't! They discount the hours of toil in which I labor for this cause in which they so triumphantly exclaimed as a matter and duty of righteousness! But we see when all the variables, figures, and costs are calculated, even their shrill cries of liberty are drowned out by the selfish accounting of jealous little men."

Morris' breathing became labored and he found himself again waiting in expectation for Haym to respond. He drank deeply from a glass of water, peeking to the side.

Haym coolly calculated his allowance— to permit Morris to dangle by his own psychologically tangled rope. It wasn't that Haym did not believe the good man or thought him corrupt; it was merely that they were fierce but friendly competitors. Finally—

"It appears it might comfort you greatly if I speak—" Haym put forward.

"Why, it would matter not to me," Morris responded, in his own inimitable urbanely self-possessed style.

"So be it, then I shall remain speechless."

The reply turned Morris' face a nice rosy shade of vexation. The men surely knew one another and one another's friends. Haym was well respected, well liked, and since in Philadelphia, had acted as personal benefactor to many in Congress in need of personal financial support. However, as Morris was the official banker of the nation and Haym the foreign upstart who quickly rose to be the most prominent broker in Philadelphia, there was a natural rivalry. Not to mention, their residences on Front Street made them neighbors. A day didn't go by in which they did not casually cross one another's paths on the street or in the coffee house. Not to mention, they would occasionally buy, invest, or underwrite, a little here and there through one another. As for the portent of time, which stood between them, Haym's purposeful stoicism outwitted Morris' attempt to hold a commanding position of authority, and he broke—

"Please, speak!" Morris decried!

Haym, with his body twisted out of shape— crookedly rose from his seat in the only officially delegated office the new government had outside of the State House of the Province of Pennsylvania. The young "old" man hobbled in a slow histrionic circle— a scene such as the wily cat cornering the overly anxious mouse. Patiently outmaneuvered, Morris silently conceded and steadily brought himself to sink into the cushion of the seat behind his desk; conclusively the two jockeying men had switched their predominant positions. In the almost three years since Haym narrowly retained his life from Cunningham's charge, his body had settled into a malformed, misshapen, aslant erection, like an old tree trunk. His infirmity included an ivory Piqué Cane and he circled in a manner between a limped stride and a lurching shuffle; his thin frame ever so slightly yet permanently positioned to be stooped when standing— and yet he was only forty-one years old. His joints, his muscles, and mechanics equaled a sum total of malnutrition and torturous punishment at the malice disposition of Cunningham. However, wrecked and ruined Haym's body was, his eyes glowed a certain glory and he had grown into a manner of spoken speech which came from his larynx with a profundity that sounded of an unflappable majesty.

"Do you know what I have found the difference to be between the European gentry and the comparable rank and file of Americans?" Haym asked Morris.

"No, I do not," Morris reluctantly responded.

"Well, I shall tell you," Haym said. "It is that the European acts and then he thinks, the American, by contrast, thinks and then he acts. But why is that? At first, I could not understand it nor understand how to understand it. Then I came to realize it was I who was unable to realize. The difference between the two breeds is a matter of virtue. But what creates this virtue? It seems illogical that Europeans wouldn't have virtue, they are not dogs. But do you know, why?"

"No, I cannot say I do," said Morris.

"I know why... and in it lies the reason why I believe the United States of America will defy the gravity of history and shine as brightly as man has ever collectively shined. You see Mr. Morris, I come from the past."

"Is that so?" Morris uttered in the forbore following of Haym's logic.

"I appear to stand before you in the present, but that is not where we stand. We, you and I, and the grave souls resisting the will of the king, stand firmly in the future. The United States, as it is, is but only five years old— it has no past. It is a slate as virgin and clean as the holiest of the holy. Has fortune ever rained so sweetly upon a land that it is not cursed with entrenched aristocrats that have organized a system to justify their lording status in perpetuity? To breathe the air of America— there is no memory upon the imprint of our national body and mind— the air is a purity of freshness that is unrivaled in the relationship of man to governess. There are no cultural grievances— there is no heartbreak from our youthful enthusiasm! I come born in heartbreak, not only as a Jew, but as a Pole! Do you understand the coarse meaning of my words? I ask you again, 'do you understand?'"

"I hearken to your words of wisdom," said Morris.

"Then hear me well. In the bark and fibers of the consciousness of each and every man in this land, there are no closed doors, which ache in his heart from the memory of failure! Men who have been denied in endeavors, claims, and aspiration characteristically wallow in rejection and focus their aim beyond justice— these are the sorts of men who create revolution to acquire what has been withheld from them. These are the wolf packs that satisfy themselves in eating hungrily, indulging in their appetite and victory, and then beholding apart from others what was held apart from them. I assure you, the life of freedom is nearer the life of restraint than the life of indulgence. This country, by contrast, is a dole of holy doves! It is no more right for England to cage us as it is a mother to bind her child's feet because it has learned to run beyond her apron."

"Yes, I see," Morris, said.

"You do?," Haym cross-examined him. "And what do you see?"

Morris had a most commanding and powerful position in public affairs, and had so for much of his life. He did not suffer fools well and was adapt at deflecting and countering the slings and arrows of suspicion and animosity. Thus, he was neither intimidated nor ruffled by Haym's exalted soliloquy. Further, he understood Haym on Haym's own terms.

"You speak of the true nature of things," Morris said rather matter-of-factly.

"Then our minds are one," Haym contentedly said.
A calm settled between them. Haym turned to retake his seat, but in the process looked back to Morris—

"Excuse my logic, but it comes born of experience. Excuse my words, but they come poetically from the heart," Haym said. "I believe in this country. For free of a past, the mind's eye can only perceive of a vision of an expected future. All other attempts at overthrowing the dynamic of lord and peasant have been rendered moot, because the past cannot be unwound by forward progress. I joined the Sons because of this virtue. I gave of my own financial affairs, note and coin, to any who have asked— for this reason. I believe in the inherent goodness and virtue in this country. However, I know what ultimately wins wars. The art of war is so well and so equally understood by the great European nations, that it is now generally considered as a contest of finances— therefore, the nation which can most adeptly incur specie to carry on the war, can generally hold out the longest."

***

Starting in 1779, Haym Salomon went into a manic overdrive! He had an elegant home and office on Front Street above Walnut, but he preferred the social beehive of the London Coffee House to conduct his frenetic style of business. If you were to pack the franticness of the London Stock Exchange, the bovine rut of every prairie, valley, and mountain top, the clogged hyperactive spawning of a salmon run, the light, heat, speed, and brilliance of a shooting star, and the perpetual motion of all the wheels in the world into a overstuffed powder keg and ignited it with fireworks, you would still lack the energy and fever by which Haym Salomon operated his financial métier.

He moved about, selling, trading, brokering, discounting, negotiating, and re-negotiating with the transporting conveyance of an octopus juggling circular saws. Always faithfully within reach, multiplying his tentacles like the appendages of a millipede was his chief clerk, a Scottish immigrant named Macrae. It was said he could take a pile of hard money— say seven English shillings and a guinea, a French Louis d'or, three Dutch guilders, two Portuguese half-joes, and five Spanish Milled dollars— and at a glance tell you how much it was all worth in Pennsylvania currency. His devotion to Haym was unwavering. They were psychic companions with the bridge between them being their ardent attachment to the means, measures, and machinations of the world of finance. Though employee and employer, their trust ran deep into the soft fleshy stratum of friendship.

Haym Salomon was in many respects a new man with a new god-sponsored lease on life! This ingest feeling was centered in the concept of "home." Though, he was not a sentimental creature by nature, he was anguished with a hole in his heart. Ever since he had agonizingly left his mother and father, he had traveled the world and but made residence after residence. There is probably a romantic notion to that, but for Haym, it was more the life of a lone wolf making his way in the world. He was struck with the psychological tribulation of "Incompletion." His mind had many a purpose, his body several houses, mansions, and abodes, but his heart never had a home. Now, to his soul's comfort, he had a deep abiding home. As incredible as it seemed to him at times, he was magnificently married, with a wife in a sanctum palace of permanence.

The most dramatic outcropping of their union was a multiplying family in bundles of love. His wealth afforded him the means to outfit Rachel as their ketubah avowed. Their home was large with furnishings to her particular desires. A block from the docks, Haym was close to the action of the shipping commerce, which delighted him and his penchant for non-stop business interests. The London Coffee House was host to the city's first merchant exchange before Haym had arrived. However, his arrival transformed it into a potent mixture of irresistible stock market, bank, clearinghouse, currency exchange, and social club! Life was beautiful and Haym Salomon was living it like a kid in a candy store.

The infectious nature of the upturn in Haym's fortunes postured a psychological shift in his personal approach to life. Imagine, if you will, that he smelled the roses and then plucked them for everyone else's pleasure. There wasn't anyone in Philadelphia society that didn't know him. He was humble, but confident; serious but comical; wealthy but altruistic; vigorous but sick. His cough gradually worsened and his body increasingly deteriorated. Nevertheless, he found a thewy gratitude and grace that had eluded him in his past quest for achievement and return to absolution. The guilt and shame over the death of his family lessened by the evil raised upon him by the Russians, the British, Walley, and Cunningham. He was convinced the devil lived, and that his dark spirit transacted through men who thought in tones of puissance. He did not judge these men, but pitied them. For he believed in exchange for the immortal power of the devil, they compromised the pleasure of peace of mind. And it was peace of mind he beheld in thought of his parents and the journey, which brought him to the present. His self-blame was dissolved into a wash of trust— that from Heaven they did not curse him.

Haym Salomon awoke every morning glad to be alive. His religiosity and fervor also grew and his adherence to Jewish law rose to an almost unbearable point for Rachel's liking but not her understanding. She was accepting of his clear-mindedness which left little room for compromise in the strictly conservative house. Haym was replete with friends, beneficiaries, and business. For the first time in his adult existence, he simply loved life. And the money— oh, the money was real good.

In the business of impersonal exchange, Haym Salomon's primary agent for the advocacy of his craft was the highly negotiable instrument known as the "Short Bob" or in more official parlances: a "Bill of Exchange." Let it be suggested that the breathtaking ascendancy of Western hegemony soared on the magic carpet that was the bill of exchange. A "draft" or bill of exchange is an unconditional order in writing addressed by one person to another; signed by the person giving it, requiring the person to whom it is addressed to follow two simple precepts: 1) Pay on demand or at a fixed determinable future time. 2) Pay a certain sum in money to, or to the order of, a specified person or to the bearer.

In Medieval Europe, bills of exchange were common and much appreciated debt instruments issued in one locale and remitted in another, usually in a different type of currency payable at the market exchange rate quoted in the locale of issue with a stated maturity corresponding to a duration up to six months. It was in mid-twelfth century Genoa that the earliest forms of bills of exchange came into being. However, the bills did not come into widespread use until the following century, when merchants, at the annual trading festivals known as Champagne Fairs, employed them. Bills of exchange became ubiquitous in subsequent centuries, primarily in Italy, evolving into indispensable financial instruments which enabled lenders to make profits via differences in exchange rates— they marked a veritable financial revolution.

The drafts carried many advantages, which were valuable for extending credit regardless of usury theory. For one, they were self-liquidating after usage. Secondly, they were easily renewable through recharge, and the rates of interest were largely predictable within certain parameters. Unwittingly, the western world was freeing itself from the bondage of hard currency and creating a new universal language of finance. The characteristics of the instrument encouraged their use by Italian bankers both as a safe means of short-term lending and as an alternative to discounted debt instruments, which were forbidden by the Church. Despite their usurious nature, merchant courts duly enforced bills of exchange, and the deliverer could sue the taker if the latter's correspondent, the payer, refused the bill. Furthermore, the legal standing of bills of exchange was concretely established by their being written in the hand of the taker, whose handwriting was known to his correspondents. They were almost as good as gold.

The "Bill of Exchange" worked as follows. A lender, known as deliverer, normally a banker, bought a bill for ready cash from a borrower, known as a taker, who drew on one of his correspondents, the payer, abroad. At maturity, the payer paid an amount in a foreign currency to the lender's corespondent, the payee. Lenders made profits on bills by having the payee reverse the process, the recharge, and buy a new bill, payable in the lender's homeland, from another borrower. Because the second transaction took place in a distant land, the second bill was purchased at a different exchange rate than the first one. The rate differential permitted lenders a chance to profit on exchange transactions. However, profit was not assured. Yet, even as wild fluctuations in the exchange rates— which were subject to the local supply and demand of specie and credit, the borrowing habits of the political authority, and so forth— could entail a loss for the lender, most bills provided positive profit. The bills of exchange performed three primary functions which were revolutionary: 1) currency exchange; 2) short-term credit-extension and; 3) trade facilitation. They originally emerged in order to support the latter, enabling merchants to avoid the costs of hiring and providing armed guards to thwart the inherent risks of robbery associated with moving specie— just as Rothschild had done when he hired armed men to accompany Haym from Frankfurt to Warsaw. Such costs were far from trivial— for example, the charge for moving bullion from Naples to Rome, a mere hundred miles, ranged between eight to twelve percent of the value being moved. The further the range, such as Frankfurt to Warsaw— 700 miles— the greater the base charge.

Simply put, a bill of exchange is a three-party negotiable instrument in which the first party, the drawer, presents an order for the payment of a sum certain on a second party, the drawee, for payment to a third party, the payee, on demand or at a fixed future date. It is distinguishable from a promissory note, since it does not contain a promise and the drawer does not expressly pledge to pay it. Nonetheless, it is functionally similar to a note. The instrument can be broken down into two distinct geographically defined types: inland and foreign. An inland bill is a bill, which is both drawn and payable within the country. A foreign bill is one, which is drawn in one country but accepted and payable in another country.

Heretofore, there are three parties to a bill of exchange:
1. Drawer (the person who is going to draw the bill; he gives the order to pay money to the third party).
2. Drawee (the person upon whom the bill is made or drawn; he is the person to whom the bill is addressed and who is ordered to pay. He becomes an acceptor when he indicates his willingness to pay the bill).
3. Payee (the person who is going to receive the money; in some cases the drawer and payee can be the same person).

The term "Bill of Exchange" is inserted in the body of the instrument and expressed in the language employed in drawing up the instrument:
1. An unconditional order to pay a determinate sum of money.
2. The name of the person who is to pay.
3. A statement of the time of payment.
4. A statement of the place where payment is to be made.
5. The name of the person to whom or to whose order payment is to be made.
6. A statement of the date and of the place where the bill is issued.
7. The signature of the person who issues the bill.

The parties involved need not all be distinct persons. Thus, the drawer may draw on himself payable to his own order. A draft may be endorsed by the payee in favor of a third party, who may in turn endorse it to a fourth party, and so on indefinitely. The "holder in due course" may claim the amount of the bill against the drawee and all previous endorsers, regardless of any counterclaims that may have disabled the previous payee or endorser from doing so. This is what saying that a bill is negotiable means. In some cases a bill of exchange is marked "not negotiable." In such cases, it can still be transferred to a third party, but the third party can have no greater right than the transferor. Another extremely important source of finance in the instrument is the ability to negotiate or discount the bill. The draft in essence provides an easier access to financing because it enables the drawer to retain a claim on all parties to the bill. Bill discounting may provide access to finance rates lower than the overdraft or loan rate the seller could normally obtain. The negotiation of a bill is the transfer of the rights under a bill from one party to another for value. However, the discounting of a draft can only occur once the bill has a definite maturity date in the future and the buyer has accepted it. Discounting differs from negotiation in that the drawer will calculate the net present value of the face value of the bill utilizing a cost of funds interest rate and a margin. The net amount so calculated is then fittingly advanced to the seller.

In late 1780, trade and commerce was not a simple task or endeavor. The marked effort and security by which to send money and goods across oceans was extraordinary. Most entrepreneurs lost their future fortunes and their nerve after a single transaction. From pirates to the gods of storm sinking vessels, the number of possible scenarios, which could doom a venture, was too numerous to count. The key to moving money and goods between far and away nations was having a network of trustworthy contacts in other countries. Haym undoubtedly had the contacts and technical skills to handle a wide range of financial transactions, both domestic and international. There was nobody in America that had Haym's network, skill, and range of talent.

***

From the time Haym settled his family in Philadelphia through the first half of 1781, his primary war-related responsibility was to engineer the sale of drafts for the French. As the French troops began to arrive, he handled the finances for the support and maintenance of their sea and land forces. The French entrusted him with 150,000,000 livres ($22,000,000,000 [£112,500 pounds]), on which he received a regular mercantile commission. The funds were earmarked for distribution for the provisions and costs of the French military during their stay in Philadelphia. Haym did one better, he reinvested a large portion of the specie besides providing the paymaster-general with all due necessity in due course of time. Haym wasn't the French Army's paymaster-general but you could say that he was the paymaster-general's paymaster. In total he sold in approximation of $600,000 in drafts to his clients, netting for himself roughly 2.5% per sale. The "one better" was upon each transaction, he gathered the profit and graciously bequeathed it upon his business rival, Robert Morris, for the Continental cause.

As comfortably settled and franchise oriented as Haym was, his life wasn't all business. During this period he laid down religious roots and joined the three hundred strong congregation of Mikveh Israel synagogue and served as a member of the governing council. He was also the treasurer of Philadelphia's society for indigent travelers, and participated in the nation's first known rabbinic court of arbitration. Furthermore, the events of the day brought him into the sordid theater of politics. Annoyed by the state's religious test oath which was required to hold public office— intentionally aimed at disenfranchising Jews— he became politically and socially as active as he had ever been since being a teenager in Leszno. Many assumed he was vying for eventual political office. However, it wasn't the trapping of power that Haym yearned for. His contentions were more virtuous. In his own subtle way, he was quietly demanding America to be absolved of the old European prejudices. As far as he was concerned, it was imperative that there weren't any limits or bars to the Jewish field of ambition, especially to positions of power. Paradoxically, his view of black Africans was not as liberal, charitable, and generous.

After their marriage, Haym had purchased a slave for Rachel. Presumably the young woman he acquired was to assist his wife in domestic chores— though more to the point— the Negro was, plain and simple: a status symbol. Soon after, to inflate his stature further, he purchased another slave. In the social mores of the time, this act of moral turpitude was as common as shivering in the cold. A great many Jewish merchants who dealt in international trade dedicated large portions of their business to the trade in African slaves. Heretofore, Jewish merchants played a minor but momentous role in the slave trade. In fact, in all the American colonies, whether Martinique, British, or Dutch, Jewish merchants frequently dominated, though they made up a very small percentage of the actual lot of traders.

The nexus of Jew's instrumental connection in the triangular trade began a century earlier in the Dutch holdings of South America. The Jews were the recipients of favorable charters containing generous economic privileges granted by the Dutch West Indies Company in Amsterdam. Free of lawful restrictions on property and trade, they came to dominate mercantile trade at most western points of the "triangle" from Curacao, Surinam, Recife, and New Amsterdam as well as Barbados, Jamaica, Newport, and Savannah.

By the eighteenth century, the most notable Jewish families from Isaac Da Costa of Charleston to Aaron Lopez of Newport to Nathan Simson in New York to Benjamin Davis in Petersburg to David Franks in

Philadelphia— families of the noble social standing, had their hands in the infamous exchange that brought slaves from Africa to the West Indies, and there exchanged for molasses, which in turn was taken to New England and converted into rum for sale in Africa. For someone as classically liberal as Haym, who raged with an internal fire for the light and liberty of mankind, it seems strange that he did not hold the same pretense toward a literally enslaved race.

Haym's benighted attitude toward and about Negroes was not in sharp contrast to the Jewish convictions of the day. Slavery was, of course, an attested aspect of the Jewish faith. Further, the practice was an archetype of man's relationship to man; in replete historical aspect across all the known cultures of the world, including the African tribes which sold members of other tribes to the slave traders that sought them for sale in North America and abroad. Many Jews, north and south, held the view that blacks were subhuman and were biologically suited to slavery, which was the predominant view held by many of their non-Jewish counterparts in America. Slavery wasn't an American phenomenon, especially to Jews like Haym. A century before Haym's birth, Jews and Christians throughout Poland were still being sold at slave markets by the Turkish Tartars. Yet, between the Christian class and the Jewish class in America, rich Jews— especially in the south— generally preferred employing white servants rather than owning slaves. This is partly because very few Jews owned plantations and their labor needs consisted of a more educated rank of people. Though, throughout the Americas, many Jews who could afford to do so, owed slaves. Again, their ownership was centered around mostly business or domestic settings, therefore a vast majority of the slaves were put to work in an urban context— such as simple clerks or as domestic servants. The bottom-line is that wealthy Jews were no different than their Christian neighbors whom they emulated with their participation in slave ownership. The best men, families, and reputations from all walks of Jewish society did not view slavery as an evil or disingenuous to their own liberal designs, and Haym Salomon was no different.

For all his enlightened broad-mindedness, Haym perceived blacks as inferior beings on a basis of social hierarchy; and his desire to endow himself with the trappings of status in the industrious sweat of owning a slave led him to not only own one but at times sell them as he might any other piece of imported merchandise. Haym wasn't a slave trader by trade nor did his measly participation in occasional auctions make a mathematical dent in the overall commodity — except of course for those in which he auctioned. Nevertheless, he always had his own slave, Joe, who by 1780 sought his opportunity and reclaimed his freedom.

A bounty was published in the Pennsylvania Packet Saturday November 18th, 1780. It read:

> Six Hundred Dollars Reward.
> "RAN AWAY from the subscriber, on the 7th inst.
> a Negroe Man named JOE, about 27 years of age,
> about 5 feet 6 inches, a thin stature and pale
> complexion; had on a brown fustian coat
> waistcoat and overalls of the same, and took
> sundry other clothes with him. It is supposed he
> will endeavor to pass as a free man, and make his
> way to New York. Whoever takes up said Negroe,
> and delivers him to the subscriber, living in Front-
> street, three doors above Arbuckle's row, or
> secures him in any gaol in the continent, shall
> have the above reward and all reasonable charges
> paid, by HAYM SALOMON"

In the relative comforts of Philadelphia, Joe's primary tasks were under the direction of Macrae. There was little hard labor involved in Haym's enterprises and Joe was taught to read, perform arithmetic, and master the currency charts. Occasionally, he was called to the service of Mrs. Salomon and duties pertaining to the upkeep of the home. His day-to-day relationship with Haym was little more than passing master and deferential servant — though Haym considered himself morally superior than a southern plantation owner and took pride in Joe's educated mind. Though the slave was educated, well kept, trusted, and virtually free to come and go, he was still encumbered with the disheartening identity and unnerving reality of being a slave. Ergo, in the hours of Tuesday, November 7th's darkness, Joe clandestinely slipped into the night a slave; and arose to the morning a fugitive.

$600. That was what the slaveowner was offering for his escaped commodity. Never one to overspend and always in pursuit of a bargain,

Haym was willing to pay no more than a pittance by the standard of the day, for the return of his two-legged property. Nonetheless, it was the same flesh body of property, which kept him alive and carried him to the safety and new god-given lease on life he was enjoying. The episode was a showcase for non-sentimental nature of Haym Salomon in the ugly colors of his personality. Though he was never bound in chains, Joe had been begging for years to be set free— feeling entitled in the light of being his master's own savior. Haym continually promised on the word, "soon," but purposefully never followed through. To some degree he was patriarchal and worried for Joe's well being. He was also arrogant in believing that Joe owed him loyalty on a debt of gratitude for Haym's years of gentle treatment, education, and excellent care. Yet, what of the fact that the slave sacrificed his own freedom to save Haym's life? Where did that factor in to the "master's" thinking? Well, in Haym's self-possessed, dispassionate, hard-boiled merchant mind, it was simply one fact of the whole equation of the circumstances and events of life. The dramatic salvation wasn't to be taken as an absolute. Sure, Haym was grateful, but as he saw things— there is always a way— and without Joe, there would have been another way that the Lord delivered him to his future.

Nonetheless, his call for reward made little headway, as the average going rate was at least four times as much and the minimum reward anyone expected was $800. Joe would never be seen or heard from again.

***

"…Let it be known to you, that Hamilton is going to endorse the charter," Morris said as he handed the application to Haym. "You're a man of money, what say you?"

Haym held the charter, which proposed a national bank and as a person who was fascinated with all instruments and institutions dealing with money, he started to study it with a keen eye. The first thing he noted was the incrediable sum of $400,000 in private subscriptions required. However, just as he did so, Thomas Willing entered.

In a certain light, he was the spitting image of George Washington, and of conduct and personality, they were cut from the same tough honorable cloth. By 1781, Willing and Morris had been partners for thirty-two years. In that time, Willing had also been a supreme court justice under the colonial government, the mayor of Philadelphia, and member of the Continental Congress— albeit he voted against the Declaration. Standing at the entrance with his eyes set upon Haym, Thomas Willing was at the height of his personal, social, and worldly power.

"Ah, Mr. Salomon," he said.

"Mayor," Haym honored him, though he had not been as such since 1764.

"Thomas, I was just telling Mr. Salomon about the charter— oh," Morris turned to Haym. "And you must agree on the name: 'The Company of the Bank of the United States!'" Morris proudly beamed.

"Yes, it flows like a salty ocean of water through an impenetrable dam!" Willing sarcastically remarked, evidently having had participated in numerous discussions about the name. "As a matter of fact, I think we should call it quite simply: 'The Bank of North America,' but I dare say that the name is the least of any of our sensible concerns.
Morris momentarily deflated a bit with Willing's gravity having replaced his levity. He turned his attention back to Haym and motioned to the document—

"The trust of the currency is of grave importance, and I see no adequate alternative but the charter," Morris exclaimed.

"Is this why you wanted to see me, about chartering a new bank?" Haym asked.

"Excuse me, sirs," Willing said. "But Robert, before you answer him. I came to inform you—"

"Yes?"

"That Charlestown has fallen."

There was utter silence. The Congress had gambled all available financial resources on the defense of the city.

"And furthermore, Major-General Lincoln has been taken captive."
The shock of the news held back the instinct of despair, at least for the time being and the men wore brave faces. However, one thing was for certain, and unsaid. The government had no more money to fight the war and the south was lost. Willing turned to exit, but—

"Mr. Willing?" Haym spoke. "May I inquire with a question?"

"Why surely, Mr. Salomon. Any question from you is an honor." Haym couldn't be sure if Willing was sincere in his statement or not. The man reminded him of European gentry, which was often known to smile at Jew but stab him in the back.

"Why didn't you sign the Declaration?"

Willing didn't know whether to be offended, angered, or reflective. Thusly, he chose honesty.

"Because, though I am a patriot, I did not think we were prepared to engage the most powerful military force this side of Heaven."

"What if Heaven is on our side?" Haym quipped.

"Then I wish for nothing more than the angels to take up arms and the Lord to take up subscriptions," Willing uprightly replied and exited.

***

In the week following William Prescott standing atop Breed's Hill ordering his men with the legacy-laden command to hold fire until they see the whites of the enemy's eyes, the Second Continental Congress severed a very tangible connection between England and America— they secretly authorized the printing of money. For all the ties and differences between the Colonies and their sovereign, the one which marked them simultaneously at odds and yet as one, was currency. From the outset of the expansion of colonization, the subjects were barred from minting their own coins. This prohibition yoked them with the British currency system as well as the use of foreign gold and silver specie. There was no official colonial money. The best the far away people could do was print their own paper credit, "new tenor," as it was known. These Bills of Credit were generally based on land holdings instead of being backed by bullion. However, in short time, with multiple loan offices and officers, local banks, and merchant-creditors offering and issuing the paper, they were wide spread through the barter-based colonies as money. British trade policy strictly forbid exchange in anything other than gold and silver. Therefore, as the bills floated upward the chain of debt from rural settlements to the harbors encompassing the circle of trade, they were unacceptable as payment, hence not worth the paper they were printed on. Parliament set about to solve this problem in 1764 with the passing of the Currency Act.

The act brought into effect the criminality of printing any form of credit or money, whatsoever. For a population devoid of the natural elements of gold and silver, coupled with a devastating trade imbalance, the new law left it without a ready-means of exchange or payment for wares and commodities. The further one ventured from the agrarian communities and closer to the city, it was more difficult to negotiate for goods and services without some form of currency. Benjamin Franklin, the colonial agent in London at the time, steadily lobbied for repels of the Currency Act, but he was only able to gain small concessions. In truth though, the subtext of the act was to curtail the colonists growing mechanisms of independence and establish through one of the greatest levers of power a government has— financial regulation— the supreme Parliament's authority over the colonies. The act did as such and effectively ended the flourishing colonial practice of printing money.

Notwithstanding the law, in the spring of 1775, the Congress was prepared to carry on a war— a struggle they issued for national independence. They had the men, the guns, the ammunition, and 2,000,000 livres ($30,607,000; [£150,000]) from the Spanish. However, the most important requisite for success in the experiment of prosecuting a war by means of paper currency is to make it command the public confidence and to secure it from depreciation— a well known phenomena in the colonies since the days of printing their own bills of credit. During the sessions of the Second Continental Congress this economic conundrum was the most expressed fear by the men at the convention. The will to fight was almost unanimous but the practical application of paying for it was short on confidence.

A special committee was convened to hastily resolve an approach to the matter. That approach proposed three distinct modes of issuing paper money, namely: that each colony should issue for itself the sum which might be appropriated to it by Congress; secondly, that the United Colonies should issue the whole sum necessary, and each colony become bound to sink its proportional part; and thirdly, that Congress should issue the whole sum, every colony be bound to discharge its proportion, and the United Colonies be obliged to pay that part which any colony should fail to discharge. Further, Congress resolved:

> "That a sum not exceeding two millions of Spanish
> milled dollars be emitted by the Congress in bills
> of credit, for the defense of America," and, "That
> the twelve confederated colonies (Georgia was not
> then represented) be pledged for the redemption
> of the bills of credit, now directed to be emitted."

So it was that each colony was required to pay its proportion in four annual payments, the first by the last of November 1779, and the fourth by the last of November 1782. On the following day a committee appointed for the occasion reported and offered the following resolutions, which were adopted:

> Resolved, That the number and denomination of
> the bills be as follows:
> 49,000 bills of 8 dollars each... $192,000
> 49,000 bills of 7 dollars each... $343,000
> 49,000 bills of 6 dollars each... $294,000
> 49,000 bills of 5 dollars each... $245,000
> 49,900 bills of 4 dollars each... $196,000
> 49,000 bills of 3 dollars each... $147,000
> 49,000 bills of 2 dollars each... $98,000
> 49,000 bills of 1 dollar each.....$49,000
> 11,800 bills of 20 dollars each... $236,000
> Totals... 403,800 bills; $2,000,000

Resolved, That the form of the bill be as follows:

> CONTINENTAL CURRENCY
> No: _____ $_____ Dollars.
> This bill entitles the bearer to receive _____
> SPANISH MILLED DOLLARS, or the value
> thereof in gold or silver, according to the
> resolutions of Congress, held at Philadelphia on
> the 10th day of May, A.D. 1775.

John Adams, John Rutledge, James Duane, Benjamin Franklin, and James Wilson were announced as a committee to get proper plates engraved, to provide paper, and to bargain for the printing of the bills. They based the currency on the loan from Spain. However, their financial obligations would quickly outweigh their physical silver and they printed a sum of paper money exceeding their means to honor it. Therefore, in time, the currency would virtually become fiat and not worth the paper they were engraved and printed on. Nonetheless, this announcement was the first public revelation of the existence of a committee appointed for such a purpose. If England ever had any doubts of the American resolve, it was overcome by the ex cathedra proclamation of this official monetary divorce.

By mid-1781, in alignment with the worsening military outcomes in the south, the financial conditions of the Congress deteriorated likewise. The most immediate solution employed was a dramatic increase in the rate of issuance, which only served to drive up inflation and depreciate the value of the Continental dollar. This was coupled with a full-frontal non-military assault by the British. They counterfeited the bills by the millions to undermine their value, confidence, and reliability.

In order to deal with inflation some states organized conventions for the purpose of establishing wage and price controls, which did little more than further depress market forces and decrease the value and wherewithal of the available money. Congress called upon the states for contributions and measures to buoy the sagging fortunes! However there was nothing additional the state could do to raise funds, the single option of selling notes was the only option but their was less and less confidence that the principle and the interest would be repaid. With the needs of the military superseding all other concerns, Congress unleashed an age-old policy of nations and kings before them. They authorized the army to confiscate whatever it needed to continue the war.

An irony to the war is that the profitable British tax system, which the Americans vehemently opposed, was the best weapon of war. By way of taxes, the English were in a better position than Congress— which had no ability to tax— to finance the war. The American aversion to taxation, which laid the framework for disillusionment from the British and was the foundation of their own, overriding tenet of central government, crippled their incorporated ability to negotiate the economics of military conflict. The newly minted United States— though in point of fact they weren't even states yet but a matter of nation states that were fighting to be united as a singular country— attempted to counteract their position between the devil and the deep blue by essentially selling war debentures with six to seven percent interest rate. However, that too was a step behind the well-oiled English mechanism for filling war chests. Britain had a variety of means, which it could tap for the funding of a war that went beyond taxation. Their numerous colonies, joint-stock companies, and worldwide trade allowed them to divert funding and rebalance the ledgers as it suited their needs. Britain simply had money to pay the foremost cost and matériel for a war and the insurgent Americans didn't. As a matter of fact it is almost strange that the colonies, which sought to be separate states in a cooperating confederation, created a premier political body to effect an army instead of thirteen individual militias. These nascent individual states were responsible for voluntarily paying a portion into the war effort though an army would not necessarily be directed in their own defense. These insubstantial powers granted to Congress were established under the Articles of Confederation. Reflecting the political environment neither the power to tax nor the power to regulate commerce was given to the political body. The problem with this arrangement was that in having no tax system to generate revenue, it was very difficult to borrow money. Rothschild made it a habit of loaning governments money because they maintained a monarchial right to tax citizens, but the Americans had done away with that governmental authority and poised themselves in a morally lofty posture but financially lower predicament. Thus, men like Haym Salomon would play larger individual roles in a national manifestation than would have ever been thought of in the previous course of human history.

***

Suffice it to say, the raw numbers did not favor the rebellious colonies. In retrospect, their courage might be matched only by their daring or stupidity. By the American decision to declare independence, the two other major European powers, France and Spain, in an attempt to weaken the English, joined the fight on the rebel's side. Thus King George was fighting three nations at once and on multiple fronts beyond the main theater of war over North American soil. The Spanish in particular used a strategy of opening small fronts in the Caribbean and other exotic locations, just to force men, money, and munitions away from Boston, New York, and Philadelphia. The total price for England to attempt to keep the colonies was £100 million (1,304,000,000 livres). However, this was an affordable sum for the rich empire. As a matter of fact, their treasury borrowed only 40% of the money it needed. As for France, heavy spending brought them to the verge of bankruptcy and many conversations were had that questioned the continuing logic of pouring more money into the Americans when it seemed they were ill-prepared, overmatched, and in a constant state of financial collapse. France itself was not as well financially codified as Britain. They were borrowing every livres they were sending to America while England could continue to accrue wealth and spend it toward the war. Britain, unlike the Congress was able to keep their suppliers and soldiers paid, while also hiring outside its boarders in employing tens of thousand of Hessians. The country had grown to incorporate a sophisticated financial system based on the wealth of thousands of landowners who supported the government, together with banks and financiers based in London. The economy hummed from Singapore to Quebec with an annul GDP above £140 million. This was in sharp contrast to the United States, which had to beg and borrow day-after-day to carry on the fight, and had only £872 ($178,000) of actual hard currency at the beginning of the war before the money arrived from Spain.

***

"…My concern is where we stand at our present rate," said Morris as he closed the door behind Willing. "This is why this bank is so important to our changing fortunes."
Haym's disposition wasn't as tense and dramatic as Morris. To a large degree, he enjoyed the pleasure of partaking in deep financial conversation. However, he realized that Morris wasn't partaking in a casual conversation; his words were building to something— something consequential.
      "And where is that in your estimation?" asked Haym.
Morris drew a shallow breath and took his time in answering the question…
      "I fear, nearer to failure than success," said Morris.
The stark even-toned manner in which he spoke conveyed a depth in the words which the words themselves could not convey without them being shouted from a man fallen into a well too deep to reach.
      "And as you have called me," Haym said through a minor coughing fit.
Morris quickly poured a glass of water and placed it into Haym's hand. Haym drank before finishing his question—
      "What is it you want from me?"
      "Your greatness," said Morris very plainly. "Show me another man who can multiply so few into so many as you do, and I will testify that I am in the presence of the Christ, himself.
      "You are mistaken. I have no greatness. Nothing have I, but the grace of God."
      "Then it is His grace through you that I require!" Morris proclaimed, almost in the intonations of a carnival barker.

"I ask that you do not trifle of—" Haym said.

"Yes-yes," Morris brought himself to a respectable demeanor. "Come, work with me."

"How so?" asked Haym.

"In assistance, in agreement, not in an official capacity— a small one, I assure you— I would not take from you so much that your duties for the French would be failing."

"My duties for the French are duties for the nation, and to this fact, there is no conflict between them."

Morris was unsure what Haym wanted to hear. So, he searched his mind with probing statements.

"The tasks facing Gouverneur and I—"

"The price on French bills are falling," Haym said.

"I assume to absorb the discount."

"The market is saturated to a glut."

"Yes," Morris admitted.

"To spend those notes now, would destroy in embryo all your hopes from that quarter and cut off the only resource which we have the hope of commanding, and shake a confidence which has been reposed in you, which the public interest calls on you to cherish."

"Then what do you suggest I do?"

"We continue to commission supplies on our personal credit, yours and mine."

"You have spoken 'we' and 'our,'" said Morris.

"I have. However, I am not attracted by your offer, Mr. Morris."

Morris was unsure as to what Haym meant exactly and vigorously pressed his argument—

"Mr. Salomon, as I see it, without an end before this year, we cannot prosecute our cause forward— I project the total cost of "Independence" to exceed sixty million pounds— frankly, there is simply nowhere more to turn for treasure."

Haym appeared as equally amused as Morris appeared desperate. Haym chuckled. Morris didn't crack a smile.

"The world is as treasured with monies as it is air, this I can assure you," Haym said.

"If you mean Holland, Adams is already working with de Neufville—"

"There are better candidates—"

"We have no way to guarantee the loans, those — "

"It will take faith!"

"A man of faith or a man money has faith in?"

Haym went silent and his smirk inverted. Morris knew he hit the sweet spot — that every man, even those with small point of pride have a vale of vanity. Now, Morris could ask for what he really needed.

***

"I came here where freedom is being defended, to serve it, to live and die for it," Casimir Pulaski said to General Washington. However, he didn't exactly mean it. By 1778, the Polish Nobleman was upset, angry, and bored — to say the least. True to form, Casimir wanted action! He wanted to fight! Even though Washington allowed him to create his own calvary unit, it wasn't given a theater to display its grand function. Casimir made it very clear to Washington of his disappointment and subtly threatened to return to Europe. Above all others, Washington believed in the Polish General and assured him that he would put him to good use — in a salient role beyond defense. It was precisely the remedy to assuage the old friend of Haym Salomon. Casimir wasn't built for defense, he was sired from the Gods of War for the aimed purpose of offensive action. The offensive action and good use was to be in the south where the British were trampling the Americans with the ease of walking through a field of daisies.

The Southern theater of the Revolution began at Charleston Harbor with the Battle of Sullivan's Island. It was a dramatic victory for the Colonials. However, after several setbacks, the accumulative strength of the British Army and Navy overtook the galvanized scrappiness of the Americans and in December of 1778, Savannah, Georgia fell.

Champing at the bit, on February 2nd, 1779, Casimir and his calvary received the orders from General Washington to proceed to South Carolina and reinforce the southern American forces under British attack. This was a front line of battle and Casimir was expected to use his men on horseback to counter the British offensive. By this time, the Royal mercenary was some 600 strong and as always, itching for a fight.

"Pulaski's Calvary Legion" as it was called, consisted of a troop of lancers, two troops of dragoons, and two hundred light infantry soldiers. They were trained to standards far beyond the standards of the

Continental Army. Casimir demanded an almost impossible standard from his men— still portions less than the standard he demanded from himself. He repeatedly tested them in cavalry tactics and when money from Congress was scarce, he used his own personal finances to assure the leigion was furnished with the finest equipment and personal safety.

In October of 1778, before they reached their eventual maxium capacity, they were first pressed into action in New Jersey, at Little Egg Harbor. It was there that American Privateers were making it a habit of raiding and capturing British supply vessels and redirecting their contents to Washington. Eventually, General Clinton was determined to directly bring this activity to a dramatic close and raze everything that stood in the harbor. From New York he sent forward the directive to "clean out the nest of rebel pirates." American Intelligence learned late of the British order, which made it a race against time; could they send a defending army to meet the Lobster Backs at Chestnut Neck before they arrived? The only option was the speed of the calvary!

However, the calvary, one hundred and seventy miles away in Baltimore, couldn't win the race! On September 30th, 1778, a fleet of nine British ships and transports, under the command of Captain Henry Collins, sailed from New York, bound for Chestnut Neck. The main attacking force was to be three hundred British regulars and one hundred New Jersey Loyalists, under the veteran command of Captain Patrick Ferguson. Governor William Livingston was warned by dispatch from Washington's camp and sent riders to warn the people. At the same time, Washington dispatched Casimir with the sound of urgency, which was music to the Count's ears.

However, with their head start, the British arrived three days before Casimir's calvary. They destroyed the iron works, the salt works, burned the plantations, and rendered useless any supplies they could not comfortably recover and transport! Nevertheless, upon arrival, Casimir set up camp with the express intent of unseating the British and Captain Patrick Ferguson— a man who in many ways was the British Pulaski. As history would unfold, Ferguson would waste no time or opportunity to take the fight to Casimir.

It had been a week and each encampment had been warily engaged in watching one another as they strategized their intentions. Enter, Lieutenant Gustav Juliet. He had deserted from a Hessian regiment in Rhode Island the prior year. He requested a commission with the

Continental Army and eventually was given a post as a sub-lieutenant with the Pulaski Legion. On October 14th, with the permission of Casimir, he organized a fishing party to go out into the bay. The party of three, led by Juliet, did more drinking than it ever did fishing and by nightfall, in a state of helpless intoxication, they spotted a British patrol. Being a man of low character, having interest only in his own odds of survival, Juliet convinced the two other dragoons to desert along with him. Thusly, they signaled the fleet and were taken aboard.

From there, Juliet, who identified himself to Ferguson as a Frenchman named Bromville, conveyed to the commander that Casimir was encamped with plans to attack and ordered that no quarter be given, whatsoever! Juliet suggested that the edict was on account of his barbaric Polish roots and that because of the bloodthirsty mandate, morale was low — not to mention the slipshod security around the Quaker homes they were occupying. Nothing the traitor said was true except for the poor security around the camp. All the while, Casimir assumed that the men had drowned, that it was unlikely that a man who had deserted once would desert again to the side he deserted from. Though he wouldn't have put it past Juliet, as he made it clear from the outset of the man's enrollment in his cavalry — that he didn't admire his style nor had he any respect for a turncoat — even as he said, "that would include an angel of the devil." Well, Casimir would soon learn that an angel of the devil was indeed whispering secrets to the enemy in the name of petty vengeance.

Pulaski might not have considered very deeply the fate of the three men on a fishing expedition, but they hadn't drowned — on the contrary. As the moon reached it's highest point, Ferguson loaded the better half of his fine unit onto boats and rowed them in the dark ten miles up river to Hickory Island where Casimir was camped. Juliet and the other two men were forcibly made to accompany the party at knifepoint.

Concealed behind an old growth of forest, in a fine cedar-shingled farmhouse, which looked out on the bay, the troops of horses, the artillery, and a portion of the infantry of the Legion were headquartered. Farther down the island road and nearer the lowlands was a picket post, occupied by fifty infantrymen under Casimir's second command: Lieutenant Colonel the Baron de Bosen.

From the heavens the first light rose at 4:00am. With it, Ferguson and his party landed on the isolated island. Immediately, he sent soldiers to guard the residents who had gathered together— at the governor's warning— for safety into one house. The house was the home of Richard Osborn, Jr.. The British soldiers drew their sword on the colonists and forced Richard's son, Thomas, to lead them to Casimir's camp. He marched them across the island when they came to a narrow defile and then to a bridge over what was called, "The Ditch" on Big Creek. To their surprise, there was no sentinel, just as Juliet said. This was without question a criminal neglect on de Bosen's part, when he knew the enemy was so near. Then, Ferguson crossed the bridge, leaving fifty regulars to secure a retreat. The British silently proceeded about a mile over a rough corduroy road made of tree trunks laid over swampland and across salt meadows until they came to the island road. A singular unprepared sentry was guarding it. They fell upon him before he could even fire a shot, and drove a sword through his belly with clenched anger constructed on the rumor that Casimir would give no quarter. One man dead. Ferguson carried the troops further in the shadows of first light to the picket post were the infantry slept.

"Charge!" screamed Ferguson and his men rammed their bayonets into every man who was awakening from their dream states! Half a mile away, Casimir awoke by sound of the commotion! Meanwhile, de Bosen charged out of the house drawing his weapons with great speed! With a pistol firing and a sword swinging, he fought the murderous British! Yet, the sheer numbers overcame his bravery and his body was pierced from head to toe until he fell twitching into the serene condition of lifelessness.

In minutes the butchery was all but absolute! Forty men lay dead or bleeding to death, while five were taken prisoner and five others fled into the woods! Ferguson set the house and the field ablaze and his men hurried across the "The Ditch." As they tacitly destroyed the crossing, Casimir Pulaski appeared from the smoke and fire with malevolent indignation in his eyes. Immediately, he took to discharging his firelock with a speed and accuracy which was unseen by any of the soldiers receiving fire, including Ferguson! The fizz, ignition, crack, whiz, and thud— men were falling one after another until the stunned fascination wore off and Ferguson led them beyond the range of fire! The tide was high and the creek couldn't be crossed by a mount. The British faded into the brush and the breaking day. For the time being, Casimir had to settle for being alive and killing only a few.

Little Egg Harbor wasn't Pulaski's first taste of battle since arriving in America. He came looking to drink thirstily of British blood. However, his thirst went unquenched and his relationship with American commanders outside of Washington proved tenuous. Unquestionably, Casimir was a prickly figure, especially if he wasn't getting his way. As often happens in tight hierarchies, outsiders are not welcome by those who didn't invite them in. So was the case with the Continental Army and Casimir. The Polish general could not wield power as he was used to, and much of his military knowledge, experience, and recommendations, were ignored by Washington's underlings. And yet, before even receiving a commission, he literally, famously, and personally saved General George Washington's life at the Battle of Brandywine. He also saved the army from a surprise attack and humiliating defeat at Warren Tavern in Massachusetts. Plus, he took heroic part in the American defeat at the Battle of Germantown. Casimir wintered with Washington at Valley Forge, where he argued that the season and weather should not preclude attack. He brilliantly directed troops for General Anthony Wayne, which brought a victory to the Americans during a skirmish at Haddonfield. Everyone who fought with Casimir was in awe of his courageous reckless abandon combined with seasoned intelligent calculations. In many ways, had he been in the position of Washington, the Americans would have headlong seized the initiative and most likely overwhelmed the British by sheer audacity. However, his evermore-spirited tactics — while still chivalrous — were beyond the more measured approach the British-weened Americans were used to conducting battle. It was as simple a contrast as the fighting style of the wolverine to the well-mannered head butting of rams. They looked at Casimir as almost a savage; not to mention his thick Polish accent and barely comprehensible English made for untenable communication. Nevertheless, Washington knew he was an asset. If Casimir wanted to fight; plunge into the heart of defeat and intrepidity wrestle victory into the grip of American possibility, Washington would give him the chance. Savannah had been lost and maybe Casimir Pulaski could return it.

***

In point of fact, the Americans were rather naive in regard to the overriding financial mechanisms in consideration to the support of military institutions and the prosecution of a wide-scale war. The intellectual high ground and the enthusiasm, which founded the belligerent Declaration of Independence and followed its ratification was tamped by the daily vicissitudes of sustained hostility. The British, who lacked the intellectual high ground but retained a principled academic rectitude, saw themselves as the aggrieved party. Thus, they vigorously engaged the Americans on solid-ground with a force and ferocity which made it clear they had no intention of further negotiating piddling grievances— this was a war of paramountcy. The winner would have the New World without opposition. If that was to be for the Americans, it simply meant that the British would go home for good and they would govern themselves; but if it was for the British, it signified something graver and much more punitive. It meant that the heads of Jefferson, Washington, Adams, Madison, Franklin, Paine, Chase, Harrison, Morris, Rush, Revere, Hancock, Hamilton, Henry, Salomon, and many more would be offered up on a silver platter to King George; served cold with a side of dipping sauce made from French and Spanish blood. For the Americans— who the British saw as power-hungry lawyers and politicians who sought to increase their minor Colonial importance by duping a simple folk into reckoning they were shackled by arbitrary unjust policies— the revolution was truly a matter of life or death. For the British and the commanders in the field, they bristled— for it was their army which saved and protected the colonies from the encroachment of the French and Spanish and the threat of the Indians— but barring being killed in battle, this was but yet, just another imperial campaign. All the same, war is fought through armed men but its key component is money. The British were flush with the means to pay for the war, which they perceived as a strategic advantage and needed only to fight on and wait until it culminated into an American surrender. Surrender wasn't an option to those who bestowed their signatures to the king, so they had to find a way to figuratively pay for their lives.

So it was that Congress authorized the printing of bills, but taxes were the issue. The bills themselves were not designed to be permanent currency, but a collective effort to centralize the financing and funding of the war. Each colony was required to redeem its share and to pay the coin called for at the end of four years, with three more annual payments to follow. Virginia owing the most and Delaware the least. When redeemed, each bill was to be cut through the middle with a circular punch an inch in diameter, and then returned to Congress to be publicly burned. However, the money was so easily procured and the demands upon the treasury for war contingencies so urgent that within five months three million more dollars were issued than was actually backed by coin.

The naivety on Congress' part was four fold. One, in the idea that after the expected wealthy purchased their share of notes, that each average citizen would buy enough from its state to finance a substantial portion of debt. Secondly, they never considered how much money would truly be needed over the course of many years. Thirdly, as an entity, Congress didn't foresee all the demands for money that running a government and war would procure. Lastly, there simply wasn't that much coinage in the country. Thus, as Congress needed money, they did the only immediate thing they could do. They printed more money. However, like governments and bodies of unchallenged power before them, their satiety was never reached and the printing press would not had stopped, had it not been for Robert Morris.

Until it stopped though, with each promise Congress made, each debt they incurred, they printed more money to account for it until $200,000,000 of Continental Currency had flooded the market, not to mention the overactive printers counterfeiting the same currency for the British, further undermining the value.

In the scheme of things, the method of redeeming its share of the money was left to each colony, and it was presumed from the outset that this would be done by local taxation. However, it was taxation, which lead them to war. The public consciousness, which was framed on the overreaching simplistic argument of living under governments, which did not directly tax, was the prevailing understanding to the non-educated set. Basically, many really believed that the United States would never tax its citizenry and therefore they would not support leaders and politicians that urged the government to do so.

As inflation grew and the value of Continental money fell, Franklin and others begged Congress to stop the presses and get the house in order— to obtain permission from their constituents to tax them. Yet, "taxes" was a political death sentence and no member of Congress was going to risk their seat in request of taxation. The fear of the politicians was very real. One broadside issued in Philadelphia read:

"Cursed be the Congress man or men who dare
tax the free men of North America."

These were the conditions and the atmosphere in which Robert Morris was entrusted with the critical task of leading the financing of the war.

To make matters worse, General Washington's overall strategy wasn't doing Morris any favors. Afforded with ample countryside to maneuver his forces and unable to match those of the British, man-to-man or canon-for-canon, Washington chose to engage in a war of attrition. It wasn't in the aggressive headlong tradition of Alexander the Great or Hannibal Barca but it was the most convincing strategy in the face of the facts. He had a smaller army, navy, and treasury. Washington's skillful leadership can be summed up as wary, vigilant, and canny. He reduced the possibility of losing his army by never engaging in an all out offensive. His hope was that by staying the course, the British just might tire of war. However, this didn't serve well the culling of the financial deficiencies Morris was daily dealing with. Washington was always needing and asking for more.

***

"...Let me share with you in a candid honesty I reserve only for myself," Morris said to Haym, while starring out the window. "If we survive, we will have problems after this war. The promises the Congress has made can't be kept in full and the depreciation of the currency will undoubtedly cause economic collapse. If this nation is be a nation, no matter the lateness of the hour victory is won, in time the chime will strike the real financial cost of this engagement, and when that bill comes due and, there won't not be enough jails for all the debtors that will ensue."

"You have my full support," Haym said sympathetically. "There is no financial cost too great if this country can become a nation based on the principles this war has been initiated."

Morris stepped away from the window; turned and faced Haym —

"Only, I tell you, only if sound fiscal policy is adopted — otherwise we will not stand as a nation but as separate factions jockeying for crumbs as do pigeons around an old maid. For a nation at war, which desperately needs money, the Congress cannot seem to even agree on the enactment of a five percent toll. I don't expect a lot from men who derive their powers on the favor of other men."

Morris sat himself down at his desk and shuffled through the papers. Haym grew antsy, as it seemed his counterpart was nervously delaying his point.

"Mr. Superintendent, was there more to our matter than the mutual arrangement by which we'd work together on the country's pecuniary needs?"

Morris's face grew somewhat red with anger and he squeezed his fist tightly, then unwound it before slapping his hand on the desk—

"Roderigue Hortalez and Company! I hear through my brother— he hears through Silas Dean— there are rumblings that our good fortune to begin this war was on credit. What do you know of that?"

"Why, I have no part," said Haym.

"I know you have no part, but as a superintendent for the French you might have information!"

"I assure you that I have none and am not privy to any that I am withholding."

Morris accepted Haym's cool answer with a calm spinning of the wheels in his mind.

"Do you know what comes with money? Enemies. And with enemies comes intrigue— lies, myths, and division," Morris said.

"I ask you, to entertain your question, assuming there is no insult directed at my loyalty or involvement. Who negotiated the agreement?"

"There is nothing to fear by my question," Morris quickly assured him. "Mr. Lee was our agent."

"I suppose you should ask him," Haym said.

"Yes, I suppose I should."

"If I may, what was the arrangement?"

"The Two Bourbon Courts would bestow upon us a gift of two million livres, to be split equally between them. But even before then, supplies had been shipped on a non-scheduled basis— finding their way through the ports of Spain, France, and Holland. Many of our captains picked up arms and ammunition in personal trading ventures. Moreover, much important trade of this nature had been going on through the Spanish ports in the West Indies—

"Yes, of that I am well aware," Haym said.

"My first detail as the Superintendent was to examine the records. It appears that the Spanish have further furnished us with 1,870,000 livres, but it also appears that the Congress has only credited the French. Why is that— theories abound. Is it because the Spanish have not formally recognized our nation? Is it because we have not envoys on their soil? Are we cursed with Francophiles among our ranks? I don't know! But the Spanish are questioning our appreciation and the French our ability! And now, I come to hear that the French assert that the money and the munitions were a loan. We are not in control of our independence in this state of dependence!"

Then, Morris fell silent, deafly silent. It was all but uncomfortable. He stared at Haym as though he held a secret, a knowledge from beyond understood human acquisition. For his part, Haym had a measure of pity for Morris' troubles but no immediate answer in conversation.

"I have done all I can do— I have bought of our own futures, outfitted several units with personal capital— I have ventured so far as to take out loans in my own name— exceeding, mind you, a million dollars for this army while the States themselves have done as much— or as little as give the Congress meat and vegetables," Morris said in full exasperated breath.

Then, Morris went so far as to hold up accounting ledgers, receipts, bills, and alike to substantiate his diatribe.

"Add, here, and here if you like, and in total you will find that of all the States combined, we have a national contribution of less than a half million dollars to the financial welfare of this war. Mind my words as an echo, in part of your own sentiments: this began as a war of bullets, but it had been deduced to a war of money."

It was clear that Morris' heart was heavy. Haym knew he was asking for money but it was also obvious that he wanted something more. His frustrated rant continued—

"All the money now at our command, and that which we may expect from the States to come, will not do more than satisfy the various engagements which will by that time have fallen due. I have ceased all printing of Continental Currency and my responsibility requires me to place us on firm financial footing. The only way I see fit is a new financial institution whose money is backed by bullion. Now, if we cannot procure a loan from the French or the Spanish, where am I to get the needed specie for the bank?" Morris asked.

Again, there was silence. Then—

"Tell me true, you are holding millions in coin for the French, are you not?"

If Thomas Jefferson and James Madison were the geniuses behind the Constitution, then it can safely be implied that Charles Gravier, Comte de Vergennes was the real genius behind Revolution. The Americans had Benjamin Franklin— "Chief of the Rebels" as the English called him— Silas Dean, and Arthur Lee in Paris on their figurative knees. They regularly met with Vergennes and Luzerne in an effort to procure a constant flow of money to support Washington. The French were already reinforcing America's motley and discombobulated army with money and military supplies, but by artful artifice. Vergennes was determined to lessen the influence and power of the English and Russians. There was little the American cause could do to dampen Russian domination of the eastern part of Europe and Asia. However, as a British colony, a revolution could swing the balance of western power back to the Bourbons. Vergennes reveled in this storybook opportunity. He went so far as to conspire against the unpopular Anne-Robert-Jacques Turgot. Turgot was the man who saved the French economy and had the trust of Louis XVI. Turgot warned of raiding the coffers on schemes against Britain by proxy of America. Vergennes would not be denied by the safe-minded bean counter as he saw the brilliant but off-putting man, and played a very helping hand in forged letters attributed to Turgot, which scandalously attacked Marie Antoinette. Every move the Americans made from the moment of the Shot Heard 'Round the World, was in some form of consul with Vergennes. It was Vergennes' tacit support, which drove the engine of Congressional confidence.

By 1779, Vergennes wanted an emissary in the colonies whom he could implicitly trust with money. Conrad Alexandre Gérard de Rayneval had been the French Ambassador. As a matter of fact, he drafted the Treaty of Alliance, which stated that France would support America in the event of military hostilities by the British. It was a somewhat ironic document in the middle of a war, but it set the stage for France's formal declaration of war against England. However, England beat them to the punch and immediately declared war on France once they were informed of France's recognition of the colonies as the United States, an independent nation. Nevertheless, Gérard's high statesmanship did not match his personal propriety. His method of bringing greater favor to France with the new nation was to lavishly subsidize many of its best-known citizens, such as Thomas Paine. Furthermore, he used French money to gift members of

Congress. Much of what he did was in secret and purposefully not placed into written correspondence. All in all, Gérard was perfectly competent but he was also a bit of a bon vivant. As Vergennes prepared to send a large military force and the funds to provide for them, he wanted an attaché on the ground better suited to stewardship, military matters and was formally acquainted with the United States money matters. His choice for this role was: Chevalier de la Luzerne.

Haym and Luzerne met early in 1779. Haym arrived on the recommendation of Rochambeau. The two Frenchmen were very close and in constant contact. Luzerne wasn't expecting Haym, but arriving on Rochambeau's direction and the fact that Haym spoke fluent French, made him immediately welcome. On their first meeting, the two men spoke at length. The conversation advanced the idea of Haym working as an official broker for both the French consulate and the officer of Paymaster General. This was the second chance opportunity Haym had been looking for to rebrand his brokerage. It was also an official title he desperately personally and professionally desired. It would, he thought, gain him unlimited access and entry to the confidence and trust of money, just as he witnessed such a title married to officialdom did for Rothschild.

For Luzerne, employing Haym showed a prudence and foresight he believed would impress Vergennes. The truth was, though the French economy was recovering on the prior wisdom and stewardship of Turgot, it was still weak and unstable, plagued by an outrageous national debt. The majority of the money France was borrowing was coming from the Dutch on an interest rate of four percent. By 1779, they had already borrowed 750,000,000 livres (£56,250,000 [$209,000,000]) and the interest payments alone comprised half the government's total revenue. If Haym Salomon could sell French bills, then maybe much of the French North American campaign could pay for itself. As it turned out, Haym's work alone paid for much of General Lafayette's expedition after 1779. Spanish and Dutch officials saw the advantage of having a man like Haym Salomon and when they couldn't find their own Haym Salomon, they employed him in the same capacity as the French until the respective country's shipping could break the British blockade. All of this business earned Haym more money than he had ever accumulated or lost in a lifetime of gain and loss.

During the time in his life, which Philadelphia comprised, Haym made himself into a pillar of society, and especially the Jewish community and the Congressional fraternity. Many a founding father and participant of the war were reliant on his charity, including but not limited to: Thomas Jefferson, Edmund Randolph, James Wilson, Joseph Reed, Baron Von Steuben, Theodore Bland, James Madison, Joseph Jones, John Mercer, General Thomas Mifflin, Robert McPherson, Arthur St. Clair, and even Rachel's cousin, David Salisbury Franks. He gave with no expectation or requirement of return.

As active and full as Haym's life was, his health remained a source of constant concern. Rachel not only nursed and cared for the children but soothed and tended to her husband's occasional bouts of coughing, nausea, and night sweats, which came and went infrequently but savagely. Usually three days of fever or more would leave him bed-ridden, vomiting, dizzy, and trickling blood from his mouth or his nose. Then, the fever would break and his strength would gradually return. Soon, he would be back to the coffee house, a dervish in relentless motion. However, it was evident that his body was slowly deteriorating from the inside out and there was nothing anyone could do about it.

***

A violent coughing fit suddenly overwhelmed Haym. He swiftly turned his back to Morris and pressed a tight covering to his mouth. Helpless but politely, Morris went about pouring another glass of water as the fit was subsiding. Haym removed his hand from his lips and stared at the spattered pattern of blood in his palm. As Morris approached, Haym quickly wiped the hand clean with a handkerchief.

"I say, what say the doctor about your condition?" Morris kindly asked.

"Oh, only that it is not much," Haym, said.
It was a very telling moment. For Morris who was well versed in the vagaries of politics, he noted that Haym did not tell a convincing lie. Though he had known the man for two years and hadn't had a discredited business transaction, in a world as Morris contended— "money"— which comes with enemies— there were always stories, positive or negative about everyone. As a merchant, common sense led one to veer toward the middle of rumor for the truth, that is unless personal experience was involved. Be that as it may, Morris was a constant victim of scandal and

unflattering accusations and in that moment, his respect for Haym and trust of him instantly rose to a place in which friendship was able to take root in Morris' jaded heart. Nonetheless, Haym personally didn't approve of anything less than the wholeness of truth. Yet, for something as personal and victimless as his fib, he gave himself permission to be disingenuous. The doctors had not told him that it was "Not much." As a matter of fact he was told it was Consumption— and he was living on a volume of borrowed time. Only, no humanly individual knew for sure just how many units of the abstract measurement the volume contained.

"Do you know the first time I encountered you?" Morris asked in the most vulnerable and genuine of tones he reserved for moments in which no position needed to be advanced.

"If you did not speak to me, I assume not," said Haym.

"You were escorted into the assembly room of Congress, you recalled how you had just escaped from the gallows."

"Yea. Yea, I remember."

"I admit, I was awe-struck by your presence. There you were, as though dropped from a mountain top, and though you prayed for employment, you also took the time to enter a plea for a fellow prisoner."

"Mr. Demezes, yea— I recall," said Haym.

"I thought, what a remarkable man, still concerned about another while he himself is still wrecked with abuse and destitution." Morris said. They held one another's gaze, until finally—

"Excuse my competitive nature over the years. You are more of a man than any I have ever known."

Haym accepted the peace without sentiment— acknowledged in silence of protest. Morris turned back to his desk with the intention of sitting, when suddenly, they spoke at the same time—

"Why do you inquire as to my responsibilities to the paymaster," Haym said.

"What of this charge against you?" Morris said.

"You speak of the securities?" Haym asked.

"That I do. I hear the figure is $50,000."

"Yea, but I contend it is but a small matter of legalities, and not fraud. Though I fear my defense will be overcome by the roaring sound of the sum drowning out the whispered tones of the facts."

"Who is handling your case— your defense?"

"I suspect I will have Mr. Wilson do so."

"No, I shall do so! Misunderstanding or mistake should not be reason for an honest man to be imprisoned. Present me with the facts of the case and fear nothing. As your criminal attorney, I vow that you shall not be convicted of anything, except maybe that of undimmed piety."
Morris didn't tell Haym, but before the hour, in some reaches of his psyche he wished for Haym's prosecution and conviction. However, it was clear to him that Haym Salomon would not knowingly cheat anyone. Morris was intent to use his position and influence to countersue the complainant and save his needed friend from default, disaster, and scandal.

"Why, thank you," Haym said.

"It is not worth the mention, what is right is right," Morris responded.

"Mr. Superintendent, what is it you need from me in my capacity as a broker to the French?"
The plain talk turned Morris from his overconfident self-possessed pizzazz to darkly serious.

"The specie," he said. "The specie."

"In the form of a loan?" Haym incredulously asked.

"Not necessarily. But, a deposit. A substantial deposit— the first depositor into the new bank."

"I see," said Haym. "To date, how much have you accrued in subscriptions?"
Again Morris, took his time, played with the exercise of deep breathing and shifting focuses, until finally—

"Thereabout $70,000," Morris said somewhat reluctantly.
Haym fell into a certain degree of intellectual shock!

"You need over $300,000!"

"Precisely," Morris said, "In gold or silver."

***

"When the dying flame of day
Through the chancel shot its ray,
Far the glimmering tapers shed
Faint light on the cowled head;
And the censer burning swung,
Where, before the altar, hung
The crimson banner, that with prayer
Had been consecrated there.

And the nuns' sweet hymn was heard the while,
Sung low, in the dim, mysterious aisle.
Take thy banner! May it wave
Proudly o'er the good and brave;
When the battle's distant wail
Breaks the Sabbath of our vale.
When the clarion's music thrills
To the hearts of these lone hills,
When the spear in conflict shakes,
And the strong lance shivering breaks.
Take thy banner! And, beneath
The battle-cloud's encircling wreath,
Guard it, till our homes are free!
Guard it! God will prosper thee!
In the dark and trying hour,
In the breaking forth of power,
In the rush of steeds and men,
His right hand will shield thee then.
Take thy banner! But when night
Closes round the ghastly fight,
If the vanquished warrior bow,
Spare him! By our holy vow,
By our prayers and many tears,
By the mercy that endears,
Spare him! He our love hath shared!
Spare him! As thou wouldst be spared!
Take thy banner! And if e'er
Thou shouldst press the soldier's bier,
And the muffled drum should beat
To the tread of mournful feet,
Then this crimson flag shall be
Martial cloak and shroud for thee."
The warrior took that banner proud,
And it was his martial cloak and shroud!"
— Henry Wadsworth Longfellow
Hymn of the Moravian Nuns of Bethlehem at the
Consecration of Pulaski's Banner

In April of 1779, Casimir Pulaski and his calvary unit arrived in Savannah. At that hour, full-scale war or siege had yet to materialize. Major General Benjamin Lincoln, Southern Commander of the Continental Army, knew that the seaport city couldn't be liberated and taken without naval support. Therefore, in the meantime, he directed skirmishes in the territory between Charleston and Savannah and waited for naval and French assistance.

General Sir Henry Clinton was exasperated with the degree of difficulty in fighting in the northern cities. He identified the problem with patriot support from the residences of the cities and towns. One idea, which came to him, was to divide a portion of his superior forces and send them south where British loyalty ran higher and American military defense thinner. To capture the south, he thought, would tighten the noose around Washington until the rebels sued for peace. Thusly, in December of the previous year, Lieutenant Colonel Archibald Campbell wrestled control of the city in a rather blasé military affair. With victory in Savannah accomplished and the British colors flying high, General Augustine Prévost, a surly old Swiss-Born Brit, to secure the prize, later joined Campbell. Campbell quickly establishing outposts in the region as Prévost sought to recruit local Loyalists to the flag.

On September 1st, after months of wait, Lincoln's wish and request was granted. Vice Admiral Comte d'Estaing brought a fleet of forty-two ships north from a victorious campaign in the Caribbean which saw him capture St. Vincent and Grenada from the British. Upon his arrival, Prévost and Campbell dug in and the Siege of Savanna, in which the Americans would try to recapture the city, began.

A variety of factors go into victory as it pertains to war. Besides, money, men, and munitions, the quality of the individual solider may play a role superior to the static realities of any other factor. When it came to the French Admiral d'Estaing, "boldness" would never be ascribed to his approach and character. Thus the siege the Americans undertook was woefully uncreative and allowed for a rather simplistic but successful defense for the British.

The offensive began with d'Estaing forming a line as he waited for Lincoln and the Continental Army who were about one hundred miles away. In response, General Prévost set to the construction of the city's defenses, ordering boats to be grounded along the banks of the river, then manned defensively. Smartly, Prévost also ordered a group of 800 men under the command of Colonial John Maitland in Beaufort, South Carolina, to hold their position, but be ready to advance in support of the city if needed. In the meantime, Benjamin Lincoln left a camp in the area around Charleston and joined General Lachlan McIntosh at Ebenezer. Together, the Continental Army advanced and began to take position around the city on September 9th. With the arrival of the opposing force, Governor James Wright, who recently was placed back into position as governor with the British capture of Savannah, ordered all able-bodied men to assist in building Savannah's defenses. Both Lincoln and d'Estaing knew that the siege would not be one of a great duration, for Britain would find out about the naval blockade and send enough ships to break through d'Estaing's line; not to forget that it was hurricane season. In reality, d'Estaing's greatest concern was his own skin. Nonetheless, it was Lincoln's belief that the British would surrender if their escape routes were cut.

General Lincoln and Admiral d'Estaing met on September 16th, at the Admiral's headquarters in Thunderbolt, five miles from the city. They began strategizing how to complete the encirclement of the British forces. However they were going to do it, the allied generals believed that the unrelenting hands of time were anything other than at favor to their objectives. Their meeting of the minds wasn't without disagreement; as a matter of fact it was entirely void of agreement whatsoever. The two men made countless compromises in strategy to one another, which lead to almost no strategy at all. The only thing they could agree upon was a shared hope that Prévost would surrender without a fight.

The following day, d'Estaing issued his surrender demand to Prévost. In return, Prévost accomplished something that didn't require much effort, he outsmarted them. Prévost acted as though he was seriously considering the demand while hastily improving the defense of city. By September 23rd, the city was fully invested although Prévost did call for the troops from Beaufort, who apparently got through the Patriots with little difficulty. Puzzling as it was to Casimir Pulaski, Lincoln did little to improve his position over that time. He seemed only to wait for an answer that Pulaski vehemently explained was never going to come.

On October 4th, d'Estaing, at Pulaski's urging and his own fear of Britain's navy or Mother Nature arriving, quit twiddling his thumbs and opened a bombardment for the ages. However, it did little more than light the sky for the entertainment of the dug in enemy. Prévost was completely undeterred and continued his task of securing the city's defenses. Eventually, even the obvious occurred to Lincoln and d'Estaing, and they agreed to attack the British positions across a broad front. On October 9th the twinkling auroral sidereal of light broke the morning darkness ahead of the diurnal course of the day accompanied by a cool breeze from the rolling Atlantic. Seizing on the fact the Americans had for once superior numbers, d'Estaing's plan called for five groups to move forward, concentrating on a salient in the British line at Spring Hill, where a group of South Carolina militia appeared to be holding the line. Some of the finest American officers were now involved including Lincoln, McIntosh, Lieutenant Colonial Francis "The Swamp Fox" Marion, and Casimir. Pulaski and Marion expressed strong disagreement with the plan, but being the good soldiers they were, they dutifully obeyed orders.

The agreed upon stratagem called for a diversionary assault on the British left, followed by the main thrust and attack of French and American troops on the British right at the Spring Hill redoubt. The infantry was set to serve as a follow-up force. As for Casimir and his legion, he and his fighting men were to launch a cavalry charge like a mythological horde of banshees with the witchcraft of death at the tip of their swords whenever a breach occurred in the defenses. In reality, this was in the tangible hopes of creating a wild havoc among the enemy's troops; and so all together, combined, and consented, was the rather unimaginative plan on paper.

As one can imagine, nothing went as proposed. To begin with, a heavy fog descended across the flood plains and a lack of clear directions delayed the French columns marching in the dark. By the time the entire force was assembled it was 7:00 o'clock in the morning, three hours later than the attack was planned— when darkness was to have been employed to hide the troop movements. In the light of the delay and the natural rise of morning, the British amusingly watched them assemble. The light gave away their strategy like a man playing poker with his private hand of cards on the table for everyone to see. Thus, as the assault began, it seemed to the unsuspecting Americans as though the British intimately knew their entire stratagem. And as the dark machineries of fate would have it, the British did know. For they benefitted from a cowardly deserter the night before slipping across into their lines and relying the orders of attack; consequently the Red Coats were able to strengthen the defenses of the

Spring Hill battery by withdrawing units from those points where the feints were planned.

From the start, the American and French attack moved forward against a cross fire of artillery! From the front, the British were blasting holes in their lines with deadly and accurate cannon fire. From the rear as well, several ships in the river threw in their shot, which created a crossfire that quickly brought an eruption of confusion rippling down the line of American formations! As it turned out, the British redoubt to the left front was chosen by d'Estaing for a direct assault as he believed it would be defended by inferior loyalist ranks, when in fact, these troops had been reenforced by Maitland's experienced hard-bitten band of Scots from the back-country. Only rabid dogs could face them without fear. Meanwhile, the advancing troops stood out in their white uniforms, which did little to camouflage their position or disguise the accuracy of British fire. As it was, death was having an excellent morning and as a matter of fact, d'Estaing was twice hit by a rifle round. Nevertheless, no matter the intensity of rifle and cannon fire, the Americans courageously just kept advancing on the Spring Hill battery.

Against his better nature, Casimir was forced to stand back and wait. He could see the heavy fire the lines were taking; momentarily being bedeviled with disarray and disorder— many times he was prepared to signal the charge— but they would quickly reassemble and continue to press forward. However, when Casimir heard that d'Estaing was wounded and at the same time spotted a new gap in the line, he waited no more. Maybe it was too early, maybe he went too far, beyond his support, or maybe he was simply ready to charge himself into immortality. Whatever the reason, Casimir gave the signal and the cavalry charged like hell on horseback!

Pulaski furiously, if not recklessly, led his troops into battle— straight for the grinding teeth of the crossfire between batteries. He was going to race through the rent formation and over the insurmountable odds into a heroic capture of the hill! His mount galloped in a satisfaction matched by his brimming will to victory, over confidence, unequaled pride, and beautiful arrogance! "Opłata! - Opłata!" he screamed! He, and fifty horsed men following him screamed in kind! It was a opera of "Opłata!" Then, a wailing screech of the perpetual motion of circular iron covered in rags discharged the full battle sounds in the air with a vacuum of silence split into a thin noise of projection, like that of destiny in the distance. The mass of small metal balls packed tightly into a canvas bag collided and ruptured into the groin of Casimir Pulaski, cutting him down off of his horse to the ground, where he for the first time in his life lay without the independent strength to rise!

A general retreat was sounded after the soldiers had withstood the enemies' fire for nearly an hour; but not before the Spring Hill battery was carried by the South Carolinians, under the Swedish officer, Curt von Stedingk. Lieutenants Hume and Bush planted the regiment's colors on the little hill, but were both gunned down moments later. It was a matter of honor that the banners not be lost, so as the regiment retired, Lieutenant Gray attempted to save them and was mortally wounded himself. A soldier named Jasper, then carried them back and handed the shredded standards off to his comrades; but he too, took a mortal wound and his soul retired of his body a short time later. So too, the same fate of eternal return would overcome Casimir Pulaski two days later.

***

By June of 1781, it had only been a month since Morris was appointed the first Superintendent of Finance and the Agent of the Marine. However, in that time, much had he already done. He instituted a myriad of reforms, including reducing the civil list, significantly cutting government spending by using competitive bidding for contracts, tightening accounting procedures, and demanding the federal government's full share of support of money and supplies from the States— a thankless task which had no end. He also introduced the proposal for a new private national bank, which he contended, could revive their economic prospects and provide liquidity. Morris had agreed to become Superintendent on the single righteous condition that he be able to continue with his own personal business ventures. This inevitably led to conflicts of interest and a blurring of the distinction between private and public business. Congress, more or less, accepted the matter of an inherent influence peddling because the business network Morris had created was able to accomplish things the legislature's rudimentary administrative apparatus could not. At the same time, a mounting list of people distrustful of Morris' motives grew, including some in the Congress. A variety of people went so far as to assert that he had a personal desire to power that bordered on dictatorial. The smears, murmurs, and duplicity marred his appreciation of men; and coming to the sudden conclusion that

Haym Salomon's personal character was a cut above, meant something to him personally. Though, at all times, Morris undoubtedly appreciated Haym as a man of action and one who understood the nuanced issues relating to finance— but lo and behold, even as a Jew, he was actually better than those backbiters, those unprincipled fartleberries, those sidewinders of mercantile commerce.

Morris lived on the edge of keeping his sanity, where the blood pressure runs high, the heart races like a thoroughbred, and for every solution there are two more problems. To boil it down, the issues the man faced stemmed from financial policy dictated by the compromises of political committee, cronyism, and an overall lack of farsighted detail. Albeit, Morris knew he couldn't single-handedly save the new United States from all the financial problems facing it, but remarkably, he adhered to a larger scope of vision: the establishment of sound fiscal policy that would outlive the age. He was the right man at the right time, he not only focused on details but he might have been the only individual in America who saw the war itself as only an opening act. What Robert Morris believed— which no one else even conceived— is that a country, like the life of a man, is defined mostly by its financial well being. What good is a government if it lingers in debt and is enslaved by the financial will of others? He saw that a nation which didn't possess a strong dynamic currency and economic assests couldn't harvest its own natural resources; that eventually such a people would be forced to sell its land and labor cheap on the international market of monarchial vultures. All the good government in the world, all the rights and freedoms of natural law equaled to a piddling of nothingness if the average wage was too low, prices too high, imports to scare, and inflation out of control. He took the job of Superintendent as seriously as Washington did the generalship. Employing a needed farsightedness and attention to detail, he energetically addressed an enormous amount of business, ranging from compensating a farmer for livestock requisitioned by the army, to personally taking a hand in supplying the troops. It almost goes without saying, but by bringing a measure of order and central direction to American finances, his power and influence grew, yet instead of wielding it for his own gain, in point of fact, he sacrificed a large proportion of his own best interest for that of country. Of course though, above all, the main problem rested in mobilizing credit. This is why he turned to Haym.

***

"…And I have a plan for a new currency," Morris professorially said to Haym. "As a matter of fact, I have written a pamphlet, 'On Public Credit,' have you read it?

Haym shook his head, having not read it, but he gave nice mien as though to indicate he would find the opportunity to do so quite interesting. Morris quickly grabbed a copy and presented it to him—

"Furthermore, I must share with you my intention of monetary decimation!" Morris said somewhat excitedly.

Morris and Haym were still standing away from one another and Morris— standing above his chair— had yet to sit. Haym's body was weighing more on his cane than it was before and he needed to take a seat. He was leaning toward the one directly across from Morris' desk but it appeared that he might not make it. Morris came around and quickly helped him to the seat.

"Is that so?" Haym said with interest and surprise. "'Decimation.'"

"Yes! I propose it be ten to equal one!"

"Fascinating!"

Then, as before, a silence neither could impede suddenly fell upon them as Morris' anxious nature for answers and conclusion overcame his patience for smalltalk.

"So, as I have spoken," Morris nervously bit into the truth. "Will you be of assistance… in the name of the nation, that is?"

The second part of his pray to Haym was rather tender for a gruff no-nonsense man. The tone made an impression upon Haym, which reminded him of the last time, he saw his father.

"I shall speak with Monsieur Luzerne," Haym said.

Morris definitely wanted quite more of a reassurance, but as he stared back into Haym's face, he detected a stoic surety that gave him reason for more than confidence. He knew Haym would in some way comply to the request.

"You are a good Jew," Morris said in a more complimentary way than the articulation sounded.

"Are all Jews not created equal?" Haym responded— not offended, but neither pleased.

"Oh, you will admit, will you not— that some are not as good as others," Morris said. "But I guess that's true of all peoples."

On Thursday, May 17th of 1781, General George Washington of the Continental Army and Jean-Baptiste Donatien de Vimeur, Comte de Rochambeau gathered at Joseph Webb's home in Wethersfield, Connecticut. This was proposed to be a meeting of the minds; a military conference by the respected commanders of the allied forces to devise what Washington hoped would be his finest hour.

The host, together with his business partner, John Carter, served as general contractors of nonmilitary supplies for all French Expeditionary forces in America. Just as the old saying goes, "An army marches on its stomach," Wadsworth and Carter's involvement was deemed crucial for the logistical support of any combined military operation. The room was large enough not to feel crowded but was well occupied with further distinctions of importance and rank. Lafayette, Alexander Hamilton, and Lieutenant Colonial Louis Le Bègue de Presle Duportail, one of the Continental Army's French volunteers— all who acted as interpreters— were engaged in this hastily devised conference. Washington, who had been briefly headquartered in Webb's home, had ready with him an eight-page outline for an operation against New York City in the hope that he could convince Rochambeau to agree to such an action before the onset of winter.

Once the salutations came to a close, the men took seats at an enormous rectangular oak table. Stately, with their backs as straight as personal power can display itself, Washington and Rochambeau sat on opposing ends. The French general opened the conversation by politely asking for paper and a quill. Joseph Webb was called into the room; he exited and returned with a fine feather quill, gold inkwell, and cotton-weaved paper. Rochambeau used the writing utensils to draft his questions in column form on the left-hand side of the paper. After each question he wrote in his native language, it would be translated and discussed among the Americans. Then, Duportail translated the American's answers in a column on the right-hand side of the page for Rochambeau to read. For Washington, the focus, purpose, and whole desired outcome of the conference was the achievement on, as he called it, an "operation against New York." He had been longing, yearning, and urging such an attack ever since the French forces had landed, three years ago. To the side of his mind devoted to military calculations, now was the time! The math promoted his thinking. For Clinton had dispatched forces to the Chesapeake in support of Cornwallis at York. Thus, Washington inferred by logic that less men concentrated on the defenses of the city made it vulnerable to a well-orchestrated combined Franco-American attack. However, the other side of his mind — the political and personal side — was even more adamant about taking the city. The British occupation of New York was a psychic thorn in Washington's side. The occupation — or recapture as the British saw it — was a conspicuous symbol of the continuing British presence in America. The Continental Army and America at large expected, almost demanded, an attack on the city. It was also the scene of the country's, as well as Washington's, most humiliating defeat. Its capture would serve as an act of redemption or psychic healing.

Rochambeau, on the other hand, was apprehensive of such an undertaking. He stressed and argued that even the combined Continental and French armies did not sufficiently outnumber the British forces defending the city, and if they did, which they didn't, any attack was doomed without corresponding naval support. So it was that the writing went back and forth before eventually Washington was forced to concede to Rochambeau's rationale for not attacking the British in New York before winter. Maybe next year with the arrival of the flowers in bloom, the renewal, rebirth, and regrowth of springtime, infantry reinforcements and an armada from France! However, Rochambeau did have a plan of attack, one in which he thought not only was possible but could decisively tip the scales of balance. He scribbled on his paper and the ink postulated the name: "York."

To Rochambeau's mind, he preferred to head south to conduct an operation against British forces in the Chesapeake Bay, where Cornwallis was camped. He contended that if the combined forces could lure Cornwallis's army into a general engagement, being the only British force not devoted to a purely defensive position, that they might yet inflict a decisive blow. Lafayette, who had shadowed Cornwallis agreed and noted that de Grasse and the naval support needed was already in the Chesapeake Bay. It was a matter of cutting off one-half of the head of the snake, right between the eyes!

Although Washington remained focused on New York, the side of his mind concerned with the personal and political found a tasty morsel to chew on in the idea of chasing Cornwallis out of his home state of Virginia. He recalled all-to-well the destruction — wrought first by British Major

General Leslie's invasion in 1780 and later by the inglorious Benedict Arnold's command. Furthermore, of the many bitter lessons he had learned as the Continental Army's general, one was that being flexible and deviating from a fixed option was more often an advantage than a disadvantage. Washington finally came to agree that York would be the target of their offensive.

As Washington and Rochambeau huddled over maps, the American general was concerned by the logistical realities of marching two combined armies five hundred miles in comparison to the shorter one hundred he was financially prepared for before. Washington's army was austere and skeletal compared to the French contingent. Strangely, the French and the English both brought their European sensibilities to this latest North American war. The French army was encumbered by a number of family members, civilian volunteers, employees, and contractors, both male and female, known collectively as "camp followers." To provide for his army's supply convoy, for example, Rochambeau contracted for fifteen brigades of wagons, or two hundred and ten vehicles, each drawn by six oxen. This required the hiring of twenty-nine men to act as drivers and conductors, plus fifteen cooks, most of them women. In contrast to the austere conditions in the Continental Army, where officers' servants were often drawn from the ranks, many of Rochambeau's officers personally employed theirs. Since these attendants had not been brought from Europe, American civilians were hired, a boom in the labor market. Each French general officer had ten or more servants, and even a lowly sub-lieutenant often kept two servants and three horses. This practice possibly added as many as 1,000 domestics, the equivalent of an infantry regiment, to the requirement for provisions. The additional horses may have raised the number of animals to 3,000 head, thereby increasing the requirements for forage.

Though Washington clearly saw the logic in pressing a campaign south, such a march would require even more logistics, which meant even more money than the money he already didn't have. Wadsworth and Carter were consulted as to what would be needed to reach York. They hurried their calculations on a five hundred mile wagon train and came up with a figure of: 2,000 horses, 2,000 oxen, while artillery required the acquisition of another 500 horses, 600 head of cattle at an average weight of 400 pounds, with another 400 head in reserve, 400 sheep every week for the soldiers' meat ration, 4,000 bushels of corn, 40 bushels of oats, 200 tons of hay, 50 tons of straw, and 100 cords of wood. This was an incredible expense and for Washington, it came down to expense. The general needed to know the financial cost. "$20,000" Wadsworth told him.

Washington sent an urgent dispatch to Philadelphia to fetch Morris. Morris arrived four days later. They combed over finances, or lack thereof. Washington pleaded with him to find a way to finance the campaign. Morris called for more time; the new bank he assured him would change their financial fortunes. For once, Morris' farsighted vision belied the present reality as Washington saw it. If the nation were indeed— for all intensive purposes— bankrupt, then it would be impossible to make it through the winter, let alone continue the fight beyond the year. Washington stressed the need to use this time on the offensive. To their credit, they both recognized that it might be, not only their last chance, but also their best chance. Yet, Morris came back to the same set of woeful facts. There were no funds left and no credit presently available. Washington was indifferent to the protestations and gave Morris a most eloquent and astute command, "Send for Haym Salomon."

***

XXVIII

YORK

"You will, by the dignity of your conduct, afford occasion for posterity to say, when speaking of the glorious example you have exhibited to mankind, had this day been wanting, the world had never seen the last stage of perfection to which human nature is capable of attaining."   *George Washington*

3 September 1781 - 7 a.m.
     Maj. I. Franks

      ...It is not common of me to meditate on time, but the abiding protracted labor of war is starting to feel long. The five years, the "It" of it all — manifestly constituted into shape, form, and sensation — It has been inflamed in pain around the British musket ball lodged into my thigh; It measures itself daily in the mercurial medicines I have been given for my acidity and alkalinity; It carries itself night after day and morning after night in the tensions and relaxation which the doctors have coveted with lettings of my blood; not to mention minutes in calomel and hours in jalap — I do not exaggerate that these five lingering years feel like but a short ten or twenty centuries! Of God and grace — of life and freedom — I cogitate; I will honor the Lord and my savior Jesus Christ and take no pride upon outfitting myself in the name of this cause; there can be no greater gratitude than mine to be nurtured in the bosom of their eternal grace with the blessing of their temporal purpose of life in the shadow of my self-induced impending deaths. Yet, I wonder through these artful strokes of the pen — I wander in focus to the prize — it is time eating away at me as the termite does the wood — it is time rendered in injury and course of disease throughout my body. I am sick but I shall will it away; I shall indubitably fight forward in steel requite. Who am I to live for anything but the glory of Christ and I question not his service to this engagement of conflict— we all look the same, the agents of heaven and hell, but our affinity and axis is in the shape of our hearts. Take heed to the need of strength— to be strong, and I take heed— wishing away sickness and wishing upon victory— in the name of America as host to the glory of the resurrection.

I suppose there are other things to mind than time, unfortunately weather is often one of them. It is exceedingly hot but they drive us harder than ever. The General— General Washington, I mean— informed us we were heading south several days ago, only he would not let us know where. I think he is diverting the whole of the company to make an assault on Cornwallis, though such an effort would counter his stated intention to us to reclaim New York. Ever so, we march somewhere— but who knows where? For my part, I had to see that the men had provisions! Again, this wasn't easy as my body sought to betray my orders. Though, I report my spirit took the day. Even so, the coffers have been empty of all but spiders! It has been getting harder to find suitable sustenance. Lo, it is beyond me to fail! I shall never fail the General nor the nation...

***

...it is hot; incessantly hot. The air, although we are within sight of the salty Atlantic, it is placid and rudely still. In impulse, I would give a years' salary for but a minute's breeze! The heat has been oppressive. Even upon evening, the setting of the sun brings but little relief. Morning, noon, and night, sweat courses its way from my brow to my cheeks, which invites a host of winged pests. We continue to dig in the best we can but the ground is soft and the water table high. Several lives lost over the past few days, mostly Negros. Two more, today. What tally in sum I couldn't be sure; officers don't keep count and our movements don't afford the luxury. There are two types of Negros, those who belong in paid service to the men and those who escape bondage by asylum under our ensign. The latter — we push them; as it is, threaten them a little, talk of returning' them back to their wretched masters! Yes, I tell you, they'll dig till they collapse. I take pity — drive into their undeveloped minds — better for them to die free than live as slaves! Do they think the Americans on their own will free them? Just as soon as they free their farm-raised swine instead of slaughtering them into the meat of bacon. I frequently tease them with the name James Somersett. But only I get the laugh. They know nothing.

On high orders from the Commander-in-chief, General Cornwallis has decided this is the best of all places to set camp. They say it is called "York," just as in Yorkshire. I say it should be called "Ague!" the home of the mosquito. Already since leaving Richmond, many men have contracted malaria and I have witnessed them treat these poor souls. Their blood is drained until they faint; at which point they are administered a dose of opium or mercury, which ever is more plentiful; and follow the regiment of treatment with the application of freshly killed pigeons tied to the soles of patient's feet. Still, I have yet to come upon a one who has been in remission by this highly artistic method of care. The only thing I have ever known to work is powdered bark from

Spanish controlled territories in the southern hemisphere, but at war with those Catholics, we cannot acquire it as such. - Further, it is rumoured that the enemy's "brain trust" is preparing to attack New York and our men are positioned as reinforcements. Delicious. It is a two-day march from where I scribble these thoughts. We will be ready!

Capt Lieut. John Royal

Ritchie, 42nd Highlanders - 3/9/81

***

6 September 1781 - 11 a.m.
    Maj. I. Franks

...Three days ago, we marched into Philadelphia. I would say our full company is a quarter over half of ten thousand— all are tired and hungry. Ashamed to say that the French, once again, outshone us; including many of our own ragged officers. They were almost twice as many of them than us and dressed finer than peacocks. They marched past the dignitaries of the Congress emboldened with a pomp and circumstance we never thought to have. I didn't know to laugh or be ashamed. They dressed in gleaming white broadcloths. Even their hats were decorated with pink and white plumes from what avian genus I am wholly unsure. They proudly stood in direct contrast to our unwashed clothes, faces, and souls...

***

...General Cornwallis was confident that General Clinton was on his way with reinforcements, but rumours abound and the truth, so to reveal itself, finally has. That dastardly de Grasse had arrived before him and Admiral Graves. General Cornwallis wasn't expecting this; none of us were! Graves fought gallantly, but the French fleet, so far, has proved impenetrable. Washington— a dullard by my humble estimation— did not attack New York! Common sense just as much military sense says that he has found out about our position and is planning an assault on our location. But General Cornwallis does not attribute common sense nor military sense to the American. However, if his Excellency General Clinton cannot get through de Grasse's defenses, this would prove fatal. I pray and demand of the good Lord that common sense does not fall upon his head as the apple did Newton's. God is good. But he might be better if he brought the fight to us. We are ready!

Capt Lieut. John
Royal Ritchie 42ⁿᵈ
Highlanders - 6/9/81

***

7 September 1781 - 6 a.m.
Maj. I. Franks

...The company made close to twenty-eight miles, today! General Washington is driving them hard, while being secretive as to where we go. By the compass, the needle points south, but how far? He knows something, only he isn't saying. He only asks incessantly if any word from de Grasse. The general personally wants to see any messenger in private! - Several men have complained of blisters on their feet, but most, like myself, remain silent and grumble beneath our breaths.

Visited relations; sister Rachel and brother-in-law, Haym. Their family has grown. Given the audience by request, I suggested to our General that he remember my brother-in-law as a potential source of additional income. Our stores are so low; it is questionable if we could sustain a mounted offensive. I doubt he will heed my suggestion, nevertheless, I felt it my duty to do likewise…

***

…Hardships turning in our favor. Fresh meat and vegetables from those in proximity to our camp. I led a variegated horde of Negros and we invaded every acre and farmhouse, and cellar like a swarm of locus. A mile east and a mile wide, it ground, the pens, and the storehouses are as clean as freshly falling snow. I predict war to end by consensus of population and one more good thrashing of Washington…

Capt Lieut. John
Royal

Ritchie, 42nd
Highlanders - 7/9/81

***

11 September, 1781 - 1 p.m.
    Maj. I. Franks

    …Rose an hour before the sun. General Washington rose just as early. We shared breakfast. There was a rosy glow about his countenance. The good man mentioned more than

once that he had not been home for six years —
that it had been so long since he last set foot on
such firm and familiar ground. As for the war, he
said little but did muse aloud of utilizing an
overland route to York. He seemed to be favoring
Sparta Road. He is anxious and desires a quick
strike. - Traveled on. Many near collapse; the
hottest sun one could ever know.

***

...laid the better part of the day to repairing
ammunition. Also washed and stitched waistcoat.
The night passed on the enjoyment of whiskey. It
had been hidden on the express agreement of
secrecy; under a Great Union. Those assigned to
the secret, myself, Alston, Innes, and McLean
enjoyed ourselves mightily...

Capt Lieut. John
Royal

Ritchie, 42nd
Highlanders - 10/9/81

***

12 September, 1781 – 1 p.m.
    Maj. I. Franks

…Pushing hard! Twenty-five to thirty miles a day! On the wane of summer's heat, I swear both man and beast are near collapse, moving as slowly as though walking on their knees. From the quarters of the general's staff, I listen closely and I understand General Washington is resolved to reach Captain Bartholomew. He examines papers, accounts, and maps and he waits on a dispatch from the Superintendent. Oft he uses his own finances to cure ills of a strategic nature. He outfits Intelligence. For the solider there is little more he can do than press the case to those who must press the case that we may all press on in battle. However, without forked tongue and the innocence of curious mind, is it far from ordering supreme education by passioned observation? Maybe I am dumb, but it seems that outside of the deathbed or the flowing loss of lifeblood, men of fashion meet in relaxed social settings that disregard the matter of fidelity to the vicissitudes; and bend the realities of events in a time warp of suspended substantiality. I wonder, did Charles I wake in mornings and admire the magnificence and vista of the sea from Hurst? Last eve, Washington surprised us all by receiving his staff at his own Mount Vernon home for the most splendid dinner. I swear, no expense was spared, even while there is no expense to spare below rank! Though, I was impressed with his hospitality. General Rochambeau arrived several hours later. It was then that we were finally told about the new objective- York! We make for York!

***

...Rainy. No movement still. More scouts have been sent into the villages to procure fresh provisions. Many countryside are Loyalists, but occasionally we deride those who counter in the suggestion that our rule is brute. Though— any that act with disdain— we have been told to ignore, unless accosted with insults— then we thrust a bayonet into their enthusiasm for haranguing...

Capt Lieut. John Royal

Ritchie, 42nd Highlanders - 11/9/81

***

13 September, 1781 – 8 p.m.

Maj. I. Franks

...I furthered correspondence from Comte de Grasse to the General. He stated a firm control of the Capes. The General was suddenly confident and praised the Frenchman as a commander that could seize the initiative! For the first time, I have heard words emitted from the General's lips that projected the prospects of victory. I admit that I do not possess the momentous vision— why should I? I see in small proportions, but very exact. Nonetheless, I am confident in our general and that his expectations will manifest. For the night, the battle cries are mute, but tomorrow we continue to march toward the defensives at York. I pray the Lord endows us with favor...

***

…The weather continues to dry. It is in the hushes but some are questioning encampment at this location. We are dug in and to move now would most surely place any approaching army at our backs. To the south we have protection; to the north they either wait ignorant that we've dug in or they march straight into our ready. From what we hear— spoken in musings— is that the "Terrible" has been scuttled. I never knew the old girl, but as I see it, a watery grave for her could portend trouble for us…

Capt Lieut. John
Royal

Ritchie, 42nd Highlanders - 13/9/81

***

…I write this day at night. It is cooler and the clouds have dissipated. About six o'clock this afternoon we were unarguably alarmed with Intelligence that the Americans are within sixteen miles of camp and moving closer. There we have it. The rebels hanker with fever to pursue this war to defeat on the field of battle. We'll give it to them; the righteousness of Lord and King demands the spilt hour of their reckless blood…

Capt Lieut. John
Royal

Ritchie, 42nd Highlanders - 14/9/81

***

30 September, 1781 – 3 p.m.
   Maj. I. Franks

...Incredible fortune! We marched two days from Williamsburg to York— exhausted— to discover that the Red Coats had already abandoned three of their forward works. This has rejuvenated the men! We quickly turned them. Our enemy's guns now face toward them with sun glinting promise and confidence! To see their shoddy defense— this may read scandalous, but I can only describe their handiwork to drunken women with hammers. Have we overestimated Cornwallis?

This has even raised my own spirits. Cornwallis has indeed placed himself in an unwise situation. To suggest the position is indefensible and they are posed only for defense would be akin to suggesting a bird is born of wings to fly! They hang like fruit, adjoined to the tree by the mere matter of time. If I didn't know better, I would think them amateurs, but I do know better, and my further evaluations will be done on patience and level headedness.   ...Salty— but I say, is our commander ungifted with the power of locomotion? The dilatory nature of our final preparations does not incite confidence. Why is General Cornwallis so calm? He does not seem to have any sense of urgency as others around him urge we construct a more gifted fortification.

***

The officers know we cannot hold for long — dare I say that all the men know as such, too? Does he not see our position is wholly swamp-ridden, mosquito-bitten and unacceptable? It as though he is resolved to retreat into the ranks of the navy. The rebels have heartily begun digging trenches on the slopes around our position and we hear them with nighttime vermin-like intensity in all that they do. Without a meaningful shot we have ceded the higher ground. The best tiding I can commit to draft is that the clouds are not numerous and those that drift across the moon are diaphanous. The bright light slows their progress and the opportunity of glister and shadow has privileged us with wounding several as they raised their shovels...

Capt Lieut. John Royal

Ritchie, 42nd Highlanders - 30/9/81

***

7 October 1781 – 1 p.m.   Maj. I. Franks

...I stared with disgust at the Meteor today — it seems obscene to me now, that Union Flag in the canton — flying over York — what right do they to the liberty of men? A parent retains but the right of child until they are a child no more. Where does the Magna Carta derive its powers but on the frail morality of law? Such a tenuous proposition to say the least. We derive our claim to liberty on the basis of divine authority. So it is divinity, which separates us from the English. When I returned from the reconnaissance this morning, it gave me pride to gaze upon the blue background and six-pointed stars fluttering in the night's air. I promote the understanding that it is a direct symbol of Heaven.

My health is failing me. The wounds throughout my body swell and inflame in the humidity. My ink is also running short, as is my paper but the good news is that we are preparing to mount a full assault; I advise the devil that he is not stronger than eternal fate...

***

...I have come to an intersection of cruel honesty and cautious pessimism by way of efficacious disillusionment. Suffice it to say — we are in a sorry state of physical and moral ill repair. My conviction of our readiness has dissipated by virtue of the panorama lent my mind through the optical lens of my eyes. Per order of Lord Murray, I set about the camp today examining high and low, every inch of the trenches and the fortifications. The astonishing amount of gambling, drinking, and cavorting with all the camp's prostitutes struck me as having increased more than at any time during our campaign. This is not to forget that many of our soldiers are reduced to wearing cowhide tied on their feet for shoes. The surety by which I composed prior entries was founded on our having dislodged Lafayette's forces and pursuing the initiative up the James. To our disappointment we were never able to engage the French coward in full battle. But now as I have come around the entire camp, I am appalled at the size of our entourage. We have a thousand of black followers of the flag. I have none, just being of a minor rank, but now that I count on my own hands, I claim across this chronicle that it appears, nearly every soldier, even those of my rank have a Negro carrying provisions whilst the officers all have three or four doing such duty! That does not even count the one or two Negresses for cook and maid. We have lost all discipline and resemble more a horde of wandering Arabians than an English army. I also hear that Cornwallis himself is sick, so sick he does little to meditate on tactics. I have never been so afraid as a solider or felt such little time to correct a mistake...

Ritchie, 42nd
Highlanders - 7/10/81

Capt Lieut. John
Royal

***

...The Americans have surrounded our position, but it appears that the General has been correct to assume that the enemy has no artillery. Not a single cannon has been fired from the hills above. Soon, we are told that General Clinton will reinforce us. The word is out that we are affording Negro runaways with fair wages and sustenance. They are flooding our banks, though many arrive with smallpox and die before their human good is exhausted. In Portsmouth, they struggle with Cornwallis order to O'Hara to care for sick negros and properly feed them though it is of no use to their fate. Then, he is to forward march and reinforce our encampment. However here, I must say, our general puts those of strong negro constitutions to well use. They are a second division within our own division— foraging more than they consume. Our stocks and supplies of horses, meal, feed, and provisions is higher than ever has been. If this is to be a siege, than we are well afforded against the rigors of time, assuming our population does not swell beyond our means. Be that as it may, all able-bodies are clasped by the hand at our redoubts, yet disease has stricken us with a labor shortage. It feels as though the skies above us are gray and over the hills where the Americans hold claim, the sun shines...

Ritchie, 42nd
Highlanders - 8/10/81

Capt Lieut. John
Royal

***

9 October, 1781 – 6 p.m.
Franks

Maj. I.

...We stand, forty-one cannons in place— the sentence of death awaits— the throaty announcement from the raven, the pet of the Grim Reaper must warble through the anticipating nerves of our old brothers. We wait only for the General to throw his arm down and shout out his command to fire! Let us stand nervously, let us tremble a bit, we bring the destruction of bodies, souls, and tyranny in the path of man's advancement! So righteous am I in this statement, I forget the shivers of sickness that accompany my breath. We have not traveled this distance only to stand idle! But wait... the command to fire has indeed been given!

***

...Above me is the most terrifying and yet brilliant sky. So it has been day and night for over forty-eight hours. We are being besieged by civilians huddled under the cliff face at the edge of the river and rushing to our defenses at the slightest length of silence between canon fire. I have not seen for myself, but it is going down the line that Cornwallis has moved his headquarters into a cave. Under rock he is saved from the carnage— the ships sunk in the river, the houses on fire, and piles of mutilated bodies and scattered body parts that silently speak to each of us still alive to witness to look upon them, "Are you next?"

Capt Lieut. John
Royal

Ritchie, 42nd
Highlanders - 11/10/81

14 October, 1781 – 10 p.m.
Maj. I. Franks

...Five days and the flat landscape 'round York is
riddled into craters so deep, one could bury a
stable of horses! Today we stormed the redoubts
and chopped through the defenses! The reports
sounded like a parade of a rapid double-time
band of drums! I am overwhelmed with
excitement! The General believes they will attempt
to use the cover of darkness to evacuate on boats
down river! But no! He has no intention of letting
Cornwallis slip through his grasp! He has sent
word to Admiral de Grasse to block off the River!
Cornwallis has no option but to fight! From where
I stand, the forces of providence are fixed under
our flag. I stand in the Virginia of the United
Colonies, just above earth and just below
heaven...

***

15 October 1781 – 10 a.m.
Maj. I. Franks

...4,000 rounds of shelling exploded at their feet,
in their ears, and before their eyes! Now we curse
them with the otherworldly echo of dampen
communion. Redoubts captured; let them chew on
the fat of that.

My ears ring and my heart still pounds. I am exhausted with excitement and the solemn fact of the flies I see buzzing over their camp, like some Biblical prophecy and the slaughtered and bloated horse carcasses floating in the river, drifting with the tide, bumping against the shattered hulks of British ships. I see bands of Negros in British uniforms running from the camp; many appeared disfigured— smallpox for sure. They should know they run back toward their enslavement but I guess they run blindly toward the sun. The intensity of my excitement is admittedly muted. The beautiful turned to the ugly; the smell of victory turned into the stench of the enemy's defeat; the music of reports quiet to the roaring sound of pain. The garrison burns. I wish to close my eyes and it all burn to ashes. Though, I suppose I would still smell what I seek not to see anymore.

***

…We rot. The influx of people from Portsmouth put a more terrible strain on our supplies than I could have ever imagined. It came down to a diet of putrid ships meat and wormy biscuits. In turn, we became weakened by the hard labor of reconstructing blasted fortifications with one arm and firing upon a motivated enemy with the other. The surgeons are the busiest of us all and the rivers of blood are pink instead of read, a sure sign of anemia. I am waiting to die. What more is there to do? We are all waiting to die, the only question is how? Typhoid? Smallpox? Malaria? Each has reached epidemic proportions. We are hemmed in on both sides by both the French and the Americans. We over 20,000 deep in breath and heartbeat but I estimate no more than 3,000 of us can still pull a trigger. Clinton has never relieved our suffering and a partial retreat is unlikely to succeed. Our provisions are now almost exhausted and our ammunition totally. God help us, finally…

Capt Lieut. John Ritchie, 42nd Royal Highlanders - 15/10/81

***

XXIX

NATION

"'Tis done. We have become nation."   Benjamin Rush

Pierre-Augustin Caron de Beaumarchais was born Pierre-Augustin Caron. He was French. He was also an adroit arms dealer, an artful diplomat, a brilliant financier, an incredible inventor, an accomplished musician, a famous playwright, a courageous publisher, a spearheading revolutionary twice over, a successful satirist, a fugacious spy, and a born watchmaker. Yet, of all these qualities and vocations, he was above all: a catalyst of destiny. His presence on earth served as the single most important incitement, which brought into existence the United States of America.

Of the two hundred and thirty-nine battles, skirmishes, invasions, captures, sieges, and expeditions that define the American Revolution, the United States was only involved in one additional conflict after the Siege of York. It took place six days after Cornwallis surrendered to Washington — the Battle of Johnstown; in the middle of New York State was another decisive American victory. For the British, the American Revolution didn't end with the Americans. They would be engaged for two more years and thirty-seven subsequent battles against the Spanish, French, Dutch, and the Indians of India, on every continent except Australia and Antarctica.

On September 3rd, 1783 the British officially had had enough. In the Hotel d'York in Paris, France, the Treaty of Paris was signed by David Hartley, John Adams, Benjamin Franklin, and John Jay. The two page document spelled out ten key points and began with an encouraging preface which declared in short that the combatants: "forget all past misunderstandings and differences" and seek to "secure to both perpetual peace and harmony." The summary of the ten articles of peace were as follows:

1. Acknowledging the United States to be free, sovereign and independent states, and that the British Crown and all heirs and successors relinquish claims to the Government, propriety, and territorial rights of the same, and every part thereof;

2. Establishing the boundaries between the United States and British North America;
3. Granting fishing rights to United States fishermen in the Grand Banks, off the coast of Newfoundland and in the Gulf of Saint Lawrence;
4. Recognizing the lawful contracted debts to be paid to creditors on either side;
5. The Congress of the Confederation will "earnestly recommend" to state legislatures to recognize the rightful owners of all confiscated lands "provide for the restitution of all estates, rights, and properties, which have been confiscated belonging to real British subjects (the Loyalists)";
6. United States will prevent future confiscations of the property of Loyalists;
7. Prisoners of war on both sides are to be released and all property left by the British army in the United States unmolested (including slaves);
8. Great Britain and the United States were each to be given perpetual access to the Mississippi River;
9. Territories captured by Americans subsequent to treaty will be returned without compensation;
10. Ratification of the treaty was to occur within six months from the signing by the contracting parties.

In point of fact, the terms of the signed treaty, which was extremely generous to the victorious new nation, was negotiated the year before. In April of 1782, Adams, Franklin, and Jay acting as the plenipotentiaries representing the Congress of the United States were in Paris to discuss with representatives of the King, the formal surrender of Great Britain and a corresponding instrument of peace. With the thrashing at York, the tide of the war for the British more than proverbially shifted — it was simply over. All that would be left was a surrender ceremony. And, said ceremony took place two days later. Cornwallis, humiliated, cowardly, and downright unprofessional, did not attend citing an undiagnosed ill feeling in his stomach — otherwise known as "defeat." Sent in his place, his second-in-command, General O'Hara, first tried to surrender to the Rochambeau who directed the British officer to Washington who in turn refused the indignity of rank and directed him to General Lincoln. As O'Hara handed Lincoln his sword, the British band played the most appropriate of tunes: "The World Turned Upside Down."

Ultimately, Cornwallis surrendered 7,087 officers and a further 840 sailors from the British fleet. All were made American held prisoners of war, including General Cornwallis.

Richard Oswald was selected to open negotiations with the contingent of anxious Americans. He appeared to many in the British brain-trust to be an excellent choice because he came with the resume of having lived in Virginia, was thought to possess a philosophic disposition similar to Franklin, and was known to share equivalent views to that of the world-famous opinionated elder statesman. As a matter of fact, Franklin would later remark that Oswald was a man with an "Air of great simplicity and honesty." A backhanded compliment indeed for a man who carried himself with an air of great profundity and self-appointed virtue. As far as the British were concerned, Oswald was the right man for the enterprise. However, he turned out to be altogether the wrong man for job.

As is often the case when one shines the light of history through the glass prism of time, all the spectrums of intrigue reveal themselves rather neatly in a stacked sequence. The end of the American Revolution is usually understood through the small particle of capitulation by Cornwallis — at what became known as "Yorktown" — instead of the international conflict the war had grown into for the British Empire. In light of their humiliating vanquishment at York, the leaders in Parliament decided that the offensive campaigns in North America required a more modest approach. They elected to cease any counter-offensive actions from New York or other bastions they held such as Savannah in favor of whipping up on the friends of America in locale where they may have overshot their ambitions. For France, Spain, the Dutch, and England, the war had widened beyond the American struggle for independence. The main reason these European countries entered on the American side was to weaken England and lap up spoils from all four corners of the world where they thought she would naturally thin her defenses. Through the fall and following winter, British colonies in the Caribbean fell to enemy forces, as did Minorca. With anti-war forces at home growing in power, Lord North's government fell in March of 1782 and was replaced by one led by Lord Rockingham. He was sympathetic to the colonial positions on taxes, which served as the spark that ignited the war. He believed he could put the genie back in the bottle by repealing all the unpopular Parliamentary acts and still keep the colonies with the British spear of influence and territory. This was the political sea change that Benjamin Franklin had been waiting for!

Upon learning that North's government had fallen, Franklin, still in Paris, wrote to Rockingham expressing a willingness and even a desire to begin peace negotiations. Rockingham faced a complex dilemma. He was willing to cease all military action against the Americans. However, they were allied with the French and the Spanish, whom he wished to crush wholesale! One fact appeared too obvious— to continue any conflict against the Americans for the piece of the pie that was the thirteen colonies, jeopardized the whole pie that was the rest of the world. Rockingham understood that peace was a necessity that had to be made sooner or later; he elected sooner. However, from Franklin, there was a catch; he made it clear that the terms of the United States' alliance with France prevented the making of any peace without French approval. On its face, this would be unacceptable to the British and contrary to the territorial claims they still held on the colonies. It meant only one thing, that the United States were no longer a British subject but a full-fledged nation. Rockingham, as representative of Parliament and the King, took the position of flatly denying the acknowledgement of American independence as a precondition for beginning talks. However, in truth, they were just trying to buy time.

The English reluctance to actively participate in negotiations with the Americans under the auspices of their right to exist was due in large part to their knowledge that France was experiencing financial difficulties and a sliver of hope that military fortunes could be reversed. As is common in diplomatic circles, the stated position is belied by the actual actions. Officially there were no talks between the American delegation and Great Britain; but in actuality, Oswald was sent to meet with the Americans while Thomas Grenville was dispatched to begin talks with the French. The negotiations between Oswald and Franklin, Jay, and Adams— as would be expected— proceeded slowly, because the foundation of their understanding and relationship toward one another was in dispute. Oswald was there more as a ploy and the Americans had already made their stance quite clear, that without recognition of their sovereignty, there was nothing to discuss. As fate would have it, the mastermind, Rockingham, died in July of 1782 and Lord Shelburne became the head of the British government. Despite the fact that the British had all but conceded the colonies, the tide of war was turning back in their favor in many parts of the world. Now, the French Army outside of the United

States were reeling. Therefore, they stalled for time as they coordinated an effort with Spain to capture the continental jewel of Gibraltar from the British. Additionally, the French sent a secret envoy to London as there were several issues, including fishing rights on the Grand Banks, on which they disagreed with their American allies. The French and Spanish were also concerned about American insistence on the Mississippi River as a western border. In September, Jay learned of the secret French mission and wrote to Shelburne detailing why he should not be influenced by the French and Spanish. In this same period, Franco-Spanish operations against the English in Gibraltar were failing, leaving the French to begin debating method of exiting all the conflicts they had engaged themselves in.

While all parties stalled for time, bickered among themselves, and positioned their arguments via copious correspondence— by sheer chance General Washington entered into the fray in a most unexpected way. In corresponding with Washington, Franklin became aware of a letter Shelburne had written to the general before he was made Prime Minister, which conceded the point of independence. This was a bombshell! It meant that Shelburne was simply carrying the old political water of Rockingham and not speaking his own mind— he didn't believe in his own lies— they were political policy, slants to jostle position, a knowingly untenable stance of kabuki theater. Again, the Americans got lucky and were ready to exploit the opportunity.

The next time Oswald came around to the Hotel d'York to discuss the future between England and America, he found Franklin, Adams, and Jay, armed with the guilty truth on a piece of parchment signed by the man who was the Prime Minister. Oswald and Shelburne found themselves cornered by honor and the truth. Finally, the issue of independence was laid to rest in the favor of the Americans. A new spirit grew over the triumvirate and real negotiations began in earnest.

Oswald and Shelburne proved to be pushovers. They fought for virtually nothing in return for granting the United States independence without another shot being fired. By November, Thomas Jefferson had joined the American delegation and each article had been drafted; alone, this peace treaty would have ranked Adams, Franklin, Jay, and Jefferson in the pantheon of men through one of the greatest feats in diplomatic history, if this was their singular worldly contribution in their lifetimes. Thankfully for America and the ages, this birth certificate of the nation might have ranked as one of the smaller triumphs of these three great Founding Fathers. However, there was one more surprise in store.

In late November, Henry Laurens unexpectedly arrived at Oswald's Paris residence where the two sides were finalizing the treaty; two days before the preliminary articles were to be signed, he more or less, stuck his head into the room and joined the negotiations — he was after all, the American minister to the Netherlands. Laurens was a born and raised South Carolinian who was a delegate to the Continental Congress. Nevertheless, Oswald's acquiescence to this rather spontaneous inclusion owed more to a friendship and his own financial entanglements in South Carolina than to diplomatic pressure.

Laurens and Oswald went back a ways. The year before when Laurens was held in the Tower of London, having been captured at sea, it was Oswald who furnished the bail for his release. Laurens was significant in negotiating Dutch support for the war. On his return voyage to Amsterdam — at the insistence of Robert Morris — to plead for more money, his ship was intercepted by the British Navy. Laurens had on his person the article of the U.S.-Dutch treaty and various dispatches. He hurriedly tossed them in the water but the British retrieved them and the next thing the Dutch knew, war was declared against them! As for Laurens, he was transported to the Tower to be tried for treason. However, Oswald and Laurens went much further back than the year before. Oswald owned a slave factory on Bance Island, in Sierra Leone, Africa and Laurens had acted as the agent for his slave cargo in Charleston. In these facts laid the reason why Oswald was the wrong man for the British job of negotiating peace with America. Oswald had his own post-war plans for America. He intended to become a plantation owner in South Carolina on land Oswald had recently purchased from Laurens. The British negotiator had a stake in America being as strong and prosperous as it could be following the scars of war.

On November 29th, on the eve of signing the preliminary agreement, a hastily written amendment was scribbled in the margin of Article Seven, to prohibit "carrying away any Negroes or other property of the American Inhabitants." This was Laurens' doing. Up to that point the contentious issues had been nothing greater than fishing rights. None of the four other American negotiators had thought it necessary to include a clause about runaways. To Jay, Adams, and Franklin, they were shocked and amazed that Oswald agreed without pause. As a matter of fact, they were prepared to chastise Laurens and remove him from the talks if this sudden power play proved impassioned. What the addition to the article meant was that every former slave which ran under the British colours for safety and freedom would have to be forcibly returned or resold on the market as the British withdrew from the United States. It made the British complicit in the inhuman act of enslaving a man as property. This would end up being the most despised characteristic for the British Army and public of the whole affair that was the war.

In the end, the treaty marked not only the beginning of the United States but the end of the political career of Shelburne and Oswald. Richard Oswald was sacked before the official signing, replaced by David Hartley to do the thankless honors. He never made it to South Carolina. He died two years later, in disgrace. Shelburne was removed from office just as swiftly and the Duke of Portland succeeded him. The only thing Benjamin Franklin asked for and didn't get was— Canada.

***

To what degree does unprincipled or less than virtuous motivation cloud history's judgement of right or courageous action? This would be a question in the case study of Beaumarchais. The man who wrote arguably two of the most famous literary works of history, "The Barber of Séville "and "The Marriage of Figaro," began his life in Paris as the only boy out of the six children of André-Charles Caron, a well-respected watchmaker, and the former Louise-Nicole Pichon. As a child he proficiently learned a trifecta— the violin, the harp, and the flute. However, his father had already mapped out his destiny— or so he thought— the moment it was announced that his fourth child born was a boy. Caron, as he was still known then, by birth was to become a watchmaker, and this he did. He absorbed all he could from his master father and showed a likewise skill by earning a patent from the French Academy of Sciences for his invention, a new form of escapement mechanism, which became a standard innovation to new watches. He was only twenty-two. Yet, Caron was a dreamer, a schemer, a go-getter, a bon vivant. He wanted fame, fortune, title, prestige, recognition, and glory— to name a few of the opulent adjectives in life. He assumed such would elude him if he were to remain a simple watchmaker. Consequently, his opening step into the dance of self-construction and identity— the venture into the creation of something grander than his father's bestowal— was a passionate marriage to

Madeleine Francquet. She was a frequent customer— wealthy, a widow from an officer of the court, ten years older than Caron, and overly flattered by his handsome features and gregarious nature which was trimmed in encomiastic flirtation. They married, but within a year she died suddenly of typhoid. The tragedy left Caron not so much heartbroken as it did somewhat well to do. He wasn't rich and her lawyers who never approved of the marriage, did their best to cheat him out of what they could, yet still they could not deny his assumption of the small estate they lived on, from which he took his new magniloquent name: Beaumarchais.

Beaumarchais quickly set about remaking himself. He was given an audience at court and after sagaciously selling a watch to the mistress of Louis XV; he gained the king's attention, trust, and favor. Louis made the attentive watchmaker the music teacher to his daughters. However, for Beaumarchais, being viewed with suspicion by the other members of the entourage for his lavish fashion of wearing naked ambition— intrigues, adventures, and petty lawsuits quickly followed. The main problem was that Beaumarchais was arrogant, indignant, and tactless in his affairs with those he perceived as being critical of his avaricious enterprise of self-promotion. In one case, which demonstrates his refined lack of subtlety and dash of moral equivalence— he lost a suit in court, but instead of lawfully making restitution, he made a stink. He accused his opponent of bribing the judge even more generously than he had himself! Yet, being the type of person whose nature it was to look disparagingly upon those he considered inconsequent to the designs of his ends; and to look up with an ingratiating saccharine grace upon those whom he perceived could greatly benefit him— Louis' opinion of Beaumarchais remained high.

The next eleven years of Beaumarchais' life was dramatic and sensational. Beaumarchais was talented, but he wasn't necessarily a genius. What he was, was a dreamer, an opportunist, a hustler, a squeaky wheel, and fated for importance. His fundemental ambitions were wealth and fame. Seizing upon an opportunity while the music teacher for the Royal family, he resigned, went abroad and became rich. In his return to France, he prevailed through a series of unjust court cases, which made him a celebrity. Then, his talent for art brought him fame through his popular plays. In spite of the good fortune— as with everything in regard to Beaumarchais— for every bit of sweet there was equal taste of bitter. He spent his earnings as quickly as he made them. His plays were eventually banned. His civil rights stripped and his efforts to attain a position in government was repeatedly denied. Finally, the time that no man knows when and if it will come— the foreordained hour of divine aegis— arrived for Beaumarchais in the form of the request for his presence before the Foreign Minister, Charles Gravier, comte de Vergennes.

***

"… Bon jour," Vergennes said, as Beaumarchais approached him among the citrus trees in one of the Versailles gardens.
Vergennes wanted to begin their meeting informally, comfortably, and unofficially. He arranged for Beaumarchais to be brought to him on a morning between two orange trees. When Beaumarchais reached Vergennes he held his hand out but Foreign Minister simply gestured from him to sit.
"Vous êtes l'auteur" Vergennes asked.
"Oui, Le Barbier."
Vergennes had his man; he stood up—
"Comme."
The two men began walking; plied to their senses was the magnificent aroma of orange blossoms. They spoke for over and hour— Vergennes lead the course of the conversation and focused it mainly on Beaumarchais' recent espionage work as an agent for the king— tracking down a crossing dressing enemy of the state. Then, the trek circled until it ended in Vergennes chambers in the south wing of the palace. Once Vergennes closed the door behind them, he drew his breath and plunged into the heart of the matter—
"Do you have the letter?" Vergennes asked.
Beaumarchais revealed a rolled parchment from the leg of his trousers. Vergennes quickly looked over it.
"Exactly as you wrote— good— very good."
"And, I inform you that I have met with the man," Beaumarchais said.
Vergennes was a bit shocked, even unnerved, which Beaumarchais could see and intended to quickly reassure him—
"The Mayor of London arranged our encounter."
John Wilkes, the Mayor of London, was a radical and no friend of King George. He openly mocked the monarch and Vergennes knew that Wilkes' involvement meant there was no double-cross involved.

"You have read my report, his name is Arthur Lee, and I agree that if we promote the disillusionment of the Colonies that the cost to England will render her like a damaged hull in the middle of the sea!"
Vergennes looked deeply into Beaumarchais, sizing up the man as one would a slave with interest to purchase. Beaumarchais volleyed between transfixed and embarrassed at the depth of Vergennes' penetrating attention. Finally —

"Yes, I have read your reports," Vergennes stated as he started his descent into the intended purpose of coming together. "They are well-written, concise, detailed, and accurate. It is exactly what I am looking for in a special agent."

"'Special?'"
Thanks to your correspondence and their concluding passages, I am in the market for something else in an agent, something unique."

"'Unique?'"

"Beaumarchais, you are an enlightened and prudent man, you know men, and I do not doubt that you would make a good bargain."

"A 'bargain?'"

"It is your good fortune that this American has reached out to you. For I doubt that another among the king's agents would have written such an insightful and compelling argument —"

"Why, thank you, Minister — I beg you to understand that the Colonies are a simmer — which shall boil — but I tell you that London is hotter still! There is little consensus as to the right action toward the Americas — they cannot decide between the carrot and the stick. And, we monsieur, to our advantage, can decide it for them!"

"You are a champion of liberty?" Vergennes asked him.
Before Beaumarchais could absorb the offsetting question and formulate an answer he hoped would please the minister, Vergennes spoke for him —

"Of course you are, if it serves your own liberties."
Beaumarchais didn't know if to agree or disagree and so he simply smiled along with the cagy old man.

"I — we, are exceedingly concerned to find the breech between England and America has widened. But, when I read your series of suggestions — let us call them more properly, "alarms" — which I did so privately — be aware that no one else as read them —

"Oui, monsieur," Beaumarchais said as an unspoken promise of silence.

"Without passion, mind you— I analyzed every word— you were urging that a commitment to the Americans would encourage them the encouragement to strike at the links of their bondage. Poetry— it was poetry. Yet, it lacked one thing—"

"And, what was that?"

"A plan."

In the silence of being confronted with his insufficiency, Beaumarchais tried to make up for it by reiterating this perspective—

"It is true, I have not conceived of a means to answer the American's needs but I say that such a vast and incredible nation as America is invincible, especially having behind her as much territory as is necessary for military retreats, even when the English have seized all their coastline, which is a long way from happening. All intelligent people are therefore convinced in England that the colonies are lost for the metropole and this is also my opinion— as you have studied."

"Fear nothing, for now, you have convinced me, Beaumarchais, you have brought me to see events anew."

The minister rolled up the letter from Lee and indicated to Beaumarchais that he intended to keep it. The agent couldn't protest but agreed nonetheless. Suddenly, there was a feeling of emptiness for Beaumarchais— was that all there was? Was it that he was being dismissed for having a vision but no proposal of action? Was this meaningless tête-à-tête the whole reason why he was called?

"But, Minister, if I may— what more might you require from a man like me?"

"Beaumarchais, I do require something from you: something incredible character— that only a man like you can accomplish."

"I assure you that I am well-versed, trained, and fit for many tasks!"

"Ah, but a man like you is best at, is truly what we need—"

"Oui, but what do you presume I am best at, monsieur?"

"Why naturally, being someone other than your real self."

Beaumarchais was stunned by the astute observation, insulted by the recommendation, and proud all at the same time. Nevertheless, he was ready to agree to anything Vergennes suggested.

"Whatever is bad for England, is good for France— this operation must have essentially in the eyes of the British Government, and even in the eyes of the Americans, the aspect of an individual speculation, to which we are strangers... I will give you, secretly, a million livres. You will endeavor to persuade the Court of Spain to unite in giving you another. With the two millions, you shall found a great commercial establishment, and at your own risk and peril you shall furnish to America arms and everything else necessary to sustain war. Our arsenals will deliver to you arms and munitions, but you shall pay for them. You will not demand money of the Americans for they have none— but you can ask return in their staple products."

Beaumarchais stood unsure what to say. He was being asked to run a shadow arms company in which he would either receive all the credit or be sliced by the razor sharp risks of espionage conducted on the highest level of government sanction— it was walking on a high wire without a pole or a net. However, the glorious possibilities that rested in success— the probable government advancements, the prestige, and the power, all flashed across his mind! Vergennes patiently waited for him to speak, for he knew what Beaumarchais was thinking— he could read uncomplicated minds as easily as a pamphlet. Finally, Beaumarchais' eyes focused as though threading a needle, and he exclaimed in epiphany—

"My Lord, to combine public interest and private advantage— is truly a master stroke of morality!"

Roderigue Hortalez and Company would be the name of the fictitious business Beaumarchais ran under the secret directive of Vergennes— before the Declaration of Independence, before the victory at Saratoga, this was the lifeline for the United States. The company was Vergennes brainchild but it was born from the seed of Beaumarchais' enthusiasm and germinated in his pleas from London.

This was Beaumarchais' finest hour. He organized the clandestine logistics, the network, the shipping, and the subterfuge with the flare of a maestro. He moved from the continent of Europe clothing, tents, mortars, bombs, gunpowder, cannon balls, cannons, muskets, and even men through the Dutch island of St. Eustatius. The administrative operation of the company conducted business through the Connecticut merchant Silas Deane, who was sharing a covert trade agency with Thomas Morris the half-brother of Robert Morris. The French did everything they could without openly supporting the Americans. Washington could not have taken Boston without Beaumarchais. Morris could not have rallied and gathered subscriptions in time without Beaumarchais. The United States of America could not have fought the British toe-to-toe with Beaumarchais.

From Annapolis, Maryland, the Congress of the Confederation—which had fled Philadelphia afraid of the soldiers marching in demand of their backpay—ratified the Treaty of Paris on January 14th, 1784. Great Britain did likewise on April 9th, 1784. Signed and ratified versions of the document were exchanged in Paris on May 12th, 1784. The British troops withdrew from New York in December of 1783 and sailed home. George Washington disbanded the Continental Army and intended to retire to his plantation. So it was, that by the civil tip of the pen, albeit from the conquest of the rifle, overnight, the United States of America was larger, at peace, and independently free. Four million people strong, the country expanded north as well as aggressively westward; more than doubling its size—a new Antebellum South emerged and the Ohio Valley was open for business. The treaty fixed the boundaries of the United States quite neatly to the topographical geography. In the Northeast, the line extended from the source of the St. Croix River due north to the highlands separating the rivers flowing to the Atlantic from those draining into the St. Lawrence River, thence with the highlands to lat. 45°N, and then along the 45th parallel to the St. Lawrence. From there the northern boundary followed a line midway through contiguous rivers and lakes, including the Great Lakes to the northwest corner of the Lake of the Woods, thence due west to the sources of the Mississippi—which were not then known. The Mississippi, south to latitude 31°N, was made the western boundary. On the south, the line followed the 31st parallel east to the Chattahoochee River and its junction with the Flint River, then took a straight line to the mouth of the St. Marys River, and from there to the Atlantic. The one concession due the British in these boundaries was that the navigation of the Mississippi was to be open to the citizens of both nations.

By the closing months of 1783 and into the next year, the Stamp Act, the Intolerable Acts, and the word "Colonies" was all but forgotten. However, the financial state of the country continued to decline. The currency was stabilized but worthless. The Articles of Confederation, which the government was operating by, still gave no power to the Continental government to tax. The thirteen separate states united under the cause of revolution now turned their causes inward and began fighting amongst themselves like irascible neighbors. Furthermore, they all neglected to pay their portion of the federal debt, leaving the Congress to begin a debate about ceasing interest payments to France and Spain—

Spain especially because they still refused to recognize the United States as an independent nation due to boundary disputes. The Dutch, however, would be spared the inconvenience and default in the likelihood that they would loan them more money still. Yet, for all the little aches and pains of birth, the country itself, was wondrously jubilant, filled with pride, and unquestionably the master of its fate.

***

Haym brought in the news that the war was over in his own individual way— with unembellished prayer. It was November 26th, 1783, and a broadside was posted outside of the London Coffee House. It announced the signing of the Paris Peace Treaty and a full text of the America's conquest. Upon hearing and then seeing— Haym, in the winter afternoon, removed himself from the cafe and left Macrae to the unfinished business of the morning; then he excused himself from his home, leaving Rachel with the children, and made… his wintery way to the synagogue. In the mile that he traversed, it appeared that crowds and enthusiasm had gather momentum— fireworks and spontaneous dancing in the street greeted him with greater intensity block after block. Finally though, he was alone— in the temple— alone with YHWH. It was a sober intimate moment, flecked with details in bits of memory that a man acquires when he has lived a life mostly in lone struggle. He whispered in the slightest breath and strained to crush a tear welling in his eye.

"I did this for you— just as you did it through me," he said to his Lord.

"Thank you… thank you… thank you."

"Bless this country, oh Father, please bless this country—"

"I did— did I not?— I did, Father— as you required of me?"

"I do not seek to claim credit. I seek only that which is mine by nature and to bask in understanding."

"Is this for us? Is this land, this country— is it for us?"

"Let it be for us, the Jews, let it be for once, for us— I speak again— let it be for all displaced— for all."

"But, Father, but is this! — Is this the land… this country… this United States… is this the land of the milk and honey… for Your people, Father— Your people?"

"Is this the work you called me to?"

Haym had paused between each question and without a word or a feeling from God; he spoke his next anxious question. However, after his last, a tincture of sound, a titillation of feeling pulsed through his body with the surge of a tiny voltage of electricity; and he heard or felt what seemed like the taciturn word of the Lord.

He slowly brought himself from his standing position in which his eyes peered up and unhooked the mangled hinges that connected the various parts of his splintered body, to a prostrate position level to the floor. He lent his ear to the carpet as though the sound of holiness from above and within was rising up from below the floorboards. In the normal hour he felt painfully uncomfortable in his frail misshapen frame — an energized unlimited spirit being shackled by a debilitated and feeble construct. Yet, suddenly, he felt himself leave his body. It was as though he could discern his clothes hanging more freely and the weight of his aches and pains dissolve into a suspended animation, which held him in a pool of weightless purity. Though, as it was, he gently shook inside, a fearful shake — an overpowering sense, as one might experience in the presence of something so large and awe inspiring that one's own significances renders their defenses defenseless. The quivering of his heart, lungs, liver, loose bones, and bodily cavities contributed to a subconscious sense of vulnerability that was scarier than if all the guns of the world were simultaneously pointing at him in anger. However, just as magnificently, a supernatural warmth and soothing sensation like that of hot cider swallowed into the hollow inside of a cold body, wrapped around his aura; and his exterior self stayed firm and unrattled. There he was, his stomach pressed to the floor, fallen in the breath of the Almighty; his perceptual mind slowly processed the communication with a bittersweet assimilation into his learned brain, and finally he responded to God in a certain sense of confusion, loss, and heartache —

"You will take me when the work is done?"

***

Haym's work surely wasn't done. Morris further employed Haym's midas touch in all the financially tight spots Congress found itself in — this included the marching soldiers who wanted their back pay. They collected their anger into a focused mob and entered Philadelphia headed straight for the assembly of men, which promised them remuneration for their toil in war. Morris himself, as the Superintendent, fled ahead of the mob with the other members of Congress while pleading to Haym that he leave no stone unturned to incur the money to pay the men-at-arms. Per usual, Haym fulfilled Morris' request and the soldiers were duly paid.

For Haym, Morris' almost flippant reliance on him wasn't insulting. On the contrary, it gave Haym a personal satisfaction and mild air of superiority. As a matter of purpose, he had gotten what he personally wanted most from the Superintendent, an official title. So anything asked of Haym, subconsciously seemed to him more of an acknowledgment of his worth than an inconvenience or a matter of being put upon. With his immodest moniker, he regularly placed advertisements in the newspaper offering his service, proudly showcasing his rarified status.

"Haym Salomon, Broker to the Office of Finance, to the Consul general of France, and to the treasure of the French Army, at his office in Front Street, between Market and Arch Streets. Buys and sells on commission bank stock, bills of exchange on France, Spain, Holland, and other parts of Europe, the West-Indies, and inland bills, at the usual commissions.

He buys and sells loan office certificates, Continental and state money, of this or any other state, paymaster and quarter-master generals notes; these, and every other kind of paper transaction (bills of exchange excepted) he will charge his employers no more than one half per cent, for his commission.

He procures money on loan for a short time and gets notes and bills discounted.

Gentlemen and others, residing in this state, or any of the United States, by sending their orders to the office, may depend on having their business transacted with as much fidelity and expedition as if they were themselves present.

He receives tobacco, sugars, tea, and every other sort of goods, to sell on commission, for which purpose he has provided proper stores.

He flatters himself his assiduity, punctuality, and extensive connection in his business, as a broker, is well established in various parts of Europe, and in the United States in particular.

All persons who shall please to favour him with their business may depend upon his utmost exertion for their interest, and part of the money advanced, if desired."

Yes, finally, he had his high-minded denomination, "Broker to the Office of Finance." To Haym, it was a badge, really— a statement, a coveted mark of his arrival and acceptance, despite being a Jew. In point of fact, when Haym wasn't present, Morris would generally refer to him as "The Little Jew." He meant nothing insincere or sinister by it, but for Haym it was disparaging, nonetheless. Haym very much wanted to be what he was not— a nobleman by way of birth; of blood— not in an effort to be among a class but in the idea of not being classified as something "other" for the fact that he was a Jew. He admired Meyer's stated intention of living beyond the walls of the Judengasses. However, he believed that it would not endear him to the gentile community, that they would accept his money, smile in his face, but snicker behind his back. Meyer did not subscribe to religiosity, as it would in some regard remind him of his own "otherness," and create a natural wedge between those he wished would see him just for who and what he was; like them— flesh and blood. No, Haym took another tact to compensate for his own underlying self-loathing. He immersed himself in God. Instead of separating his identity from his heritage and race he chose to identify with it— to internally and emotionally elevate his race to the Torahanic status of chosenness. And, all of this became more important and pronounced as the struggle for independence ended. Haym had a vision of America and for America in which Jews weren't separated into two branches nor tied to the old stereotypes that defined them as subhuman. In America, Jews were not to be subjects— they were not to be told where to live or how to live, nor were they to keep to themselves. The government would not dictate to them what taxes or tolls that would be paid separately from the masses. As he saw it, they would be a united part of the masses! In America, to be Jewish would be just as sovereign as to be the king of the world. This was Haym's vision— this was the land in which such a lofty ideal could be achieved— and by God, he played his part perfectly to achieve it.

The war was over. Haym yearned to drink of the liberty he adopted and lent his name, reputation, body, soul, and life for. He had a certain expectation that the Lord had in store for him a life of profound fulfillment and contentment for a job well done. He already stood on a foundation of being rich, powerful, admired, trusted, and well pleased with himself. However, the Almighty — graced in a logic, purpose, and higher reason intertwined into the fibers of every soul, possibility, and ensuing times to come — had quite another plan for Haym Salomon, one beyond the self-interested human's perfunctory perspective of a better nature.

***

XXX

AFFLICTION

"We are not so sensible of the greatest health as of the least sickness."
Benjamin Franklin

Of course no one could see it, but Haym Salomon's lungs were heavily scarred. His prolonged cough had reached a zenith and his phlegm was as horrifically thick and dark as one could imagine. He knew he was afflicted with the disease consumption. Everyone who knew him knew it, even though it was not dared mentioned as anything other than a common transient ill. Nonetheless, the unsightly truth was that the red-hooked shaped bacteria which had multiplied and dwelled within Haym's body was killing him faster than he actually knew.

The fact of the matter was, that the disease of consumption was nearly as ancient as humanity itself. Long before the onerous disease began decimating humans, it afflicted cattle. Between 8,000 and 4,000 BC, when cattle became one of man's client species, the bacteria responsible for consumption infected humanity through man's ingestion of the cattle's milk. However, after 1,000 BC the strain of the disease wildly transmuted into something more vicious and direct— an airborne virus that attacked the lungs. Consequently, it suddenly and rapidly spread through the simple acts of coughing or sneezing. By the first millennium BC, consumption was an endemic on the wind and throughout the world and it could be found in the earliest recorded telltale symptoms of the cough, expectoration, hemoptysis, and wasting away, in the library of Assurbanipal, king of Assyria. Those same symptoms and those same microscopic viruses, which infected the world— over 2,700 years later in the Livingston Sugarhouse prison, were inhaled by Haym and took deadly root in his lungs.

Since contracting the disease, its progress in Haym's body had been atypical. Consumption first appears as nothing more than an intractable cold or flu. Then it may lay dormant for a period, as if the afflicted vanquished the cold. Over time it would reappear in the various forms of fever or cough; escalating a little worse each time. And, even though the disease may lie in a quiescent inoperative condition in the human body for months, years, and sometimes decades, eventually it rises to a vigorously active state— and only twenty percent of those who contract a strain of the infection survive. With consumption, it was mostly a matter of "if," not "when" — the rapid decay and wasting away of the body would begin? When was the end near enough to see in the emaciated cheekbones, scrawny forearms, and dull eyes? It was an affliction of deterioration; a malady of the rapid acceleration of unprofitable time. The internal advancement of consumption was in all inevitability going to gruesomely evolve from manageable to ghastly for whomever hosted it in their respiratory organs; they were going to be consumed in an increasing depletion of the mechanics of the body's ability to function. Haym Salomon, too, could not defy the bearing of that macabre fate.

***

By 1784, everything in Haym's life was a dream upon a dream come true, except that is for his health. So well respected was he in Philadelphia that it was said, "his endorsement on a note made it 'undeniable.'" He was a master Mason. He was the chief contributor to the construction of city's only synagogue. He maintained the single most successful brokerage house in the city, despite a post-war depression and Robert Morris' personal jealousy. He was universally acknowledged as the most intellectually and politically important Jew in the country after having spearheaded the repel of the religious oath which barred Jews and other non-Christians from holding public office in Pennsylvania. He was proud to be Jewish and openly protested those who disparaged Jews as money-grubbing and profiteers from the "War for Independence." He was known in Congressional circles for his generosity and personal faith and trust loaned in species for the Continental Army's efforts at victory. By his own accounts and position with the French, he gave liquidity to the country's Bank of North America. Of all people directly responsible for the new nation, Robert Morris, knew the unseen value of Haym's direct hand in the United States' fruition and fortunes of war. Besides the money he raised, he also advanced in specie over $211,000 to Morris and entered into other transactions with the government to the tune of over $353,000. Additionally, he held numerous promissory notes totaling $92,000. In all, the sum that Haym advanced to help the war's cause was over $658,000.

He was roundly respected as a man devoutly of God. He was a husband and a father of three. He was a son of liberty that gave his all for God and country, from being a courageous spy to coordinating the financial obligations which allowed the promise of America to be violently born, against the wishes of the most powerful monarch and army in the world. Yet, the time had come for change, again. Philadelphia, beyond its own control, was losing its charm for him. Surely it was the city of his greatest combination of success, stability, and joy. Nevertheless, it was founded upon him on the run. His eyes, his heart, his business sense, and his family cast their gaze northeastward. There was something about New York, which called to him. Philadelphia was a refuge, just as Amsterdam once was, but New York was home, to some degree as home as Leszno— now starting to be referred to in Europe as Lissa— once was. These were the cities in which he began fresh, one in which he was born into the world and the other in which he was reborn into his divine purpose. Lastly, Rachel also missed New York and desperately yearned to return.

***

Jacob Mordecai was born under a lucky star. However, it can be assumed that at the moment he emerged from the birth canal, the star was temporarily eclipsed by a shadow of darkness. In a lifetime of being an early riser and yet a late bloomer, Jacob would play a small but disastrous role at the end of Haym Salomon's life, before he would discover his own true calling.

In the winter of 1783, following Washington's triumph at York, young Jacob Mordecai, all of twenty-one years old— only eight years after being a boy rifleman in Washington's army — was urging his stallion to pick up his pace and carry him from Philadelphia to Richmond as fast as it could. By this time, Jacob wasn't a solider anymore and hadn't been at any other point in the war. No, he found his way into the mercantile business working as a clerk for one: David Franks in Philadelphia. At this juncture in his young life, Jacob had two magnificent reasons to ride into Richmond on the full speed of his mount. Firstly, his stepfather, Jacob I. Cohen arranged for him to take a junior partnership in his Richmond mercantile and investment firm of Cohen and Isaacs— thus to be: Cohen, Isaacs and Mordecai. And secondly, he was deeply, madly, and purely in love.

Judith Myers was her lovely name for a very lovely girl. She was still in Philadelphia and as taken by Jacob's handsomeness as he was by her pulchritude. He wanted to marry her more than anything else life had to immediately offer him. In Philadelphia he was struggling to find his way in the world and was in no measure ready to provide for a wife. This position in Richmond he viewed as his invitation to call on her hand. He rode there with sweet memories of her and composing in his mind a draft of conversations as if they were still in the same room. The moment he arrived in the Virginia city, he settled into a long love letter extracted from those thoughts and endeavored in ink to request her heart and hand in ever lasting matrimony. She returned the missive granting his wish with equal desire. For the next four months, Jacob toiled at his profession and saved every dollar for the future destines to come.

As winter died into spring, on the air of fresh life, the time had come for the two to become as one. Jacob traveled to New York where Judy and her family— like many other Jewish New Yorkers who had left the city during British occupation— had returned. Jacob arrived as handsome as ever, more successful than he had ever been in life— a junior partner of a firm, and qualified flush with money. Judy had been anxiously awaiting his return, encased in the frozen memory of love, and entranced by Jacob's having made good on the perils of business. So, it was that on June 16th of 1784, the marriage contract was signed and Judy's finger was host to a circular golden cast symbolic of the promise of eternal love. Life could not have been sweeter for the boy born under the eclipsed star.

A man's life is defined by the control of his character in the overall success or failure of his endeavors, but it is uncontrollable misfortune, which creates the structure of a man's life. The structure of Jacob Mordecai's life would follow suit. The day before the wedding, Jacob and Judy were called to the drawing room of her humorless father. The young couple, of the same age, sat closely to one another, grinning with intense love on their faces. Then Judy's father began to speak. He started with congratulations and support for their union. However, he admonished Jacob for holding to the idea that he could take his daughter to some "backwoods," "backwater," country town such as Richmond. He wouldn't allow it! Jews, as he explained did not belong in the south, among the aristocratic uneducated gentile southern culture! "Jews must stand together!" he demanded— in the cities— in the cities in which there was a network of support! Was there a synagogue in Richmond, he asked? Of course there wasn't, and there alone his point was definitively made. In closing, he was willing to give away his beloved daughter to the enthusiastic young man she so deeply adored, but only if they remained within a safe distance— New York, Philadelphia, Boston, Providence, but not Richmond! Judy was not in the habit of opposing her father— she simply wasn't raised that way— and the couple sat together, with Judy unable to object, and Jacob unwilling to protest. He was the traditional lover, not a fighter, and thereupon had no other option but to comply.

Following the ceremony, Jacob deferentially made his way south back to Richmond to dissolve his part of the partnership bestowed to him in grace by his stepfather. He was expected to return with his bride in tow but instead walked into the firm with a forlorn look on his face, which telegraphed there was a problem. Jacob went about telling his story before his semi-stunned stepfather and partner Isaiah Isaacs. He expressed his appreciation for the position and disappointment that he had to excuse himself from the opportunity and partnership. Once he finished, he braced himself for a storm of indignities from his stepfather, and they came with the fury of a hurricane! "Backstabber!" "Weak!" "Turncoat!" "Fool!" It was to an uncomfortable and acrimonious disillusionment to say the least. Nevertheless, Jacob asserted the tender of his resignation and asked for his rightful share of unpaid dividends.

The truth was that Jacob Cohen wasn't surprised by the unexpected development or his stepson's impractical choice of romantic love over the fundamental business of self-sufficiency. Cohen quickly opened the books and went about settling the accounts between them. Again, Jacob was the weaker personality of the parties and did not receive a settlement of debts and commissions to his liking or favor. His stepfather showed no mercy and rewarded his stepson with just enough to afford him the four day return journey to New York. To a large degree, Jacob was embarrassed and in trying to make some sort of amends, apologized for his "behavior" but explained that he was in love— and that he believed that love was more important and lasting than business.

Jacob did not have a head for investment, a mind for finance, or an entrepreneurial spirit. However, he was confident and determined to make his way just enough, that his love and his marriage could blossom. He wasn't looking to be wealthy or powerful, all that was necessary was an adequate supply to provide the sustenance of home, warmth, and intrinsic comfort to Judy's simple taste. Luckily for him, the opportunity presented itself in the form of Haym Salomon.

***

"...I beg you, Mr. Salomon to allow me to repeat how much I appreciate this opportunity," Jacob said.

"You have thanked me enough," a preoccupied Haym replied."

"Ye, Haud yer wheesht! Quit yer blether! " Macrae piped in. Jacob always found Macrae quite intimidating and as time went on, he would do his best to direct any of his thoughts, concerns, ideas, and solutions to Haym. Though Haym was only forty-four years old, he seemed to be more an old man of seventy. There was no day-to-day consistency in health. His coughing fits increased and grew in great intensity at times— so much so that words Haym was going to say were all but lost as he excused himself to cough; only to return wiping his mouth and having forgotten his chief point. At times it looked as though Haym wasn't long for this world and yet in a day or two, his condition might be as bright and healthy as a caterpillar having turned into a magnificent butterfly. Trying to soften the kicked-up dust of Macrae's grit, Haym turned to Jacob and extricated his next words between yet another a fit of coughing—

"Thank me with good work— with profit— not words, young Jacob."

"Yes, sir, of course," Jacob said.

"That'll be your desk," Macrae unenthusiastically pointed to a over-stuffed banker's desk in the corner.

Macrae was no big fan of Jacob's. Haym had essentially done this boy a favor— as a member of the Philadelphia congregation— and made him a partner, although he had no real experience to speak of. The Scot would have worked for Haym since he arrived in Philadelphia and loved the man like a brother, if wasn't Jewish. Not only that, he came off as short to people; gruff. He enjoyed his drink greatly, which fostered a snippy curtness, which ran slight against Haym's sensibilities. Though, Macrae might have agreed to all these descriptions of his character, he didn't think they should preclude his becoming a partner. Yet, Haym never offered him one, nor did he consider it. Haym was a Judeophilia and as much as he cared for, needed, and appreciated Macrae, he was never going to share his business with a non-Jew.

As Jacob came on board, Haym wasn't looking for a new partner, though he was slowing down a bit and Macrae found himself handling more transactions than he ever had and taking a full management role in the firm. Jacob was the product of a non-Jewish mother and an elderly father of the congregation. In 1760, they were European immigrants who settled in Philadelphia. Even though, Jacob's mother converted for the sake of marriage, their union was rejected by the tiny Jewish congregation of Mikveh Israel. Almost twenty years later, when Haym was elected an elder, he reversed policy and invited them to join the synagogue. From then on, the Mordecai's had strong ties to Haym and when Jacob had nowhere to turn, he knew the one man would give him a break.

"What do you think… in this economy?" Jacob blasted across the room. Haym and Macrae stopped and looked at one another, they weren't used to a boisterous voice. However, Haym remained gracious —
"We must guard against enthusiasm."
The wit wasn't lost on Jacob. Yet, his question wasn't out of the question. Immediately following the victory at York, business continued to boom for Haym, and he carried on his much needed support of Congress. The fledging government's debt grew to the point that it couldn't even borrow from it's own bank — the Bank of North America, the institution chartered by Morris. At Morris' request, Haym continued to rescue the country with private loans from Holland and France that only Haym had the network of old associates to access. However, as 1783 turned to 1784, Haym's firm began to experience financial losses. This prompted him to plan moving his business to New York where he thought he could expand, including creating a stock exchange. He bought buildings on Wall Street and organized a network of financiers to envision New York as a new financial capital of the world. In the meantime, in Philadelphia, he took up the patriotic and expansive fervor sweeping the country and invested in a variety of proposals, including the airship company that Morris had invested in. The ballon, like many other wild-eyed ventures never got off the ground. Haym was ahead of his time but losing money for it. Furthermore, he had a good portion of his credit locked into cargo shipping a sail across the oceans while his specie was not only dumped into investments but engaged in the costs of a growing family and numerous petitioners of Congress, including Morris. Nevertheless, he relied on the fact that he had his government investments, which he could always cash in, essentially retrieving his own borrowed money for Congress in liquid. This perspective of his options would prove to be one of the few financial miscalculations Haym Salomon ever made or was simply the product of the worst timing in the world.

The American economy in 1784, you could say, was landlocked. Even though there were no military battles between the United States and England, the British were still fighting the French and the Spanish and going out of their way to blockade the flow of goods to American markets. England stopped trading with the United States as it had done with it's old colony and they were successively winning battles in the West Indies which disrupted the European trade to America. Coupled with the incredible debt the United State had incurred through war— and straddled with interest payments to France, Spain, and Holland— the American economy was as stagnated as a puddle of dirty water. For Haym Salomon, to make matters worse, he had been sick much of the year— for periods which at times lasted weeks— and Jacob Mordecai became the principle investor in Haym's firm. It was the equivalent of leaving a nursing baby at the teat of its father. The firm got on with Macrae handling the specie as always and debt collections while Jacob supervised the shipping investments and insurance transactions. Unfortunately, Jacob was either poor in his choices of business or haplessly unlucky in their outcome. Nevertheless, Haym was hemorrhaging money and he knew it.

On Saturday, January 1st of 1785, officers of the government arrived at Haym's home. Weeks before, concerned about his finances and ready-cash, Haym had petitioned the Congress for repayment of his loans. At Haym's request, Morris himself, made sure that the petition was handled promptly, mostly as matter of acknowledgment for Haym's selfless service to the country. The first day of the New Year was a beautiful one. Not only was the weather pleasant for a winter's day but Haym basked in a new solace that was as gentle, peaceful, and emotionally profound as he had ever known. For one, Rachel was busily going about the house starting to pack various items in the exciting and expectant return to New York. Haym found a wonderment in the children gathering around him as he read prayers aloud, just as his father used to. There was a contentment, a fulfillment, a sense of overgrown joy spreading from the heart and breaking through in feeling of beams exuding from the fingertips.

The government men that arrived did so with a sheaf of documents. Haym had made his petition to Morris but had not tabulated the debts nor presented a formal request. Therefore, for the time being, he was going to be required to sign a series of affidavits and an official claim.

However, after Rachel received them at the door, Haym entered the anteroom and blisteringly dressed the men down for having the nerve to request of him a business transaction on the Sabbath! It was a bit embarrassing to Rachel and she protested. She asked him to think of Morris, to keep his temper in check, and to receive the documents for the next day at which time he could sign them and have the men return for them. She went so far as to take them herself, but Haym forced her to hand them back. Haym refused any further discussion of business and told the men he would call for them on another day in the week to proceed.

Man can never be sure of tomorrow. And Haym Salomon had no idea that on his next tomorrow, the dawn of eternity would rise for him, as it does every creature scheduled on God's on time.

***

XXXI

ETERNAL RETURN

"And this be our motto: 'In God is our trust.'"

Star-Spangled Banner

Man is a peculiar creature. Of all the living personalities burdened with mind, heart, and soul that are scattered about the earth and in the kingdom of mortality, it is only man which has conceived of a consciousness consisting of something of a figure beyond his immediate senses which is larger and more powerful than himself. This figure is an almighty deity, a demiurge more mercurial than quicksilver, more enigmatic than the core of the earth, and more puzzling than a ball of lightning. Up for grabs between the terrible truth and the beautiful lie — counterbalanced in tottering and teetering symmetrical rationalizes are the urges, notions, cravings, will, disposition and nature of volition, otherwise known as the natural element and emotion: the human heart. The beautiful lie is that the salts of the earth can quench the inner thirst. The terrible truth is that God will not judge us by what we achieve but by what we don't rebuke. Superimposed against the personal will of man, the sentimental relationship with God seems cold, indeliberate, and impersonal. It is not the attainment of the joyful glory of God, which the individual souls of mankind take umbrage with; it is the specific and designated path of perceived disasters in which the victorious glory appears to require. So it was, that Haym was bedeviled by Yahweh. Why was he sick? He was still young for a man; still awakening to the glory of God. Why were things as they were when finally they came to be?

Haym Salomon was forty-four years old, with three children and a pregnant wife. He was also the proud uncle that presided over the birth of a new nation. It was firmly establish in his heart that the metaphysical mind of God could not be so arrogantly calculated with the limited physical variables of understanding that the temporal intellect of man could foresee. Thus, he labored in his mind, "Why... why?" However, it wasn't a cry or a weeping question. No, instead it was gentle, comforting — an almost beautiful plea. For hours at a time, he would suspend himself in silence and listen with both his ears and his untamed intuition. He heard different mumblings in various pitches, as though operatic spirits were singing over one another, and he could feel a gnawing in his gut. Yet, he couldn't make out the tonal conflict of the prima donnas into a concrete answer to the atonement.

Further still, his silence, was oft interrupted by his blood splattering coughs. The room itself was fragrant with a suggestive hallmark— the trance hint of a pervasive spoor, the fetor of a colony of roosting dark angels biding their time on the misty particles of plasma that floated throughout the air. For hence he had come from his mother's womb covered in fluids and streaks of blood, so hence he would eternally return.

***

It was the first dusk of Thursday, January 6th, 1785. Haym had been bed-ridden since Sunday with a steady fever of 103°, at times rising as high as 105°. On occasions he was delirious, thrashing his head from side to side, speaking in foreign tongues, and calling for "Yankel" to slow the horse and bring the cart to a stop! He was almost drowning in his own perspiration— though the window and winter wind drove through the room night and day! His pulse beat so fast as to be visible and he had the look of a skeleton wearing waterlogged, blood splattered undergarments. In this condition of dire straits, in the context of discernment and the prayer of hope, Rachel refused all who came to see him, either on business or personal call. This included Macrae, Fitzsimmons, Wilson, Morris, and Madison. This was understandable if you take into account that of the nominal daylight and evening hours set aside for social activity, Haym was for most of them in a pitiful state of consumption. He was swollen and weak, flecked with ulcers, and somewhere in between reality and arid illusion. He moaned and complained of his stomach being rot and corroded and he would not eat, causing the bacteria in his mouth to multiply and his breath to be untenably foul. Not to mention that his cough dreadfully echoed in the death note of B flat minor, sending chills down the spine. Poor Rachel was doing all she could to stave off the inevitable. She followed every doctor's recommendation. Though it was cold, she kept open the bedroom windows in the hopes that fresh air would counteract the disease. On a French doctor's advice she served her husband his own urine, spoonfuls at a time. The children and she would pick the freshest fruits and vegetables and feed him in tiny portions, which he consumed in moments of clarity illuminated by love and gratitude. However, by January 6th, Haym could hardly breath. She didn't know it but his lungs were bleeding and infected with abscesses. The passing change of death was imminent, and that, both of them did know.

The only remaining resonance of a voice Haym had left was a faint whisper from the little bit of air his body could produce. After a few words, his lungs would gasp! Then they desperately expelled an inconsequential puddle from the pool of blood and fluid accumulated in his chest cavity with a series of coughs in wet bloody hacks!

As Rachel stood beside Haym, she went about lighting candles to foil the natural spell of day's duality. He called her down to his lips. She was seven months pregnant and still only twenty-two. Per usual, she offered him fresh food, but he refused it. She loving forced yet another spoonful of his own urine down his throat, and though he swallowed it at her insistent behest, his intention upon calling her was instead to be heard. As she dropped the spoon back into the jar, he motioned for her to close the windows but she barked of the importance of fresh air! He had her shutter them anyway. It was clear to her that he was giving up and finally she bowed her head in the same hopeless defeat and lowered her ear to his lips.

"Be with me," he said.

Then he motioned for her to sit beside him, to relax, not to leave the room, as she normally would do before returning again to tend to him. In this sought position they tenderly held hands. In a short time, she wept.

"I love you," he whispered as best he could.

She absorbed the sentiment and dotted his forehead with love and kisses.

"Fear not, my dear," he said. "It is my calling, now."

Her eyes wet and tearing, he raised his trembling hand and wiped the dribbling droplets away.

"You must be strong," he said.

She turned her face away. She didn't want to hear that! He extended the feverish bony fingers of his hand out toward her protruding stomach. She took it from him; raised her blouse, and held it flush over her naked belly. The baby kicked and they warmly delighted in feeling it together.

"If it is a girl, we'll name her Rebekah," she said.

"No, name her Rachel," Haym insisted.

Rachel blushed but shook her head in disagreement.

"I think it's a boy," she admitted. "It kicks so hard."

They smiled at one another as she eagerly held his hand to her skin. The baby continued to kick and Haym gently closed his eyes and concentrated on the closest sensation of his child that he could forevermore behold.

"We'll name him Haym," she said resolutely.

With the eager anticipation of pleasing another, Rachel expected Haym to be touched if not outright ecstatic. Instead, his eyes turned upward before he turned back to her and reclaimed his hand—

"I must see and speak to the children," he said.

***

Ezekiel was the first to enter the room. The dusk of a short winter day was overcoming the sun and the room grew in multiple grayness and shadow. The boy was a stout six and half years old. Yet, he was already crying as he looked up at his dying father.

"Why do you cry, my son?" Haym asked in his strained tone.

"Because mommy said you're going away."

"That is right, I am going away."

"Why, Papa?"

"Because our Father has called me."

The religious reference to being stopped Ezekiel in his tracks, as it would have his father thirty-five or so years ago. He, too, was taught and drilled in the Law of Abraham.

"Like you have called me into the room?" Ezekiel asked.

"Much the same, my son."

"But why does he call you now, Papa?"

"Because it pleases him, I suppose."

"It doesn't please me," Ezekiel cried.

"Then it is today that you, my son… you have received your inheritance," Haym said in somewhat sad but an elevated whisper. Ezekiel stared back, simply dumbfounded—

"The inheritance of human consciousness," Haym concluded. "Isolation."

"What does that mean, papa?"

"That you now know yourself separate from your parents, your sisters, and… your God. You are now your own self— your own person— your own "I." My son, the journey of your long life has now but begun." Ezekiel stood absent of the faintest clue as to what his father meant, but as his father shivered in fever, dripped in sweat, and coughed in blood, the little boy couldn't hold in the overwhelming feelings welling inside. He didn't know what the word "Isolation" meant but he was feeling it. As the outside body can feel hot and cold, his insides were experiencing isolation and loneliness like an external force beyond his control; no different than standing without shelter in the mists of a storm. He tried to be strong and hold it in, but...

***

Rachel led Sallie into the bedroom in which Haym was quartered. The little girl had been frightened of the room since Sunday when her father's illness took a dramatic turn for the worse. Accosted by the smell, the freezing temperature, and adolescent premonitions, Sallie simply refused to enter, going so far as to throw a temper-tantrum at the threshold, which her mother led her. But, at this terrible hour, by heavy-handed persuasion, Rachel forced her along.

Sallie was but five years old, adorable to the eye, shy as a june bug, and clinging to the leg of her unforgiving mother. Rachel pressed her forward and militantly presented her to her father. Their daughter quaked and sniffled back the tears of her tantrum. But, with a soft touch, her father stroked her long auburn hair. Glancing across her cheek, rising up under the hair above her ear and rolling back along the side of her head; stroke after stroke the quiet language of love constricted around her fear and throttled it with fondness. Before he finished a ninth or tenth caress, Sallie embraced her dying daddy for dear life!

"Papa, will stop being sick? Please papa, please!"

***

The darkness consumed the dusk and night fell upon the candle-lit room. Next to the bed, Rachel sat in a rocking chair with Deborah. The two year old was asleep across her lap. Rachel's eyes were going in and out of sleep, themselves. Haym looked on them with veneration and the thoughts of all he had experienced to reach the company of their love.

"Rachel-Rachel," he whispered in spits of blood.
She gently opened her eyes; naturally kissed the baby, and positioned her ear toward him.

"I believe the hour is here and the moment is nearing," he spoke.

Her eyes welled, as she knew not what to do or say. He seemed so calm and agreeable, that it was in all honesty, disquieting to her.

"I left instructions with Macrae—" he started to say when a fit of coughing silenced him and he thrashed him about!

Catching his breath and turned from that thought, he held out his arms for Deborah. Rachel handed her to him. She was asleep but her eyes popped open as she found herself held in the air looking down at her father.

"You will never be able to know how much I love and adore you," he said in a throaty whisper, which she couldn't hear.

"Papa!" the child said with a smile and a carefree laugh!

But Haym was weak. His muscles shook and were starting to give out. Rachel took the child back from him and his arm fell to his side with no control whatsoever. A little melancholy resignation set in and Haym turned to his wife who was coping with the uneasy reality that he would die any second, right before her eyes. He wanted to reach out and place his palm to her abdomen again but he was too weak and she was too agitated. Instead, she desperately grabbed his face and frantically kissed him about it, saying—

"Why? Why is this? Why? Don't. Please. Why?"

Her tears literally showered him, but he was mute and unmoved. The strength that remained, he carefully saved for one more task.

***

"My dear..." he breathed.

Suddenly, she stopped kissing him and slowly removed her hands in a certain freight that he was going to tell her now that he was already dead. However—

"Hand me-hand me—" he struggled to say.

She knew what he wanted without him even needing to finish the sentence or point to the object. Dutifully, she grabbed the prayer book, the siddur, with the stitched six-pointed star, and handed it to him.

Upon receiving it from her, he drew the deepest breath he could and found the power to refrain from coughing. For a final moment he sounded of himself—

"Quill, if you would?"

Rachel quickly dipped a turkey feather quill in ink and handed it to him. Sitting up and wheezing, he wrote quickly, but thoughtfully. Rachel looked upon him with some amazement as he showed a sign of life. Hope renewed itself as he handed her the book.

"Let it lay open and dry. Reserve if you will— reserve the book for our child still nestled inside you. It is all they may ever have of me— the words I wrote are to she or he— that they may know I loved and thought about them."

With that, all the strength Haym had mustered was expired and he sank into the bed even a little deeper than he laid upon it before. The renewed hope deflated and Rachel thought she could already see his soul departing his body and the room glowing blacker than the candle could sustain light.

"Leave me now, my dear. You must leave me now," Haym said. Resigned to her fate, she followed his order with a tinge of personal resentment and clasped Deborah's hand to exit—

"Bye papa!" the little girl said, though she didn't know the full profundity of her words.

Rachel looked at him one more time through watery eyes. They shared a look of finality, which she saw upon someone for the first time in her life, but it was a look that Haym had become very accustom to. Thereby, she closed the door. In unison, the candles all went out into streams of smoke and the room was completely pitch black.

***

Haym laid there, still alive. Impatient and eager, the scampering sounds of angels of darkness cursed the silence with their heavy breathing, but Haym ignored it altogether. His mind turned inward to the outward thought of God. There he lay in his ephemeral state, a man that risked his life and fortune for the ideals of a country that was not his own. He wished to believe that he answered to a higher calling. However, he knew that in the whole of his time in life, he was riposting to a fire for liberty and freedom that burned within him from the day he first heard Exodus. So it was ironic— in fever yet again— at that moment, that Haym finally and completely surrendered. God could have him now, if that was what God wanted. He had already learned that to resist the Will of God was as futile as to resist Newton's Laws of Motion.

Nevertheless, there was still some conscious peace in the man, maybe it should be called pride, but it was a judgement of peace. The meaning of America, the manifestation of what was ultimately his life's work— though he never intended it to be— was a source of triumph. To his mind, the world gained a beauty it never had before. It gained a garden of natural law that placed the individual sovereignty over the rights of government and monarchy. It was the opposite of the Judengasse and the districts of ethnic homogeny. He participated and performed all he could to bring into existence a state in which a child born would not be restricted by the station on their arrival or by the sins of their father upon ascendence. On the contrary, in a new outlook to the history of humanity, the child could achieve, as they so desired by the volition of their own ambition. There would be no more despotism! There would be no richer, lazy kings and princes to arbitrarily set rules and enrich themselves! There would be representational government in which a new chapter of mankind would begin!

With the momentary reminiscence of his life recalled and remembered, it quietly faded away. There were no more sounds to the memories; no more spoken words heard. The silence was followed by the vision of all the years distorted into a single figure of his father's finger in the glow of candle light, guiding his eye from right to left across the pages of the Torah— until even that evanesced into the edge of the candle flame growing out of mental proportion.

In the sweat and fever, his temperature lowered to a calm sensation, much like being submerged in a warm ocean of water. He could not speak anymore but his inner voice chanted, "Yahweh-Yahweh." His eyes closed. The darkness he could no longer see grew darker in the same terms of falling down a deep well at midnight. However, within his own sight, a pinpoint of light emerged in the distance. "Yahweh-Yahweh," he called. The call echoed back to him "‏בֵּן — בֵּן‏."

His heart stopped beating and his spirit escaped the cage of his body through the various orifices until it levitated above him in a misty brilliant silvery shade of energy. Haym Salomon was dead.

Within his mind the emerging light grew closer and the operatic prima donnas now sang in perfect concert at a full volume. It was an extraordinary and ancient hymn. Meanwhile, the light rose into a golden arc closing into a shinning lustrous circle. Within the circle was a kind of luminescent, but something brighter than light; brighter than each and every sun combined and exploding together as one. Yet, it did not blind him at all. He could see clearly— and more clearly— clearer than through the lens of a telescope! Haym Salomon in his state of life upon death could see: nothingness!

Beyond the panoply of stars in the universe, planetary bodies, phenomenons of space and time, persons and people of sight and sound, there was a "nothingness" that shimmered in iridescent flakes of invaluable impressions of unconditional love. The closer he came to the light, the more familiar the song grew. It pulsated, as it ranged from a crackle of notes, like a soothing campfire to a melody of giggles, like that of an infant. Finally, the light of all the nothingness fully consumed him in a totality of singularity. Within it, the warmest and most snug feeling of contentment and "home" dissolved Haym's consciousness into an individual all-encompassing singular thought: "Is."

***

"But with respect to future debt; would it not be wise and just for that nation to declare in the constitution they are forming that neither the legislature, nor the nation itself can validly contract more debt, than they may pay within their own age, or within the term of 19 years."   Thomas Jefferson

In the dust of Haym's return, the tally of his life did not match its moral weight in the balance of the ambit sublunary scales of hallowed justice— such is often the case in the compounded strata of human interaction with the course of divine providence. For his God— Yahweh, and his country— the United States, Haym Salomon suffered, toiled, and gave not only of his fortune and life, but selflessly consigned the self-identified meaning and purpose of his very soul. However in the process, nothing was lost, left behind, or carelessly placed in a classification of indifference. His words and deeds matched his thoughts and feelings— his efforts and his strides matched his desire and will— his heart was a worthy stanchion to the sacrosanct foreordained advance of his deific spirit. Unfortunately, for those who stood in his dust, inherited his legacy, and were burdened with his financial debt, the light shone upon their character makes for a somewhat unseemly image.

At the hour of Haym's death, he had in his ledgers:

Loan Office Certificates worth............ $110,233.63
Treasury Certificates......................... $18,244.88
Continental Liquidated Dollars............ $199,214.45
Commissioner's Certificates............... $17,870.37
Virginia State Certificates................... $8,166.00
TOTAL............... $353,729.43

However, his outstanding obligation to creditors was in excess of $45,000. This was owed to a personally disastrous end to 1784. The enormous Spanish merchant ship "Sally," was in return and to his consignment, on which cargo and hull he was invested in to the sum of $50,000; his estate on the expedition sustained almost total loss, owing to the failures and disasters among merchants of those days, to whom the property had been consigned and by whose advice it had been undertaken. The limit of Haym's prosperous tally of accounts was $44,732, which Rachel, as the administrator of the inestate, honorably delivered in full under the guidance of James Wilson, Thomas Fitzsimmons, Matthew Clarkson, Joseph Carson, and Eleazor Levy. Yet, the remaining balance of unpaid debt still left her $560 in the arrears to wanton creditors. In an attempt to cash out the $353,729.43 of government securities devastatingly bequeathed upon her, she kindly entrusted the advice of James Wilson, Haym's attorney.

Acting on behalf of the State of Pennsylvania and the Congress, David Rittenhouse, the State Treasurer and James Wilson reassuringly advised her to give them the certificates and securities. As it was proposed, owing to market factors and liquidity, there was a possibility that she might not receive in return a full measure of the expectant amount. Nevertheless, with Rittenhouse acting in official capacity, they confidently promised the widow that due remittance was shortly forthcoming. As Rachel waited for receipt of payment, her short promised wait became an unfulfilled eternity. Rittenhouse, regarded as the preeminent intellectual in America, was primarily an astronomer and a treasurer only by right of trade. Though he was an honest and competent treasurer, during 1785, he was wildly engrossed in another of his highly prized and innovative instruments: the man-made diffraction grating. For Rachel this would mean that at worst James Wilson was executing her financial arrangements or at best, she was temporarily forgotten. By 1786, Rittenhouse on behalf of the state was forced to ignominiously explain the unexplainable— that in short, they had regretfully lost the certificates and thereby had no way to accordantly calculate the claim. It was a suspicious explanation to say the least. Nevertheless, the claim would go unpaid in full. Straddled with a baby at her breast and three other small children, ages six, five, and two— Rachel was a widow and her fatherless children whom were born into wealth were suddenly irrevocably impoverished.

Owing to a lack of finances, family, and the admiring passions of David Heilbron, pregnant a year into her second marriage, Rachel petitioned the orphans court and requested the appointment of guardians for her children: Ezekiel, Sallie, Deborah, and Haym M. Salomon. The baby Haym, who was born three months after the passing of his father, was given to the Gomez clan, a well-known and respected leading Jewish family. Sallie, who was seven, was placed with Joseph Andrews. Eight years later, Sallie and Joseph, twenty-six years her senior, would be married. They would also have eleven children. Rachel married David Heilbron and after moving to New York and having a child, they emigrated to Holland. Following the birth of a second child, Rachel returned to Philadelphia less her husband and children, and lived out her days with but only a strained relationship with her children until her death in 1818.

***

Haym M. Salomon, the fourth and last child of Haym and Rachel Salomon, served as a captain in the Navy during the War of 1812. However, he made his way in life as a mercantile merchant in New York City. Much like his father, he dabbled in countless crafts, products, services, and goods. His considerable political connections afforded him unique business opportunities, which he strived to capitalize on. In the footsteps of his father, religion and faith played a prominent role in the younger Haym's life. He ascended to the presidency of the Trustees of Congregation Mikveh Israel, though he tended to approach his faith with a considerably lax demeanor than his father had. Financially, he was successful but in the grand scheme of things, much less so than his father. Yet, the good, simple, and gentle man managed to substantially provide for his extraordinarily large family.

By 1827, at the age of forty-two, Haym M. was married to Ella Hart, the daughter of another Jewish financial hero of the Revolutionary War, and together they had produced eight children— with twins on the way. Ella's father, Jacob came from the same upper stock of patriotism and business acumen as Haym's father.

Jacob Hart immigrated to America in 1775 from Prussian Bavaria, settling in Baltimore. He quickly established himself as a heady ready-to-make a deal merchant, and also a great believer in the wondrous glory of the American ideal of liberty.

When General Lafayette visited Baltimore and elucidated— as only sharp-dressed flamboyant Frenchmen can do— to the population of the great eternal needs of the army, Hart organized a subscription of all the Baltimore merchants, Jew and gentile alike, for a loan to the commander. A leader among men, Hart headed the list, making himself the largest of the contributors, throwing in his lot at £2,000 against the full loan of £5,000. In three years time he married; welcomed Ella into the world; and moved to New York where he emerged as an important member of the Jewish community, serving as parnas of Shearith Israel upon its reopening.

And so it was in the year 1827, that due to the public publishing of the journals and records of the Continental Congress— and in them a passing mention of his father-in-law, Haym humbly wrote to the Treasury Department of the United States. He inquired as to the unpaid securities and Continental notes of his father, which were subject to the dubious neglect of the State of Pennsylvania. He wondered if there were corresponding records of any of the transactions, which the Continental Congress might have documented in their journals.

Mr. Joseph Nourse, Register of the Treasury of the United States since the time of the Revolution replied from Washington to Haym M. Salomon:

> "I have cast back to those periods when your
> father was agent to Office of Finance; but the
> inroads of the British Army in 1814 deprived us of
> every record in relation to the vouchers of the
> period to which I refer." He was referring to the
> War of 1812 and the British burning of
> Washington D.C.."

Haym graciously accepted the explanation and did not inquire about the matter for the next fourteen years.

In the fall of 1841, Haym M. attended a lecture at Harvard University where Professor Jared Sparks was giving an electrifying lecture on the American Revolution. He touched upon Jewish contributions and singled out Haym's father and his tremendous philanthropic nature. In three year's time, this gave cause to Haym M. contacting Mr. Sparks and reconstituting his family's initial efforts to claim remuneration on Haym Salomon's investments.

***

The Franks family post war story is varied but the single thread that runs through the matriarchy is a duplicitous nature owing to self-interest above cause or ideal. David, Moses' brother and Rachel's uncle was placed on trial November 9th of 1778. At the behest of Congress, based on written letters of an improper nature and dangerous tendency to the enemy, "intentions inimical to the safety and liberty of the United States," he was held in the newly erected gaol of Philadelphia.

The letters in question, which framed his predicament, were cumbersome in their many topics but two things in particular caught the eye of the Americans. For one, he admitted that the discreet income streams, which they had cultivated through the years of double-dealings, had dried up. Therefore, he, David, was considering an immigration to London instead of supporting the patriot cause as some— he lamented, in their unholy divided family— which he found great disappointment in. The second item of contention was an inquiry to the general costs of war provisions in London. He suggested to Moses a surreptitious scheme in which they could privately purchase the supplies cheaper in London and resell them to each side of the battle in America. The nascent federal government, which arrested him, decidedly remanded David to the State of Pennsylvania, which, it determined, was better, equipped for a legal proceeding. This was the equivalent of a farmer catching a pig and awarding its custody to an abattoir.

In Philadelphia, he and his out-of-control socialite daughter were public enemy number one. By that change of venue, Franks knew his life expectation was severely reduced and he did everything he could to ingratiate himself with his jailer, similar to the tactics of his niece's husband. Ironically, at the same time, Haym was entering Philadelphia from his New York Provost-break.

Charged with an indictment of High Treason and the public perception of guilt by association, he fearfully faced the gallows. Everyone on his side of the Franks family was cause for his association of guilt, but it was his daughter, Rachel's cousin, Rebecca that made the public's blood particularly boil.

The Franks in Philadelphia were the high-society of Loyalist circles, intermarried, intermingled, and interlaced with lawyers, politicians, and generals. Rebecca was well known and despised for her Meschianza, an elaborate fête attended by over 400 given in honor of British General Howe. Her father was one of the attendees and if the American leaning public of Eastern Pennsylvania could, they would have hung every one of the 400. While David awaited his fate, from London, Moses was working overtime to devise a means for his brother's release, including pleading with Washington for a prisoner exchange. Further working against David was the fact that being imprisoned restricted his ability to provide prisoner rations for British P.O.W.'s held by the Americans. A real twist of irony. His contract though wasn't with the British but the Continental Congress. He worked for them but was expected to be reimbursed by the British, of which he alone was responsible for. David's incarceration directly led to the starvation of British prisoners, his own bankruptcy among creditors, and greater vitriol from the Congress who were ultimately burdened with the expensive unwanted task.

David Franks had labored under worry of a graveyard dead verdict for six weeks. Finally came judgement day. The adjudicating event arrived, embodied in the twelve men of citizenry which life or death hung in the weighted balance. As it turned out, the men of Philadelphia were honorable men, American to core. They rejected the trumped up charge, even in a time of war; covered their eyes and consolidated their bias behind Lady Themis. Their verdict was composed on the lack of sufficient evidence. Reluctantly, officials released Franks behind British lines after what he deemed to them was an unnecessary incarceration. To his point, he was just a businessman, though, less the wealthy one he once was. As for Rebecca, she hightailed on the waves in a family owned packet ship straight out of America! Few left in Philadelphia wept.

Three years later, arising from the British defeat at York and the handwriting on the wall— David would scuttle and make like his older brother, daughter, nieces, and nephews before him, and take up residence in England. For he and his wife, the change of address was Bath. Almost the entire clan of Franks chose a similar path and traveled outcome. However, born and raised in New York, for David, both he and his wife yearned for their old friends and the nostalgia of Philadelphia, which continued to swish and swirl in their minds like a pleasant hangover. Hence they returned in 1783 and David began a new brokerage firm. Yet, in the slow cyclical waltz through the intervals of life, the intersection of time and space in one instance can be steeped in the masquerading illusion of an infinite magical moment; but returned to at some later next, the juncture renders itself the fantastical verisimilitude of a bloody thorn stabbed into the heart. Thus it was that the old nostalgia was faded into memory and definably dead and buried with the defeat of the British.

David found Philadelphia a second time around to be a tough go. His wife found the old society very new and unforgiving. Most significant factor though was that David's landholdings had lost a large degree of their value and his inability to convert them into cash strained his attempts to mirror their once opulent lifestyle. Stricken with Yellow Fever, they set off for a return to England and in the course of the voyage; he prepared to give death a big kiss and drafted his last will and testament.

During the years of their early adulthood, Moses and David acted as proxies— colonial lineages of the business operations of their father and his father's businesses before him. They ran the British commissary during the French and Indian War, involved themselves in the Indian Trade, and all worthy capital ventures north, south, east, and west. The typical dynamic of their relationship saw Moses discreetly operating the financial logistics and David, the expansionist, belligerently executing the ground administration. In concert, the brothers, bit their tongue of political voice— though David had signed the Non-Importation Agreement demanding a repeal of the Stamp Act. Nonetheless, in a tradition inherited from their father and race, they placed their Jewish heritage and personal self-interest before country— be it England, in any course, a country that rejected their humanity and citizenship. Though, this is what made America different! Haym saw it! Pulaski saw it! Kościuszko saw it! Hart saw it! Jews had been home without a country, and in countries without a home for centuries! America offered the Jew not only freedom and liberty, but equality! Nevertheless, the Franks vowed their allegiance to contracts more than charters or constitutions. For David's part, he left the faith all together for a Christian wife and her Christianity, as did Moses' son, Isaac. But they were also not men of God; God did not fill their hearts, their thoughts, or their unsatiated appetites— they were men of opportunity. Their wisdom lied in the prudence of speculation and the reduction of risk.

Moses Franks appears complex to understand. His son is a revolutionary war hero and his daughter marries one. Yet, he himself, though a true believer in life, liberty, and the pursuit of property, disassociated himself from politics except to size up another, fumble for angles to push product, and touch the heart of a person's mind. He was an individual of great learning and artistic talent, but the streams of his sweat were undeniably formed on the love and labor of business pursuits. As a matter of fact, gifted as he was, Moses designed many of the family's company ships, which led the way in countless nautical advancements.

Yet, outside of the soothing sounds of the violin, his talents were rendered supplementary. To rape the natural resources of America would not even begin to describe the furor in which he sought to exploit the avenues of commerce. Everything from tree trunks to cotton, the Franks would harvest and send to England. He had his own personal liberty and freedom, and for his mind and money, he knew what it was they were founded on: man's insatiable rapacity— an ever-present market force acquired at variable rates.

Unremarkable in his remarkable disassociation and disinterest, Moses left for England before the opportunity presented itself in which he could lay his eyes upon his first-born grandson. By such time, the various income streams the family utilized were balkanized by the factions of engaged war. It was difficult and dangerous to do business on either side. With his daughter's hand given away in a personally fortuitous arrangement of her affections and advancing into the half-light age of sixty, he fled for greener pastures before what he feared would be a turning tide. In his mind, to stay in beloved New York or Philadelphia, left open the possibility of all possibilities being in play. Anything could happen, including being charged with treason, just as his brother would soon be.

In England, Moses built himself a brick mansion overlooking the Themes and renewed his interest in law and completed his legal studies. Otherwise, he quietly lived out fifteen years of remaining days and nights in the safety and comfort of his family's holdings.

Isaac, Rachel's brother, was a fine man. Once he rejoined Washington's army in New Jersey, besides being a confidant, he was appointed a forage manager— someone who hunts down food and provisions. In 1781 he was commissioned to the Seventh Massachusetts Regiment in West Point.

Discharged from the army in 1782— due to poor health— Isaac settled in Philadelphia, near to his sister. Owing to his father's largesse, he engaged in land speculation, slavery, banking, and other mercantile activities. He eventually acquired a inspiring piece of real estate in Germantown, which in time he loaned to George Washington. However, over time, Franks' prosperity declined and he was forced to declare himself "indigent" and survived off his meager veteran's pension. No longer a practicing Jew, he died with a Christian burial in 1822.

On April 30th, 1789, George Washington had been inaugurated in New York City as the first President of the United States of America under the Constitution. For the oath-taking ceremony, the Bible was opened to the 49th and 50th chapters of Genesis with two engravings facing the text: one representing the blessing of Zebulon, and the other the prophecy of Issachar, symbolizing the similarity of the States to the tribes of Israel. Gershom Mendes Seixas was one of fourteen clergy officially presiding over the affair. Seixas, maybe to be considered the most important intimate Haym Salomon every made, would live a long fruitful and full life which would stretch into his country's first war following independence.

As the hazzan was in attendance at the celebratory birth of the nation's new government, he was also present for the solemn funeral and burial of his great friend, Haym Salomon. The holy communion of the meeting of their souls in mind and morale was a conduit of the summons of God's Perfect Will. Seixas always remembered it as such — as the merciful rivers of heaven flooding their banks and delivering the Israelites to the city on the hill. They the two men were spoken for from the day they were born, though they would not known it until theirs set upon one another. And with Haym's laid into the earth in which he adorned with the manifestation of God's Truth, Seixas left Philadelphia and returned to the beloved Synagogue which still held the spirit of their first encounter — the love of two men combined in divinity larger than their separate recognition of God.

Throughout Seixas' life, he rose in importance, stature, and recognition, but never any further in the rabbinical order. Nevertheless, he was regarded and esteemed by all in the new country's Jewish community and beyond the Jewish faith, including the affections of President Washington and those in government. Paradoxically, for all Seixas patriotism and past advocacy for war with England — if that's what it would take to be a free nation — he was also a staunch pacifist and opposed the War of 1812, while vigorously defending an old friend between he and Haym: President Madison.

The body of Seixas' life's work was replete with multiple historic accomplishments, which for many men, one of them alone would have represented a proudly lived; including his charter of Columbia College, later to be expanded to Columbia University. Gershom Mendes Seixas was a good a man that America has ever seen. He bountifully received and bountifully gave. He did what most aspire to but failed to achieve: he truly lived by his ideals— believing that the very purpose of a fortunate person's life was to help others, regardless of whether they were rewarded for their generosity. He didn't sign the Declaration of Independence or the Constitution, but without his spirited conviction, it could be argued, those documents would have been longer in ever coming.

The contribution of Robert Morris to victory in the American Revolution, the dynamic and stable monetary policy of the country, and to the eventual wealth of the nation— a wealth greater than any nation in the history of the world, cannot be understated. His presence in the history of America is as critical and vital as George Washington. During a significant portion of his life, Morris was quite possibly the richest man in the nation and the most personally and politically financially responsible. Yet, toward the end of his life, he would spend thirty months in debtors' prison. Ironically, that experience too, was a major financial milestone for the country, which would one day become the financial empire of the world.

Following the end of the war, Morris was still personally flush with money. He built the most magnificent mansion in Philadelphia which he offered to the young country as a presidential palace until Washington D.C. was completed. George Washington and John Adams would conduct their presidencies from his residence. As the nation was forming, Morris' political clout and presence didn't diminish. He was elected to the Constitutional Convention where he gracefully paid one political debt and bestowed one elegant honor. The political debt centered around his arrangement of his longtime assistant Gouverneur Morris to be appointed to the Pennsylvania delegation of the convention. Gouverneur made the most of the opportunity, writing the final draft of the Constitution. As Amendments, the structure of government, and the tug of war between states and federal rights was hotly debated; Morris primarily played the role of church mouse. He knew his day in the sun had come and that in many ways— two years after the war— to some he had grown long in the tooth. Instead, he could take solace in the convention being the grandest part of his life's manifest. All through the hot and humid summer, Morris said very little in the hall, sparing most of his intellectual thought and political wisdom for Gouverneur. When there was something he deeply objected to or wanted proffered— that the debate might move in certain direction— he tended to run it through James Wilson, a fellow delegate and his personal attorney, who had also been Haym's lawyer before his passing. Interestingly, it was Wilson and Gouverneur who took to the floor more than any other two men during the convention. Paradoxically, the honor Morris would bestow wasn't politically motivated though it was political in nature. It was Morris who nominated his friend, colleague, and man he held in the highest esteem for the country's good fortune, George Washington, for the role of President.

Two years later, as Washington assembled his cabinet, Morris was the first he sought out. The ex-Superintendent of Finance was the obvious choice for Secretary of the Treasury. However, Morris declined the offer. Instead, he used the opportunity to pay another political debt. He suggested Alexander Hamilton for the position. All of the monetary policy with which the United States based their finances was from the mind and conversations of Robert Morris and Alexander Hamilton. Morris loved Washington for his grit and he appreciated Haym Salomon for his might, but it was Hamilton who was his kindred spirit. Morris detoured his own political career to something slightly outside the direct line of fire and served as U.S. Senator from the great state of Pennsylvania. Though no longer glared at under the microscope of Congress, he was active with forty-one Senatorial committees and even reported for many of them. As Hamilton proposed new economic policies, they found powerful Congressional support through Morris. This wasn't surprising, for each of those new economic policies were principally based on Morris' old pamphlet, "On Public Credit."

Morris' financial portfolio was varied and numerous. He purchased enormous swaths of land, becoming the single largest landowner in America; invested in airship companies, iron mills, theaters, icehouses, greenhouses, and many other interesting capital ventures. As he had always done, he made some here, lost some money there, but in the balance was richer for his endeavors. However, in 1794 he set upon building a mansion to rival European royalty. It was an unwise decision in a weak economy by a highly leveraged fortune. With the French Revolution raging, an anticipated loan from financiers in Holland failed to materialize when the Dutch entered the conflict. A combination of the Panic of 1797 and the Napoleonic Wars, which followed the Revolution, ultimately wrecked the American real estate market. For Morris, who heavily borrowed on his land holdings for ready-cash to pay debts, suddenly found himself a very rich man in dire straits. He couldn't borrow enough hard currency to pay his creditors and they sought their relief as though he was just any other debtor, and not the man who created the economy. Morris was arrested in February 1798 and imprisoned for debt until August of 1801.

Morris wasn't alone in the falling fortunes of many Founding Fathers. Though the fall for some came on the cause of his own own financial collapse, as much of what he invested in was mimicked by his old compatriots. Morris had both friends and enemies in high places. As his enemies picked his political bones and filled his empty seats of power, his friends in Congress passed the nation's first bankruptcy legislation, the temporary Bankruptcy Act of 1800, in part, to legally spring Morris from prison. The great man spent the rest of his life in a penniless retirement until his peaceful passing on May 8th, 1806.

***

In 1844, sparked by Jared Sparks, Haym M. Salomon retired from his mercantile business and made it the remaining quest of his life to bring glorifying justice to the memory of his father. He went about collecting evidence, acquiring affidavits, and constructing a case to present to Congress. In the process, a little political patriotic storm gathered around him. Great names of the day like: Clay, Calhoun, and Webster came to his defense as a cause celeb!

Growing up in the hazy myths about his father's passing, Haym M. intended to avoid such calamitous misadventures, which beset his mother. As a matter of fact, he went so far to advert the disastrous mishap his mother had with the Probate Court of Philadelphia losing her security certificates that he offered the remaining unsigned securities the family retained, to President Tyler for safekeeping. Left to the care of a sitting president, he had no worries of their guardianship. Additionally, Haym M. visited the Secretary of the Treasury, Mr. Walter Forward and impressed him a large sheaf of Revolutionary documents which he also left to his care in the expectation that just deserved reimbursement would soon follow.

On March 3rd of 1847, he entered into the well of the House. It was the final calendar day of sessions in a Congress that oversaw expansion, change, and prosperity at breakneck speed. Of his various instruments of evidence, they were little more than notarized recollections, reflections from the letters of founding fathers, and even favorable correspondences from the likes of the new President James K. Polk. His clincher, grand finale, knock out punch, stroke of grace! — was to be a signed document he had obtained nineteen years early from the administrative office which had received his mother's securities and papers all those years ago. It read the inventory what they took into their possession:

> 58 loan-office certificates
> 19 Treasury certificates
> 2 Virginia State certificates
> 70 commissioners' certificates
> Continental liquidated certificates
> Totaling: $353,744.45
> I certify that the above writing is a true extract
> from the original inventory and appraisement of
> the personal estate of Haym Salomon deceased
> filed in the register's office Philadelphia on the
> 15th February, 1785.
> (Signed) John Geyer, Register.
>
> Given under my hand and seal of office this 28th
> May, A. D. 1828.

Armed with the two presidential letters, which validated the obvious right to his claim, Haym M. expected a day of victory. Instead, he was offered a day of optimism. Being the last day of Session, the 29th Congress decided to table the matter for the next Congress, with a favorable recommendation.

***

The Revolutionary Claims Committee of the 30th Congress took up Haym M.'s claim, Number 504. The committee had been in existence under one name or another since 1813. The varying members had examined thousands of claims and pensions since the early days of the body. The right to petition the government for redress of grievances is among the most fundamental individual rights guaranteed in the First Amendment to the Constitution. From the earliest days, Americans had freely used the right to petition Congress, and by the time Haym M. appeared, the hallowed branch of government had already presided over 250,000 claims.

Representative Dickinson presented the claim and Haym M. spoke eloquently of his father, though it was all-anecdotal from the educational notes of Professor Sparks. What he was able to speak directly of was the tally of emotional hardship and family divide that preceded the basis of his claim. He didn't seek restitution for being given up by his mother as a child. He defended her actions with grace on the grounds that she was an overwhelmed woman who knew little of his father's business and was bullied by lawyers, creditors, and administrators, not to the mention the liability of the Congress and State of Pennsylvania. He mentioned that of the entire estate, which was handled by men outside of the family, she received a grand total of $3,000 for the value of the household goods four years after his father's passing! He declared by his presence that he was only asking for that which was rightfully due he and his sister Sallie by record of his father's contributions. Then, he presented a letter from Madison. It read:

> "Dear Sir: The transactions shown by the papers
> you enclosed were for the support of the delegates
> to Congress, and the agency of your father therein
> was solicited on account of the respectability and
> confidence he enjoyed among those best
> acquainted with him."

The next item of evidentiary worth was a letter Madison addressed to his colleagues years before Haym's death. It read in part:

> "I have been a pensioner for some time on the
> favor of Mr. Haym Salomon." "I am almost
> ashamed to reiterate my wants so incessantly to
> you. The kindness of our friend in Front Street,
> near the coffeehouse, is a fund that will preserve
> me from extremities; but I never resort to it
> without great mortification, as he obstinately
> rejects all recompense. To necessitous delegates he
> always spares them supplies."

However, impressive the affidavit and letters were, the Senators inquired about simple direct proof that payment was owed. Haym M. blushed as he was forced to explain his inability to procure much that he had taken years to attain. For instance, the Post Master General informed him that the archive of material he requested in return from President Tyler had inadvertently been lost in the mail. Likewise, the Treasury Secretary was unable to locate the Revolutionary documents bestowed upon him. To some degree, it seemed as if Haym M.'s claim was fraught with either mismanagement, misfortune, or a warm sticky combination of the two. Undaunted Haym M. carried on his train and trail of circumstantial evidence. He produced a letter of Don Francisco Rendon to the Governor General of Cuba. It read:

> "Mr. Salomon has advanced the money of 10,000 Spanish dollars for the service of his most Catholic Majesty, and I am indebted to his friendship in this particular, for the support of my character as his most Catholic Majesty's agent here, with any degree of credit or reputation; and without it, I would not have been able to render that protection and assistance to his Majesty's subjects which his Majesty enjoins and my duty requires."

Further Haym M. pressed on, and presented similar letters from the French embassy at 150,000,000 livres, roughly $747,000; all of which passed through the hands of Haym as the French banker. Through mercantile commissions he increased the sum to an exponentially larger amount of which the capital investment he devoted to the republic. The daybook and ledger of the Bank of North America exhibited a receipt by Robert Morris of nearly $200,000 in coin. The Bank of North America kindly supplied him a detailed accounting of his father's transaction and they read as follows:

> "The account of Haym Salomon with the Bank of North America appears to have been early as the beginning of its operations, from January, 1782, and only to January 1784, occupies fifteen entire pages of the ledger. The first forty other entire accounts, beginning also from first of the ledger, occupy, in all, but fifteen pages. The same appears the proportion of the amount of his account when compared with the others.
> The following are the balances, as appears in the bankbook of Haym Salomon, for those periods, as

they are in the same handwriting as the ledger of the bank:

February 1, 1782:	$23,253.00
April 23, 1782:	$32,233.00
June 26, 1782:	$46,569.00
August 14, 1782:	$18,238.64
May 2, 1783:	$14,144.35
July 1, 1783:	$11,005.62
August 25, 1783:	$14,854.27
March 31, 1784:	$26,743.74

Respecting the examination of the deposition of the amount charged in the undermentioned checks or drafts to the account of Haym Salomon, paid to Robert Morris and to superintendent of finance:

August 1, 1782:	$20,000
August 9, 1782:	$10,000
August 27, 1783:	$20,000
October 8, 1783:	$6,000
October 13, 1783:	$6,000
October 17, 1783:	$6,000
October 27, 1783:	$3,000
October 30, 1783:	$5,000

The above with thirty-three other orders, amounting to upwards of one hundred thousand dollars, exclusive of the above, of various dates and amounts, appear all charged as having been paid to Robert Morris, in the daybook and ledger of the bank.

The account of Robert Morris himself begins July 17, 1782, and ends may 6, 1783, being about the same period of time as Haym Salomon's account, as examined. The credit side consists principally of two discounts— $22,625.20. The only cash deposited by him was $9,822.06, which appears to have been received from Haym Salomon, as Haym Salomon's account is that day charged with the exact amount stated as paid to Robert Morris.

I have examined the charges in the account of the ledger of the bank against Haym Salomon, of various dates, as received by the following persons: Jefferson, Wilson, Ross, Morris, Harrison, Pendleton, Madison, Randolph, Jones, who are said, in history, to have been members of the Congress of the Declaration, or of the subsequent session of the revolutionary legislature, and found them to agree as to dates and amounts, as well as the sums and dates of those charged to Haym Salomon, as paid to general St. Clair, General Mifflin, and Baron Steuben, with the charges of the same in the bank books.

Respecting, the disposition of the funds charged to Haym Salomon, at the bank, as made payable to the persons undernamed, who according to the journals of the revolutionary Congress, examined, as per certificate of librarian of the House of Representatives of the United States, August eighteen, eighteen hundred and forty-eight, and according to an exemplification, marked F, from files in the Department of State, signed James Buchanan, Secretary of State, with the seal of that department, papers of old Congress, number 137, page 193, were agents, consuls, chargé d'affaires, and ministers of Louis XVI of France and Charles III of Spain, our allies of the revolution, I found by examination of the payments to Roquebrun said to have been the treasurer of Rochambaud's army, August 2, 1782, August 15, and August 18, 1782, amounting to $61,404.38, which several amounts are credited on the same days in the account as received by Roquebrun from Haym Salomon.

Sieur De La Forrest, consul general of France in the revolution, is credited with twenty drafts, amounting to $31,434.39, charged in the bankbook and ledger to Haym Salomon.

John Holker, consul of King Louis; the amount as payable to him is also charged to Haym Salomon's account.

Sieur Barbe Marbois, chargé d'affaires of the King; the checks charged, as far as examined, as for amounts received at the bank from Haym Salomon, by him, were credited on the bank ledger as received by Marbois from Haym Salomon.

Chevalier De La Luzerne, the French ambassador of King Louise XVI, so friendly to this country in the revolution. All the checks charged, or so many as were examined, stated as payable to La Luzerne, were also charged on the ledger of the bank to Haym Salomon, as paid the chevalier; and the only cash deposits of the latter agree precisely with the amount named on the check payable to him.

Don Francisco Rendon, the secret minister of Charles III, of Spain, in the revolution; the amount and date of the check charged, as payable to him, agree precisely with the ledger of the bank, as charged to Haym Salomon.

J. HOCKLEY
Cashier of the Bank of North America

The son of Haym Salomon couldn't have done much better. He impressed the committee mightily. There was only one question for many of the senators that seemed to elude a rational explanation. That question was, how could Wilson and Rittenhouse have lost the vouchers and still they have never surfaced? Haym M. could only speculate and suspect innocent incompetence and in time some clerk enterprising in the value of the future requisitioned them for the signatures of Washington and the others.

Led by Senator Frederick A. Tallmadge of New York, the committee found that it could ascertain for certain if the administrator of Haym's finances did not receive a small percentage, which was paid for that class of debts of the government some years after his death. However, from the evidence in the possession of the committee, the patriotic devotion of Haym Salomon to the cause of American Independence cannot, in their judgement be questioned. In the view of all the facts, they were induced to consider Haym M.'s father as one of the truest and most efficient friends of the country in a very critical period of its history, and when its pecuniary resources were few and its difficulties many and pressing. Therefore, they arrived at the conclusion that Haym M. was eminently and undoubtedly entitled to relief. The only question remaining to be considered, was the manner in which it should be allowed.

However, for this figure to be determined, the federal auditor would have to respectfully reexamine the evidence and come to a just amount considering the nature of Continental Currency and what value it held in relation to the gold standard dollar. Unfortunately, this process of examination would take a generous degree of time. Therefore, they offered Haym M. a simple calculation. The full monetary and numerical measure of his claim in the indemnification of something other than hard currency. He could have $353,729.43 of the equivalent value in land grants.

After a brief thought, considering his advanced age and the complex difficulties in dealing with land — he respectfully declined. Instead, he confidently felt it prudent to patiently wait for the auditor's report, expecting it to be within the calendar of the 30th Session, which encompassed a full remaining year. Puzzling, as it would be, it was the best offer he was going to receive from Congress for a long time to come.

***

Ezekiel Salomon died young, two years shy of his father's youthful eternal rest. Just like his father, he lived a full and prosperous life. He joined the navy at a young age and was privy to much adventure, including fighting in the First Barbary War in Africa. He had a healthy amount of distain for his mother and upon both of their returns to the United States, it was he who initiated the revaluation of his father's unresolved war lending. Her assistance wasn't forthcoming and he was forced to take action against her and Thomas Fitzsimmons — a signer to the Constitution — for documents relating to the property of Haym Salomon, and upon a promissory note drawn by them and endorsed to him.

Ezekiel was an exceptionally brave man who showed valor in the war and at times of trouble. His service was well noted, respected, and rewarded by the Navy and the government. A math wiz— like father, like son— he was charged with operating the U.S. Bank in New Orleans. Socially, he was a 32nd Degree Freemason. It was from this vantage point in which he sought to restore his father's legacy to its rightful place among the founding fathers— many of whom were direct recipients of his altruism, not to mention the whole of the country by the sum result of Revolutionary War. In 1821, at the age of forty-three, he contracted an undiagnosed illness and died very shortly thereafter. In writing to his brother, he reminded him of the responsibility, which they uniquely bared to a man who was more than their father, if not their father at all except in the biological architecture of love. That is he, Haym Salomon, an intercessor— a holy ghost! And that "He" is always with them, in the spirit of the republic being a nation of laws and not of men; in the manifestation of the sooth that all men are in actuality created equal; and he is hypostatized in every inch of the copper and steel sparkling at the entrance of the shinning city on the hill— in the living words of his life welcoming the exiles, the tired, the poor, the huddled masses yearning to breathe free; the wretched refuse of teeming foreign shores and Judengasses all over the world— the homeless tempest-tost Jew and gentile alike. Ezekiel implored his young brother to recognize that all free men, from Jews, to Catholics, to former slaves, must remember to pay homage to Haym Salomon— so that what was a world devoid of equal liberty may never rise again.

***

Haym M. Salomon had to wait two years before the Treasury responded to the 30th Congress' inquiry as to the appropriate means to calculate what was owed to the remaining Salomon descendent. Facing the 31st Congress, Haym M. was accompanied by some of his children and grandchildren. Now, it was Cullen Sawtelle, of Maine, who presided over the proceedings. The Salomon family sat anxiously before the committee as Thomas L. Smith, the First Auditor of the Treasury Department was called to testify as to his findings.

"State your name for the record," Sawtelle said.
"Thomas L. Smith, Esquire."
"Your position at the Treasury Department, sir?"

"I am the chief auditor, Senator."

"Sir, would you please be good enough to answer simply yea or nay, to the following questions, arising out of the case of Mr. H.M. Salomon now before the Committee of Revolutionary Claims, of which I am the chairman."

"If I am able," Smith said.

"All right then. First, can you find that any of the annexed described paper was funded after the present government was established by Rachel Salomon, relict of Haym Salomon, or by either of the children of Haym Salomon, namely: Ezekiel Salomon, Sarah Salomon, Deborah Salomon, or Haym M. Salomon?" Sawtelle asked.

"Well—"

"Please, allow me to finish my questions first, then you may answer them one at a time."

"Very well, as you wish," Smith deferred.

"Second question," Sawtelle began. "Can you find whether any of said Revolutionary paper was ever funded or paid to Thomas Fitzsimmons, Matthew Clarkson, Joseph Carson, or Eleazor Levy, administrators of Haym Salomon? Third question, can you find that said Rachel Salomon, wife of the deceased, or any of the children of Haym Salomon, ever funded any kind of Revolutionary paper at all, or any number, or amount, after the new government was established in 1789? And lastly, can you find that the above Revolutionary paper left by Haym Salomon, was ever funded or paid to any person or persons at all after the adoption of the present Constitution? Now please, you may answer." Smith patted his brow from the humid conditions, inside and outside the building. He followed minor preening with a gulp from a provided glass of water. Then, he opened his briefcase, removed four large files; shuffled in his chair, then cleared his throat.

"Are you prepared to answer?" Sawtelle inquired.

"Yes, Chairman, I am," Smith said assuredly. "Well Chairman, proposing the four questions, requesting me to answer simply yea or nay, I have the honor to state that, after a careful search through more than ten thousand pages of records of funded certificates of Revolutionary debt, being the entire series of said records, page by page— for they do not appear to have made indexes previous to the present century—"

"I'm sorry about that," Sawtelle said rather humorously.

Everyone present laughed, including Haym and his family, though they were nervously anticipating the next words to come out of the auditor's mouth.

"I have to give a negative answer to each and all of the your inquires, which I accordingly hereby do."

The words were a bombshell. Haym was disheartened. However, Senator Sawtelle rose to his defense and simply tabled the matter for the time being.

Haym M. brought the claim back to the 35th, 36th, and 37th, Congresses. Each time the bill received a favorable report out of committee. But as it moved a long the process of passage it was hampered by delays; placed at the bottom of dockets and pushed, while more pressing bills on wars and railroad superseded it. Ultimately, up to that time, Haym had no powerful sponsors and therefore a lack of thrust into a united action forsaken the claim from ever becoming legislation and money in his hand. The government frequently acknowledged a monumental debt was owed, but appeared to have no urgent intention of paying it.

***

EPILOGUE

"Our country is in danger, but not to be despaired of. Our enemies are numerous and powerful; but we have many friends, determining to be free, and heaven and earth will aid the resolution. On you depend the fortunes of America. You are to decide the important question, on which rest the happiness and liberty of millions yet unborn. Act worthy of yourselves."   *Joseph Warren*

The discordant echoing racket of tick-tock — tick-tock reverberated in intermittent sinusoidal waves of motion throughout the nearly empty Senate chamber. The only objects to bend or alter their paths were one old man and adolescent pages preparing for the day's legislative activities. At nearly fifty, the Senate Clock, or the "Ohio Clock," as was its enigmatic epithet, was no spring chicken by the modern standard of usefulness but youthful in the art and mechanics of time. She was an elegant but gainly old behemoth of dead dark wood standing at the south entrance of the new two-tiered Senate chamber. It thrummed, tick-tock — tick-tock — in marks and strokes of the unfeigned transference of the limited progress of the third dimension. Tick-tock-tick-tock — through, in, and around all sixty-two desks waiting to be occupied by men of connected tissue, frames of bone, and rushes of blood. It throbbed and pulsed, tick-tock-tick-tock — into elapses and advances of the casual countertransference of the fourth dimension. Tick-tock-tick-tock — penetrating through the dreams inside the soul, the minutes and hours of heaven above as below, and into and out of the imprisoned ghost of Haym Salomon indefinitely lost to impersonal bills, motions, and votes.

The round glass face of the timepiece indicated a mean solar time of three minutes to two o'clock in the afternoon. One-by-one, the stately men representing the 38th Congress of the United States filed in, taking their place in the interference of the ticking sound waves.

The distinguished President of the Senate and 15th Vice President of the land, Mr. Hannibal Hamlin, was absent. In his place, President pro tempore, Daniel Clark of New Hampshire was presiding. The heavy-smoking, irascible, horseshoed mustached man arrived behind the full hoard of his colleagues. Upon his entering, a page brought the large double doors of the chamber to a tight close. The tick-tock-tick-tock ceased in the measure of a shooting star that burns out beyond the horizon. The spacious and still unpainted assembly subsequently rustled with only the motley susurrous sounds of humanity. Then, Clark took the embellished seat set against the arched Roman vaulting.

Simultaneously, having trudged nineteen more stairs, Haym M. Salomon reached his balcony perch, from which he peered down on the sinew of men who would cast his fate and approbate their respect on the ghostly memory of his father— for whom they would not exist in their orotund form. Reverend Bernard Nadal opened the session with a thoughtful prayer to the God that administered over the providence of war, which beset them. Amen, and Clark dutifully initiated the session with the presentation of a petition from Adam Gurowski, praying that the horse cars in the city of Washington may be allowed to run on Sundays; which was ordered to lie on the table.

Haym M. had seen his own prayer and petition left lying on the table more than once, but he knew for sure that June 24, 1864, was going to be a lucky day for the name "Salomon." Clark had been the chairman of the Claims Committee and oversaw much of Haym's joy and shared his frustration, but in charge of the day's proceedings, Haym M. was sure he would bring the bill from committee and the House to a vote. Right on schedule, the first order of business was a claim from the Claims Committee, George H. Plant. It was only a matter of moments before his well-favored petition would be introduced and maybe his prayers answered. Next was a bill about the navy and then one about a state militia.

Haym M. Salomon was a few months shy of eighty years in his skin and karma and below him "Yea" and "Nay" were sounded off with either regular boredom or enraptured fury! Some debate was had; a little pompous, self-indulgent display here and a bit of arrogant strutting and boisterous theatrics there. Nevertheless, it was fast and furious, one bill after another was tabled or voted on. Then finally, like the sun breaking through the clouds, his turn struck with what sounded as though an alarm!

"Mr. Salomon," the honorable Mr. Morton Wilkinson of Minnesota shouted, knowing Haym was in attendance. "How long must a man wait?"

It was Wilkinson whom the Senate referred the claim to for a sixth time. They demanded an exhaustive and thorough investigation and Wilkinson sure gave them one.

"Mr. Salomon, the senate recognizes your inquiry and each in this room have properly read your grievance against the United States Government, as pertains to the monetary restitution of stated loan during a most troubling time in this nation's history. We, as a body, are grateful and indebted to your father, Haym Salomon, for his ferocious dedication to the Revolution and the establishment of freedom! He is a shining example of service and the epitome of self-sacrifice in a most noble cause. Now, let us vote!"

With each vote loudly cast, Haym was grasping his father's prayer book and wiping escaped tears more slowly than they coursed down his wrinkled cheek. He listened anxiously to what he finally believed was to be the long-awaited acknowledgment of his ancestor's honorable work. For nearly twenty-five years, he had implored the highest governing body of the country to favorably address the issue and make remuneration for which his mother, Rachel, his brother Ezekiel, and his sisters Sallie and Deborah, were unable to collect. On a tension filled second reading, with the last mind changed and the final vote recorded, Senate Bill 331 was passed. It read:

> "Be it enacted by the Senate and House of Representatives of the United States of America in Congress assembled, That the Secretary of the Treasury be, and is hereby, authorized and directed to cause to be paid, out of any moneys in the treasure not otherwise appropriated, to Haym M. Salomon, only surviving son and legal representative of Haym Salomon, deceased, or to his legally appointed attorney or attorneys, administrators or assigns, in lieu of the indebtedness due from the United States to said Haym Salomon at the time of his death, as the same appears from the inventory filed by his administrators on the fifteen day of February seventeen hundred and eighty-five, in the court of probate in Philadelphia, and sworn to on the fifth

and sixth days of August, eighteen hundred and forty-six, the sum of three hundred and fifty-three thousand seven hundred and twenty-nine dollars and forty-three cents: Provided, That the said Haym M. Salomon, or his legal representatives, relinquish all further claim upon the government on account of such claim."

Mr. Wilkinson made the following report to accompany bill:

"The committee on Revolutionary Claims, to whom was referred the memorial of Haym M. Salomon for indemnity for advances of money made by his father to the United States during the Revolutionary War, have had the same under consideration, and respectfully report:

The claim of the memorialist is one of undeniable merit. It is for money advanced to the Revolutionary Government when the public credit was exhausted, its Treasury bankrupt, and specie almost impossible to obtained. It has been repeatedly examined by some of the ablest committees of the two Houses of Congress and always reported upon favorably, with a bill for the relief of the memorialist; but the great magnitude of the papers and vouchers required so protracted an examination as to place it last on the calendar at each session, and never to come within the reach of final action.
The facts show that Haym Salomon, the father of the memorialist, a native of Poland, settled in this country as a merchant and banker before the Revolution and was a zealous supporter of the war for independence; that he was a man of unquestioned integrity, great financial resources and ability, and enjoyed the highest confidence of our public men of the time, as is shown by the most abundant proof, as stated in the reports of

the various committees; that his large, private fortune and the proceeds of his extensive commercial earnings were freely applied to the use of the Revolutionary Government and its various public men, and the agents of foreign governments friendly to our cause, whose supplies were for the time cut off; that during the war he was imprisoned, with Stockton and others, as early as the year 1775, at New York, in the loathsome prison called the 'Provost,' where he contracted the disease which ended in his death just at the close of the war and before any steps had been taken to secure the same or by the Government to reimburse him for the large amount he had advanced for its use.

When he died he left a young wife not familiar with our language and four young children, the youngest, the present memorialist, being some three weeks old, at the time when all matters, both public and private, were in a state of the greatest depression and confusion and necessarily exposed to corresponding hazard and neglect. The inventory of his private estate, as filed in the probate court in Philadelphia on the 15th day of February, 1785, exhibited among other things the following public securities as forming part of its assets, viz:

Loan-office certificates: $110,233.63
Treasury certificates: $18,244.88
Continental liquidated dollars: $199,214.44
Commissioners' certificates: $17,870.37
Virginia State certificates: $8,166.00
Total: $353,729.43

After a careful inspection of disbursements, and payments by the Government from 1781 to the formation of the present Government in 1789, it appears that no part of this indebtedness was ever paid to Haym Salomon or his heirs or that any payments whatever were made to him or his representatives; and in an official statement of the first auditor of the Treasury, in answer to questions propounded by the committee of the House of Representatives when examining the same subject, with a certified copy of these evidences of debt before him, that officer stated that no part of the sum had been paid or funded by anyone since the formation of the present Government. It is therefore conclusive to the mind of your committee that no such payment ever has been made and that the same is still a valid claim for proper indemnity in favor of the memorialist. It is also proved by the original checks and vouchers before your committee that Haym Salomon advanced in specie to the 'Superintendent of Finance' of the Revolutionary Government (Robert Morris), at various times and in various sums, to the amount of some $211,678, for which amount the original checks are before your committee, excepting two or three which are mislaid, but are well vouched for and referred to in former reports.

The evidence before your committee also proves that Haym Salomon advanced to the Government six promissory notes, amounting to 34,758 pounds, 18 shillings, 2 pence, Pennsylvania currency, or in Federal currency about $92,600, for which the original receipt of M. Hillegos, Continental Treasurer, is presented, showing that it was for the use of the United States.

There is also before your committee the promissory note of Haym Salomon for $20,000, payable in 30 days to the order of Robert Morris, which shows by the bank and paid by Mr. Salomon at maturity, whose name is erased, and Robert Morris is still on it. There is no doubt that this note was loaned to Mr. Morris, for the reason that a receipt was given bearing even date with

the note, 'July 25th, 1783,' and there is a
memorandum endorsed on the note to that effect,
so specifying. And considering that Mr. Morris
was at that time exclusively engaged in
financiering for the government, which was
greatly in need of means, it is most likely the
proceeds of this note were so applied, though the
memorialist does not claim it as part of his
demands against the Government.

It is also proved by the vouchers before your
committee that Haym Salomon provided the
means to support the ambassador of the King of
Spain, Don Francisco Rendon, who was in secret
alliance with the Revolutionary Government and
whose supplies were cut off by the British
cruisers. This fact was acknowledged in an official
letter from the minister to the governor general of
Cuba, and the original orders uncanceled, to the
amount of 10,000 Spanish dollars, are before your
committee, showing that the amount was never
paid. But the memorialist does not, nor never has
asked this Government to pay that sum.

All the reports from the committees of both
Houses show that Haym Salomon supported from
his private means many of the principal men of
the Revolution, who otherwise, as stated by
themselves, could not have attended to their
public duties, among whom are mentioned
Jefferson, Madison, Lee, Steuben, Mifflin, St. Clair,
Blond, Mercer, Jones, Monroe, Wilson, and others;
but the package of vouchers containing the
original letters and orders from these parties to
Mr.Salomon, with the important confidential
statements of these parties, together with many
other important as well as interesting matters of
fact, have all disappeared from the proper files in
the case since the adjournment of the last
Congress, and no search has been able to find or
discover them. It is supposed they have all been

extracted for the sake of the original autograph letters and signatures they embraced. But sufficient of their contents has been preserved in the former reports to show their accuracy, and the importance of the relief granted to those who devoted their whole time to the public service, and wherein the patriot Madison says, in 1783-

'The expediency of drawing bills on Virginia, even the most unquestionable, has been tried by us in vain. I am fast relapsing into pecuniary distress. The case of my brethren is equally alarming. I have been a prisoner for some time on the favor of Haym Salomon. I am almost ashamed to reiterate my wants so incessantly to you. The kindness of our friend near the coffeehouse (Haym Salomon) is a fund that will preserve me from extremities, but I never resort to it without great mortification, as he obstinately rejects all recompense. To necessitous delegates he always spares them supplies, etc.'

The distressed condition of the public men of the time is corroborated by Mr. Morris, superintendent of finance, who, in 1781, wrote the president of Congress that 'the Treasury was so much in arrears to the servants in the public offices that many of them could not, without payment, perform their duties, but must have gone to jail for debts they have contracted to enable them to live,' etc., had they not been favored with assistance.

It was in a crisis like this that Mr. Salomon not only aided the Government directly, as we have seen, but sustained its public men without reservation or security, trusting in the honor and gratitude of the American people when independence should have been secured.

As evidence of the ability of Haym Salomon to make the advances before stated, your committee have before them the sworn statement of the cashier of the Bank of North America, taken from its books, showing that after making all these payments and loans his bank account at the end of each consecutive quarter during the time referred to averaged a surplus of from $11,000 to $46,000; and the same sworn statement also proves, from the same books, the advance of the large sums stated to Robert Morris; and indeed, in all respects corroborate the financial character and responsibility of the father of the memorialist. The sworn statement also proves the advances made to the various public men of the Revolution before mentioned, showing the orders or checks upon which the money was paid.

The committees of the last Congress state that 'In order to be satisfied how far payments of the whole or any part of these advances or Government obligations have been made, have had brought before them full exemplification of all the revolutionary expenditures and payments anterior to the formation of the present Government, but do not find that there is any evidence of such payments having been made to the father of the memorialist or to his heirs or legal representatives after his death.'

'That the accounts rendered by the superintendent of finance have been carefully examined, and no discharge of any of any of these obligations can be found.' That 'a like search has been made in the private accounts of Robert Morris, as stated upon his oath while incarcerated for debt in the year 1805, and no payments to, or charges against, Haym Salomon appear in any shape.' And the first author of the Treasury states officially that no such payments have been made since the formation of the present Government, which is conclusive evidence that there is justly due the memorialist a large sum.

The evidence before your committee shows that the memorialist has been diligent in pursuing his claim. At the death of his father, in 1785, his brother, the eldest of the family, was but 7 years old. When he arrived at maturity, he found the large real estate owned by his father all sold, and no account rendered of anything. Steps were taken to pursue such rights were as were visible, and among others, this demand; but as the evidence was scattered, and they were compelled to earn a livelihood by their industry, things moved slowly. Early in this century, his elder brother dying in the discharge of public duties, far from home, the memorialist took charge of it, and has pursued it by every proper means in his power.

Many of the survivors of the Revolution, who were the compeers and knew the sacrifices made by Haym Salomon, wrote encouraging letters to the memorialist on the subject. Among these may be mentioned one from James Madison in 1827 who, among other things, stated;

'The transactions shown by the papers you enclose Were for the support of the Delegates to Congress, and the agency of your father herein was solicited on account of the respect and confidence he enjoyed among those best acquainted with him,' etc., and concludes with the wish that the memorialist might be properly indemnified. But, without amplifying, there is sufficient to show that the memorialist has been vigilant in the pursuit of his rights, and though he has had numerous reports made in his favor he never could get his case finally acted upon. The aggregate of the indebtedness or demand of the memorialist against the Government and of the monies advanced to the public men of the Revolution, as shown by the papers and recognized by all the committees of both Houses, which have examined the same, may be stated thus:

Government obligations of the various species before stated: $353,729.43

Specie advanced at various times to Superintendent of finance: $211,678.00

Haym Salomon's six promissory notes: 34,758 pounds 18 shillings and 2 pence; or, in Federal currency, say:$92,600.00

Making a total of: $658,007.43

Besides the note of $20,000, evidently loaned to Robert Morris, and the $10,000 and upward advanced to Don Francisco Rendon, the ambassador of Spain, and an indefinite amount advanced to the many of the most devoted men of the Revolution, which is not enumerated or claimed by the memorialist.

In former reports in favor of the memorialist it has been recommended that a bill be passed appropriating to him the amount of Government obligation held by his father at the time of his death, viz, $353,729.43, except the report of this committee made at the last session."

The verdict of Haym's final attempt to recuperate funds he believed his father had lost to the Federal Government, although favorable to him, was ultimately nothing more than a hallow victory. It was the darkest hour of national finances for the United States. Salomon P. Chase had just withdrawn a loan from the market for want of acceptable bids, and the capacity of the country to lend seemed exhausted, so by extension was it's ability to immediately remedy a dying man for a batch of almost one hundred year old loans. The currency had been enormously inflated and as William Fessenden took reigns of the treasury at the sudden departure of Chase, he declared that no more currency should be issued until finances could be sured.

Akin to a Greek tragedy, Haym died within seven months of his triumphant day. With his passing, after a year of non-compliance, the government was shouldered with a claim for relief by his son Samuel. He headed an enormous contingent of brothers, sisters, and cousins who sought the expectant funds. However, after two years of ignoring his pleas and with most of the descents being of substantial means, including Samuel who headed a private bank, they petitioned the government for something new, a simple coin. The Salomon clan sought a gold coin in honor of their grandfather for which in return they would renounce all claims. By 1893, fifteen years later, their wish appeared to be granted, as this too, was taken up by the Congress and favorably voted on. Yet, was history repeated and the coin went unstruck.

The Haym Salomon matter presented itself again on the nation's sesquicentennial— 1926. A committee headed by Samuel Oppenheim, the lawyer and Jewish historian, conducted a thorough examination into the Salomon claim. According to Oppenheim's findings, the claim now was chiefly based on securities Haym had owned at the time of his death, which were represented as issued in payment of "loans" he made to the Continental government. By his examination and discretion, it was Oppenheim's point and impression that Haym in fact did not have the money to make such substantial loans. This followed that those securities recorded as "money" at the time, were largely depreciated, and some plainly common "investments." Oppenheim asserted that their possession, even prima-facie, did not indicate that they represented original loans to the government. Moreover, Haym was a known dealer in those very securities, and bought and sold them on a regular, if not daily basis. This contention was in accord with Haym's own advertisements. Therefore, in his hands there was even less reason to suppose they represented advances in such sums, which he had made to the strapped government.

However, Oppenheim in his meticulous handling of the evidence, went further and retained the history of the securities involved and listed in detail the "inventory" and "account" of Haym Salomon's administrators soon after his death, respectfully and separately: Thomas Fitzsimmons, Matthew Clarkson, Eleazor Levy, and Joseph Carson. Oppenheim's evidence appeared to show that nearly all the certificates issued pre-dated Haym's near improbable arrival to Philadelphia and his direct financial connection with the government. Oppenheim didn't stop there— he upped the ante and produced photostat copies of the original surrogate court records of Philadelphia, which presumably showed that the proof submitted by Haym M., was false in that the bulk of the securities which he owned at the time of his death, on which the claim of loans to the government rested, were described in a document purporting to be officially certified in 1828 as "liquidated currency," whereas they were "un-liquidated," according to the original records, thereby increasing nearly all the amounts involved by a multiplication of forty fold. According to the prevailing law, under which "un-liquidated dollars" were scaled down to 1/40 of their face, in accordance with a measure of their depreciated value, making a holding of about $10,000 figure as $400,000 liquidated; this undisputed fact constituted four-fifths of the whole estate. The succeeding finding or assertion of import Oppenheim leveled against the hundred year-old claim was that the Philadelphia Surrogate Court records affirmatively attest from the administrators of Haym's account that the bulk of the remaining securities were turned over by them to his chief creditor, the Bank of North America, to be applied to the reduction of their claim, when sold. If such was the case it is without question as a financial institution, as an instrument of liquidation, that they most likely turned them in to the government or otherwise disposed of them, and the government or the states, after such transfer, owed the money for which they were to be redeemed to that bank, and not to the Haym Salomon estate. Oppenheim's committee had one last deathblow to the wraith recognition of Haym Salomon. They went so far as to impugn the motives and the assertion of claims by noting that Haym never filed a claim of his own and insinuated that the prayers brought before Congress by his son forty-two years later were no more than an act of desperation over validity.

Perhaps John Geyer, the clerk in the Philadelphia public office made a mistake, when giving his "certified copy." Perhaps he assumed or misdescribed the debt and papers to be "Continental liquidated dollars" instead of "un-liquidated." Perhaps if Macrae had not met such a strange, untimely, and harrowing end, then Rachel and the children would have been well protected from the pecuniary vultures of misfortune. Perhaps the certified transcript of the administrator's accounts was fraudulently altered, after execution but before submission to Congress, with or without the knowledge or wherewithal of Haym M.. Perhaps, James Wilson, whose fingerprints appeared to be hovering over a couple inexplicable transactions and tragedies following Haym's death did not act in the most virtuous and responsible manner. Perhaps he made with some of the papers and by forgery found reimbursement from the states in which they were purchased. Though a founding father and a member of the Supreme

Court, he was a notorious serial debtor who managed to stay one step ahead of his creditor by accumulating yet more unsuspecting fools. That was until a long-in-coming day of holy justice. While still on the bench as an Associate Justice of the Supreme Court of the United States, Wilson reached the destination that all moving bodies eventually do— the end. By 1797, there was nowhere left to run or anyone remaining to turn to, and Wilson, justice of the Supreme Court, was summarily charged to a debtor's prison. Upon his release he fled to North Carolina to avoid further creditors who sought by that late stage, not only his money, but his head. As it turned out, some people have to learn their lessons the hard way— and though he was a man of keen and overwhelming brilliance— arguably the second most important personage in the whole of the shape and substance of the U.S. Constitution— he returned to land speculation in western New York, Pennsylvania, and Georgia and promoted yet another grandiose scheme to recruit European immigrants to settle there. These investments, just like all of his rides to riches, crashed over a cliff and proved to be ruinous for all involved. The judge was yet imprisoned again, the whole time improbably but duly performing his responsibilities to the court.

Perhaps the Salomon family was owed $353,729.33 plus centuries of interest. Or perhaps the figure should have been reduced to a paltry sum on account of un-liquidated value. Nevertheless, the legacy of Haym Salomon was owed a priceless re-numeration of gratitude.

Since then, other inquiries and even claims have been filed against the Federal Government. As recently as 1982, a gentleman contended to have purchased several investment documents from the French Government, which showed a face value of $4000 owed to Haym Salomon. He sought to collect $42,000,000 in interest, plus the original principle. The government rejected his claim on the ground that he was a non-heir and therefore not entitled to the compensation. What government-sponsored recognition Haym did receive came in the form of a 1946 statue erected in Chicago. The beautiful bronze showed Haym standing with General Washington and Robert Morris. The most contemporary commemorative came from the Post Office in 1975. They issued a stamp that went so far as to state that Mr. Salomon was the financier of the Revolutionary War! Even though Haym Salomon's heirs remain unpaid and he has only received passing recognition, America remains truly in his debt!

***

Before Haym M. Salomon retired from the chamber in which he was kindly rewarded with all of the acknowledgement his father's spirit and memory was obliged — the double doors opened and once again the din of tick-tock-tick-tock beat the heart of time. The aging man closed his eyes — and relived the many years of his life; remembering the bulk of the sour and the sweet, the bitter and the best times. Tick-tock-tick-tock — and gradually his own heart sung to the metronomic pace of time, a flawless sixty beats a second. His mother, God rest her soul. His brother, God bless his efforts. His sisters, may they rest in peace. The odyssey of life — the turning in circles, the heavy burdens, the great wishes, the long falls, the deep moments of love, the wails of pain to God and the shouts of joy to the angels.

"Father, I finally understand you!" he whispered. "Yes, yes I do."

And Haym M. slowly opened to the page in his father's siddur in which the great patriot spoke to him in the womb. Haym M. Salomon fell to tears yet again but for now he just let the sorrow and elegiac endearment flow, and they pattered and moistened the paper as he read the same words to himself over and over again. These were the only sentiments his father ever addressed to him directly; conscious he was going to die before the baby was born. They read:

> "My dearest child, in your dearest mother's care,
> boy or girl whom you are — though you may
> never know the touch of my face or the smell of
> my breath, may you know my true love in my
> departing wisdom. Be you, God's gardener. Plant
> your seeds of unshakable determination. Worry
> not if you live to see your works enliven your life,
> it is the lives of others in which you are entrusted
> as God's gardener."

"I planted the seed, father. This is your country, and it enlivens all who seek their freedom... their liberty... and the light of the garden of God," so he looked up and said in choked whispers. "Be you pleased with me, for all of us indebted to your works, may we remember you beyond our age and the age which follows... and all ages to come. The cost of everything deliciously so sweet to us as Americans, is but ripened fruit of your seed."

***

With that Haym M. Salomon wiped his eyes, closed his beloved and inherited prayer book which came all the way from Poland in the hands of an eighteen year-old boy, one who knew not where he was going, and,... why?

***

BIBLIOGRAPHY

Archives, Collections, and Letters

Marcus, Jacob Rader. United States Jewry 1776-1985. Vol.   1-2.
Historical Society of Pennsylvania. The T. Coxe-H. Salomon Papers
New York Public Library, Rare Books Division.
Books and Pamphlets:
    The Balloting Book, and other Documents Relating to Military Bounty
Lands, in the State of New York: Printed by Packard & Van Benthuysen, 1825. A
Committee of Twenty-five. New York, 1774. The Constitution of the State of New
York. Printed by Samuel London. New York; 1777.
        The Constitution of the State of New York. Reprinted by E. Holt. New
        York: 1785.
    A Copy of the Poll List of the Election for the
        Representatives for the City and County of NEW YORK. 1769.
        Deane, Silas. An Address to the Free and Independent Citizens of the
        United States of North-America. Hartford: Printed by Hudson &
        Goodwin, 1784. Low, John. An Alphabetical Table of the Situation and
        Extent of of the Different Streets, Roads, Lanes, etc. of the City of New
        York. New York: 1807
The Papers of Henry Laurens, vol. 16 73-4. Laurens to Gervais, 14 December 1782.
The Papers of Robert Morris, 1781-1784. Volumes 1-9.
Richard Oswald Papers, CL. Oswald's private letter to the Secretary of State on his
deliberations in Paris, 16 November 1782.

Books and Periodicals

Alden, John. A History of the American Revolution.
    New York: De Capo Press, 1969.
Amberson, J. B. Features of Early Pulmonary Infiltration.
    Am. Rev. Tuber. 45:660, 1942.
American Jewish Historical Quarterly, Volume 27.
    American Jewish Historical Society
Anderson, Dale. The Battle of Yorktown. Gareth Stevens Publishing, 2004.
Andrews, Joseph L. "To Bigotry No Sanction": The Role of American
    Jews in the Revolution. USA. Midstream, 2002.
The Annals of America. Vols 1, 2, 3. Chicago:
    Encyclopaedia Britanica, Inc., 1968.
Baack, Ben. "Forging a Nation State: The Continental Congress and the Financing
of the War of American Independence." Economic

History Review 54, no.4 (2001): 639-56.

Baack, Ben. "British versus American Interests in Land and the War of   American Independence." Journal of European
   Economic History 33, no. 3 (2004): 519-54.

Baack, Ben. "America's First Monetary Policy: Inflation and Seigniorage
   during the Revolutionary War." Financial History Review 15 no.2
   (2008): 107-21.

Baack, Ben, Robert A. McGuire, and T. Norman Van Cott.
   "Constitutional Agreement during the Drafting of the Constitution:
   A New Interpretation." Journal of Legal Studies 38, no.2 (2009):
   533-67.

Baron, H.S. Haym Salomon: Immigrant and Financier of the American
   Revolution. New York: Bloch, 1929.

Barrat, Norris, and Sachse, Julius. Freemasonry in Pennsylvania 1907.
   Vols. 1, 2. Philadelphia: New Era Printing, 1908.

Bemis, Samuel F. The Diplomacy of the American Revolution.
   Bloomington: Indiana University Press, 1957.

Bernardo, Antonio and Ivo Welch "Financial Market Runs," Quarterly Journal of
   Economics, 119, 135-158.

Blakeman, Clovis H. Haym Salomon, Financial Genius of the
   Revolution: Sons of the American Revolution Magazine,
   Louiville, KY, Spring 1984. Pp. 20-22.

Brewer, John. The Sinews of Power: War, Money, and the English State, 1688-1783.
London: Cambridge University Press, 1989.

Buel, Richard. In Irons: Britain's Naval Supremacy and the American
   Revolutionary Economy. New Haven: Yale University Press, 1998.

Bullion, John A. A Great and Necessary Measure: George Grenville and the
   Genesis of the Stamp Act, 1763-1765. Columbia: University of Missouri
   Press, 1982.

Bullock, Charles J. "The Finances of the United States from1775-1789, with
   Especial Reference to the Budget." Bulletin of the University of Wisconsin
1, no. 2 (1895): 117-273.

Calomiris, Charles W. "Institutional Failure, Monetary Scarcity, and the
   Depreciation of the Continental." Journal of Economic History 48, no.1
   (1988): 46-68.

Coil, Henry W. A Comprehensive View of Freemasonry. New MaCoy, 1954.

Coleman, Kenneth. The American Revolution in Georgia, 1763-1789.
   Athens: University of Georgia Press, 1958.

The Confidential Correspondence of Robert Morris. Philadelphia:
   Stan V. Henkels, Auction Commission, 1917.

Conway, Moncure D. Omitted Chapters of History Disclosed In the
   Life and Papers of Edmond Randolph. New York: Da Capo Press, 1971.

Davies, Norman. God's Playground: A History of Poland. NY.
   Columbia University Press, 2005.

Davis, Burke. The Campaign that Won America. New York:
   HarperCollins, 2007.

Dawson, Henry B. The Sons of Liberty in New York. Reprint. New York Arno
   Press and the New York Times, 1969.

Dimont, Max I. Jews, God, and History. New York: New America
    Library, 1962.
Dubnow, S.M. History of the Jews in Russia and Poland. Trans
    Friedlander, Philadelphia: Jewish Publication Society of America, 1916.
Dull, Jonathan R. A Diplomatic History of the American Revolution.
    New Haven: Yale University Press, 1985.
Egnal, Mark. A Mighty Empire: The Origins of the American
    Revolution. Ithaca: Cornell University Press, 1988.
Fast, Howard. Haym Salomon: Son of Liberty.
    New York: Julia Messner Inc., New York, 1941.
Ferguson, E. James. The Power of the Purse: A History of American
    Public Finance, 1776-1790. Chapel Hill:
    University of North Carolina Press, 1961.
Ferling, John E. Almost a Miracle: The American Victory in The War of
    Independence. New York: Oxford University Press US, 2007.
Fleming, Thomas. The Perils of Peace. New York: The Dial Press, 1970.
Foner, Phillip S. Jews in American History, 1654-1865, International
    Publishers, New York, 1945.
Friedman, J. H., Kastlin, G. J., and Kooperstein, M.C. Psychosomatic Factors in
    Pulmonary Tuberculosis. Dis. Of Chest. 12:539, 1946.
Freidman, Lee M. Jewish Pioneers and Patriots. Philadelphia: The Jewish
    Publication Society of   America, 1942.
Gunderson, Gerald. A New Economic History of America. New York:
    McGraw-Hill, 1976.
Hall, Leslie. Land and Allegiance in Revolutionary Georgia. Athens:
    University of Georgia Press, 2001.
Harper, Lawrence A. "Mercantilism and the American Revolution."
    Canadian Historical Review 23 (1942): 1-15.
Heckelman, Joseph. The First Jews in the New World.
    Jay Street Publishers, 2004.
Hertzberg, Arthur, ed. Judaism. New York: George Braziller, 1962.
Higginbotham, Don. The War of American Independence: Military
    Attitudes, Policies, and Practice, 1763-1789. Bloomington:
    Indiana University Press, 1977.
Hoffman, Ronald, and Peter J. Albert, eds. Peace and the
    Peacemakers: The Treaty of 1783. Charlottesville: Published for the
    United States Capitol Historical Society by the University Press of
    Virginia, 1986.
Homes, Henry A., ed. Description and Analysis of the Remarkable
    Collection of Unpublished Manuscripts of
    Robert Morris. Albany, N.Y. Joel Munsell, 1876.
Hutchinson, W.T., and Rachel, W.M., eds. The Papers of James Madison.
    Vols 4, 5. Chicago: The University of Chicago Press, 1967.
Jackson, Harvey H. Lachlan McIntosh and the Politics of Revolutionary Georgia.
    Athens: University of Georgia Press, 1979.
Jensen, Merrill, ed. English Historical Documents: American Colonial
    Documents to 1776. New York: Oxford University Press, 1969.
The Jewish Encyclopedia. Ed. Isidore Singer. Vol. 8. New York: Funk and
    Wagnalls, 1904, 1925.

Johnson, Allen S. A Prologue to Revolution: The Political Career of George
    Grenville (1712-1770). New York: University Press, 1997.
Jones, Alice H. Wealth of a Nation to Be: The American Colonies on the Eve of
    the Revolution. New York: Columbia University Press, 1980.
Kaplan, Herbrt H. "The First Partition of Poland" New York and
    London, Columbia University Press, pg. 101.
Kelly, Robert. The Shaping of the American Past, Volume 1. Prentice Hall,
    Englewood Cliffs, NJ, 1975.
Ketchum, Richard M. Saratoga: Turning Point of America's
    Revolutionary War. New York: Henry Holt and Company, 1997.
Kohn, Meir. Bills of Exchange and the Money Market to 1600. Working paper
    99-04, Department of Economics. Dartmouth College, 1999.
Knight, Vick. Send For Haym Salomon! Haym Salomon Foundation, in
    collaboration with Borden Pub. Co., Alhambra Calif., 1976.
Kohler, Max. Haym Salomon, The Patriot Broker of the Revolution: His Real
    Achievements and Their Exaggeration. An Open Letter to Congressman
    Celler. 1931.
Langguth, A. J., Patriots: The Men Who Started the American Revolution. New
    York: Simon and Schuster, 1988.
Larabee, Benjamin Woods. The Boston Tea Party. New York:
    Oxford University Press, 1964.
Lewis,   Lawrence. A History of the Bank of North America.
    Philadelphia. D.B. Lippincott, 1882.
Mackesy, Piers. The War for America, 1775-1783. Cambridge:
    Harvard University Press, 1964.
Madison, Charles A. Eminent American Jews 1776 to the Present. New York:
    Frederick Ungar, 1970.
McCusker, John J. and Russell R. Menard. The Economy of British America,
    1607-1789. Chapel Hill: University of North Carolina Press, 1985.
Morais, Henry S. The Jews of Philadelphia. The Levitype Co., 1894.
Moran, Donald N. "Haym Salomon – The Revolution's Indispensible
    Financial Genius. Rev. War Historical Article. Retrieved 2001 01-09.
Morris, Richard Brandon. The Peacemakers: The Great Powers and American
    Independence. New York: Harper and Row, 1965.
Morrissey, Brendan. Yorktown 1781: The World Turned Upside Down.
    London: Osprey, 1997.
Michener, Ron. "Backing Theories and the Currencies of Eighteenth-Century
    America: A New Comment." Journal of Economic History 48, no.3
    (1988): 682-92.
Milgrim, Shirley. "Mikveh Israel Cemetary". USHistory.org. Retrieved   2008-06-26.
Moorman, L. J. Tuberculosis and Genius. Chicago. University of Chicago, 1945.
Nester, William R. The First Global War: Britain, France, and the Fate of North
    America, 1756-1775. Westport: Praeger, 2000.
Newman, E.P. "Counterfeit Continental Currency Goes to War." The Numismatist
    1 (January, 1957): 5-16.
New York Comptroller's Office. New York in the Revolution.
    Vols. 1, 2. New York: J. B. Lyon, 1904.

North, Douglas C., and Barry R. Weingast. "Constitutions and Commitment: The Evolution of Institutions Governing Public Choice in Seventeenth-Century England." Journal of Economic History 49 no.4 (1989): 803-32.

O'Shaughnessy, Andrew Jackson. An Empire Divided: The American Revolution and the British Caribbean. Philadelphia: University of Pennsylvania Press, 2000.

Palmer, R.R. The Age of Democratic Revolution: A Political History of Europe and America. Vol. 1. Princeton University Press, 1959.

Pereswetoff-Morath, A.I. A Grin Without a Cat, Volume 2 and Jews and Christians in Medieval Russia – Assessing the Sources. (Lund Slavonic Monographs, 5) Lund, 2002.

Perkins, Edward J. The Economy of Colonial America. New York: Columbia University Press, 1988.

Peters, Madison C. The Jews in America. New York: John C. Winston, 1905.

Peters, Madison C. The Jews Who Stood by Washington: An Unwritten Chapter in American History. Trow Press, New York, 1915.

Pool, Rev. D. De Sola. The Mill Street Synagogue 1730-1817 of the Congregation Shearith Israel. New York: 1930.

Posthumus, Nicolaas W. Inquiry into the HHistory of Prices in Holland, Volume 1: Wholesale Prices at the Exchange of Amsterdam 1585-1914. Rates of Exchange at Amsterdam 1609-1914. Leiden, Brill.

Prazmowska, Anita J. A History of Poland. Palgrave Macmillan p. 199. Retrieved 29 April, 2012.

Reeves, Thomas C. Gentleman Boss. American Political Biography Press, 1975.

Reid, Joseph, D., Jr. "Economic Burden: Spark of the American Revolution?" Journal of Economic History 38, No. 1 (1978): 81-100.

Rippleye, Charles. Robert Morris: Financier of the American Revolution. 2010.

Robinson, Edward F. "Continental Treasury Administration, 1775-1781: A Study in the Financial History of the American Revolution." Ph.D. diss., University of Wisconsin, 1969.

Robinson, Henry James. The Power of the Purse. London: John Murray, 1928.

Rockoff, Hugh. Drastic Measures: A History of Wage and Price Controls in the United States. Cambridge: Cambridge University Press, 1984.

Rose, C. B. and Stanburt, W. S. The Psychology of Tuberculosis. Am. Rev. Tuberc. 28:217, 1933.

Rolnick, Arthur J. In Order to Form a More Perfect Monetary Union. Federal Reserve Bank of Minneapolis Review, Volume 17, no. 4, Fall 1993.

Russell, Charles Edward. Haym Salomon and the Revolution. New York Cosmopolitan, 1930.

Sawyers, Larry. "The Navigation Acts Revisited." Economic History Review 45, no. 2 (1992): 262-84.

Schappes, Morris U., ed. A Documentary History of the Jews in the United States 1654-1875. New York: Citidel, 1950, 1952.

Schiff, Stacy. A Great Improvisation: Franklin, France, and the Birth of America. New York: Henry Holt, 2005. Schoenbrun, David. Triumph in Paris: The Exploits of Benjamin Franklin. New York: Harper and Row, 1976.

Searcy, Martha Condray. The Georgia-Florida Contest in the American Revolution, 1776-1778. University: University of Alabama Press, 1958.

Seidenfeld, M. A. A Comparative Study of the Responses of Tuberculous and Non-tuberculous Subjects on the Mailer Personality Sketches. J. Psychol. 9:247, 1942.

Stone, Daniel. The Polish-Lithuanian State, 1386-1795. University of Washington Press, 2001.

Streeg, Clarence L. Ver. Robert Morris: Revolutionary Financier. Philadelphia: University of Pennsylvania Press, 1954.

Stryker, William Scudder. The Egg Harbor Affair, New Jersey, October 15, 1778. Trenton, NJ: Naar, Day, & Naar, 1894.

Sumner, William Graham. The Financier and the Finances of the American Revolution. Vol. 2. New York: Burt Franklin, 1891, 1970.

Swiggert, Howard. The Extraordinary Mr. Morris. New York: Doubleday, 1952.

Thomas, Robert P. "A Quantitative Approach to the Study of The Effects of British Imperial Policy on Colonial Welfare: Some Preliminary Findings," Journal of Economic History 25, no. 4 1965: 615-38.

Tucker, Robert W. and David C. Hendrickson. The Fall of the First British Empire: Origins of the War of American Independence. Baltimore: Johns Hopkins Press, 1982.

Usher, Abbott Payson. "The Origin of the Bill of Exchange," Journal of Political Economy, 22, 566-576.

Ver Steeg, Clarence L. Robert Morris: Revolutionary Financier. Philadelphia: University of Pennsylvania Press, 1954.

Vaughan, Alden T.: ed. Chronicles of the American Revolution. Originally Compiled by Hezekia Niles. New York. Grosset & Dunlap, 1965.

Walton, Gary M. "The New Economic History and the Burdens of the Navigation Acts." Economic History Review 24, no. 4 1971: 533-42.

Wharton, Francis. Ed. The Revolutionary Correspondence of the United States. Washington D.C.: Government Printing Office, 1889.

Wickwire, Franklin and Mary. Cornwallis: The American Adventure. Boston: Houghton Mifflin, 1970.

Wolf, Edwin, and Whitemen, Maxwell. The History of the Jews of Philadelphia from Colonial Times to the Age of Jackson. Philadelphia: The Jewish Publication Society of America, 1957.

ABOUT THE AUTHOR

James Arcuri, a master Storyteller, with over 70 screenplays and novels, are being produced under the Identity Features publishing and moiton picture brand. Film making and storytelling, has always been part of his life professionally since 1974.

Soon to be released on all media, motion picture and documentary films, and books.

LULLABY – A thriller, Pshycotic deception at all levels.

A GARDEN OF THORNS – A boy, who fought againt the Nazis in WW2, was awarded The Medal of Honor 70 years later for his efforts.

AMITYVILLE HIGH – the continuing series of thrillers of the famous Amityville murder story, but this time the house was not to blame, as new facts surface.

"72" - The true story of the biggest theft of drugs in NYC's history, the French Connection case in 1972. From the dirty cops to the mob, the crime didn't end.

FRANKENSTIEN RECREATED – Before Mary Shelly created her famous novel, she came across an ancient manuscript of recreation of human life.

JONES BEACH – In 1944, the race for the element of the atomic bomb was on between Nazi Germany and the United States. A Nazi Spy had that secret and had to be stopped before he returned to Germany.

CASTING A KILLER – A boy stumbles upon a murder scene while making a film and unknowingly finds something that could identity the killer.

More to come from Identity Features.

www.identityfeatures.com

Any questions, thoughts or comments, lectures or bookings, I can be reached by email: jarcuri@identityfeatures.com or identityfeatures@gmail.com

We are also on Internet Movie Data Base, www.imdb.com

Made in the USA
Monee, IL
07 January 2021